HOOKED ON ICE FISHING III

GAME FISH

Tom Gruenwald

Published by

700 E. State Street • Iola, WI 54990-0001
Telephone: 715/445-2214

www.krause.com

Please call or write for our free catalog of outdoor publications.
Our toll-free number to place an order or obtain a free catalog is 800-258-0929
or please use our regular business telephone 715-445-2214
for editorial comment and further information.

Library of Congress Catalog Number: 99-61265
ISBN: 0-87341-734-8

Printed in the United States of America

Dedication

Foremost, I dedicate this book to my savior, Jesus Christ, for without his daily love, strength, direction and guidance I am nothing. This book is also dedicated to my patient wife, loving children, parents, grandparents and supportive colleagues, whom Jesus has also blessed this world with. May I grow to be a reflection of the wonderful people you've grown to be.

Acknowledgements

A humble and most grateful thank you to my savior Jesus Christ, without your continual blessings and steadfast guidance, there is no way this book would have been possible. For my wife, Lisa, daughters Alyssa and Brianna, parents and grandparents, thanks for your loving support through the trials of writing another book. To my colleagues and special friends, Paul, Ken and Nate Grahl, I cannot express the level of my extreme gratitude for your support, loyalty and commitment. I couldn't be blessed with a finer group of friends. And to the manufacturers, guides and supporting crew for all the projects associated with production of a book of this caliber, a hearty thank you. The "Hooked on Ice Fishing" series simply would not exist without you.

Contents

Preface

Gamefish: The Things Ice Fishing Dreams are Made Of

A strong, gusty winter wind blasts across the ice, driving heavy snow through the cold, gray air. Our tip-ups, plainly visible in the distance only moments ago, are now concealed behind an icy curtain of swirling, turbulent snow.

I lean against the powerful gusts billowing my snowsuit, and crouching slightly to protect my rod, maintain a keen eye on my sonar while continuing to jig. Since this sudden, strange front blew in, fish activity has slowed, and I'm not seeing anywhere near the movement of fish I had earlier. But I feel fish are still present, and I'm not willing to quit. At least not yet.

I reel up, and carrying my sonar, move to another hole. Trying to find previously drilled holes is getting harder, as blowing snow has covered most of them, erased my established trails and devoured even my most recent footprints. Only odd, swollen, scaly gray masses of fresh snow, acting as sponges above each hole, provide evidence of any disturbance atop the ice. I press on, scooping these heavy, wet clumps from the holes, carefully placing my transducer in the water and repeatedly dropping my silver, shiner-tipped spoon into the depths.

I'm just starting to question my fishing in the face of this massive outburst of winter fury when a large target appears on my sonar. It is just beneath my falling spoon. Holding my breath, I stop, twitch the spoon, and allow it to fall. The target rises, and before I witness the chance meeting of lure and fish, my ice rod takes a wrenching dive. The stiff blank arches under the heavy weight of a powerful, hard-running fish. I can feel the stressed graphite fibers creak under the steady, thrashing pressure.

My spinning reel compensates as drag whirls off line, spraying mists of beaded water and ice into the air. Clambering, I reset the drag, and with the fish temporarily under control, turn and yell for my partner. The driving wind carries my voice well away from his ears. He can scarcely see me in the gusty shrouds of snow, much less hear my voice through the forceful, whistling blasts.

My attention is immediately directed back to the fish as another sudden run ensues. My cold reel balks in protest, and I loosen the drag while trying to maintain pressure on the fish. The line is now stretched so tight the blowing wind strikes an eerie ring as it sings around the strained line.

My arms feel weak, my hands sting fiercely from the raw wind and I find myself striving to adjust the drag with stinging wind-numbed fingertips, while at the same time trying to keep my hole free of blowing snow.

After two more runs, the toothy head of an ill-tempered, monstrous pike thrashes at the hole, sloshing a frigid mixture of ice crystals and thick droplets of water across my kneeling legs. Holding the rod high with my shaking left hand, I scarcely note the water instantly freezing against my pants as I plunge my painfully cold right hand into the icy water, and with my last grasping strength, heft the wide, heavy body of a massive pike from the water.

By the standards of many ice anglers, I've just experienced the ultimate thrill in ice fishing.

Maybe the thrill is the overwhelming initial sensation of realizing you've hooked a big fish; the split-second, frightening confusion of trying to set the hook and adjust the drag; the gripping fear wondering if the knot was properly tied or the tumultuous, nerve-shattering drama of fighting the fish. Whatever it is, this thrill is what ice fishing dreams are made of.

This book reveals strategies I've incorporated into a highly effective ice fishing system. I've done this with the hope that you, too, can enjoy such dreams. But first, we must review the foundation of this system. We'll begin with defining the term "gamefish." Many anglers consider all species worthy of winter pursuit, but a broad definition also includes the panfishes. That's something we already covered in the second book of the "Hooked On Ice Fishing" series.

For clarity, let's polish our definition of the term "gamefish" by describing what they are not. They are not "panfish." Within the "Hooked On Ice Fishing" series we have defined panfish as "any respectable species commonly caught through the ice, that at maturity in an average environment typically fits comfortably in an average-sized frying pan." Sure, a large cisco, perch or state-record crappie might undermine this classification, but notice I used the words "typically" and "at maturity in an average environment." In exceptional situations, some panfishes might not fit this definition perfectly. For our purposes, this definition will better distinguish the term "panfish" and help eliminate species such as walleyes, pike, lake trout and salmon from consideration. These larger predator species we will define as "gamefish."

Still, we must be careful, as confusion may be intensified by misnomers. Like the panfishes, many gamefish species go by regional names. I've heard pike called "pickerel" and "jacks" throughout Canada, "snakes" and "jackfish" here in the United States. Walleyes are called "pike" on restaurant menus and "pickerel" in Canada. Closely allied species such as largemouth and smallmouth bass, pike and pickerel; walleyes and sauger; lake trout and splake are often confused, even by the so-called experts.

Here's an example. A Swedish ice fishing friend and I recently met near Toronto for a winter lake trout outing. He was surprised to find we were fishing char, not some unique trophy North American trout. He felt I misled him. Like me, most North American anglers commonly refer to char as lake trout without realizing the misnomer. Looking back, I caused a friend to travel halfway around the world in pursuit of "lake trout" only to find out the fish was a species available in his home waters. Such confusion can be avoided by using proper common names, which we will refer to throughout this book.

Our secondary definition of "gamefish" will help classify them even further. As defined here, gamefish constitute any species commonly caught through the ice, NOT fitting in an ordinary frying pan, and having a place within the upper reaches of the food chain in the environment in which they're found. This is important, because limiting our definition to species found in the uppermost portion of the food chain not only helps further define the term gamefish, but also means these species are seeking smaller, natural prey—not only baitfish, but often, many of the "panfishes" such as smelt, ciscoes, or perch. This has considerable implications in our classification because it follows if gamefish follow such food sources, many of the underlying panfish patterns revealed in the previous book of this "Hooked On Ice Fishing" series also coincide with those of gamefish. That's simply because often where these panfish are found, so are the predators we're defining as "gamefish."

In addition, predators at the top of the food chain are larger in size, making them actively sought game—hence the term "gamefish." Yet because larger gamefish comprise the upper end of the food chain, they're generally less abundant than the panfishes they feed upon. Their tremendous size potential is the primary reason so many anglers feel gamefish are the things ice fishing dreams are made of.

With gamefish now defined, you might ask why I'd write a book devoted strictly to icing them. A better question might be, why not?

By our definition, gamefish are present throughout millions of acres of water around the ice-fishing world. Being on the higher end of the food chain and of a lower relative abundance than panfish, they grow large and well-conditioned. So the challenge of fishing them is irresistible to veteran winter fishing enthusiasts worldwide.

That's not to say gamefish can't become overabundant. In some environments, gamefish may procreate to the point their numbers exceed available food supplies, making them "stunted" but very active and willing to strike. This provides good fishing when action is desired over quality. Such phenomena are common with northern pike or walleye in shallow, fertile, weedy waters. However, while good from an action standpoint, excessive quantities of any gamefish are not healthy. Overpopulated gamefish knock lakes out of balance, often offering tremendous numbers of smaller fish, but few, if any, larger ones. This is a condition that may be caused by a number of physical, biological and chemical limitations.

Better balanced are lakes where populations of gamefish are reduced through natural environmental constraints. In such cases, forage is divided among a smaller number of individuals, providing greater opportunity for them to grow. These fish will be less competitive and aggressive. Such waters make better targets for more experienced, veteran ice anglers searching for the challenge of finding and catching fewer but larger gamefish.

So whether you're looking for action or the challenge of stalking a trophy, gamefish are fun for ice anglers of all ages and skill levels. Just note that because they are usually less abundant, you must learn to understand each gamefish species and develop specialized systems to enjoy more consistent catches.

Sure, folks who seek gamefish strictly for food or as a way to leisurely pass time may catch some on a variety of presentations and almost any type of gear. Sometimes, simply by putting their time in, anglers may chance onto an occasional big fish. But those who strive for the challenge of maximum efficiency have learned to use specialized tackle and techniques to become more consistent. These ice anglers have found there are a few tricks for finding winter gamefish. Specialized tactics using specialized gear, lures, baits and refined techniques improve their odds of icing a trophy greatly.

Best of all, no matter where you live within the North American ice fishing belt, such action can likely be experienced throughout the winter in waters close to home, without a great deal of expensive equipment. Combine this with the great table fare of gamefish like northern pike, walleye, trout, salmon or whitefish and you'll know why people chase gamefish. It's for the challenge, the thrill and the wonderful taste of fish.

Remember, whenever you're dealing with fish on the highest ends of the food chain, their diverse habitat and habits and inter- and intra-species relationships come into play. Your odds of making consistent catches can only be improved by closely examining each species and situation on an individual basis. Factor in the variety of lake types, water and weather conditions, and ice fishing gamefish practically becomes a science. Thus, knowledgeable, seasoned veterans typically have distinct advantages over the beginner.

Enter the "Hooked On Ice Fishing" advantage.

With the foundations of safe, knowledgeable and successful ice fishing systems and patterns established in the first two books of this series now being combined with the specialized information provided here, you'll learn to better understand each gamefish species and develop specialized systems to create even more consistent catches. Bottom line? The information provided here in the "Hooked On Ice Fishing" winter gamefishing system will help you establish solid

background knowledge that could otherwise only be gained through years of experience. That experience leads to greatly improved catches of virtually any gamefish species. It's all here at your fingertips, provided you meticulously study each individual species and the situation.

A pike is very similar to a pickerel, a walleye to a sauger, lake trout to a splake, steelhead trout to salmon, even a largemouth bass to a smallmouth bass for that matter. So general patterns can be applied to catching them. Yet all are different species with varying traits, and each responds differently to an immense variety of sub-ice environments. If you learn to better understand each fish, you'll discover it's possible to develop systematic, strategic approaches to best meet these unique situations and conditions. Then you can create consistent methods for finding and catching your target species.

Introductory concepts for such fundamental systems were outlined in the first book of the "Hooked on Ice Fishing" series. These were built into specific, commanding patterns for "panfish" in the second book. Within the pages of this book, we'll review these concepts, then build on them even further, picking up where book two left off and covering powerful methods for identifying more detailed winter gamefish patterns. If you've read previous "Hooked On Ice Fishing" volumes and some material in the beginning chapters sounds familiar, it should. Many basic concepts are reviewed within the pages of this book. Just don't miss the effective new twists and wrinkles added in for fishing gamefish.

This book begins by reviewing methods for remaining safe and comfortable in the cold, then covers how to use systematic, mobile approaches to help with locating the winter baitfish and panfish that gamefish pursue. This continues by revealing how to research your target waters using lake maps, electronic navigational aids, sonar, underwater cameras and many highly refined, never before revealed approaches and techniques. You will be able to identify the preferred habitats, behavior, habits and movements of specific gamefish species. I'll demonstrate a versatile array of productive, fine-tuned presentations covering a variety of situations and conditions, then suggest the best equipment, baits, methods and techniques for catching each gamefish species. I'll even recommend the most productive times to fish them.

The most popular gamefish species are then covered thoroughly within individual chapters.

You'll discover the specific habits of these species based on the research and experiences of the nation's leading fisheries biologists, winter guides and experts. We'll elaborate on more species-specific winter gamefish patterns, and you'll gain insight into the best angling techniques of ice pros, ice tackle designers and manufacturers throughout North America. You're sure to learn new tips that will help you catch respectable, even trophy-sized gamefish with more consistency.

These seasoned ice angling veterans realize high quality gamefish catches are seldom easy, and trophy gamefish aren't common at all. But they've also learned tricks to improve their odds. This is the exciting world of winter gamefish, one which we'll explore and reveal within the pages of this book. You'll get solid information you can use to catch gamefish in a variety of waters across the North American ice fishing belt, throughout the winter.

Regardless of your reason for pursuing gamefish, if you're a bona fide "hard-water" gamefish enthusiast that loves the adventure and challenges involved with ice fishing big water for big fish, this book was written for you.

Introduction

The Thrill of the Hunt: Locating Winter Gamefish

Few experiences compare to the challenge of deciphering consistent patterns for catching trophy winter gamefish. Like any hard-earned achievement, hours of preparation, research and experimentation can be formidable tasks, especially in rugged sports like ice fishing, where most of this work must be undertaken in bone-chilling winds and sub-freezing climes. But few can deny the rewards when powerful, hefty trophies are lifted above the ice.

Not even the most educated "expert" can locate and catch gamefish all the time, but a number of tools and techniques can tip the odds in your favor. These are the techniques we'll reveal in this book. The key to improved catches is understanding how each species relates to its environment so you can target specific locations during high-percentage times to maximize your productivity. While this process involves a number of variables and can be complex, I've found the best starting point to be choosing the proper lake type, then locating prominent sources of cover, forage and oxygen. By choosing waters offering optimal growing conditions, then understanding specific locations best meeting the fish's needs on these waters, we improve our odds of finding trophy gamefish.

The "Hooked On Ice Fishing" system for choosing the right waters, finding cover and locating forage involves 12 variables I call the "deadly dozen." Each details important gamefish-finding elements. Once you learn these factors and become adept at applying them to various situations, you'll have learned the foundation for consistently finding winter gamefish.

These variables are similar to winter panfish patterns. Have you ever jigged for bluegills or perch in a weedy bay, while successfully using tip-ups for pike? Probably. Both species relate to weeds for cover and forage. Bluegills may be there for the insect larvae and plankton, while the pike will be there for baitfish, possibly even the bluegills and perch themselves! Because all links in the food chain concentrate in one area, the "Hooked On Ice Fishing" "Deadly Dozen" formula works for all types of fish. All the deadly dozen variables revolve around the basic needs of winter fish: their preferred lake types, cover, food and oxygen requirements. Don't get confused with the complexities right now, but rather, look at this introduction for what it is: A list of important variables in elementary patterns for locating winter gamefish. We'll examine details later.

Lake Type

The first "Deadly Dozen" variable involves researching lake type. You can catch fish without such research, but the more you know, the farther you'll go.

All ice fishing waters can be classified into various categories, such as natural lakes, flowages or reservoirs, rivers, river backwaters, ponds, pits and Great Lakes bays. But these can further be subdivided. Limnologists describe deep, cold, infertile, richly oxygenated lake trout lakes as "oligotrophic," and shallow, relatively warm, fertile, bass lakes as "eutrophic." These lakes are often oxygen-starved in the winter. Reservoirs, also called flowages, can be classified into categories such as "flatland" or "highland," and there's certainly a big difference between a large, frozen river system and a shallow backwater, a shallow sand quarry and an iron ore pit several hundred feet deep. By examining these characteristics, we can establish environments most likely to harbor the species we wish to target.

Lake trout, for example, are found only in deep, cold lakes, reservoirs and pits supporting high levels of dissolved oxygen throughout the

All ice fishing waters can be classified into various categories, such as natural lakes, flowages or reservoirs, rivers, river backwaters, ponds, pits and Great Lakes bays. (photo courtesy Craig Ritchie)

year. Fishing a shallow, weedy lake would not be conducive to catching any lake trout, much less a trophy. On the flip side, if you're targeting large-mouth bass–a species preferring shallower, weedy environments– a deep, cold lake would not be the place to go fishing.

Thus, identifying specific gamefish species and their preferred environments are keys to success. So is an understanding of the structure, cover and forage available. By better under-standing the structure and cover individual waters offer and how forage species relate to them, we can better locate our target species. We could spend years investigating the winter habitats of golden shiners, spot-tail shiners, lake chubs or northern red-belly dace and it could improve our winter fishing, but for the context of this book, we'll leave that to biologists. Instead, let's focus on two more common forage species: cisco and yellow perch.

Ciscos thrive in large, deep, cold-water lakes and often suspend in deep water, leading game-fish predators such as pike and walleyes there to feed. But when ciscoes spawn in the shallows late in the winter, gamefish follow. Focusing your efforts with cisco-imitating baits and lures in deep water on large, deep cold-water lakes during mid-winter may bring excellent results. But fishing the same way with the same bait during the late season could be futile.

Fishing with cisco patterns in small, shallow lakes likely won't work because the cisco isn't likely to be a major forage fish. That's not to say cisco won't be present in smaller, shallower lakes. They could be. This is also not to imply that some gamefish won't suspend over deep holes in relatively shallow lakes. They sometimes do. But since ciscoes won't likely be present in numbers that will attract concentrations of gamefish, with the occasional isolated exception, the cisco pattern isn't worth pursuing on most shallow, weedy lakes or bays.

Yellow perch, however, may be abundant in smaller, shallow environments. Again, I'm not saying perch aren't found in larger, deep lakes. They can be, but the population will likely be marginal, and if present, probably will hold only within isolated, shallow, weedy bays.

However, if the thought crossed your mind you could pursue specific gamefish species feeding on yellow perch within isolated shallow, weedy bays on these waters, and that such a situation might offer a unique opportunity to capitalize on a possibly under-fished pattern, you're not only getting the idea, you're advancing beyond the scope of this introduction. By under-standing your specific target species, primary forage base and the environment they're most likely to thrive in, you can choose key waters, even specific areas within these waters, to better focus your winter fishing efforts.

These basic concepts can be taken even farther. If you learn to understand each gamefish species and its relation to unique environments, you can create better strategies for identifying where to find the most productive fishing. Consider the above example. While deep, cold environments aren't conducive to growing large perch populations, perch can thrive in isolated areas within such a body of water. A certain species or portion of a specific gamefish population may choose to feed on perch within these isolated areas because of reduced competition from other fish. Anglers may ignore these areas, leaving those fish to grow to trophy proportions simply because they haven't been influenced by fishing pressure. This is a simplified example, but such patterns exist.

These are not places to take the kids or beginning anglers. But they are certainly nice trips for serious trophy hunters to explore.

Gamefish inhabit various winter environments, each offering unique conditions. To be consistent, we must recognize the waters most conducive to supporting our target species, then learn how to apply the right techniques for finding their preferred forage and, ultimately, our target species.

Variable #1 Identify the lake type most likely to support a healthy population of the fish you seek, then begin searching for specific locations most likely to attract them.

Population Cycles

Next, it's important to understand population cycles. Say you wish to catch mid-size, "eater" walleyes. You start by learning their preferred lake type, then research and find such waters in your area, preferably those featuring locations meeting the preferred criteria for their primary forage. You go there, fish and don't do well.

This may be caused by a downward ebb in the population cycle. Walleyes, like many gamefish

For consistent winter success, it helps to ask a local biologist or guide what specific lake type and area waters currently feature a good population of the specific gamefish species (and size) you wish to catch.

species, experience ebbs and flows in population based on a number of environmental factors. In the case of walleyes, population cycles are strongly based on successful spawns. A couple years of cold, low-water spring seasons resulting in poor spawns may decrease the number of smaller fish, leading to a depletion in the population of new fish, leaving a few big walleyes and noticeable absence of smaller, "eating-size" fish available for several winters.

In contrast, a couple high-water, mild spring seasons can result in good spawns, bolstering the population of smaller, eating-size fish. So to be successful, you must not only choose the right waters, but also fish during an upward swing in the population of the species and size you're seeking.

Variable #2 Find the right lake type featuring a rising population cycle of the species and size of fish you're looking for.

Habitat/Structure/Cover

Once on the ice, you'll want to narrow down the amount of area to be covered on your lake. I call this finding target locations. These are areas where you're most likely to find your target species, and they vary from one lake type to the next. In river backwaters or small, shallow ponds and natural lakes shaped like bowls, gamefish may simply relate to cover like vegetation, downed timber or stumps. If distinct drop-offs or deeper holes exist, they may hold on these edges or cruise along them, perhaps even suspend over them in deep water, essentially using depth itself as a form of cover.

In larger, deeper, more structurally diverse waters where bottom features include distinct drop-offs, rises and falls at various depths, gamefish may relate to any number of areas, migrating between them as the winter season progresses. By learning to predict when, where and how far these movements occur and how long they will last, you can better pinpoint locations gamefish will hold, and estimate when migrations between them are likely to occur. Many factors influence these key locations, movements and peak periods. We'll examine these things throughout this book. For now, understand each species prefers specific habitats, structures and cover types within their unique environment—and these preferences are often dictated by forage.

Once you've chosen the correct lake, you must carefully research the locations offering the best combinations of habitat, structure, cover and forage most likely to attract your target fish—something which can be accomplished most efficiently using lake maps and global positioning systems (GPS).

Again, consider the contrast between cisco and perch. Massive schools of cisco often suspend high over deep water, away from structure and cover, where the only shelter from predators is their sheer numbers. Although perch may utilize such habitat, it's usually only when forced by environmental conditions, such as severe cold fronts, little or no oxygen or forage availability on deeper, sparsely vegetated hard-bottom structures and mud flats. Or, it simply could be they've been chased out of preferred areas by predators or competing species. Perch usually prefer to group on structures and flats offering cover in the form of moderate vegetation, wood or rock.

Variable #3 You've chosen the proper lake type offering a solid population of the species you're seeking. And you've found that population to be on an upward swing in cycle and identified primary forage types. Now you must select the areas offering the best combinations of habitat, structure, cover and forage. These areas will be the most likely to attract the fish you are after.

Depth

Another primary consideration when choosing specific locations is the depth where the best habitat, structure and cover combinations are found.

A sunken island 15 feet deep, just outside a shallow bay might be good first ice structure on a shallow lake with a maximum depth of 40 feet, but during mid-winter, a sunken island in 30 feet of water might be better. Better yet is a point running from a shallow feeding flat into 30 feet, because it offers more options for the fish. Given ideal weather conditions, gamefish might slide up the point and scatter into the shallows. After the passing of a severe cold front, you'll likely find most fish on the deep end of the point, especially if they're light sensitive species like walleye or sauger. Evaluate the structure, based on the lake type, the time of the season you're fishing and conditions.

Regardless of lake type, always start looking for gamefish around the most suitable combination of

After arriving on a "high-percentage" fish-holding location using your GPS, clear snow from the ice surface in preparation for shooting sonar readings through the ice to locate the structural edge and migration routes lining the deepest available water.

habitat, structure and cover nearest the deepest available water. That's because deep water is less susceptible to change.

Consider a shoreline point extending from a shallow flat towards a deep hole. Early in the season and during twilight periods offering mild, overcast, stable weather conditions, you might find walleyes holding within the adjoining vegetated bays or shallow shoreline flats. But, during mid-season or bright midday periods, they'll probably be near deeper weedlines or drop into deeper pockets along the point where the environment is more stable.

Just remember, the terms "shallow" and "deep" are relative. Following severe cold fronts, walleyes might move into the deepest available water. That might be 10 feet on a shallow lake, while on a nearby deeper lake, the same fish might drop to 20 or 30 feet. Depth on a lake with a maximum depth of 10 feet versus lakes with maximum depths of 40, 100, or 200 feet would certainly be rated differently, because walleyes would have dramatically different sets of conditions and location options. Walleyes feeding on ciscos in a lake with a maximum depth of 40 feet might remain near schools of ciscoes suspended in 20 feet of water. In a lake with a maximum depth of 200 feet, they might suspend in 30, 40, 50, 60 or even 100 feet. Know your water.

Depth makes a difference in another respect as well. Deep lakes, having more volume, cool more slowly in fall and warm more slowly in spring than shallow lakes. This means they freeze later in fall and thaw later in spring than shallower waters. If the same species existed in both lakes, the shallower lake, which cools first, would freeze first and offer the best early season action. For good late-ice fishing, however, the deeper lake, which warms more slowly, would likely offer safer ice fishing later into the spring.

The implications here can be tremendous. Knowledgeable anglers, know the first- and late-ice seasons offer terrific action but are short-lived. These anglers are quick to fish smaller, shallow waters during first-ice, and by the time groups of anglers find the ice solid and start attacking these waters in droves, they're moving to larger, deeper, less pressured waters that have just iced over. This allows them to extend the short-lived "first-ice" bite by moving from lake to lake. Ditto late-ice, when they fish smaller, shallower lakes first, then, after many ice anglers have put their ice drills away for the season, extend the famed late-ice season by fishing larger, deeper lakes, which are more resistant to thawing.

Variable #4 After finding the most ideal lake-type, look for the right combination of habitat, structure and cover based on time and conditions. Next, identify areas nearest the deepest water to determine which might hold fish. Choose these areas based on lake depth and the progression of winter.

How Far Winter has Progressed

Pinpointing winter gamefish can be narrowed further by considering how far the winter has progressed.

Individual gamefish species make under-ice movements, many of which involve depth changes. While these may be quite sudden, they're typically gradual, and can be predicted as changes in seasonal and daily conditions occur. Seasonally, pike will typically be found in shallow vegetation when a lake first freezes. They will then hold along or suspend over deeper weed lines, holes and structures during mid-winter before returning to shallow water as ice-out approaches. Walleyes may be scattered in shallow or mid-depth water first ice. They will typically move deep during mid-winter, then gather in large schools within mid-depth structures, holes and breaks located just outside shallow river mouths late in the season. This is where they stage prior to their upstream spring spawning runs.

Either species may move slightly deeper or shallower based on the lake type and daily conditions, because gamefish make general movements within areas of seasonal constraints. First-ice walleyes may move from deep water pockets and holes onto shallow feeding flats, often following specific paths or "migration routes," at specific times. The length and duration of these movements vary with the conditions.

Given ideal conditions and weather, walleyes might move into the shallows and feed actively several days in a row. A great deal of activity on the ice, however, might keep them from moving too far. Severe cold fronts offering significant changes in barometric pressure and bright, sunny skies might keep them out of the shallows altogether. Again, keep in mind depth is relative, so the distance, duration and depth of these movements vary depending on lake type, deepest available water and most easily accessible deep water. Water characteristics, local conditions and how far winter has progressed all come into play.

Variable #5 Always remember gamefish movements under the ice will vary with how far winter has progressed. Several biological, physical and chemical parameters also prompt or discourage these movements.

Forage

Forage is an example of one biological parameter that nearly always influences winter gamefish location. As you've likely surmised, considering this variable has been mentioned in almost every section of this formula. You might find the right lake type undergoing an upswing in population cycle and just the right combination of your target species preferred habitat, structure, cover, depth and other qualities for the time you're fishing. You might also identify primary migration routes, but if there isn't an adequate amount of forage present, gamefish won't likely congregate there.

Furthermore, if large numbers of your target species attack an area of concentrated forage, fishing may be poor simply because the natural abundance of forage creates a lack of interest in angler presentation. Simply put, the fish don't want your bait because they have plenty to eat. By the time these fish finish foraging heavily on existing food, which tends to scatter the forage, the fishing starts to improve. But then, another change in feeding habits and further under-ice movements are likely to occur.

One of the main factors involved with locating winter gamefish consistently is locating structures offering moderate amounts of forage. Excessive amounts of available forage usually result in well-fed fish and poor fishing action. Then again, areas supporting low forage densities won't attract fish. The trick is to find good "combination" areas harboring quantities of forage large enough to draw fish, but sparse enough to provide competition among individuals.

To identify primary forage bases and their relative abundance, contact a local fisheries office. Although you may discover overlaps in forage use from one gamefish species to another, to reduce competition individual species typically seek different environmental niches. Some may feed on perch amid shallow, vegetated flats. Some may chomp crustaceans along the edges of mid-depth, hard-bottom structures. Others will peck at insect larvae in deep, muck bottoms, shiners on hard bottoms, main-lake structures, or shad suspended just beneath the ice, while others slash into schools of deep, open-water ciscoes.

Even among a single species, smaller gamefish might feed on hard-bottom, shallow-water structures offering plankton while larger individuals relate to deeper, soft-bottom structures offering insect larvae, bait fish or worms. Speak with local biologists to determine the preferred forage of the species and size you're targeting on your lake. Then ask about the habits of these forage fish and locations you're likely to find moderate numbers of them. Or, better yet, ask where you can find moderate, yet diverse numbers of several preferred varieties, such as where a crustacean-filled hard bottom meets an insect larvae-, worm- and shiner-rich, soft-bottomed weed line. By learning to understand the habits of your species' favored forage bases and forage niches, you'll learn to pattern gamefish.

Variable #6: Fish where the food is.

Bottom Content

Bottom content may have a profound effect on numerous water characteristics. Like many other variables in nature, bottom content directly and indirectly effects other important parameters. Muck bottoms supply a great num-

Once the edge and migration routes along the deepest available water are identified, set out to find specific areas that are likely to be holding fish or attracting forage. This is best done using sonar because, like depth readings, sonar readings revealing the presence of forage can be taken without drilling holes.

ber of nutrients. This is a chemical parameter which produces large growths of plant and animal life, creates thick growths of vegetation and thick blooms of tiny plants called phytoplankton which float freely in the water. All these combine to reduce the clarity of the water, another physical parameter.

Lakes featuring less fertile bottom contents such as sand or rock typically feature clearer water, which allows more sunlight penetration. In turn, the bright light causes light-sensitive species such as walleye to become less active during periods of bright light, or sends them scurrying into heavier cover or deeper water during bright, midday periods. Improved clarity also allows better and deeper vegetation growth. This is a physical parameter that increases photosynthesis and its important chemical by-product, oxygen.

In contrast, darker water reduces sunlight penetration in the depths, reducing vegetation growth, slowing photosynthesis and limiting oxygen production. This is important. Consider how various forage and gamefish species have different levels of tolerance to oxygen concentration. Areas not supplying adequate oxygen will be vacated by both forage and fish. So even if you're fishing the right lake type in a location featuring a good combination of habitat, structure, cover, and bottom content, but the location you choose is without adequate oxygen, it may not support numbers of actively feeding gamefish.

Reduced sunlight penetration results in shallower weedlines. This decreased amount of cover influences gamefish depth patterns and migrations. Similarly, thick ice and heavy snow cover diminish sunlight intensity, influencing a variety of physical, biological and chemical parameters, creating varying degrees of winter gamefish activity, positioning and movement.

Different environments also often display vastly different varieties of bottom content. Although shallow, dark-water lakes typically feature a large percentage of soft, mud bottom, and deep, clear lakes are more likely to be predominantly sand or rock, variations occur. Since certain types of prey prefer specific bottom types, bottom content can heavily influence under-ice location. A sand or rock bar on a lake with a muck bottom, for instance, might provide that little something different gamefish will relate to.

Why? Go back to variable number six, fishing where the food is. Since worms are likely found in muck bottoms, and insects or crustaceans in rocky bottoms, areas where the two meet offer a

After finding specific locations offering forage—particularly those areas with the specific bottom content or bottom content transitions you're looking for—are identified, carefully position a series of holes over the area to efficiently cover water.

diversity of forage that attracts gamefish. Here, fish can peck at worms or insect larvae in the muck bottom, move a few feet and eat crustaceans or shiners on the rocks.

Variable #7 Always remember your target lake's bottom content mixture. This, along with other interrelated physical, chemical and biological variables, will tell you where the fish are likely to be found.

Inter-Species Competition

We can now delve deeper into the mysteries of winter fish location. Let's say you find the right lake type. You also identify the right combination of preferred habitat, structure, cover, depth, forage, bottom content and oxygen concentration in a particular area. You begin fishing and start catching walleyes, then the action suddenly stops.

Why? It could be the walleyes are simply are moving along a migration route or break line of some kind. Perhaps a slight shift in activity level is occurring? Or it could be another competing gamefish, such as a large pike, has moved in and the walleyes are responding by retreating into heavy cover or deeper water to hide until the competition passes. Either way, inter-species relationships are important considerations when attempting any winter fishing.

This doesn't happen often, because pike and walleyes, when found in the same environment, typically prefer not to compete and choose different ecological niches or feed most intensely during different daily periods. At times these two species will overlap for forage and such conditions will affect your fishing.

Variable #8: Consider inter-species relationships in the lake you're fishing. They often have an impact on gamefish locations.

Intra-Species Competition

Just as another species may cause a change in your target fish's feeding mood or habits, so may larger fish of the same species. Take pike for example. As you'll see later in this book, the environmental needs of pike are similar no matter what their size. Still, smaller pike have slightly different needs than larger ones, causing them to often hold in different areas. This is a key which can be used to increase your knowledge of productive patterns and consistency with larger pike.

There are times pike of different sizes utilize the same areas. When this happens, depending on the lake's balance, larger pike may chase the small ones away, slowing the feeding activity of smaller fish. Conversely, the sheer number of smaller fish may simply reduce the ability of larger fish to feed effectively. Either way, this intra-species competition will impact your fishing.

Variable #9 Consider the population cycle, density and "balance" of your target species on the lake you're fishing. This will effect fish positioning, activity levels and movements.

Time of Day

Time of day also has a pronounced effect on activity levels and movements. Some species are more likely to feed at night. Walleyes, for instance, have large eyes and see better than

Since both forage and fish move beneath the ice based on the current local conditions, monitoring their movements using sonar or underwater cameras is necessary to efficiently pattern these movements.

most prey species during twilight and evening periods. Since this is a predatory advantage, you're likely to find walleye actively feeding during these periods. Trying to find active walleyes during mid-day can be difficult, but locating mid-day schools of active, pike isn't unusual.

These fish may even share prime feeding grounds. A deep weed line can be a great pike spot during the day, and turn into a walleye magnet at night. Why? The forage is there, it's just the species have adapted to co-exist in their environment.

Time of day may also influence daytime movements. Bright conditions following passage of a cold front will send most gamefish, especially larger ones, scurrying deeper or into heavier cover, particularly in clear water. Even suspended fish may move into greater depths. However, if thick ice and heavy snow coat even the clearest water, these movements may be altered. Given extremes, light-sensitive species such as walleyes may move shallow and feed at high noon, simply because diminished light penetration allows a change in behavior. To pattern these fish, consider where such movements are

Weather

Since this variable is completely out of our control, it's the one that most commonly wreaks havoc with any winter fishing system. As with open-water fishing, sudden changes in barometric pressure, wind, heavy snows and the passing of cold fronts and their associated bright skies may dramatically influence fish activity levels and movements beneath the ice. Even experts can't explain why, but here are some weather conditions that appear to change ice fishing success:

- Stable conditions are good for fishing.
- Gamefish seem to bite better on partly cloudy days than bright, sunny days, likely because there is less light penetration into the water.
- South and west winds are good for fishing, but north and east winds are poor.
- Thin ice and little snow cover let light in, causing gamefish to hide deeper in cover or at greater depths during bright conditions.
- Thick ice and heavy snow cover reduce the sun's brightness underwater, allowing gamefish to move shallower and feed, particularly early and late in the season. Mid-season, such conditions may reduce photosynthesis, slowing or stopping oxygen production, lessening the distance of movement, perhaps even causing gamefish to move deeper or suspend.
- Gamefish usually bite well during periods of light snow. Heavy snowstorms and blizzards may cause them to hide in cover or move deep. Fishing is often poor for a day or two after a big winter storm or the passing of a severe cold front.
- When you hear meteorologists talk about warm and cold fronts, listen carefully. Warm fronts associated with low pressure systems usually bring active fish up to feed. Cold fronts and bright, high pressure systems tend to send them deep, where they're not as active.
- Finally, listen when meteorologists discuss the barometer. Many experts find fishing best when the barometer is rising, others like fishing when pressure suddenly drops.

Variable #11 Either adapt your strategies to the prevailing weather conditions, or time your trips during sustained periods of

In general, most gamefish seem to bite better on overcast days than they do on bright sunny days. Anglers can still catch them under sunny conditions by moving deeper, fishing heavier cover or refining the presentation to better match the conditions.

likely to occur based on the prevailing conditions. Ask yourself where these fish might be moving to and from—not just during, but also before and after these changing light conditions. Then try to determine how long or short these movements are in duration and distance.

Variable #10: Consider the species you're seeking and the importance of the time of day when planning your winter angling strategies. Inter-related variables such as bright skies, water clarity, interspecies competition, ice thickness and snow cover will effect the movement of the fish.

When fishing for gamefish, always consider the species you're seeking, it's location, depth and activity level along with the local conditions when attempting to choose the proper presentation.

most feature large mouths and big appetites, so it shouldn't be surprising they eat primarily larger forage items such as larger crustaceans and bait fish. Occasionally, an abundance of insect larvae, worms or fish eggs might cause them to temporarily take advantage of alternative forage bases. As anglers, we must try to match their natural feeding habits by using primarily larger, crustacean- and minnow-imitating lures and baits, but at the same time, be ready to scale down if they're feeding on alternative forage.

Often, these tendencies translate into the use of medium-light, medium or heavy action jigging equipment, including stout ice rods and durable spinning and baitcast reels with a good drag. Thin, yet strong lines and a variety of large minnow-type jigs, spoons and specialized lures can be the ticket to consistency, but at times, scaled down, lighter tackle and smaller jigs and baits will be needed. Specifically what equipment, lures and baits perform best depends on the species you're targeting, its location, depth, local conditions and timing. The fish's activity level and careful consideration of the aforementioned "Deadly Dozen" factors are also important to your success.

At times, tip-ups also play a role in successful presentation. Special heavy settings on ultra-smooth underwater, thermal and wind tip-ups allow the use of larger hooks, rigs, lures and minnows for pike, salmon and lake trout. Lightly set wind tip-ups, balance-style tip-ups and tip-downs with specialized, light rigging may be necessary when dealing with finicky, light-biting fish such as largemouth and smallmouth bass, walleyes or whitefish. Again, which model and presentation strategies best fit the situation depends on the species you're targeting, its location, depth, and activity level. Obviously there are a lot of details to consider, but since these vary greatly with the species and conditions, we'll reserve further discussion for upcoming species-specific chapters.

Variable #12 Always consider the species you're seeking, its location, depth, and activity level along with the local conditions when attempting to choose the proper presentation.

The Deadly Dozen Formula Equals Success

Nature isn't subject to any single set formula. There are many combinations of direct and indi-

mild, overcast, low pressure systems or extended periods of stable, favorable weather. Fish will bite best just before the arrival of a significant weather change.

Presentation

The final variable in the formula for ice fishing success is presentation. Once you've considered all the other factors, it's time to drill a few holes and start fishing. Knowledge of how to set, rig and use equipment and tackle comes into play.

Gamefish, by our definition, are often of substantial length and girth. With few exceptions,

Translate the "Hooked On Ice Fishing" "Deadly Dozen" variables properly, and the results will equal more consistent, more enjoyable ice fishing outings. (Courtesy Vexilar, Inc.)

rect effects that should cause you to make slight changes to your interpretation of the above factors and variables that influence winter gamefish location. We'll explore many of these in future chapters. For now, it's important to recognize these variables and understand that together, they help create a general foundation for consistent winter fishing success.

For many, the thrill of ice fishing is learning to identify key location patterns. Then you must capitalize on them by determining the proper presentation based on the environment, daily conditions, fish's activity levels and moods. Translate these variables properly, and the results will equal more consistent, more enjoyable ice fishing outings–and the thrill of the hunt.

Chapter 1

Staying Comfortable

If you've ever tried to accomplish anything in the cold, you know its trials. Trying to concentrate and remain patient during even the simplest project when you are subjected to the cold can seem impossible.

Take the annual hanging of outdoor Christmas lights as an example. Cold temperatures are enough to make most people wish they were indoors handling a hot drink instead of outside decking the halls. Simple tasks such as climbing a ladder become challenging. You must set its base in an area devoid of ice and snow and risk a nasty fall as you navigate each slippery step wearing bulky boots. Untangling those lights, ordinarily a task requiring little more than patience, becomes frustrating when wearing bulky gloves. Choosing to accept the alternative, cold fingers, doesn't make the chore any more pleasant.

Now think about spending extended periods of time in wind-exposed areas trying to accomplish tasks such as tying knots with hands that aren't only cold, but damp from handling fish or wet line. Ouch!

Bottom line? We can learn all we want about winter gamefish location and bait presentation, but there are two things required for winter fishing: safety and comfort. Without a safe approach and the comfort of dry, light-weight, warm cloth-ing, ice fishing experiences become no different than the annual hanging of outdoor holiday decor.

So, before getting into specifics about locating and catching winter gamefish, let's tackle ice safety and staying warm. As we've pointed out throughout the "Hooked On Ice Fishing" series, no fish is worth a human life. An improperly dressed angler will spend more time thinking about getting warm than catching fish. That's not much fun.

Anglers must be cautious around springs, as these areas will feature warmer water and create water movement, inhibiting ice formation.

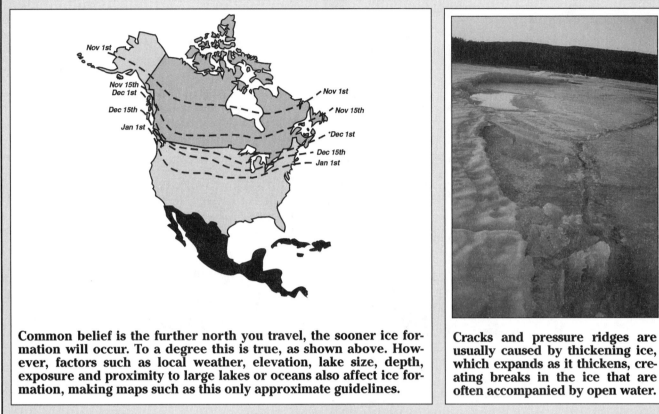

Common belief is the further north you travel, the sooner ice formation will occur. To a degree this is true, as shown above. However, factors such as local weather, elevation, lake size, depth, exposure and proximity to large lakes or oceans also affect ice formation, making maps such as this only approximate guidelines.

Cracks and pressure ridges are usually caused by thickening ice, which expands as it thickens, creating breaks in the ice that are often accompanied by open water.

Examining Ice Formation

- *Generally, the farther north you go and the higher the elevation, the sooner the ice forms.*
- *The farther away from large water bodies, the sooner ice forms. Parts of inland New York may have ice, while areas bordering the Great Lakes have none. Upper Michigan and northern Wisconsin might have solid ice, while lower Michigan, at the same latitude but influenced by the "lake effect" of Lake Michigan, might have little, if any ice.*
- *Consider lake depth, too. Ice may be several inches thick on shallow, protected water, while deep lakes in the same region might boast scarcely a fraction of an inch if exposed to wind.*
- *Ice thickness is seldom uniform. Shallow, shaded or protected bays on a deep lake may be covered with a couple inches of ice as whitecaps roll on the main basin.*
- *At most temperatures, snow accumulation insulates the ice, slowing ice formation.*
- *In-flowing creeks, channels and springs create water movement inhibiting ice formation. Pack ice, formed when broken chunks of ice blow together and freeze, pose problems because the ice is never a consistent thickness.*
- *Animal activity, such as the movement of muskrats, ducks, geese or fish can impede or prevent ice formation.*
- *Aerators, placed to maintain oxygen for fish or protect man-made structures such as docks, may prevent ice formation entirely.*

- *Cracks and pressure ridges are usually caused by thickening ice, which expands as it thickens, creating large heaves. Typically, these are accompanied by open water, and given strong winds, may expand. Many ice anglers have crossed small cracks in the morning, only to return and find they're isolated from shore by several yards of open water the same afternoon.*
- *Fishing reservoirs and flowages can be treacherous because of fluctuating water levels. If the water rises, shore ice floods, leaving unsafe ice surrounding the shoreline. Falling levels cause steep ice heaves along shore.*
- *Late season, shore ice may be open days before deeper main lake areas.*
- *Ice surrounding exposed objects such as downed trees, docks or large rocks becomes increasingly hazardous late in the season. The same is true for shallow, dark-bottomed areas. All absorb the sun's heat and transfer it to the surrounding ice, weakening the pack.*

Be cautious. Call or check with local anglers, guides, baitshops, state park superintendents, wardens, motel, restaurant and resort owners responsible for plowing and maintaining access sites or roads before stepping on the ice. If they can't tell you the current conditions, they can likely put you in touch with someone who can.

Lake depth is a primary factor influencing ice formation. Ice will form much sooner on a shallow, wind protected lake than a deep, wind exposed one.

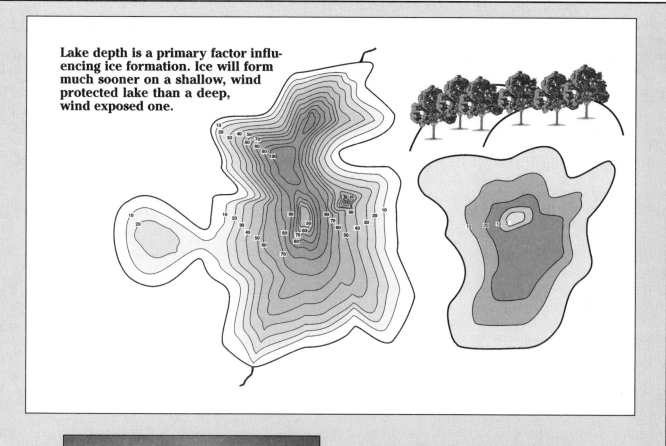

Pack ice, formed when broken chunks of ice blow together and freeze, pose problems for ice anglers because these chunks invariably consist of various thicknesses.

Aerators, placed to maintain oxygen for fish or protect man-made structures such as docks, may prevent ice formation entirely.

Fishing reservoirs and flowages can be treacherous, because rising water levels may flood shore ice, or as shown here, falling waters may cause dangerous ice heaves along shore.

Since ice safety has been covered at length throughout this series, we won't dwell on the topic, but rather, review some important points, starting with some basic information on ice formation.

Traveling Over Water

I usually walk onto the ice either pulling a packed sled or portable shelter, unless ice conditions allow prudent use of six-wheelers, four-wheelers or snowmobiles. These are lighter and less expensive than a car or truck. They are also easier to escape from should you break through and are much better for snow and ice travel.

That's not to say vehicles can't be driven on the ice. They are each winter. Then again, vehicles can and do drop through each winter. However, should you choose to drive on the ice with any vehicle, follow these guidelines closely:

• Don't drink and drive. Alcohol slows response time and impairs the ability to react.

• Avoid ice heaves and fractures, unless safely bridged by an on-ice road maintenance crew.

• Avoid excessive speeds. Vehicles traveling on the ice produce shock waves that weaken and may fracture ice. This is especially dangerous with two vehicles traveling close together. When driving at night, you can also attain speeds that require stopping distances longer than the extent of your headlights. This is a problem if you shift off course or approach thin ice or open water.

• If in a car or truck, remove heavy clothes that might impede your ability to slip out, unbuckle seat belts and lower your windows. This is espe-

cially important with power windows that can short-circuit upon contact with water. Always keep one hand on the door latch. Each of these steps saves precious seconds in the event you break through the ice.

Helping Someone

If assisting someone who has fallen through the ice, keep your distance. Lay down on the ice to distribute your weight and "extend yourself" to the victim. Throw a rope, extend an ice drill, chisel, or tie items such as belts or clothing together and without getting too close, extend them to the victim. Two people in the water can't help each other.

Most importantly, always respect the ice, and remember, "when in doubt, don't go out!"

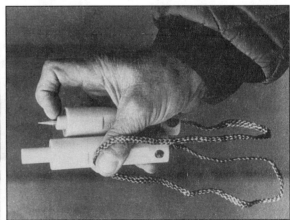

Carrying a high quality set of ice picks is smart, so in the event you do break through the ice, you can pull yourself to safety. (photo courtesy Bob Hammes)

The Quest For Warmth

Once you've checked the ice and are prepared to venture out, your next goal is to remain comfortable.

Like an athlete preparing for competition, this begins with proper fluid and food intake. Dehydration is a concern because moisture is quickly lost through perspiration and breathing. While loss of moisture to breathing may seem insignificant, in cold, dry air, your body uses up moisture quickly. During each inhalation moisture is added to the air being drawn in. Moisture is then expelled during exhalation. With your body continually drawing moisture for this process, dehydration can occur quite rapidly. The result is slowed metabolism and inadequate bodily heating.

Clothing

In addition to fluids and diet, you must dress properly. Today's cold-weather clothing is lighter, drier, warmer and offers more insulation than ever before. Use the right combination of modern cold-weather clothing, and it's unlikely you'll become uncomfortable, even while spending extended periods of time on the ice. Modern cold-weather clothing is designed to minimize heat loss, particularly in regions where body heat loss is the greatest: the head, torso, and legs. While your hands, fingers, feet, toes, nose, ears, chin and cheeks are susceptible to frostbite and must be adequately protected, heat for these areas originates from the body core and is mostly dispelled through the head, so let's begin by focusing on protecting the areas from which the most heat is lost.

Cold Weather Clothing

Start with the head, where an estimated 40% of heat loss occurs. A warm, well-insulated stocking hat lined with polypropylene is perfect, especially if it has the ability to be loosened during periods of activity. Polypropylene allows moisture to be wicked away from the skin and hair, thereby keeping your head dry. Being able to loosen the material allows you to release heat should you start to feel too warm. During peri-

Layers of clothing help insulate from the cold because they trap layers of warm air. Bulky layers of lofty materials sandwiched between polypropylene undergarments and wind resistant outerwear perform best. Depending on the conditions, anglers should add layers to warm up or strip some to keep from perspiring.

ods of minimal activity, the hood from a hooded sweatshirt and/or hooded outer garment should cover your hat to help retain additional heat, especially in strong, cold winds or during periods of precipitation.

As for the body core, most people follow the layering concept, which means wearing multiple layers of clothing. This works because layers of warmed air are trapped between layers of clothing, holding heat close to your body and insulating you from the cold. But to achieve maximum warmth, this layering must be carefully assembled. If you don't wear enough layers, you'll get cold. Wear too many layers, and you may end up perspiring, resulting in damp clothing. Since wet clothing conducts heat, it's a poor insulator. Furthermore, the evaporative process, being a cooling one, draws heat from the body, especially when combined with wind.

Other drawbacks to multi-layered clothing systems include the following:

By the time you notice you're wearing too many layers, you are often too warm and you've already broken a sweat.

The temperature range where clothing remains comfortable decreases substantially when the insulation becomes damp.

When layered clothing becomes wet with perspiration, it's often difficult or impossible to dry it without removal.

Therefore you must wear the right clothing in the proper order, based on the conditions and your activity level. Throughout the Hooked on Ice Fishing Series, I have referred to this proper layering concept as the "three W's": Wicking, Warming, and Wind-resistance. The wicking layer closest whisks trapped moisture away from your skin, keeping you dry. This can be accomplished using a variety of modern, man-made materials.

The second, or warming layer, resists heat loss by trapping pockets of warm air between your body and the cold outside air, providing insulation and warmth through layers of stabilized air. This is best achieved using layers of materials featuring very low heat-conducting properties near the skin. The more the material restricts air movement, the better the insulator. Insulation which does not absorb water, or better still, insulating materials which can entrain moisture in vapor form and consequently expel it to the outside, are best. These layers should also be able to evenly distribute moisture in both vertical and horizontal directions, allowing adequate time for the diffusion of moisture through the

WIND CHILL CHART	Wind Speed (mph/kph)	Equivalent Temperature (Fahrenheit) To convert to Centigrade - C = 5/9 (F-32)										
	0/0	35	30	25	20	15	10	5	0	-5	-10	-15	-20
	5/8	33	27	21	16	11	6	1	-6	-11	-16	-21	-26
	10/16	21	15	9	3	-3	-9	-15	-22	-27	-32	-38	-45
	15/24	16	9	1	-4	-11	-18	-25	-33	-40	-45	-52	-60
	20/32	12	5	-3	-9	-17	-24	-32	-40	-47	-52	-60	-68
	25/40	7	0	-8	-15	-22	-29	-37	-45	-52	-58	-67	-75
	30/48	5	-2	-11	-18	-26	-33	-41	-49	-56	-63	-70	-78
	35/56	3	-4	-13	-20	-28	-35	-43	-52	-60	-67	-75	-83
	40/64	1	-7	-15	-22	-30	-37	-45	-54	-62	-69	-78	-87

☐ Cold   ☐ Very Cold   ☐ Bitter Cold   ☐ Extreme Cold

Courtesy of Northern Outfitters

In a still environment, a shroud of warm air surrounds the body. Wind makes you feel colder because this shroud is dissipated by the wind, creating "wind chill factors." Wearing wind-resistant clothing helps protect from this effect by protecting the layer of warmth trapped within your insulative clothing below. (courtesy Northern Outfitters)

insulation without significant heat loss. Materials utilizing strands of fiber, or better yet, small open air cells, create the most effective, insulating pockets of air.

The third, or wind-resistant layer, blocks the effect of wind. Wind makes you feel colder because in effect, a cloud of warm air surrounds the body, but is quickly dissipated by wind. This effect creates the "wind chill factors" we hear so much about during winter.

But be careful. True waterproof, wind-resistant layers don't allow wind to cut through the material, but don't allow moisture vapor to pass to the outside, either. While waterproof outerwear is good in mild, damp conditions, such materials cause serious problems in the cold because they don't allow adequate expulsion of moisture.

In the past, this was a difficult, if not impossible clothing combination to find. With today's modern technological advances in materials, however, this balance has been achieved and numerous exceptional choices in lightweight, dry, warm, comfortable, high-quality winter clothing is available.

Of all the products I've seen on the market, Northern Outfitters patented VAETREX clothing (an acronym for "Vapor Attenuating and Expelling, Thermal Retaining clothing for Extreme cold weather conditions) is among the best. According to the experts at Northern Outfitters, VAETREX works well because it provides superior ability to retain body heat. It conducts very little heat away from the body by remaining lofty to stabilize an insulating layer of air and encourages moisture suspension in vapor form. This provides a means for both liquid moisture and moisture vapor transfer to the outside. Best of all, these features, combined with very low wind permeability, are all comprised into one dry, lightweight, comfortable layer.

This is revolutionary. Modern ice fishing involves a great deal of movement and physical activity, and the ice angler's greatest enemy is multiple layers of restrictive clothing that slow blood circulation, and worse yet, become too warm during periods of activity. This quickly leads to perspiration which causes chilling.

While cotton is warm and comfortable when dry, once you begin to sweat, it draws moisture against the skin, cooling the skin's surface and counteracting any insulating properties. Wool is an excellent insulator and even stays semi-warm when damp, but it dries slowly and becomes

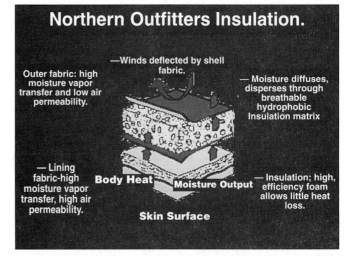

Northern Outfitters Insulation.

Of all the products I've seen on the market, northern outfitters patented "VAETREX" clothing (an acronym standing for "vapor attenuating and expelling, thermal retaining clothing for extreme weather conditions) is among the best. (Courtesy Northern Outfitters)

heavy and scratchy when wet. This is a problem, after all, during periods of activity, you will perspire. When you stop to fish and become inactive, perspiration begins evaporating from the skin. Not only does this cause chilling, especially in wind, but also drains the body of energy.

This is where modern synthetic fabrics come into play. Rather than absorbing moisture and packing down, modern synthetic materials remain lofty and transfer water away from the body to the outside of the fabric where it evaporates away. As a result, you stay warm and dry– even if you perspire–and you retain more energy. So while conventional cold-weather clothing protection is based on the idea of warmth through multiple layers of insulation, top cold weather clothing designers know insulation is not the only requirement for efficient cold-weather protection. Managing the body's moisture is equally important, because even the finest natural or man-made fabrics can degrade in their ability to insulate when they become wet. If the moisture from perspiration is not removed or managed, clothing will be rendered useless as a thermal protector.

Back to Northern Outfitters. Building on a concept derived by the Eskimos and improved using modern physics principles, their single layer, or "monolithic" clothing systems are top-of-the-line. The concept is simple and, best of all, consists of a single wicking, warming and wind-resistant layer

Northern Outfitters "VAETREX" monolithic clothing systems incorporate a moisture wicking, insulative and wind-resistant layer all into one comfortable, lightweight garment. (courtesy Northern Outfitters)

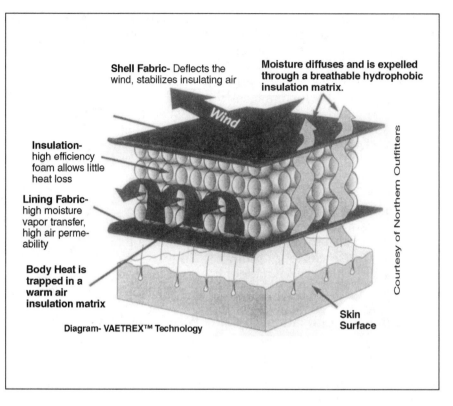

Shell Fabric- Deflects the wind, stabilizes insulating air

Moisture diffuses and is expelled through a breathable hydrophobic insulation matrix.

Insulation- high efficiency foam allows little heat loss

Lining Fabric- high moisture vapor transfer, high air permeability

Body Heat is trapped in a warm air insulation matrix

Skin Surface

Diagram- VAETREX™ Technology

Courtesy of Northern Outfitters

designed to follow two fundamental laws of physics to expel moisture.

1.) If moisture in the air is given limited opportunity to condense, it will remain suspended in vapor form.

2.) Warm, moist air will flow across a temperature gradient to cooler, dryer air. The greater the gradient, the faster the flow.

Thus, the monolithic concept used by Northern Outfitters not only keeps you warm by insulating you from the cold and wind it also expels moisture. Since moisture is not allowed to collect next to the skin or in the garment you not only stay warm, but dry. Additional advantages of this monolithic system include the following:

• The single layer of clothing is lighter and less restrictive, allowing better circulation and freedom of movement, yet effectively wicks away moisture, keeps warmth inside and protects against wind.

• The clothing effectively and efficiently retains the body's natural heat.

• There is no moisture build-up or frost layers in the clothing.

• The clothing dries while being worn, using natural body heat.

• There is a wide external temperature comfort range. Your skin will not become damp, and you won't feel overheated when inside or chilled when outside.

• Less changing of clothes is required when activities require a person to move from the inside to the outside.

Stripping layers of clothes during periods of activity isn't necessary, nor is storage, transport or access to extra clothing layers while inactive.

• While not waterproof, (waterproofing would destroy the ability of the material to wick moisture away to the outside) should the clothing, boots or mitts get wet, you simply pull them off, wring out the water, and put them back on. The outer layers of material will absorb any remaining moisture, keeping your skin dry and warm.

Essentially, this system creates the three W's layering system all in one dry, warm, comfortable layer.

To keep your feet warm, start with a pair of lightweight, PolarMax or Thermax polypropylene socks. Then choose from the variety of high-quality pack boots on the market. Companies such as Sorel, Red Ball, LaCrosse and Polartec all produce excellent models featuring modern synthetic insulating materials.

Northern Outfitters also makes a boot using VAETREX technology, which keeps your feet dry, and thus warm. One final tip: the experts at Northern Outfitters recommend loosening boot

A variety of high quality pack boots featuring warm, comfortable synthetic insulative materials are now available, so there really is no excuse for cold feet. (photo courtesy Red Ball Boots)

laces when you're inactive to help maximize circulation. Just be sure to lace them back up when you're active so the boots provide proper ankle support.

As for the hands, I recommend polypropylene-lined mitts, not five-fingered gloves. Loose-fitting, five-fingered, polypropylene lined gloves can be worn under mitts as an additional warmth layer. Why mitts? Quite simply, they keep your fingers together instead of spreading them out and dissipating body heat. Of course, mitts should also be well-insulated and lined with polypropylene. Always bring a second pair, just in case the first becomes damp.

Several companies, including Wells-Lamont and Northern Outfitters, make good mittens. The advantage of these mittens is that you can place wet hands in them after baiting or handling fish and, with such strong wicking properties, the liners dry on their own. Northern Outfitters VAETREX-lined mitts can even be dropped in water and, if you simply wring them out, in a matter of minutes the wicking action will dry the liners.

Other Factors

The other factors affecting warmth on the ice include the quality of your blood circulation and your degree of physical activity. Consider each when dressing. Blood circulation, for instance, varies between individuals, and those with poorer circulation have less tolerance for the cold.

As for the degree of physical activity, think. If you're employing the layering concept and you'll be walking two miles to a secluded lake carrying all your gear, strip down to your initial layer and perhaps a light wind-resistant layer, or you'll perspire and become chilled. Upon arrival, open the wind breaking garments during lake exploration and hole drilling. When you finally set up to fish, meaning the level of physical activity is reduced, add layers of insulation and close up the wind-breaking layer, one step at a time as your body cools.

In addition to adding or subtracting layers of clothing to adjust insulation, clothing can be loosened or tightened to adjust heat flow. Since heat rises, the human body acts as a chimney. Opening a flap somewhere near the neck or head, even at the wrists–can allow heat to escape. The trick is to do so before perspiration becomes a problem. Otherwise, try modern clothing materials such as Northern Outfitter's VAETREX.

A couple final points to consider: Tobacco, or specifically nicotine, should be avoided, as it constricts blood capillaries, reduces blood flow to the skin and reduces warmth. And remember that alcohol dilates capillaries, thereby increasing blood flow and causing rapid loss of body heat through the skin. Other problems include cosmetics, lotions, perfumes and colognes, which increase the possibility of frostbite because the alcohol content decreases skin temperatures.

Summary

When traveling from place to place on the ice, consider wearing a PFD. Carry warming and nourishing food and drink. Dress properly using modern clothing technology and the three W's system. Always be prepared to add, remove, loosen or open layers of dry clothing as necessary to suit your body and activity level. Avoid using cosmetics. All these recommendations will help you stay warmer.

Here's a convenient winter clothing checklist for your next trip:

- ❏ Polypropylene long underwear
- ❏ Polypropylene socks
- ❏ Polypropylene lined pants
- ❏ Multiple layers of polypropylene lined t-shirts or light sweaters
- ❏ Hooded sweatshirt
- ❏ Light, lined wind breaking jacket
- ❏ Hooded snowmobile suit or better yet, two piece bibbed gore-tex snow pants and hooded coat
- ❏ Quality pair of heavy duty pack boots
- ❏ Quality pair of polypropylene lined mitts, plus at least one spare pair
- ❏ Warm, polypropylene lined knit stocking cap
- ❏ Facemask or scarf

OR:

- ❏ Polypropylene long underwear and socks
- ❏ Northern Outfitters style liner, parka, pants, hooded coat or wind anorak and pants, and baraclava
- ❏ Polypropylene lined hat, socks, pack boots and mitts

The Northern Outfitters complete winter clothing system, including jacket, pants, hat, boots and mitts. (photo courtesy Northern Outfitters)

A FEW COLD WEATHER "DO'S AND DON'TS" COURTESY NORTHERN OUTFITTERS

DO:

- *KEEP YOUR HEAD COVERED, EVEN IT DOESN'T FEEL COLD. Fifty percent of heat loss occurs through the head.*
- *INCREASE YOUR INTAKE OF WATER, DRINK REGULARLY AND FREELY. You need water to prevent dehydration.*
- *KEEP YOUR CLOTHING DRY AND LOFTY. Wet clothing flattens, causing conductive and evaporative cooling.*
- *ELIMINATE ALCOHOL AND NICOTINE. Both negatively affect blood circulation.*
- *KEEP THE BODY'S CORE WARM. If the body core cools, less blood will circulate to the extremities.*
- *INCREASE THE NUMBER OF CALORIES CONSUMED. This increases metabolism, keeping you warmer.*
- *CUT DOWN ON CAFFEINATED DRINKS. Caffeine degrades the body's ability to produce and regulate heat.*
- *USE WIND SHELLS OF TIGHTLY WOVEN FABRIC OVER THE OUTER CLOTHING TO COVER YOUR HEAD, TORSO AND LEGS. Wind increases convection cooling.*
- *MAKE SURE BLOOD CIRCULATES FREELY. Tight fitting clothing restricts blood flow and increases conductive cooling.*
- *SELECT THE PROPER TYPE OF CLOTHING BASED ON THE TEMPERATURE, WIND CONDITIONS, AND ACTIVITY LEVEL.*
- *Wear more, heavier or closed clothing in extreme cold, heavy winds and during periods of inactivity. Reduce the number of layers, go lighter and loosen openings during lesser extremes in temperature and wind, and periods of increased activity.*
- *KEEP YOUR CLOTHING CLEAN. Soiled clothing is less lofty and increases conductive cooling.*
- *APPLY A SMALL AMOUNT OF STICK ANTI-PERSPIRANT TO THE FEET. Reduced sweating will help keep your feet drier.*

DON'T:

- *WEAR COTTON OR WOOL UNDERGARMENTS OR SOCKS. They collect moisture next to the skin.*
- *SPILL LIQUID FUELS OR GASOLINE ON HANDS OR CLOTHING. Super cooled liquids lower skin temperature.*
- *TRY TO DRY WET BOOTS AND CLOTHING BY WEARING THEM INSIDE A WARM CAR. Your boots will warm from the outside in, reversing the warming and drying process, forcing moisture and cold to remain next to the skin.*
- *DON'T WEAR TIGHT OR CONSTRICTING LAYERS OF CLOTHING OR SOCKS. This interrupts good blood circulation.*
- *DON'T TOUCH COLD SURFACES WITH EXPOSED HANDS. This causes conduction cooling.*
- *DON'T WEAR WATERPROOF BARRIERS IN WEATHER BELOW PRECIPITATION FREEZING LEVELS. Moisture will not be drawn from your clothing to the cold, drier outside air.*

Ice Shelters

On especially cold days, you might also want to consider the advantages of an ice fishing shelter.

Permanent "shanties" offer protection from the cold, so you can concentrate on your fishing. They're also nice when taking out kids, beginning anglers, guests new to the cold or for overnight stays. I've also used them when fishing for long periods during extremely cold weather. During those times I've used a portable shanty to move around, and the permanent shelter as a warm home base.

While all you really need is a sturdy, well-ventilated enclosure with a window and a heating device, I've even seen some pretty elaborate "shacks" in recent years, some two-storied, complete with carpet, wood stoves, tables, beds, generators for electricity, refrigerators, televisions, satellite dishes, even portable toilets.

Permanent shanties can be rented or purchased pre-built, but if you wish to build a permanent fish house, design it carefully. Be sure the design fits in your truck or trailer, or build a base with an attached axle assembly. Be sure the unit features adequate room and an organized hole set-up for the number of people you want to house. Also include the desired or required number of windows and proper ventilation. Vents should be provided near the ceiling and floor, or you risk carbon monoxide poisoning.

When using a heater or wood stove, set the controls and chimney to reduce the danger of fire. Also be sure to check laws on licensing, permits and building codes requiring windows, roofing designs, trailer safety standards, lights, removal times and name labeling–all of which vary from state to state and area to area. I also recommend use of a carbon monoxide meter. These may not be cheap, but what's a life worth? Sadly, I read an account of several young people who were asphyxiated in a permanent shanty several seasons ago. These were deaths a detector may have prevented.

Once on the ice, slip wood blocks between the frame and ice, or the unit will likely settle into the pack and freeze down. Be sure to loosen or move the unit every 10 to 15 days, especially during warm periods or later in the season. Also, be responsible enough to remove the blocks after each move rather than littering the lake.

Portable Shelters

The problem with permanent shacks is if you're not positioned over fish, mobility is limited. In today's mobile world of modern ice fishing, permanent shelters play little, if any role. Don't get me wrong, properly set over a good spot or set up by a winter guide service over a productive location, permanent fish houses are terrific. And if you want to play cards, watch football, cook out or spend an extended weekend on the ice, they're the best way to go. But if you're a modern, mobile ice angler, you have the choice of sitting out in the open or within a comfortable, portable shelter that blocks wind and offers protection from the cold.

So why not? With today's lightweight, portable enclosures, there's no excuse for not going ice

"Permanent" shanties offer protection from the cold so you can concentrate on your fishing better, but being challenging to move, often limit the mobility of most anglers.

With today's lightweight, easy to set portable shelters, there's no excuse for not going ice fishing, no matter what the temperature.

The primary function of a portable shelter is to keep you dry, dark and out of the wind–and units like this Frabill model do so with style.

fishing–no matter what the temperature. Most importantly, portable shelters provide most of the advantages of a permanent shanty. They serve as a wind barrier, reducing convection cooling, provide ample opportunity to heat the air around you, reduce conduction and radiant cooling, plus they give you the opportunity to neatly organize and store your gear during transport and while fishing. They do all this without the reduced mobility of a "permanent" fish house. For these reasons, portable shelters are becoming increasingly popular.

But choosing a unit today isn't easy. A decade ago, you could choose from perhaps a dozen models, today, there are many more. So how do you go about choosing one?

I spoke with Mark Gostisha of Frabill, a manufacturer of quality portable ice shelters, about the primary functions of a portable shelter.

"Their primary function is simply to keep you dry, dark and out of the wind," Mark said. "I suppose this could be accomplished with a refrigerator box and a $3 tarp, but today's portables offer a variety of advantages and benefits anglers should be aware of."

He gives the following considerations for anyone contemplating a new shelter purchase.

• Portables should be sturdy and close tightly so minimal snow is picked up during transit, yet should be lightweight for easy pulling or towing.

• Portables should feature molded plastic, flat floors. Wood is heavy and disintegrates in wet, freezing conditions. Flat floors eliminate the awkward hinge joint positioned in the center of the shelter.

• Canvas and nylon materials are more durable and quieter than rip-stop polyethylene. Removable material is also nice for mending damage, or drying and storage during the off-season.

• High quality, self-contained steel frames and material fastened to the floor or base are necessary to make set-up easy, even when wearing gloves or when the wind is blowing.

Collapsible, highly portable, lightweight shelters like HT's Polar Shelter, are popular with anglers packing in to fish remote waters.

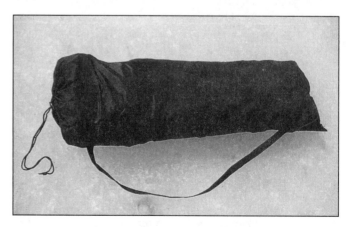

The collapsed Polar Shelter, compacted in its convenient, folded carry case.

• Windows are important for watching outside lines, and drapes help darken the tent so you can "sight fish" finicky biters.

• Arched doors make entering and exiting in heavy clothes easier. Also look for high-quality, self-repairing coil zippers.

• Portables should be tall enough to allow you to stand and stretch.

• Be sure fishing holes are large enough and spaced wide enough to be easy to fish with the intended number of anglers.

Also answer the following questions:

• Is the shelter made of durable, quality materials and workmanship?

• Is there a manufacturer warranty?

• How much does the unit weigh?

• Is it easy to set up? Easy to break down and stow away?

• Is the unit self-contained, or are there any loose parts that may get lost?

• How many people will be fishing in it, and how much room is needed for people, equipment and gear?

• Does the floor plan suit your needs?

• Can you fish effectively from it with your preferred equipment and methods?

• Is there adequate room to set the hook using your preferred rod length?

• Are ice anchors included?

• Is the lighting and number of windows satisfactory? Are they draped?

• How many doors are available? What type of zippers are used on them?

• If you plan to use heaters, does the unit have adequate ventilation?

• How compactly does it fold up?

• Is it easy to transport, carry, tow and store?

Another increasingly popular portable design is the so called "portable fish station", designed for the mobile ice angler who will be fishing alone, or perhaps with one other angler. Key features here include:

• A comfortable, built-in seat, to maximize mobility and comfort.

• A deep base, important for gear storage, and when towing this prevents kicked up snow from entering the shelter during transit.

• Canvas or nylon material, preferred for durability and quietness.

• Multiple roof positions, including closed, windbreak and open. For maximum convenience, this should be performed without taking off or adding pieces to the frame with each use, even in strong winds.

Keeping such things in mind will make selecting the right unit an easier task, especially given the number of portable models on the market today.

An increasingly popular portable shelter design is the so called "portable fish station," designed for the "on the go" ice angler.

Portable Heaters

A variety of portable heaters in an array of sizes and heating capacities are available. Some even offer accessories that allow heaters to double as cookers or portable stoves.

The primary concerns for the buyer involve choosing a unit to adequately and safely heat the size of shelter. A small one-person portable may be warmed adequately with the help of a simple camping lantern, depending on the outside temperature, wind velocity and type of material the portable is made of. Canvas for example, tends to dissipate heat.

Larger shelters require larger heaters, but guidelines are more easily established for a typical insulated, permanent house. They are as follows:

Shelter Size	Recommended BTU'S
6' x 8'	15,000
8' x 8', 8' x 10'	20,000
10' x 10' or larger	30,000

If using these heaters in a portable shelter, you'll want to increase the BTU's slightly to compensate for the non-insulated walls. For example, in a 6' x 8' portable, you might want to use the 20,000 BTU heater.

As for safety, make sure all connections are tight and any heating unit is properly vented. Be sure to keep heating units away from shelter walls, gear and loose clothing. Preferably choose a heater with built-in heat shields. Always be sure you have adequate ventilation, and as I recommended for use with a permanent shelter, carbon monoxide detectors are good investments.

Bear in mind that most small, portable heat sources are designed for outdoor use and should be properly vented. Also, be sure the model you choose properly suits the intended use and that the unit is properly installed. When done cor-

A variety of portable heaters in an array of sizes and heating capacities are available. Just beware! Such heaters are designed only for outdoor use within freely ventilated spaces. These are not intended for indoor use, as such practice risks carbon monoxide poisoning or asphyxiation.

rectly, ice shanties can be safely heated. For safety's sake, I'm listing the symptoms of carbon monoxide poisoning:

- Headache, dizziness and drowsiness
- Nausea, vomiting, extreme sleepiness
- Heart flutter, shortness of breath

Should you feel any of these symptoms, get into fresh air quickly and seek medical help immediately.

Chapter 2

Better Understanding the Under-Ice World

To me, the most fascinating part of ice fishing is exploring the under-ice world.

There's a lot of frozen water out there, and it comes in many forms. Natural lakes, reservoirs, ponds, pits, Great Lakes bays, river backwaters and even rivers. Each offers unique under-ice environments created by a variety of physical, chemical and biological conditions. These factors vary from one body of water to the next, each time you fish, throughout each day and during each season. Factor in the size of these waters, the structure, cover, water clarity, local weather, how far winter has progressed and the species present, and the complexities of the under ice world become more clear.

Furthermore, each gamefish species responds to these unique sets of conditions in its own way. Pike are genetically close to pickerel, walleyes similar to sauger. Yet each is a different species with different preferences, habits and responses. Consistent success depends on learning how these individual species relate to each unique environment. By learning about the species we want to catch and combining this knowledge with the ability to skillfully classify their environment

and identify the conditions they're subjected to, it's possible to adapt strategies for locating fish more consistently.

To do this we must review basic lake classifications, their unique physical, chemical and biological factors and how they influence general winter gamefish location, movements and migrations. Once we've outlined some general patterns, we'll apply this knowledge to use of lake maps and electronics. This will allow us to establish specific location patterns, movements and migrations in future chapters.

Where To Begin

Patterning winter gamefish begins with evaluation. When you catch fish, ask yourself why. What type of lake are you fishing? Where? Were they on bottom or suspended? Why were they there? How far has the season progressed? What kind of structure and cover are present? How deep are they? What time of day is it? What's the water clarity? Are the conditions sunny or overcast? Is the barometric pressure high or low? How many fish did you hook? What size were they? Did they bite continually or just periodically? Were they aggressive or passive? Did they bite for an extended period of time or a short time? Did you catch a mixture of two or more species? What were they feeding on?

Take this process a step at a time, each time you fish, every time you drill a hole, with each drop of a lure. Identify "fixed" factors such as lake type first, then work your way toward other variables, such as depth, structure, bottom content and water clarity. For anglers wanting to explore and make sense of the unknown, it's there, waiting to be patterned, and the satisfaction of discovery can be momentous.

I experienced this recently while fishing northern Wisconsin. The evening before the first day of fishing, my fishing partners and I stopped at a local restaurant and overheard two ice anglers discussing their fishing. I couldn't help but inquire how they'd done. They explained how they'd carefully reviewed lake maps to identify potential walleye structure, entered those coordinates into a GPS, located them, and used sonar to search them. They investigated three bars and found fish on one, but were disappointed to find they were perch.

Misconstruing the stereotype that walleyes hold on hard-bottom bars, they had proceeded to a large, clear, mid-size sand-bottom lake of moderate structure and fished three pre-identified bars, but returned after catching nothing but perch. We sat reviewing their maps and talking for three hours. I didn't know what had happened, but had a theory, one I set out to prove.

The next morning, local biologists confirmed the lake held a tremendous population of walleyes. They also confirmed this sprawling body of water was gin clear and offered reasonable structural diversity. Being 8:00 a.m., however, we chose to pass on this lake, at least for the moment. Getting a late start, we instead chose a smaller, shallower, stained-water flowage nearby, and managed to each pull a limit of walleyes by 10 a.m. before the action slowed. Knowing walleyes are light-sensitive, we deliberately chose this shallow, stained-water environment where they would likely be more active in the mid-morning. By 11:30 a.m. we moved to a mid-depth, clear water lake featuring a weed line from 15 feet to 17 feet deep. We set lines for pike, and after four hours of good action, packed up. Time to try our new lake.

Here we met our new friends coming off the ice, disappointed. I felt bad. These people were fairly knowledgeable and well-versed in the use of their equipment. What they appeared to be missing was a basic understanding of the lake environment. The gin-clear water and sand-gravel bottom with only sparse vegetation didn't provide enough quality cover for walleyes to feed in during the day. I suspected these fish were feeding at night. Since these guys had basically thrown in the towel, I asked for their GPS coordinates. Heck, the two days they had spent outlining these structures shouldn't go to waste!

The first bar was mid-sized and shallow, the second small and isolated, and as these anglers had indicated, neither held fish. The third was a large, elongated shoal gradually stair-stepping from a wide, shallow flat into a deep, main-basin hole. We caught perch right on this break, immediately.

As darkness set in, the perch bite stopped and the walleyes moved in. We not only caught our legal limit, but ended up with two fish of more than 4 pounds, one 6-pounder and one we estimated at close to 10. The next morning we ran into our friends, who asked the inevitable, "How'd ya do?"

The best winter patterns vary from lake to lake and species to species. Ice anglers must recognize this, then maintain open minds. (Courtesy Northland Tackle)

Careful not to hurt anyone's pride, we explained the situation and showed them our catch, then invited them to fish with us. Since the weather was relatively stable, we again fished the smaller, stained flowage for walleyes that morning, tried pike mid-day, then came back to spend the evening on their lake. We did well. They were delighted to see their structure produce, and reviewing the situation, learned an invaluable winter fishing lesson.

They had done most everything right, but missed several important pieces of the puzzle that made the difference between a great catch and no catch. First, they limited themselves to three structures on an immense, structurally diverse lake. Secondly, the shallow, mid-size bar and isolated deep reefs offered little cover, forage or migration possibilities. The large, elongated bar, however, offered cover, structural diversity, a migration route from deep to shallow water with numerous holding points and forage. It was a good choice, but the walleyes had adapted to feeding at night.

The best winter location patterns vary from lake to lake and species to species. Anglers must recognize this and maintain open minds. It's okay to have some pre-conceived notions about fish location and patterns, after all, we must start somewhere. But good ice anglers, regardless of where they fish, continually evaluate. What is the lake type? Where are active gamefish likely to be found given the time of winter and day, and when are they most likely to be active? Once a fish is caught, they ask why the fish are there. What type of structure and cover are the fish relating to? What forage? Are they just moving through, holding there because of specific conditions, or because they've been forced there by changing weather, inter-species competition, oxygen depletion, or a combination of the above? And if gamefish are attracted to specific spots, why this particular one and not another? Were these fish holding within cover on the deep, shaded side, or shallow sunny one?

Answer some of these questions and you can learn to pattern winter gamefish.

Are Gamefish "Smart?"

Gamefish have small brains, and respond by instinct. They cannot think, rationalize, review situations or determine the outcome of their actions. Like any animal with pea-sized brains, they can merely be conditioned to respond or not respond to various stimuli.

I've had salmon nab a bait beneath a tip-up, shake loose from the hook, then come back when I jigged the minnow. I've caught the same pike twice in one day, had lake trout smack a lure, get hooked, break free, then come back for more. I've watched schools of walleyes beneath the ice strike blue and silver jigging minnows with reckless abandon. Then, after catching several, I noticed the remainder became tough to catch.

Were they smart? No. When I'd switch to black and gold, they would strike again, then stop biting-until I switched to chartreuse. Why? Probably because some fish were more conditioned to react to specific colors. When all the active fish conditioned to respond to blue and silver were caught, the action stopped. By switching to black and gold, then chartreuse, I improved my catch. When the fish in that school stopped hitting those lures, I switched to a spoon and caught a couple more, and when the action really came to a halt, still managed to nab one more on a jig and minnow.

This is like the friends my young daughter recently invited to her birthday party. Served trays of finger Jell-O, blue was preferred, followed by red, and noticeably fewer children took the green and yellow. The kids showed preferences. Almost all of them, excluding two, ate Jell-O. Most wanted blue or red, only a couple chose green or yellow. One didn't care for Jell-O at all, the other complained of a stomach ache and wouldn't eat.

Fish are similar. Most might prefer blue, some red, a few green or yellow. Some may not want any because they're not hungry or environmentally stressed and won't eat.

Another analogy: If 10 people look at a restaurant menu, a couple might order the same selection, but it's unlikely all 10 will choose the same item. Some may prefer chicken, some will eat fish, some will go for the soup and a sandwich. And in rare instances where everyone chooses the T-bone special or pizza, they won't likely all order steaks prepared the same way or pizza with the same toppings. Some might not feel well and will just pick at their food or not eat at all, even if it's good.

Gamefish respond similarly. If there are 10 fish in a school looking at my presentation, a couple might strike a jigging minnow, but it's unlikely all 10 will strike the same lure. Some may prefer spoons, some bladebaits, some a jig and a minnow. If they're all vulnerable to large tube jigs, I'll likely have to vary the lure action, color or depth to attract them all. Some may not "feel well" and won't feed. That's not to say we can't come back

Predictable fish movements often occur throughout the winter. Figure them out, and you won't be left in the cold.

and try them the next day, or later that evening. Given different conditions, you may get some of those fish to strike.

Back to our original point. While gamefish can't think, they do respond, and if we can determine their responses and reactions to certain sets of conditions, we have the upper hand. That's because we have the ability to think and we know these fish may respond similarly to similar sets of conditions. Maybe we can't always explain why, but we can learn to predict how gamefish might behave based on repeat observation.

This can be taken farther. Consider a late-ice pike movement toward spawning grounds. Based on lengthening days, pike instinctively move shallow sometime between mid-winter and late-ice. If we can identify spawning grounds and areas where mid-winter pike hold, usually the deepest available water adjoining shallow spawning grounds, then identify the path they use to move between the two areas, we can increase our odds of locating them repeatedly under the same annual conditions. Similarly, predictable move-

ments may also occur throughout the winter. Figure them out, and you won't be left in the cold.

We know that gamefish move into specific areas at specific times, spending transition time between them in dormant, semi-active or active feeding states. If we can locate fish in specific places between these areas and identify periods of feeding activity, then determine what conditions stimulate movement we increase our winter catch. To really pinpoint our target fish we need to know how fast our target species moves along the route, how far they will go, and when, where and how long they will remain in active feeding states. Again, the fish aren't deciding to move, they're merely responding to stimuli. Identify these stimuli, and you'll catch more fish.

Determining Primary Gamefish Locations

Begin by determining the lake type best matching your target species preference. Is it a pond, river backwater, shallow natural lake, deep natural lake or reservoir? Examine the lake's physical qualities such as maximum depth, water clarity

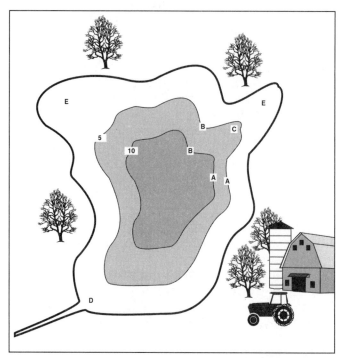

Successful ice fishing begins with evaluating lake type. In a small pond environment, features such as drop-offs (a), turns in bottom contours (b), slots of deeper water extending shallow (c), inlets and outlets (d) and shallow bays (e) are often the most productive structures.

and bottom content breakdown. Are the conditions favorable to good fishing?

Next, contact a local fisheries office to confirm that the population cycle is high or on the rise. Note primary forage bases. If the forage consists of small sunfish, perch, smelt or cisco, look back at Hooked on Ice Fishing II: Panfish and review their habits, movements and patterns. Productive gamefish location patterns often coincide closely and knowing these can help you to determine precisely when and where your target species is most likely to move from the adjoining deeper water and pursue these "forage" fish.

Also review the types of habitat, structure and cover available, bottom configuration and irregularities, including the more complex, less visible attributes such as temperature stratification, current, springs or oxygen gradients. Remember, not all structure is created equal. Any location where two or more of these factors meet or overlap is a high-percentage location. Find a rocky or gravel

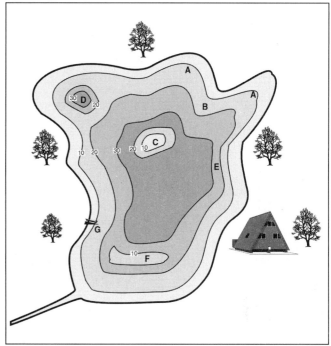

Small, shallow natural lakes feature slightly more distinct fish attracting structures, such as shallow bays (a), points (b), sunken islands (c), deep holes (d), drop-offs (e) and bars or shoals (f). Also try to find the most convenient access points (g) closest to your intended destination.

point extending from a deep, 45-foot muck-bottom hole butting up against a gravel bottom. If it has a moderately weedy secondary point extending toward a vegetated, sandy main-lake flat leading to a shallow, 5-foot spawning flat you'll be doing fine. Since this physically changing, diverse structure leads through several layers of strata from shallow water to the more stable, deep-water environment it provides a great laboratory for experimentation. This type of area will not only offer depth, bottom content and cover variations, but will also include areas of subtle temperature gradients, oxygen concentrations and varying cover and forage availability.

Gamefish will likely feed on specific locations along that point, depending where forage is concentrated—but they'll move and feed only during specific times. Exactly when varies with lake type, how far winter has progressed, the time of day, inter- and intra-species competition and weather. As anglers we can note the current conditions, make an effort to predict where and when possible movements to and from these locations might occur. Then we test the theory.

Yes, this can be challenging. But if you check with local biologists, guides and anglers to iden-

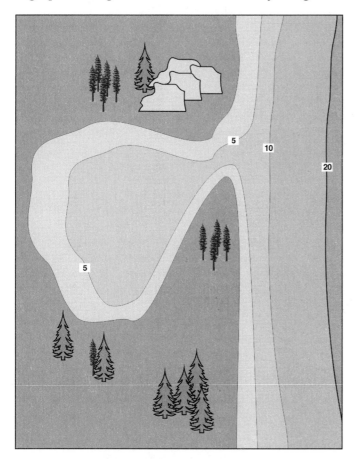

River backwater areas are often shallow and feature minimal structure. In most instances, deeper pockets, slots and deep edges in vegetation or wood graced with a hint of refreshing current are primary fish-holding areas.

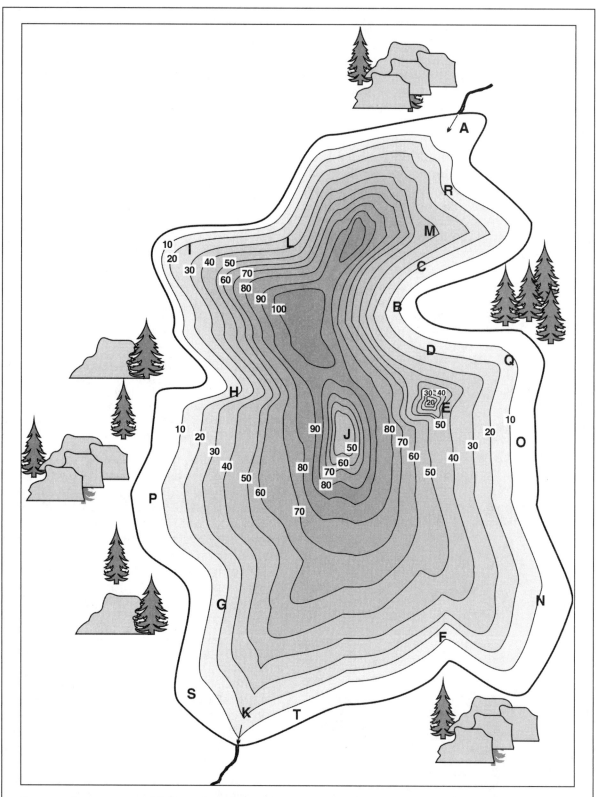

Larger, deeper natural lakes often feature more complex and diverse forms and varieties of habitat, structure and cover, including inlets (a), points (b,f,g,h,l) turns (c,d) sunken islands or reefs (e,j) slots of deeper water leading shallow (i,m) outlets (k) and shallow flats (n,o,p,q,r,s,t). With more complex environments come more complex winter patterns.

tify target lakes featuring populations of the species you want to catch, you can start to determine where, based on the conditions, gamefish are most likely to be. From here, you must determine if and when any movement between these depths takes place.

During most winters, gamefish prefer deep water because they're cold-blooded and heavily influenced by environmental conditions. Deep water is preferred because it's the most physically and chemically stable and the most protected from environmental change. I've also found that

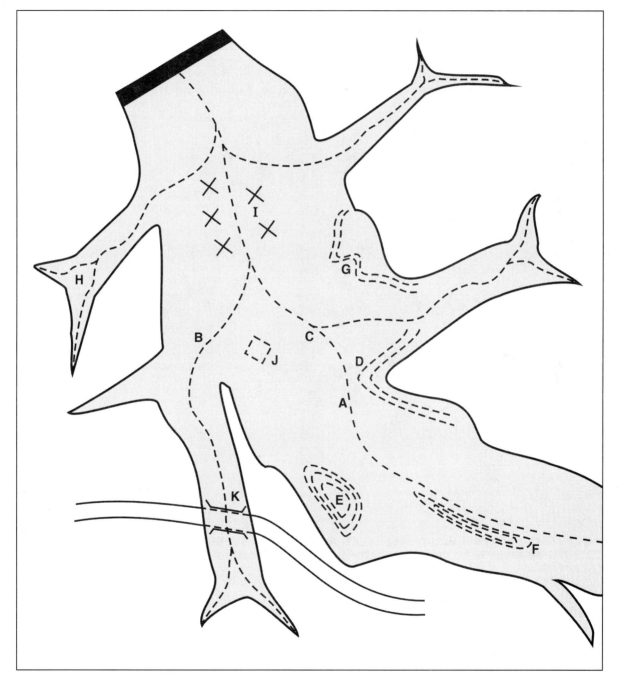

Like natural lakes, reservoirs (in some areas they're called "flowages") come in a variety of sizes, shapes and depths. They also offer structure unique to reservoirs, including the main river channel (a) secondary river channels (b) intersections of river channels (c), old building foundations (j) even submerged roads and bridges (k). In addition, they may feature points (d), sunken islands, reefs and rises (e), shoals lining the old riverbed (f), bars (g), shallow coves (h) and flooded wood and stumps (i).

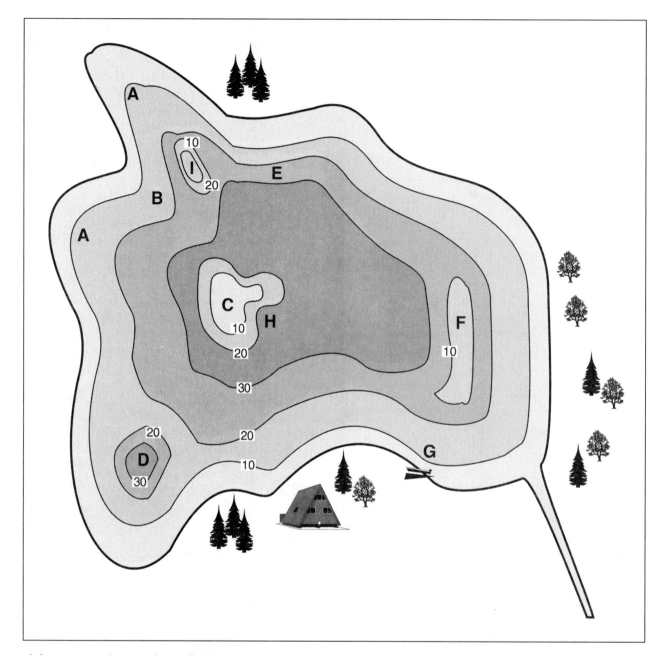

A key to consistent winter fishing success is trying to find and determine which structures your target species is most likely to be using during the time you're fishing. Bays (a) might be productive during early or late ice, but deeper structures such as points (b), sunken islands (c), deep holes (d), deep weedlines (e), bars and shoals (f), deep mud flats (h) or rock piles (i) might be more productive during mid-winter, depending on the species being sought, the current weather and water conditions.

the bigger the gamefish, the more important deep water is. In fact, if your target is a trophy, it will likely be found in the deepest available water in the area you'll be fishing. Take our sample point. It's extending from a shallow, 5-foot flat toward not only a hole more than 45 feet deep, but a hole which also happens to be the deepest water in the area. There's a good chance the largest fish will relate to this area.

With the best deep-water holding area now identified, begin considering movements. Start with basic movements between shallow and deep water and where they might occur. Then, secondarily, consider how local conditions might affect these movements. If the days are getting longer but you're fishing well before ice-out, start by fishing deeper water. If the ice is beginning to darken and the spawn isn't far away, try shallower water.

When searching for the best structures, focus on the most structurally diverse features leading from shallow to the deepest water in the area because deep water offers more environmental stability for winter gamefish. Here, the side of the point adjoining the deeper hole would likely hold more gamefish than the shallower side.

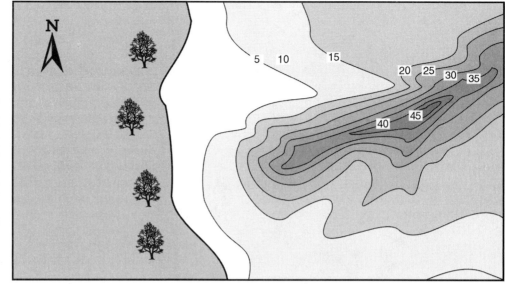

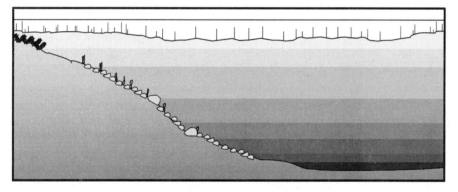

Diverse structures leading from shallow flats to the deepest available water in the area offer an increasingly more stable environment passing through a variety of potential fish-attracting features. By leading through several layers of depth strata often offering changes in bottom content, cover, temperature, oxygen concentrations and forage, such structures offer great laboratories for experimentation.

Gamefish will likely disperse over a diverse structural feature, holding at specific depths based on the lake type, how far winter has progressed, the time of day, weather, inter- and intra-species competition, cover and the availability of forage.

When targeting any winter gamefish, be sure to factor in the influence of the current weather conditions on the lake environment you're fishing.

Don't forget the influence of weather. If a cold front passes and brings bright, high skies and changing barometric pressure, bait fish generally respond by moving into heavier cover or deeper water. Mild, hazy conditions might draw them out and the gamefish will respond similarly. Only they will typically hold slightly deeper. Such knowledge combined with a mobile, open-minded approach should allow ample opportunity to locate active fish.

Some species like largemouth bass, or even more notably, smallmouth bass and catfish, seldom move at all. Instead, they congregate heavily in relatively small, specific home areas, rarely moving far at all. Get on top of them, and the action can be incredible. Fish 10 yards away, and you may not catch one all winter.

We will look at specific gamefish species and how the fish relate to structure in future chapters. For now, let's begin with some general winter patterns. The information will be based on how far winter has progressed and some basic influencing variables, beginning with ice-up.

General Winter Gamefish Patterns

During late fall, most gamefish move into deeper, more stable water. As ice forms and winter stratification begins, gamefish tend to hold deep, making only short, scattered movements from deep water holding areas towards cover and food-laden shallows. Given suitable shallow-water structure, cover, food, minimal fishing pressure and cooperative weather, gamefish are likely to remain shallow longer.

As the season progresses, shallow cover and forage often become diminished, and fishing pressure takes its toll. Yes, gamefish may make occasional movements back and forth from deep to shallow water. In general, most of the fish found in the shallow waters at this time are small. During mid-winter, larger concentrations of gamefish, especially large ones, relate to deep water flats, drop-offs and mid-lake structure, starting with features adjoining productive first-ice areas, then gradually moving deeper.

However, movements between the two areas may occur. Gamefish holding in deep holes adjoining long points, reefs or bars leading to shallow water offering cover and food will, sometimes

General winter gamefish movements occur each winter. Most gamefish will hold deep in fall, and begin making movements into shallow water to feed once the ice forms, tending to remain in the shallows longer if cover, oxygen and forage are available and the weather is cooperative. By mid-winter, shallow water movements usually become shorter and less frequent, until later in the season when many gamefish species feel the urge to spawn and begin migrating shallow again.

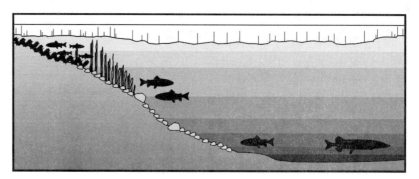

move along the edges and onto the tops of these structures, perhaps even into the shallows. The degree and duration of these movements vary with the conditions.

If fresh, green, oxygen-producing weeds persist in the shallows throughout mid-winter, plankton will thrive and grow, bait fish will move in. Should a path be available for gamefish to follow from deeper mid-winter haunts this combination of cover and food may attract gamefish periodically throughout the winter, if conditions are right. If one variable is missing, say the weather brings a cold front and bright sunny skies, gamefish may still move, but they won't move as far. Instead, they may make only a slight movement toward the shallows, stopping on some combination of structure and cover along the migration route. This, of course, depends on the severity of the cold front and degree of brightness.

By late-ice, most gamefish begin moving toward shallow spawning areas, but will still drop into deeper water if conditions dictate. Again, the distance and degree of these movements vary with the conditions. As spawning time approaches the movement will not just be sporadic. It will likely be an all-out migration of actively feeding deep-water schools. These fish will move into the shallows often causing the classic "late ice bite."

High-Percentage Locations

Again, these movements are based on instinct, so if we can logically identify where and when such movements and migrations will occur, we increase our odds of locating and patterning active winter gamefish.

To increase consistency, we must fish areas offering the greatest combination of features, or locations likely to attract the largest numbers of active gamefish under the broadest variety of conditions. Applying the deadly dozen variables, we know what areas increase our chances of finding fish. We also know structures close to the deepest available water in the area will produce fish. Just keep in mind this may not necessarily be the deepest water in the lake you're fishing, but the deepest water available near the high-percentage area.

Say your lake features a maximum depth of 40 feet. While possible, it's unlikely gamefish will be stacked on the bottom in 40 feet of water, even during the most severe conditions. It's more likely that gamefish will position themselves near the deepest water available in the area. In a structur-

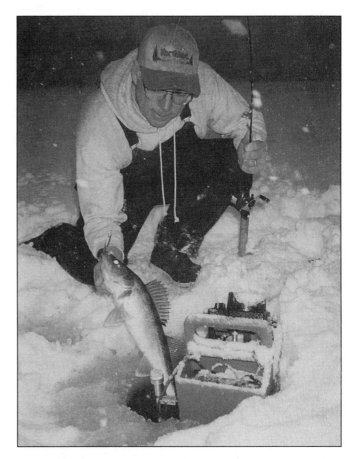

Winter fish movements are based on instinct, so if we logically identify where and when such movements and migrations occur, we can increase our odds of locating and patterning active winter gamefish. (Courtesy Northland Tackle)

ally diverse lake, this might consist of an elongated shoreline point or bar extending from a shallow feeding flat into 25 or 30 feet of water. In a smaller lake, they might be found in a bay with an average depth from 4 to 6 feet, offering a hole running 10 to 12 feet deep. Either way, check these areas out. You're likely to find gamefish holding and moving in or around these deeper pockets. Just note these areas may be large in scale, and often require the anglers to be mobile to pinpoint precise migration routes and holding areas.

Deciphering Migration Routes

The next trick is to determine where and when these fish move between water of different depths. You've also got to figure out if these are temporary movements, or regular seasonal migrations. While gamefish can't think, they seldom move haphazardly, either. They instinctively follow the comfort

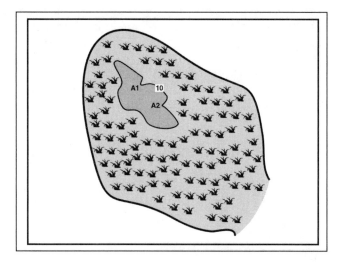

Game fish often relate to the deepest available water, which in a shallow bay averaging 4 to 6 feet deep might be a hole running 10 to 12 feet deep. Just keep in mind such areas may be quite large in scale, so finding specific areas of cover and forage-holding "micro-structure" on such a feature, like fingers or projections (a1, a2) would be good places to focus your efforts.

of migration routes leading from deep water into the shallows, and often, the same paths back. Depending on the environment, these routes may be along the outer edge of a weed line, depth break or structure such as a point, reef, hump, underwater river channel or the edge of a bottom content change. Whatever it is, the path usually runs between the deepest water in the area and the food-producing shallows. It will also usually consist of a distinct edge differentiating it from other surroundings.

Once identified, the next questions are when, how frequently and how far the movements are. Start with when and how frequently. If gamefish are moving through or holding in a certain location early in the morning, are they also coming through in the late evening? Are these fish making partial or secondary movements during late morning and early afternoon and stronger runs early in the morning and the late afternoon? If so, specifically when and how often do activity levels peak? Are these patterns occurring only during certain times during the winter or all season long? You

Once you've identified a primary fish-attracting structure, the next goal is to determine a potential migration route and, given the conditions, how far your target species is likely to travel along it. By doing so, over time you will note distinct patterns and the conditions causing various movements.

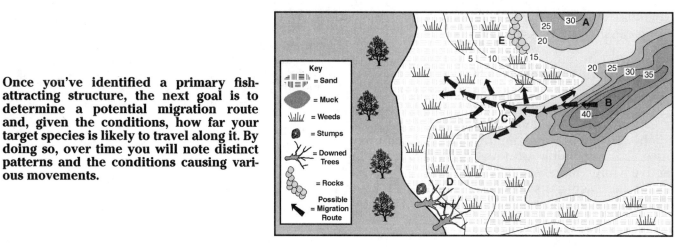

After possible migration routes are determined, search for distinct features gamefish may hold along as they travel. This may be vegetation (a), wood or stumps (b), rocks (c), fish cribs (d) or more subtle features such as a depth contour, bottom content change or transitions in temperature or oxygen concentration. Such places are "holding areas" for migrating gamefish.

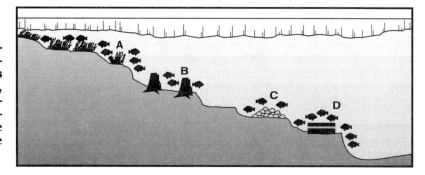

can get this information by contacting local anglers or guides, but the best way to find the answers is to fish the area.

Also note how far these movements occur. If the migration route leads between a flat that's 3 feet deep and a hole that's 40 feet deep and 200 feet long, are the fish moving into the shallows and dispersing or are the movements on a smaller scale where gamefish are only coming part way up? Are these regular daily movements at certain times of the year? How does the degree of movement vary with given conditions?

I've often noted that under mild conditions and overcast skies gamefish move onto shallow vegetated flats and feed heavily. During mid-winter or brighter, more unstable daily weather conditions, gamefish may still move up the migration route, but will move a shorter distance. And given a severe cold front, gamefish may simply move down the route into deep water, then hold there, perhaps even feeding within the deep water. As knowledgeable winter gamefish anglers, it's up to us to discover such patterns.

Why is this important? Gamefish are not aggressive, but rather, only become active during certain times. This primary activity is often centered around specific areas, depending on the conditions. These activity periods usually occur on shallow feeding flats, but might happen on what I call "holding areas" along migration routes. These holding areas might consist of a secondary point, a patch of dense weeds along an otherwise sparse weed line, a cut, a pocket or a projection along a break. They could also include series of stumps along submerged river channels, fish cribs placed along a rocky break line or a rock pile. Basically, a holding area will be anything providing differing cover that may attract forage.

Also understand, just as migration routes can be huge and holding areas can be a challenge to find, both can be small and very specific. This is why you can fish right beside someone who is snapping fish after fish, while you go without so much as a nibble. It happens with panfish, but is more frequent and frustrating with gamefish such as walleyes, salmon, steelhead, even eelpout. On large, deep, natural lakes, elongated points, bars and reefs several may serve as migration routes, and secondary structures as tiny as an 8-foot wide finger might constitute a holding area or define the exact path of movement. The next day, that path may be 3 feet wide, 3 yards away.

On a large reservoir, the route might be the junction between a main and secondary river channel several miles long, with submerged roads and flooded bridges, building foundations or stump fields constituting holding areas. That's a lot of ice to cover, especially if the fish follow only specific, narrow paths.

On small, shallow lakes, however, the weedy fringe of an eight foot pocket the size of a car in the midst of an otherwise three foot vegetated flat might constitute a migration route, and a larger, more dense clump of weeds, change in vegetation type or height, subtle depth or bottom content change might constitute primary holding areas. This makes finding fish somewhat easier, but still, primary fish activity will likely be focused. It's up to you to find the ones your target species are using.

Many anglers ask how to identify these spots, and the answer is to actively search them out. I recently had a devout winter eelpout fanatic explain he and a partner had been fishing a northern Minnesota lake. They located a beautiful main-lake point leading from an expansive shallow spawning flat to deep water. They were marking eelpout and catching fish. However, they simply weren't experiencing consistency.

We decided to fish it together. After confirming the lake supported a population of eelpout the size we wanted to catch, identifying primary forage bases and seasonal habits, we went to the lake and immediately began evaluating the area, based on the immediate weather and water conditions.

First, was the nearby deep water the deepest water in the area? Was there any secondary structure or microstructure available? Cover? Were there any secondary cover combinations holding the desired forage? What was the water clarity and bottom content? Was there any potential migration route from deep to shallow water? Where? And what about potential holding areas and their locations?

Further investigation found that yes, the deep water nearby was the deepest available in the area. We also identified a large, elongated hard-bottom break extending out between deep water and a shallow flat. This was a holding area supporting good quantities of baitfish. Repeated fishing had proven this an excellent eelpout spot just before sun-up and just after sundown during periods of stable, overcast weather. The best fishing occurred in mid-February when eelpout were moving from the deep hole toward the shallow flat preparing for the spawn.

So why weren't my friends catching fish consistently? Quite simply, eelpout were using this migration route, but only during stable weather at twilight. They were feeding mostly on the secondary, steep break. Even here, the fish moved through quickly. By simply fishing along the point and the adjoining flat throughout the day, these anglers were periodically able to tempt occasional passing fish to strike. To consistently catch fish they needed to be on the secondary break during the right times.

Since then, we've also found periods of overcast, stable weather cause eelpout to move onto the shallow flat earlier in the afternoon and stay later the following morning. But, during severe cold fronts and high, bright skies, movements are of shorter duration. During unstable weather, restricted movements take place along a relatively narrow and short migration route. During these times, even in a good spot, you may catch nothing while fishing a hole a foot away from someone catching several fish an hour. Simply fishing the edges of a specific migration route without targeting specific daily paths based on the conditions will result in less action, perhaps no catch at all.

Consider another example. Two anglers head to a local lake before daybreak, drill holes above some shallow green weeds, and are fishing just as the sun cracks over the horizon. For two hours, they catch pike consistently, then the action stops. They continue fishing hard all day, but get no consistent action again until late afternoon. Why?

The fish could be simply sitting there, only becoming active early and late in the day. But unless we're fishing a shallow, weedy river backwater, pond or lake this is unlikely. More likely,

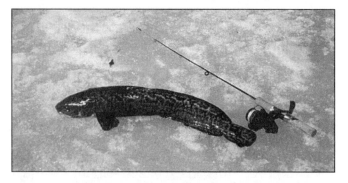

As the author learned while fishing winter eelpout—"They're not pretty, but they fight." He claims that even when fishing a high-percentage area, it's possible to fish a hole a foot away from someone catching several fish an hour, while you catch nothing. Fishing the edges of a general migration route without targeting specific daily paths and holding areas will often result in less action, perhaps no catch at all.

these pike moved into shallow weeds early and late in the day and are moving into deeper water during midday. If these anglers had located the deepest available nearby water and the likely migration route between the shallows and the depths, they would probably have been catching pike during mid-morning and mid-afternoon on holding areas along the migration route. They may even have caught them along deeper weed lines or holes during midday, and still taken good catches from the shallows early and late.

Again, these daily movements vary in timing, and will seldom be the same distance or duration. The same two anglers might return the next day after the approach of a cold front, fish the shallows and catch nothing, simply because the pike didn't move shallow. However, by identifying the migration route, they could simply follow it down towards deeper water until they encountered fish. It makes a big difference and there's more.

Under ideal conditions featuring cooperative weather and light penetration, good structure, cover and food availability, these pike might move into the shallows, spread out for long distances and prowl there for lengthy periods of time. Under less than ideal conditions, these fish might simply move towards mid-depth areas, hold tighter to the migration route and stick close to the protection offered by dense cover. Given poor conditions, the fish may not move at all, but simply hold deep. This requires an entirely different approach. By recognizing that such movements are occurring, then trying to decipher just where, when and how the fish are responding anglers will have more consistent winter gamefish catches, simply because they, unlike the crowds, are aware that fish are responding to the conditions.

Too many ice anglers set up and experience strong flurries of action for short times, with long dead periods between. They'll do this day in and day out, and smugly joke about how the fish bite for a while, then turn off. Many won't even recognize their flurries of action were coming during specific times when fish were moving through. Sure, a straggler or two might move in to confuse the issue, but essentially, these people are missing the obvious.

Remember, gamefish adapt to their environment based on lake type, habitat, structure, cover, depth, forage, oxygen availability and light penetration. These adaptations are often made through slight adjustments in location and position along established migration routes. Some gamefish species adjust faster than others, and some are more sensitive to particular changes and therefore react more strongly. It's up to you to figure out the particulars.

Pay attention! The greatest environmental changes take place in shallow water, where most ice anglers like to fish. But where folks like to fish and where they'll actually catch fish are usually two different places. Shallow water temperatures, light and oxygen conditions can vary dramatically through winter, even during the course of a day. Small fish hiding in the shallows may not be bothered much by such variations unless the changes are extreme or severe. But larger gamefish are bothered, and since the fewest changes take place in deeper water, gamefish holding deeper are usually not only larger, but they are also spending less time adjusting to such factors. That allows them to focus more on feeding. This can mean bigger and more consistent catches in deeper water. Yet many anglers will sit in the shallows waiting for a bite, with no regard for this important point.

Notice throughout this entire discussion, I haven't given much regard to water temperature. This is because with a few exceptions, temperature variance really isn't great beneath the ice. Secondly, gamefish are cold-blooded. So while the water is cold, other than the fact their metabolism is slowed, temperature really doesn't affect them.

However, shallow water is slightly colder and subjects the fish in shallows to dramatic swings in light penetration, oxygen availability and activity on the ice. All these things affect gamefish location, movement and positioning. The deeper water is more stable and less susceptible to such variables. Consequently, gamefish are often more "comfortable" in deeper water. While movements and feeding activity among deep-water gamefish may be limited, we also know these fish still must feed. If we can determine when they feed, the fish can be caught.

Given severe conditions, deep-water gamefish may seldom move at all, but I have found even when they don't move, they often become active at the same time they would otherwise move shallow given better conditions. Otherwise, feeding activity in these deep fish may be accompanied by only a slight movement towards or into more productive shallower water. Again, depending on the conditions these feeding forays may be intense, but short-lived.

Again, gamefish don't think. They don't move shallow because they think food will be there. They simply instinctively move when they get hungry and adequate food isn't available where

Gamefish adapt to their environment based on lake type, habitat, structure, cover, depth, forage, oxygen availability and light penetration. They make location and behavioral adjustments to these factors both seasonally and daily. Smart ice anglers do the same.

they're holding. As they move, they follow the safety and comfort of established migration routes, and when they encounter food within a depth range offering the best combination of food and "comfort" they stop to feed. Thus, by evaluating the conditions when feeding occurs, we can determine how far fish move and how long they will remain active in particular areas given the noted conditions. That's called establishing a pattern.

Again, always locate the deepest water available in the area and identify possible migration routes from the depths to the shallows, then evaluate and learn through experience the conditions and locations causing the strongest and longest migrations of active fish for the time you're fishing. Doing so will increase your consistency. Set up in the shallows and sit there, and you may catch some stragglers, you might even experience a couple brief,

Gamefish instinctively move when they get hungry and adequate food isn't available where they're holding. (Courtesy Northland Tackle)

intense flurries of activity, usually early or late in the day when these fish move shallow to feed. Follow the fish, however, and you can stay on more consistent action throughout the day.

More On Structure, Migration Routes

Be careful where you begin searching for productive locations and their associated migration routes. Again, not all structure is created equal. Many productive-looking structures don't extend all the way down from shallow feeding flats to the deepest available water. That makes them poor migration routes. They might extend down, but not offer adequate holding areas. Or perhaps they connect to only a small, steep-breaking flat not supporting much cover or food. Be sure your structure extends from the deepest available water to a vast, cover-laden flat offering cover, oxygen and food.

Don't forget to consider the deadly dozen variables. On a river backwater or small natural lake, the deepest water in the area might consist of little more than a 12-foot hole within an otherwise shallow bay or flat. In a large, deep lake, it might be a 40-foot hole adjoining a gradually breaking shoreline point. On a river, flowage or reservoir, this might be the deeper river channel adjoining a point extending from a shallow flat. Exactly where along these features gamefish move, when, how

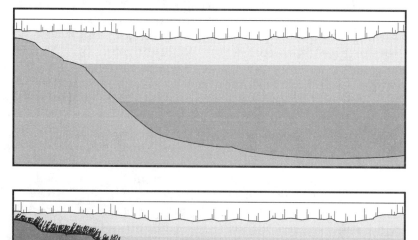

Just as all structures are not created equal, neither are migration routes. A good migration route should feature a gradual, structurally diverse, stair-step drop leading from the shallows to the deepest available water, and should offer a variety of holding areas extending right to the break lines all along the drop.

long and far they move would be dictated by the structure, water and weather.

In addition, some structures might be shallow, some deep. Some might have gradual drops, some might have steep drops, some will look like stairs. Others will be elongated, some will be round. Some will feature hard bottoms, some bottoms will be soft, some will be a mixture. Some will feature turns, bends, fingers and irregularities along their edges. Some will extend from shallow feeding flats to the deepest available water in the area. Some won't. Some feature cover such as rocks, weeds, or stumps. Others don't. The variety is almost endless.

Structures can be abundant, large and found at a variety of depths. I can't tell you specifically which ones will hold fish, nothing is etched in stone. I can tell you it's important to establish the best patterns by strategically moving to locate the particular structures, secondary structures, cover, migration routes and holding areas. If you continue following this mobile, open-minded approach every time you fish, you'll learn to better understand where and when to find active gamefish, even during the toughest conditions.

Positioning

Once the proper combination of features and active gamefish have been located, consider the position of fish on their holding area. Are they holding directly on the bottom or are they suspending? If the sun is bright, are they holding on the sunny or shaded side? If current is present, are they facing it or hiding behind a current break?

This may vary with the time and conditions you're fishing, but be aware of different positions and note how the fish respond. Often, you can drill holes in various spots, fish them, then note specifically where your target species is holding and most active under a given set of conditions. You'll soon note that characteristic movements, times and patterns vary by species. You'll also discover specific areas most likely to attract certain species under specific conditions.

Smaller gamefish are likely to hold shallower on the feature, while larger fish hold slightly deeper. Such positioning might be intensified during severe weather conditions or intense light penetration. Less significant positioning movements, which are more difficult to understand, may be caused by predator/prey movements, forage movements or lack of oxygen in the depths. Be aware of these. Learning exactly where active fish position themselves under various conditions is imperative to consistent success, especially when conditions get tough. This not only involves separating good-looking structure from truly productive structure and cover, but carefully evaluating details of fish positioning.

Under good conditions, I locate potentially productive areas, identify possible migration routes and holding areas, then look for gamefish holding along primary break lines adjoining deep water. I especially like cover-laden primary break lines leading from deep to shallow water in a stair-step fashion. And if these stair-step break lines offer irregular, cover-laden secondary features like smaller turns, slots, fingers and points gradually leading into various depths the better the chance they'll hold and attract gamefish. Combine this with features, cover and oxygen in the preferred

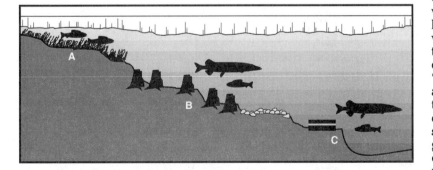

Winter gamefish movements along a migration route vary with the conditions. Given a cloudy, overcast day during a warm front combined with suitable shallow cover, forage and oxygen availability, winter gamefish may move along a migration route into shallow feeding flats and disperse (a). This would be an example of "ideal" conditions, a time when most ice anglers experience good catches. Given the opposite conditions—bright, sunny days following a severe cold front—some small fish may linger shallow, but most gamefish are likely to move into the deepest available water at the base of the migration route (c). Most of the time, gamefish are likely to make only slight movements, and hold somewhere in-between (b).

Once migration routes and holding areas are identified, you must pinpoint how gamefish are positioned on them. The fish depicted here are holding on the deep edge of the holding areas, facing one direction. These fish could simply be relating to the deep edge, but this might also happen to be the shaded side or the side sheltering them from a current flow. You might also note if the fish are relating only to weeds, wood or rock, or specific features located within a particular depth strata. Remember, pattern the fish.

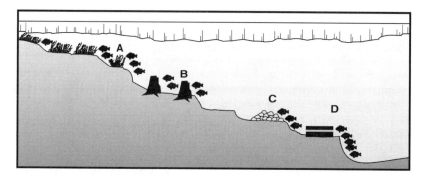

depth range for the time you're fishing and near the deepest available water, and you're likely to find active gamefish using them. And don't forget to not only identify, but thoroughly examine specific holding areas and the position of fish on them to help better understand why they're holding there.

Pattern the fish! Are they holding on a particular holding area at any particular depth? On the left or right side of the structure? Deep or shallow? Is it shaded or sunny? Are the fish preferring such edges featuring hard bottom, soft bottom, or bottom content changes? Along the base of the cover near bottom, or suspended along the edge? How high? If you're on a steep break, could there also be varying temperature or oxygen breaks fish may be relating to? Is a current present, and how are the fish positioned in relation to it? The more such details you uncover, the better.

Summary

We've covered a lot of material here, so let's review the main points. First, we've established that gamefish utilize their survival instincts to respond to weather and water conditions. The fish are most likely to use structures and their associated break lines offering the best combination of features, cover and forage as migration routes or travel corridors. The most popular of these will feature smaller breaks or "holding areas" that fish can relate to and use as rest areas along the way. How far they will travel any given day varies with seasonal and daily conditions.

When conditions are poor, gamefish may not move to even the first major break line. When conditions are favorable, they may move far beyond, into the shallowest areas on an adjoining structural feature. If conditions warrant, they may hold

there for several days. It's up to you to evaluate the conditions, find the right combination of structures, secondary structure and cover for the time you're fishing. This can be achieved by asking yourself the following questions when you catch several gamefish in a specific area: Why were the fish there? What led them there? Where did they come from? What spots along the migration route might be likely to hold the school, even if only temporarily? How are they positioned on these features? Given the conditions, figure them out, and you'll see your winter catch rates soar.

An overview of good structures and potential migration routes. As winter anglers, we would have to identify which feature is closest to the deepest available water, is most structurally diverse, offers the best possible migration route with the best combination of holding areas, cover, oxygen and forage for the species and conditions we're fishing.

Again, let me emphasize, the best combinations of structure and cover available are most likely to attract and hold gamefish. But these aren't necessarily large and distinct. On smaller, muck bottom "dishpan" style lakes, you might find that a dredged boat channel, a deeper pocket on a shallow, vegetated flat, areas of different bottom material, weed lines and edges, even slight bottom contour changes of 6 inches become significant to fish. Use your knowledge and investigative skills. Always look for structure where movements might occur. You may be surprised what you find.

Also, remember that different species may be holding on different types of structure at any given time. Pike might be holding on a hump with a tall weed line, while walleyes are holding along a hard-bottom/soft-bottom transition at the base of a deep underwater bar. Don't make the mistake of mixing the patterns of various species. To reduce inter-species competition, gamefish don't always, but usually, follow distinct patterns, based on their environment.

However, a single species may be relating to two or more locations at the same time, even on the same lake. Some large pike in a deep water basin might be holding deep along a 17-foot weed line, while in an adjacent shallow basin, small ones may be holding shallow on a weed line bordering a 6-foot hole. To combat such behavior and complications, be mobile and versatile.

Other Considerations

Finally, keep in mind that while established patterns may be repeated from winter to winter, they can change. Water fluctuations in a reservoir may leave some structure dry as water recedes, or make new structure available or better during periods of increased flow. Stumps in a flowage or reservoir may rot away, dredging may change current flow, shoreline development and construction of causeways, bridges, fish cribs or other man-made structures may change bottom configuration and depth. These are all things which may change movements and migrations. Again, be mobile and versatile. If you can find the right locations during periods when weather and water conditions are favorable on the best seasonal structure near the deepest water available at the right time, you may establish patterns that produce year after year. Just be aware that they are subject to change.

Gamefish often distribute themselves by size. Large pike might hold along a 17-foot weed line in a deep-water basin, while numbers of smaller fish hold shallow along a weed line bordering a 6-foot hole in a vegetated flat. (photo Courtesy Berkley/OTG, Inc)

This can all be further complicated by conditions such as local weather. Of all the deadly dozen variables, weather is out of our control. Yet it has a major impact on making conditions unstable and thus causing fish movements and changes in fish activity. These changes can occur from hour to hour, day to day, week to week or month to month, depending on the conditions.

When cold fronts pass, bringing high, bright skies and changing barometric pressure, gamefish typically move into cover lining primary migration routes and follow it down to the deepest available water where light penetration is reduced and environmental conditions are more stable. These movements may be modified and less intense in lakes featuring dark water, thick ice or heavy snow cover. Changes in gamefish movement, positioning and activity will likely take place until conditions stabilize and at least some cloud cover returns following passage of the front.

Now take this a step further. The effects of cold fronts may last several days, depending on the severity of the front and the number of days required to gain some cloud cover. If a minor cold front quickly passes and mild, overcast days with light snow return, gamefish may become active and start moving in a day or two. However, if an especially severe cold front or two moves through and keeps the days bright, movement and feeding activity may be minimized for several days.

If you're fishing during a bright-skied cold front and have a choice of lakes, pick deeper ones with some water color and good populations of the species you wish to catch. This way, you increase your odds by fishing waters with a solid number of fish. And, the water conditions will allow slightly higher degrees of fish movement and less impact on activity, despite the front. The general guideline following cold fronts is: the brighter the condi-

tions, the less movement, less activity and tougher the fishing. The darker, the easier.

Accordingly, you can surmise winter gamefish won't always be active. Even during ideal conditions, no fish feed all the time, and since their metabolism is slowed, it takes time for food to digest, so they don't have to feed as often. Still, I've caught pike with a couple good-sized minnows sticking out of their mouths. So remember, gamefish may have already fed, but you can still make them strike if you fish the right presentations in the right manner.

This brings us to another facet of catching winter fish, the presentation. This is a topic we'll touch on in future chapters. For now, understand if you're able to identify various factors and how gamefish react to them; then piece all this together in a workable system, you'll learn to locate active winter gamefish with more consistency. With experience, you'll learn to build on these basics and fine-tune solid, strategic approaches, making you a better winter gamefish angler.

Chapter 3

"The Search for Gamefish"

By now you've probably realized elementary winter gamefish patterns coincide with basic winter panfish patterns. The same thing is true of searching for gamefish using electronics–with two major distinctions.

First, gamefish are usually less plentiful than panfish, making them somewhat more difficult to find if you don't pay attention to detail. Secondly, gamefish tend to hold somewhat deeper. Yes, these are generalizations. There are simply too many lake types, variables and influences to etch anything in stone. That's ice fishing, and it can be a humbling sport.

But there are tendencies. Even if you've never fished through the ice before, after reading the preface, introduction and first two chapters of this book, you should have a pretty good idea how to stay safe and warm while locating winter gamefish on a variety of lake types. You should also have a general understanding of seasonal and daily movements, migration routes and an awareness of the possible pattern variations that may occur as a result of local weather and water conditions. The next step is learning how to use this knowledge to find these areas efficiently.

This is accomplished by combining our basic definition and understanding of gamefish with the deadly dozen variables and another important concept, winter lake stratification. Then, we can put everything together through the use of lake maps, navigation systems and high technology sonar and underwater cameras to pinpoint structure, microstructure, secondary cover, forage and fish. Combine this with a willingness to be mobile and versatile, and you'll understand the "total approach" to modern ice fishing.

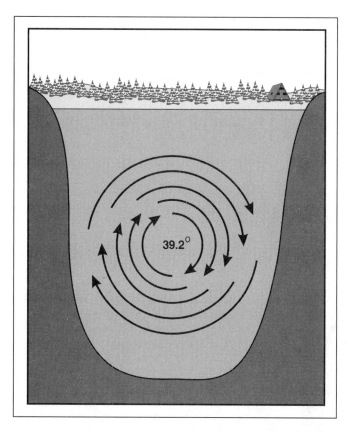

As air temperatures cool surface water to 39.2 degrees F.—the temperature at which water is heaviest and most dense—surface water sinks, dissolving summer stratification, making the lake a uniform 39.2 degrees. This renews oxygen concentrations throughout the lake.

Following fall turnover and the formation of ice, winter stratification results in the coldest water just beneath the ice (33 degrees F.) The densest, warmest water (39.2 degrees F.) pooled on the bottom.

Winter Lake Stratification

In summer, lakes stratify with the warmest water on top, coldest on bottom, and a layer between that cools quickly. Specifically, this layer cools one degree centigrade for every foot of depth. In fall, shorter days, less direct sunlight and colder air reduce surface temperatures until they become colder than the water below. As this surface water cools, it becomes heavier and sinks. This process continues until surface water reaches 39.2 degrees F. At that temperature water is at its heaviest. At 39.2 the surface layer and middle layer dissolve, and with the help of fall winds, lakes mix to a uniform temperature of 39.2 degrees.

When surface water cools below 39.2 degrees, the maximum density and heaviest state of water, it becomes lighter and rises above to rest on top of the 39.2-degree water below. When the surface reaches 32 degrees, it freezes. Frozen water mole-

cules expand, and becoming less dense float on the liquid water below. With an insulating layer of ice now covering the surface, surface water is 32 degrees, water just below is slightly above, and as you go deeper, the water warms slightly until it reaches bottom, where the heaviest water pools at 39.2 degrees.

Some anglers believe this causes gamefish to go deep, toward the warmest water–so they fish the bottom, and sometimes catch fish. Remember, while important, temperature is not a leading factor in winter gamefish position. Cover, food and oxygen are.

Consider first-ice. When ice and snow cover are relatively thin, sunlight penetration is good and plant life is abundant. With the autumn mixing of the water just completed, both shallow and deep water support good dissolved oxygen counts, so gamefish often hold near bottom where temperature, cover, food and oxygen intermingle in favorable degrees.

During mid-winter, however, ice thickens, snow cover increases and light penetration decreases, reducing weed growth and oxygen production in the shallows. Sealed by ice, there is no mixing. Deep water oxygen is often used up. Now fishing on bottom, where the water is warmest, could be obviously inappropriate because cover, forage and oxygen levels may have dwindled.

At the same time, water just beneath the ice supports oxygen producing plankton which also acts as a food source. But such areas are closer to bright light, and usually offer little cover. So as winter wears on, foregoing their desire for deeper, warmer water and cover, gamefish may abandon oxygen-reduced shallows and oxygen deficient depths, and begin relating to remaining green vegetation on shallow flats and main-lake structures. Or, on some small, shallow lakes with no current influence, fish may suspend over deep, main-lake basins where life-sustaining oxygen and forage are available. Some might think

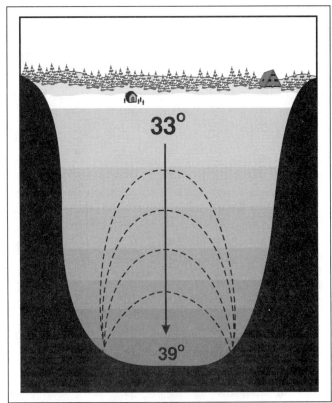

Mid-winter, ice and snow cover thicken, and sunlight penetration, plant life and oxygen distribution is reduced. Depending on the species, lake type and a variety of other related factors, gamefish will seek structures or break lines along structures peaking out within specific depth strata intersecting the best combination of features, cover, oxygen, forage and temperature. Pattern the fish!

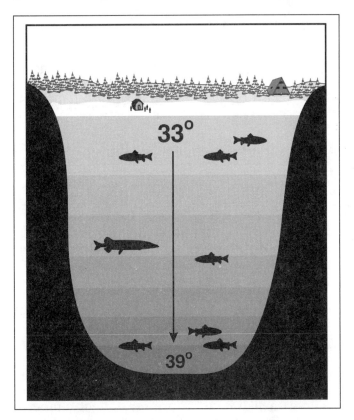

First-ice, when ice and snow cover are relatively thin, sunlight penetration is good, plant life is abundant and oxygen distribution is good, and gamefish may position themselves at a variety of depths.

with gamefish more concentrated, catches would be easy. But unless suitable structure offering adequate mixes of cover and forage are available within this oxygen layer, these fish seldom feed aggressively, and you'll have to use specific techniques to catch them.

Right before ice out, the situation changes again. Openings develop in the ice, allowing relatively "warm" meltwater to enter. Since ice is approximately 10 percent less dense than water, it floats approximately 10 percent above the actual water level. During mid-season, the weight of water and snow may push the ice below this level, and as longer days and warming sun cause melting, ice is relieved of this weight and eventually "pops" back up above water level. This causes warmer, oxygenated water to flow through openings, drawing gamefish.

At this time of year sunlight penetration also increases. This effect is especially prominent

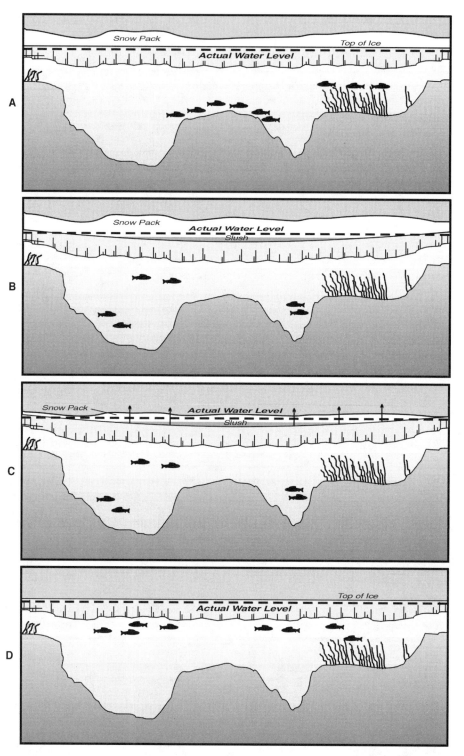

During early ice, snow settles directly on the ice (A). Gradually, the snow deepens, bending the ice and forcing it beneath the actual water level (B), forming slush. Right before ice-out, the snow begins melting, and the reduced weight of the snow pack allows the ice to "pop" back into position (C) causing oxygenated, warming melt water to seep through openings. This often increases feeding activity and, on some lake types featuring low oxygen conditions, may even draw gamefish, causing them to suspend in the oxygenated water directly beneath the ice (D).

near shallow spawning bays, where many gamefish stage to spawn. With sunlight causing vegetation and plankton to rebound and warm water runoff flowing under the ice, gamefish eventually move shallower and become more active.

However, since water temperatures remain essentially stable throughout the winter, temperature doesn't generally have a substantial bearing on gamefish location. But consider this: Could gamefish relate to winter's slight temperature breaks as they do more prominent summer stratification? While this theory might seem far-fetched, fish may relate to subtle temperature breaks, say, perhaps, from 34 to 35 degrees. It

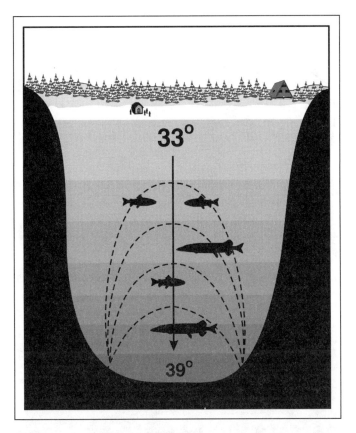

Since temperature differences vary only a few degrees in winter, temperature doesn't usually have a significant bearing on gamefish location. However, experienced anglers have noted gamefish suspending or holding along structures topping out at specific depths. Some feel these fish may be relating to subtle temperature breaks within the water column.

may sound unlikely because these breaks aren't very pronounced, but in some instances, they could affect winter gamefish positioning.

Temperature also becomes significant if you pinpoint an inlet or underwater spring–spring water, for example, remains a constant 50-something degrees all year. This is, of course, considerably warmer than the 33 to 39-degree surroundings. These "spots on the spots" often are micro-environments that seem to be seldom noticed by most ice anglers, but they are often critically important to consistently locating active winter gamefish. Such areas also offer additional cover, oxygen and forage, creating high-percentage areas.

Maintain a sharp eye. Search for structure and migration routes, then locate specific micro-structures and holding areas offering the best combination of features falling within the depth zone most likely to support a combination of cover, food, oxygen and yes, even temperature, for your target species.

Deep-Water Gamefish

Just remember: some gamefish may not relate to obvious structure. They might hold on subtle, deep-water features or suspend over deep, open water. In deep, well-oxygenated waters, deep-water gamefish may be heavily concentrated, less stressed by environmental conditions and less affected by fishing pressure. Here, large concentrations of active, deep-water gamefish such as walleyes, lake trout, eelpout and salmon often go untouched–yet they can be caught. They can be caught because they're protected by depth, and likely to remain active barring barometric changes, storms, cold fronts or activity on the ice. With gamefish species like largemouth and smallmouth bass or channel catfish holding in deep, tightly grouped concentrations, often the only chance of catching them is to fish deep.

These are fish many ice anglers pass up, thinking it takes too much work to pinpoint isolated deep-water schools. That's a mistake. Thanks to

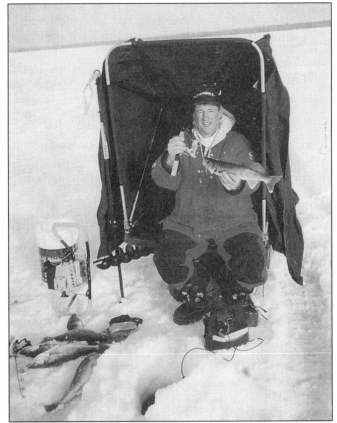

Deep-water gamefish such as these walleyes often aren't strongly pressured because they're difficult to find. Knowledgeable anglers using electronics have proven that while walleye are a lot of work to find, the extra work is well worth the effort.

today's accurate lake maps and modern electronics, it's possible to find and fish several deep schools in relatively short periods of time.

Lake Maps

The process of finding productive locations begins before you're on the ice. Consider the lake type, depth, structure, water clarity, the weather and species you're targeting, then review a lake map.

Reviewing lake maps and marking potential high-percentage locations is crucially important to consistent success. Assuming you've talked to local experts to confirm your target waters offer a good population of the species and size you want to catch, this process should involve the following procedures:

1) Identifying the lake type.
2) Choosing an accurate, well-marked lake map. Preferably, this will be one featuring tight depth contours for better definition, plus recent fisheries survey information, fishing tips and pointers from knowledgeable anglers. It should also have a listing of lake characteristics.
3) Noting lake characteristics such as maximum and average depth, water clarity, primary bottom contents, cover types, forage and fish species present and their possible inter-relationships.
4) Locating the best structures featuring the best desired combination of structure, secondary structure, depth, bottom content

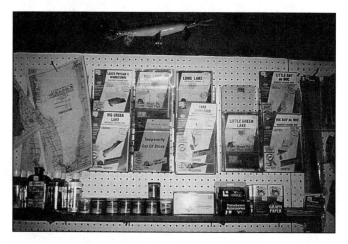

Purchasing and reviewing lake maps, then marking potential high-percentage locations prior to setting out on the ice is one practice separating expert ice anglers from the novices.

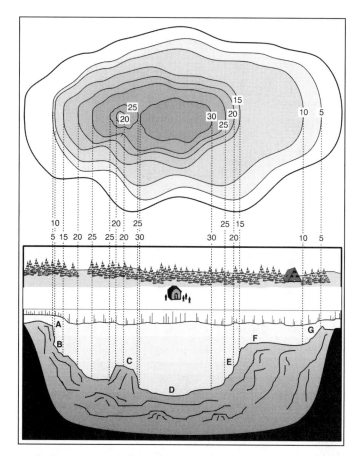

Lake maps are indispensable tools, because they take three-dimensional lakes and place them on 2-dimensional paper. Areas such as shallow bays (A, F, G) drop-offs (B, E) sunken islands (C) and mid-lake flats (D) are transformed into a series of connecting depth contour lines, allowing enterprising anglers to better visualize the bottom layout and structure hidden beneath the ice.

changes, cover, cover combinations and edges, inlets, outlets and springs, river channels or man-made cover like fish cribs or submerged roadbeds. All these should be within the desired depth strata and adjoining the deepest water in the area.
5) Identifying structures most likely to hold fish at the time you're fishing. Variables include lake type and depth, weather, sunlight intensity, water color, and available forage.
6) Locating the deepest water in close proximity to these preferred structures and any adjacent shallow feeding flats. Then identifying potential migration routes between them and potential holding areas along them.
7) Noting the probable position of fish based on light intensity and the day's wind direction. Yes, even in winter, wind has an effect on the water beneath the ice. It often creates sub-

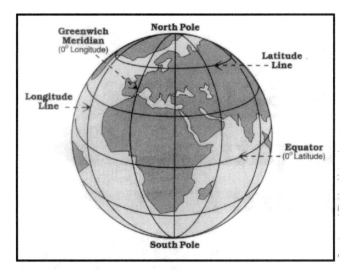

Lines of latitude and longitude encompass the earth. The precise locations where these lines and their fractions, read in "minutes" and "seconds," intersect are called coordinates, which can be saved electronically on Global Positioning Systems, so you can locate them repeatedly with the press of a button. (Courtesy Fishing Hotspots)

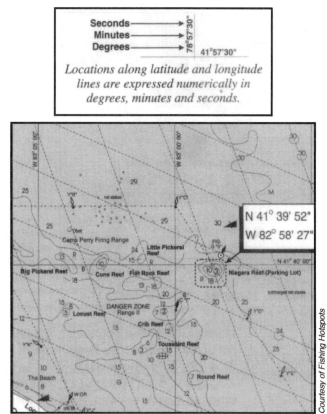

Locations along latitude and longitude lines are expressed numerically in degrees, minutes and seconds.

In the past, GPS mapping cartridges were expensive and inconvenient accessories. Today, some models are packaged with CD ROM accessibility, allowing you to use your PC to download virtually any map directly into your receiving unit. This same software also allows you to interchange specific waypoints, icons or plot trails from your unit to your PC and back. (Courtesy Fishing Hotspots)

tle, sub-ice currents, and gamefish may position on the windward side or lee sides of structure.

8) Identifying the nearest access points to these locations

9) On larger waters, entering Global Positioning Systems (GPS) coordinates into your GPS receiver, then using a compass or GPS and scale on your map to determine the direction and distance from your access point to the preferred structure.

10) Reviewing where you intend to fish and how deep so you can pack the proper gear. If the water is clear and features only light cover, lighter tackle may be necessary. If the water is dark or deep and you'll be fishing heavy cover, heavier rods, lines and lures might be required.

Once on the ice, use your lake map and GPS to move efficiently to your fishing locations, and use your sonar and underwater camera, your underwater eyes, to review what's below and locate unmapped hot spots.

After making notes, meet with knowledgeable anglers to glean additional information. Have them mark areas offering potential, and combine this information with your own based on our winter gamefish system. Now, you're almost ready to fish.

Before finalizing your initial strategies, carefully consider all the variables and how they might affect winter gamefish location. The key isn't necessarily to determine where fish will be, but to eliminate unproductive water. Here's how.

GPS On Ice

While use of a compass and lake map can help accurately locate productive areas with little investment, this is the hard way of navigating on ice. Global Positioning Systems (GPS), demand no time-consuming manual calculations to determine direction and distance to specific locations.

GPS is not only fast, but accurate. Coordinates for targeted locations are simply taken from your map, entered as "waypoints" on portable, hand-held GPS receivers, then recalled at will, allowing movement directly to intended locations, repeatedly. When you locate potential waypoints, give

Using a GPS, especially on expansive waters, is the key to efficiently closing in on pre-marked high-percentage locations. Saving access sites as waypoints also makes the GPS a good safety tool in the event you become disoriented in darkness or a "whiteout." (Courtesy Lowrance Electronics)

knowledgeable anglers can also be a productive way of communicating specific hot spots and patterns.

GPS has the capacity to read out to thousandths of a minute in latitude and longitude. That means it is accurate to within about 6 feet. Well, the military version is that accurate. In the name of national security, the military deliberately scrambles civilian signals through a process called selective availability. GPS satellites broadcast two signals, a commercial Standard Positioning Service (SPS) for civilian use, and a Precise Positioning Service (PPS) exclusively for military access. GPS has the poten-

Global Positioning Systems allow you to take coordinates for intended locations from your lake map and enter them as waypoints. The receiver will then lock onto your present location and the waypoint, then lay out your course of travel and guide you to that specific location. (Courtesy Lowrance Electronics)

each a number, record that number on your map, and store this number along with a reference name and other notes in a waterproof, tearproof logbook such as the one available from Strikemaster Ice Augers. Anytime you wish to fish that location, simply review your lake map, recall your waypoint, press the "Go To" button, and watch as the receiver provides a "map" on the plotter screen indicating the direction and distance to the requested waypoint. Some units also provide speed of travel and your estimated time of arrival.

If you find new or secondary "hot spots" while on the ice, simply push the "save" button, which automatically stores your present coordinates in electronic memory. You can then add information to your logbook, such as the time you were fishing, the species caught, and productive presentations. Exchanging such information with other

Any time you wish to travel to a specific waypoint, enter the waypoint number assigned to represent that location's coordinates, then watch as the unit guides you to that location quickly and accurately. (Courtesy Lowrance Electronics)

tial to direct you close to your intended location, but not right on. Several manufacturers use a technique called Differential GPS (DGPS) to somewhat compensate for military interference and increase accuracy, but still, this signal is not as accurate as the military's PPS.

Regardless, GPS saves time by efficiently moving you near your pre-planned locations quickly. And with today's models offering in-use charge adapters for connecting to an ATV or snowmobile, better receivers with improved sensitivity, better accuracy and faster satellite lock-on, well, you can't go wrong.

New features are also generating new on-ice tactics. Icons, for example, allow you to mark specific spots where you've caught fish, and plot trails so you can outline specific structures, weed lines, or

features electronically. Combined with today's mapping capabilities, such things can all be marked as the GPS simultaneously indicates your current position by a blinking cursor on the map.

In the past, these mapping cartridges were expensive accessories. You needed to purchase accessory cartridges for specific areas, making them major investments. Today, some models are packaged with a CD-ROM, allowing you to use your personal computer to download virtually any map directly into your receiving unit. The software included with these units also allows you to interchange specific waypoints, icons or plot trials

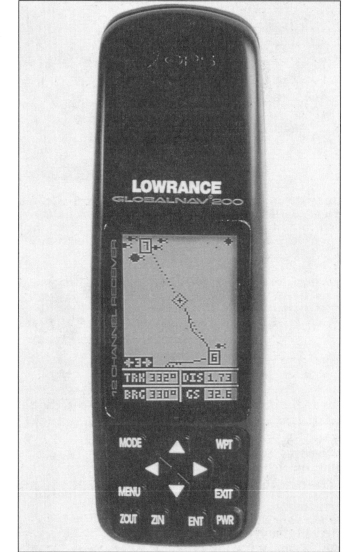

GPS units save time by efficiently moving you to your pre-planned locations, allowing you to try fishing several high-percentage locations with ease. This will increase your odds of success. (Courtesy Lowrance Electronics)

Once at your intended location, GPS features such as event markers (or "icons") and plotter trails allow you to outline specific structures or secondary features electronically. (Courtesy Lowrance electronics)

In the past, GPS mapping cartridges were expensive and inconvenient accessories. Today, some models are packaged with CD ROM accessibility, allowing you to use your PC to download virtually any map directly into your receiving unit. This same software also allows you to interchange specific waypoints, icons or plot trails from your unit to your PC and back. (Courtesy Lowrance Electronics)

from your unit to your PC and back. You can also exchange waypoints with other high-tech ice anglers.

Now factor all this together. After reviewing a map, gathering information and locating specific desired coordinates, you can not only drive right to them, but by using your GPS mapping unit along with sonar and a squirt bottle of water, you can "run" the structure, laying out a plot trail and outlining the structure as you watch for fish. As you do, you can mark icons for specific locations holding fish, and interesting areas of microstructure or secondary cover. You'll now have a highly detailed map of that specific structure, and be able to fish it with efficiency, learning details about specific patterns in a fraction of the time it took before this technology became available. In essence, you can see basic patterns appearing right before your eyes. If you wish, all this information can be electronically saved.

Now sonar comes into play.

Sonar

Once you've outlined the targeted area using your GPS, you'll want to see the structure's layout and pinpoint high-percentage combinations of microstructure, secondary cover, forage and fish. Provided you know how to set your unit and interpret the appropriate signals, sonar enables you to decipher depth, bottom type, cover, forage and fish. If you are good at it, you can even estimate

Courtesy of Vexilar, Inc.

Once you've outlined the target area using GPS, you'll want to visualize the structure's layout and pinpoint high-percentage combinations of secondary cover, forage and fish using high quality sonar, such as this Vexilar flasher. (Courtesy Vexilar, Inc.)

the species, the approximate size, the depth, their activity levels and responses to specific presentations.

Since basic electronics concepts were covered in the first two of the "Hooked on Ice Fishing" series, I'll assume you already understand sonar basics. But to make sure we're fully covering winter gamefish patterns, let's review.

Most "modernized" ice anglers are now using some form of sonar. If they don't, they at least understand the advantages of using sonar. I'd be lost without it. Without sonar, I wouldn't be able to find precise depths, structures, bottom contents, secondary cover, forage or fish. I can't determine specifically what depth my bait is off bottom, and unless fishing clear, shallow water, I certainly can't efficiently monitor fish activity and their responses to my presentations without sonar.

Sonar, namely Liquid Crystal Graphs (LCGs) and flashers, are arguably two of the most valuable tools modern ice anglers can use.

Liquid Crystal Graphs

Let's start with liquid crystal graphs (LCGs). Today's LCGs function better than ever before. Thanks to features such as Lowrance's "Clearvision" they're easier to read in bright sun. With a growing number of vertical pixels combined with today's "zoom" features magnifying images several times, resolution is better than ever.

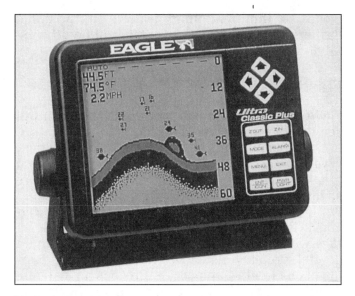

Today's liquid crystal graphs feature an increasingly larger number of vertical pixels for better resolution, and numerous features that are advantageous to the ice angler. (Courtesy Lowrance Electronics)

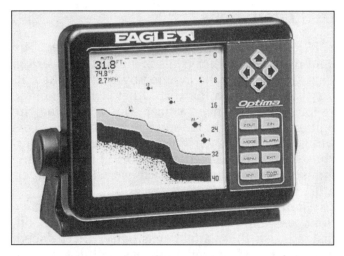

LCG features such as Lowrance's "greyscale" enhance the ability to determine bottom topography and secondary cover, and help separate fish from the bottom. (Courtesy Lowrance Electronics)

Additional features, such as Lowrance's "greyscale," also enhance the ability to determine bottom topography and secondary cover, and help separate fish from bottom clutter. Other options include side scanning transducers for taking readings to the side, split screen features for viewing two different areas at once, zoom screens for zooming in on specific depths or features, even modules capable of incorporating GPS functions into the unit. These are all features flashers simply don't offer.

Split-Screen zoom features are especially helpful. Say you're fishing 40 feet of water and have located a school of walleyes directly on the bottom. With the press of a button or two, you can split the screen into two windows, and have the left side of your screen showing the entire vertical column, and the right side "zoomed" in on the fish. You'll still see the overall picture on the left side of the screen, so you're covered if fish come through at another depth—but by utilizing the zoom feature and splitting the screen, you can also program the unit to reveal only the lower sector of this column, say the 30 to 40-foot depth range, on the right.

Not only does this allow you to zoom right down to where your lure and the fish are, but also focuses the entire, broad-face pixel width into a smaller area of coverage, providing better resolution and hence, more detailed coverage. Say you're in 30 feet of water, using a unit featuring 30 vertical pixels, or one pixel per foot resolution. Zoom in the entire screen from the 15- to 20-foot range, and you'll now have resolution of six pixels per foot. That makes a significant difference.

LCG Limitations

There are drawbacks to LCGs, however. The fluid operating the crystals is subject to freezing. This situation can be avoided by keeping the battery at maximum power. Other tricks include keeping the unit near a heat source, turning the unit and screenlight on and leaving them on. This will generate heat while fishing. You can also purchase nitrogen-packed units or units featuring industrial-grade fluids that will withstand temperature to minus 40 degrees.

Another concern for LCG ice fishing applications is automated settings. Turn them off. Instead, use the manual sensitivity, chart speed, gray scale and screen darkness settings so you can customize your picture. One of the keys to improving response time with an LCG, for example, is to increase scroll speed. This can best be accomplished by turning off the automated setting and manually maximizing chart speed. You can also achieve faster scroll speeds by turning off the digital sonar, which provides digital depth reading. Simply put, faster scroll speeds adjust the pulse widths of the transducer, improving resolution and making it easier to mark baitfish, plankton and fish. It also helps you to note movements and responses.

While some LCG manufacturers claim signal return is instantaneous, the symbols representing these signals are generally slightly behind the "real-time," instantaneous flasher responses. But technology is getting closer. The experts at Lowrance offer a "Fast-Trak" feature. This is a verti-

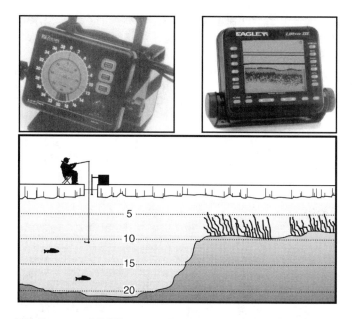

Flashers and LCGs reveal the same information, just in different ways. Here, the flasher on the left and LCG on the right reveal two fish positioned at 12 and 17 feet, and the angler's lure at 11 feet. Note how targets appear as elongated lines, rather than objects, on the LCG. This is because you're stationary, and the target is being repeatedly marked.

cally oriented "flasher-style" reading that appears alongside the liquid crystal display screen. These readings are almost instantaneous, just like a flasher, meaning this is closer to real time. If you lift your lure, it will move almost instantaneously on this display, similar to a flasher. And, by making the adjustments we've just reviewed, you can get closer to the "real time" feature of traditional flashers, plus enjoy the advantages of liquid crystal display.

Flashers vs. LCGs: A Comparison

When you work a bait below a flasher, you will see the lure's response and movements instantly, not with a moment's lapse like you will with liquid crystal graphs. Even the best liquid crystal graphs, set on their fastest chart speeds feature slight delays.

Good LCG results have been attained with Zercom's Real-Time Sonar RTS. The biggest advantage with this unit is thanks to direct-drive liquid crystal circuitry instead of traditional multi-plexing pixel circuitry, the entire screen is an instantaneous "Fast-Trak" style readout. Set on the 0 to 15-foot range, your lure and fish look immense. When fishing gamefish in shallow water—a river backwater for instance—the definition is outstanding.

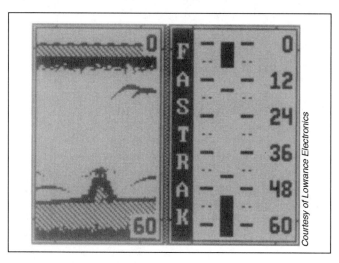

Courtesy of Lowrance Electronics

Lowrance's "Fastrak" feature allows you to see the bottom using the LCG picture, yet also splits the screen to reveal a flasher-like view on the right. (Courtesy Lowrance Electronics)

However, some ice anglers believe that traditional liquid crystal graph "history" is beneficial. Should you look up just as a fish quickly moves through while using a real-time flasher, the image would be gone. You'd never know it was there. On an LCG, if you look down a split-second later, you'll still see the mark briefly, providing a second chance to bring your bait to that level and work the fish. Objects appear elongated on an LCG—with the pixel farthest to the right being almost instantaneous. The farther left you go, the older the signal. That's the pixel "history" I'm referring to.

Still, others will argue instantaneous response doesn't matter much. When jigging for active gamefish, they'll say, simply knowing you've found fish at a specific depth and knowing precisely where your bait is relative to the fish is enough to get action, Even with a momentary delay in the signal response, you still get this information.

Maybe. But at times, evaluating specific jig movements and immediate fish response is very important. Drop a jig down a hole in clear water and watch how fast a walleye can inhale and expel that jig. You'll see what I mean. Instant feedback simply lets you make split-second decisions to hook short-striking or light-biting fish.

This is where the advantage of a flasher comes in handy. Flashers provide instantaneous readouts—meaning any movement of the lure or the fish shows up on your screen as it is happening. Other general flasher advantages include manual sensitivity settings, meaning you can adjust and fine-tune your sonar to the point you can read even the smallest ice lures. You can even tell if a minnow is ripped off a hook!

Most manufacturers won't set the automatic sensitivity modes on LCGs this light, because the average operator wouldn't be able to see fish easily. But when you're trying to tempt largemouth bass with an ultralight ice lure and you want to see that lure on screen, using an LCG it's like trying to track a stealth bomber on radar. The thin, knife-like edge of that vertical ice jig is difficult for the pulse of a sonar unit to pick up. But, set correctly, a good flasher will show these fine targets. This is why so many ice experts prefer manually adjustable flashers.

Simply put, flashers provide controlled resolution. Unless they are turned off, if this option is available, automated control settings spontaneously adjust gain as the computer deems necessary. Even in "manual" mode, slight compensations are made beyond user control. This makes focused readings difficult. When you

Unlike LCGs, flashers provide instantaneous readings, meaning any movement of your lure or fish appearing on your screen is happening at exactly that moment and depth indicated below. (Courtesy Vexilar, Inc.)

set the gain and suppression on a flasher, however, even pulses are maintained. This is an important characteristic, because automated changes slow transducer pulse, decreasing resolution and making precision readings like measuring fish response time or marking fish close to bottom almost impossible. Once you adjust your gain and suppression on a flasher, however, there are no needless automated changes.

Remember, you're stationary when ice fishing, so depth remains the same. Unless you move to another hole, there's no need for further adjustment. Flashers are also more cold-weather compatible, thanks to direct-drive circuitry. Instead of receiving pulses from the transducer, sending them through multi-plex drivers and a series of liquid-filled pixels like most LCG's, a flasher's direct drive digital signal circuitry sends pulses directly to a neon bulb, LED or direct-drive liquid crystal display.

Flashers

One of my favorite models is Vexilar's FL-8SLT, which features a neon flasher bulb that pulls sensitivity levels in three colors. Sensitivity is easy to read, because signals in the center of the transducer cone appear in red, to indicate a strong signal; orange, an intermediate signal and green, a weak signal. This is much akin to watching a meteorologist showing the strength of a storm system, using color as a guide to intensity, with the darker colors indicating stronger intensity. The only difference is while television stations use virtually any color of the spectrum to show intensity, the neon LED bulb on the FL-8SLT flasher is limited to three. But it still makes for easy interpretation. Zercom's Color Point offers similar advantages.

Units without color readouts indicate signal strength by the width of the uniformly colored signal–thicker being stronger and thinner being weaker.

Just don't abuse this setting. Too many anglers adjust sensitivity so their lures appear deep red. That's overkill. What you want is to make your lure appear green or green with an orange or yellow fringe. By turning the sensitivity weak on the bait, any slight reduction of the signal shows. In other words, if a fish appears near the bait and steals the minnow off your jig, the green line will thin or the orange/yellow fringe will disappear. This is more difficult to see if your sensitivity is set too high and the lure and bait appear thick and red.

More importantly, when a fish enters your cone you'll see it in green, as it approaches your bait, it will turn orange, then red. This allows you to tell if a fish is approaching or moving away from your bait. By watching how slowly or quickly the colors change you can learn how active the fish are. To

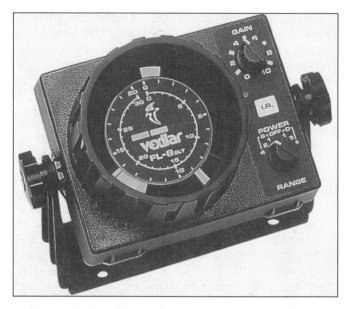

Vexilar's FL-8SLT, the market's first "three color" LED bulb flasher. On this model, sensitivity is improved and the screen is easy to read and interpret because strong signals register in red, intermediate signals appear orange, and weak signals are green. (Courtesy Vexilar, Inc.)

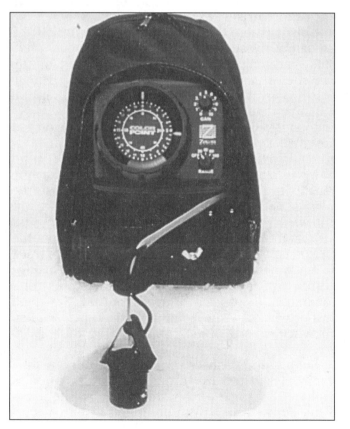

Zercom's "Color Point" flasher, the market's newest "three color" LED bulb flasher, offering an incredible 1.5" target separation. (Courtesy Zercom Marine)

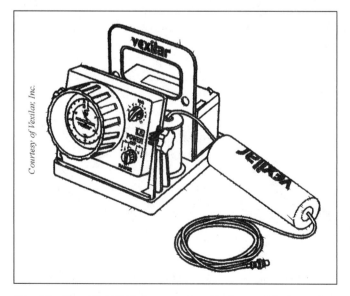

Courtesy of Vexilar, Inc.

The Vexilar FL-8SLT three-color flasher with interference reduction and self-aligning transducer is one of the most popular flashers for ice fishing use. (Courtesy Vexilar, Inc.)

date, no flasher other than Vexilar's FL-8SLT or Zercom's Color Point offers this feature. Zercom claims the Color Point offers an exceptional target separation of 1.5 inches. I'll discuss that in depth later. Vexilar's resolution is also exceptionally good. The FL-8SLT has 530 LED segments, so if you're on the 20-foot scale and divide the depth by 530 segments, you can see why objects below appear in such good detail. Amazing!

Liquid Crystal Flashers

Flashers are also available in direct-drive liquid crystal displays. This might seem like a contradiction when using the terms liquid crystal and flasher in the same breath, but note I said direct drive liquid crystal display–not multi-plexing liquid crystal graph. Zercom's Clearwater Classic was the first unit to incorporate such technology. Zercom claims the Classic, which reads like a flasher but utilizes LCD technology, is so sensitive tiny ultralight ice jigs can be seen in 40 feet of water. The Clearwater Classic's cousin, the Clearwater Pro, features electro-luminescent backlighting, a battery charge indicator, gray scale for bottom determination and reads well in sunlight.

The Clearwater series also features Time Variable Gain (TVG) to show true bottom and display fish equally at all depth ranges. This make secondary cover such as weeds easier to read, and provides the ability to easily mark and differentiate

Zercom's Clearwater Classic, the first "direct drive" liquid crystal display flasher, combining the liquid crystal advantage of less power draw with the flasher advantage of instantaneous readout. (Courtesy Zercom Marine)

The Zercom LCF-40 liquid crystal flasher featuring time variable gain (TVG) which insures targets remain consistent in relative size. In other words, big fish create big marks and small fish create relatively small marks. (Courtesy Zercom Marine)

fish or other objects among them by simply adjusting the sensitivity. The Clearwater Series also features super-sharp gray scale display for easy recognition of bottom content, weeds and other structure. This helps to identify fish holding tight to the bottom. With Zercom's backlighting system, readings will show up even in bright sunlight, and marks indicating your lure show up clearly whether you're fishing just beneath the transducer or fishing just off bottom.

Electronically, the Clearwater series features fast cold-weather response time, low battery current draw, 1000 watts of power, and target separation of 2.5 inches for seeing fish, including those holding tight to bottom. This engineering has led to an entirely new category of high-definition sonar: high-definition liquid crystal flashers.

Desiring to build better liquid crystal units for ice fishing, and understanding the basic ice fishing advantages of flashers, Zercom Engineers have improved and advanced flasher technologies and incorporated them into the LCF-40 liquid crystal flasher. Like traditional flashers, the LCF-40 operates on real time. Thanks to their "direct-drive" circuitry, when you lower your bait you'll see it dropping instantaneously. On many LCG's, multiplex drivers operate 10 or 20 pixels each, one at a time. Zercom's direct-drive liquid crystal display (LCD), features one driver per pixel, meaning pulses from the transducer are immediately received by each individual pixel instead of being sequentially transferred through several. Mathematically, this makes Zercom's response instant. You can see precisely how fish react to your motions. In addition, Zercom uses a special military-grade fluid that remains tractable down to -50 degrees F. On most liquid crystal units, fluids aren't designed for such extremes, and the combination of multi-plex drivers and reduced fluid speeds result in delayed signal response.

Zercom's LCF-40 also offers Time Variable Gain (TVG). This patented feature insures targets remain consistent in relative size: Big fish appear bigger than smaller ones, regardless of depth. On standard flashers, larger fish appear as smaller marks in deeper water. The shallower they come, the bigger they look. There's no way of determining relative size...unless multiple fish pass through at precisely the same depth. Resolution is also consistent on Zercom flashers. Once set, targets can be picked up little as 2.5 inches off bottom.

Another Zercom feature is the gray scale, a feature allowing each LCD segment to operate independently. Benefits? When small fish appear, they register as a light mark, while larger fish appear dark. With TVG, this remains constant throughout the entire vertical column, not just the horizontal plane you're fishing. This enables you to differentiate relative target size from just under the ice to the bottom. This also allows you to evaluate a fish's response to your presentation. Fish on the outside edge of the cone appear as a light, "fuzzy" gray, become solid gray as they approach the middle, then turn dark when they reach center. Nice, because you can tell when fish move into the cone toward your lure, or out, away from the lure.

The LCF-40 also offers 1,000 watts of power, making readings in deep water more clear and allowing fabulous target separation. It's not difficult, for example, to discern fish moving through light weed growth on the bottom, or to see fish holding tight to the bottom. In fact, instead of two small perch looking like one larger mark, the LCF-40 will show two distinct marks. This power, combined with TVG, also results in no "surface clutter" along the first few feet of your screen. This is outstanding when fishing shallow. And with all this power, Zercom units feature a low current draw, 50 milliamps compared to a typical 350 milliamps. Obviously, with seven times less current draw, batteries last seven times longer. Zercom engineers claim their units will run 100 hours on a single charge, although daily charging is encouraged to prolong battery life.

Finally, Zercom's liquid crystal display is highly visible in bright sunlight at virtually any angle. Electro-luminescent backlighting is available, providing a pleasant, evenly dispersed light across the entire screen for night angling. The only major drawback I've noticed with these LCD flashers is the amount of interference that can occur when fishing near other anglers using sonar. The only way around this is to try to find a transducer operating at a different frequency. This can be a difficult proposition, because most sonar operates at 200 kilohertz. However, I know Zercom is producing the Color Point in 150 kilohertz units, and I suspect as more sonar is used on ice, other unique frequencies will be instituted to help reduce interference.

Cone Angles

This brings us to cone angles—which determine the amount of water being covered by your sonar. No matter what unit you choose, cone angles come in various sizes, but you must understand the advantages of each in order to select the unit that's right for you and correctly interpret what it's telling you.

Sonar units feature various cone angles. Narrow cone angles concentrate the most power within a smaller area, making it easier to determine the precise depth at which fish are holding. Wider cone angles cover more area and thus reveal more fish, but you won't be able to determine precisely where they're holding as easily. Because the fish are so much farther from the cone center they will likely appear slightly deeper on the screen than they're actually holding.

I prefer units featuring narrow cone angles because their power is more concentrated within a smaller area, making it easier to determine the precise depth at which fish are holding. Although wider cone angles cover more area and presumably mark more fish, those located on the outside edge of the wider cone are so much farther from the cone center they may appear slightly deeper than they really are. Hence, you won't know precisely where they're positioned.

This is why today's "duo range" or "three-way" style sonar units have so many beneficial ice fishing applications. These units actually feature two or three transducers in one. On the duo range unit, one is a narrow cone, one is a wide cone. Duo-range transducers, something pioneered by Vexilar, offer both a 9-degree and 19-degree transducer in one. The problem narrow cone transducers had in the past was their bulky design, which wasn't conducive to ice fishing. Vexilar has changed that.

On three-way units, all three transducers feature narrow cone angles; one pointing left, one right, and one straight down. On most of these units you can employ any one alone or all three in a composite picture to create a wider cone angle. Some of these LCG units even provide depth cursors that indicate the exact depth of suspended targets, which takes some of the confusion out of reading marks when operating wider cone angles.

For most applications, it's best to utilize the center narrow cone to concentrate power and achieve better target separation—especially for fish on the bottom—then take advantage of the wider cone under special circumstances, such as when fishing for wandering schools. If a school starts moving away from your current position, you can check the general direction it's moving by enlarging your cone angle. Simply relocate the school using the side cone, move toward them, then switch back to the narrow cone as you jig. Although you won't be able to pinpoint specifically which direction fish are heading, you'll have a general idea which way to move, and you'll find the benefits of this strategy tremendous.

If this cone angle stuff sounds confusing, start from this point: a wide cone angle is often suitable for use in less than 40 feet of water, because you can see more fish. Your resolution may not always be as great, but it's good for fish finding. A narrow cone angle, however, like tightening the spray nozzle on a garden hose, allows you to channel the same amount of output into a smaller area, providing more power so you can see smaller objects more easily, or see any object better in deep water.

Sonar blind spots, or "dead zones" are areas that are missed by sonar pulses, so objects within these areas will not be revealed on your sonar screen. Blind spots are largest and most prominent when you're fishing over a drop-off (left), but while thinner, also occur even on a relatively flat surface (right).

Blind Spots

Many ice anglers also haven't heard of sonar "blind spots," or "dead zones," which essentially means fish seemingly in the cone along the bottom are present but won't actually register on the sonar screen. The width of this blind area is thickest at the outside base of the cone, narrowest in the center, and based on the unit's cone angle and the capability to sense, distinguish and display fish holding tight to the bottom. Wide cone angles feature wider dead zones. Narrow ones, focusing more power into a smaller stream, reduce these blind spots. Blind spots are also most significant when you're positioned directly over a steep drop.

There's currently no technology available that can be used to eliminate this phenomena. If you lower a lead depth finder or heavy lure to bottom, gradually raise it until it appears on your sonar screen, then measure this distance on your line, you'll know the thickness of the dead zone at cone center.

Target Separation

Another related concern is target separation, something I promised to touch on earlier in this chapter. As a rule of thumb, the smaller the target separation, the better. Say your sonar offers a target separation of 4 inches, and four small panfish, swimming uniformly one on top of the other two and half inches apart, move into the cone simultaneously. The unit would display them as one target. If they were 4 inches or more apart, however, they would be revealed as four separate targets. A unit with a 2.5-inch target separation, would mark the fish as four separate marks.

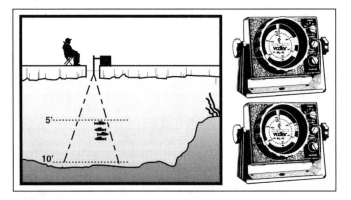

Target separation is another concern when choosing a sonar unit. Models featuring smaller target separation are better, as depicted here. Say the top sonar unit shown here had a target separation of 4 inches; the bottom unit a target separation of 2 inches. If four small fish, swimming uniformly, one on top of the other two and a half inches apart entered the cone, the top unit with a target separation of 4 inches would display one target. The bottom unit, featuring a target separation of 2 inches, would display four individual markings.

Now all that's left is to note the specific position of marked fish, in other words how they're relating to the structure. Are they suspended? Holding tight to the bottom? On the sunny or shady side? Over hard or soft bottom? Are they holding within any specific depth or cover? Such questions would be tough to answer without sonar, but with it, they are relatively easy.

Underwater Cameras

Now for one of the newest and most controversial twists on fishing technology: underwater cameras. These underwater viewing systems are basically comprised of a specialized, precisely balanced underwater video camera that can be lowered into a hole. Provided the water is relatively clear and there's enough outside light penetrating through the ice they will display a continuous, instantaneous picture of exactly what's below. In deep, dark or turbid water, conventional lenses aren't sufficient to obtain clear visuals, but infrared models can make up for this disadvantage.

Either way, the picture can be displayed on virtually any TV monitor. For convenience, small black and white units are usually preferred. On some models, monitors may even be included with the unit. Special adapter plugs can also be hooked up to transfer the image to a camcorder for recording. With sonar you can only make an educated guess as to what species are below and what forage and

set of environmental circumstances your gamefish are relating to. With underwater video you can confirm specifically what species you're seeing, how many are present, their position and even identify the forage. Heck, with the lens in a fixed position, you can even watch how the fish react to your lures and baits, much as you would when sight-fishing in clear, shallow water. If you use a VCR, you can play it back and review your day's fishing in the warmth of your living room!

Many versatile, mobile ice anglers find these units cumbersome, bulky and a detriment to their mobility. But they also realize the value of the under-ice details they can provide. Personally, I've found them fascinating, and if possible, will opt to carry one along, if for no other reason than simply to key on specific locations, like notches along a weed line or pockets in shallow weeds. To me, the drawbacks of underwater cameras are the extra weight during transport, the lack of ability for some models to penetrate deep or dark water, an especially irritating occurrence during "prime time" twilight and evening bites, and the worry of damaging an expensive lens or TV monitor while traveling. They can also distract from your fishing concentration.

Their advantage is the ability to show what's beneath the ice better than any other technology. If used properly, they provide the ability to identify and monitor specific fish-holding locations and confirm your interpretation of what your sonar is showing you. They also allow you to observe reactions to your presentation, and using the camera lens as a reference, provide a better

The Aqua-Vu underwater camera, which allows you to lower a video camera lens beneath the ice and display the image on a TV monitor.

indication of their specific direction of movement. Just lower the lens, flip the unit on and observe.

With a bit of research, background knowledge, mapping technology and the use of GPS radio navigation systems, sophisticated sonar and underwater cameras, you can learn to eliminate unproductive water and close in on winter gamefish much more quickly.

Batteries

One recurring problem with using electronics on the ice is battery power and life. Given harsh, cold conditions, batteries are more prone to trouble. Standard, heavy-duty batteries lose power quickly in the cold, and aren't adequate for operating electronics for long-term field use.

When using a hand-held GPS, for instance, alkaline batteries are your most affordable bet, although the more expensive nickel-metal hydrate or lithium batteries are better if you want to invest in batteries offering the best thermal characteristics. Some nickel-metal hydrate batteries also offer re-charging capabilities, charge quickly, and feature no "memory," meaning they can be recharged at any capacity from near-dead to fully charged without reducing the capability of the battery to receive a full charge.

For operating sonar, lantern-type batteries, even alkaline models offering greater longevity in cold temperatures don't have the power and "endurance" to handle cold weather for extended periods. They're difficult if not impossible to recharge, making them expensive. Motorcycle bat-

Gel-cell sealed lead acid batteries are the battery of choice for most professional ice anglers using sonar and underwater cameras, because they are small, don't leak and are relatively easy to care for. (Courtesy Vexilar, Inc.)

teries are a step up, but they are bulky and heavy. If they are tipped, they will leak acid. Despite these disadvantages, motorcycle batteries feature longer ampere hours. By using motorcycle batteries, you'll somewhat sacrifice longevity and convenience for larger capacity.

To best prevent cold-weather battery problems, my preference is the 7-amp sealed lead-acid power pack gel-cell battery. They're relatively small and lightweight. They generate excellent power, and are very capable of operating even the most power-draining flasher type sonar for 16-24 hours of continuous use. They can run an LCG for 30-40 hours of continuous use and will light up a liquid crystal flasher like the Zercom LCF-40 for 100 hours or more. Most underwater cameras will run the better part of a day without a problem on one full charge.

Gel-cells feature a thick, putty-like electrolyte solution inside. This is pressed between the battery plates and doesn't flow. They won't leak if tipped, but, like an acid battery, they function best when upright. While it is not likely to occur, gel-cells are subject to freezing. Although power is drained faster, if you're packing in to a distant fishing location, 1.2- or 4-amp gel-cells are much smaller and lighter than the 7-amp model. A fully charged 1.2-amp gel cell should provide power for a full day's fishing, and a 4-amp will provide a good 60 hours. By the way, a cold battery has 1/3 of its overall capacity lost just by cold temperature, so larger, fully charged batteries will provide the most power.

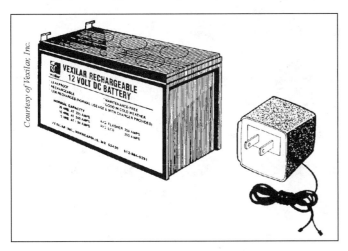

To best prevent cold-weather battery problems, my recommendation is to use a 7-amp sealed lead-acid power pack gel-cell type battery. (Courtesy Vexilar, Inc.)

When it comes to charging gel-cells, the engineers at Zercom Marine recommend charging your batteries after every seven or eight hours of use. Charging on a trickle charger is normally good for a satisfactory charge, but, don't overcharge your unit. Your charger should be a high-quality, 15-volt "smart charge" unit, and a volt meter should be used to monitor the charge. When the charge reaches 14.5-14.8 amps, discontinue the charge, or you'll risk permanent damage to the battery. Vexilar and Nature Vision both produce chargers that automatically shut off at the correct voltage, eliminating the chance of overcharging.

Then again, don't under charge, either. Placing your battery on a regular charging schedule as recommended by the manufacturer will double the life of your battery, and you should always charge them before storing. Periodic supplementary charges during long-term storage is a good idea to prevent "sulfating." Finally, keep your batteries clean by occasionally wiping them with water or a cloth dampened with alcohol. Otherwise, the standard rules of battery care apply.

Transporting Sonar

Once you've chosen a unit featuring the desired cone angle and a battery, you'll need something in which to transport your sonar. You can build your own case, or buy a commercially produced box such as Vexilar's P-160 or Winter Fishing Systems "IceBox." These are perfectly suited for transporting sonar on the ice. Vexilar and Zercom also offer sonar "kits" which include carrying cases, sonar units, a battery, battery indicators and chargers all in one package.

Most portable flashers and LCGs are available in compact, hard plastic protective or zippered, vinyl cases. Just be sure your chosen model is compatible to today's gel-cell batteries. Lowrance, for example, offers a "Porta-Power Pack", a self-insulated battery compartment that will accommodate either gel-cell or D cell batteries.

Underwater cameras should be self-contained, with a plastic case to store the lens, cable and monitor.

Preparing Your Sonar

The next step before heading onto the ice is correctly setting up your unit. Have your battery adequately charged, and be sure your transducer is level, providing the most power and best read-

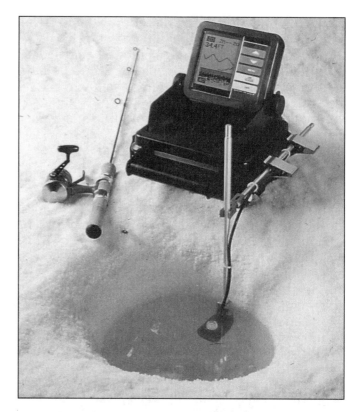

Most portable LCGs are available in compact, hard plastic protective cases to protect the unit from damage during transit. (Courtesy Lowrance Electronics)

Underwater cameras should be self-contained, with a plastic case to store the lens, cable and monitor. The Aqua-Vu shown here also shades the monitor for easier viewing in sunlight.

out. Many modern sonar units designed for ice fishing now feature self-aligning transducers that automatically level themselves. If yours doesn't, set the unit on a level surface, adjust the transducer perpendicular to the ground using a level, then glue a leveling bubble on top of the transducer. Some sonar units include such bubble. If yours doesn't, check with a local sporting goods dealer, they should know where to get one.

Finally, be sure the transducer and power cords are properly and tightly connected, wipe the face of the screen clean with a damp cloth, plug in the transducer cord and power connectors to the battery, and step onto the ice.

Setting Your Sensitivity

Once on the ice, you'll need to occasionally correct your power settings.

Start by dropping your lure halfway to the bottom and turn your sensitivity all the way down.

Most of today's sonar units designed for ice fishing now feature "self-aligning transducers" that automatically level themselves when suspended in the ice hole. (Courtesy Vexilar, Inc.)

You won't see much. Turn it up slowly and the bottom will show up. Turn it more and you'll see your lure. It's not that the lure didn't exist previously, it just wouldn't show up at the previous setting. The lesson? You must control such settings, and continually adjust them to be able to see specifically what you're looking for. One limitation of sonar units is knowing what they're telling you, and how to set them so they tell you what you want to know.

This is especially important when other anglers around you are also using sonar. Since they're at the same or near same frequency, your unit is shooting electronic pulses and waiting for the return, and also receiving misdirected pulses from other nearby units, causing interference. This is much like being in a room with several radios. Play just one, and you can hear it distinctly. Tune a second radio to a different station, and it's harder to focus. The more you add, the more difficult it becomes to sort things out. Ditto for sonar.

Vexilar has helped reduce this problem by offering patented, interference reducing circuitry on their FL-8SLT. The simple press of a button changes the signal, reducing interference. If two or more people are fishing close together, say in a fish house, by pushing the button an equal number of times you can synchronize the pulses–the closer you get, the less interference will occur, because pulses from both units are operating at the same frequency. The more times you press the button (up to a possible eight) the more interference will be reduced, although each press also slows the pulse rate, pulling you slightly away from "real time" readings. This must also be adjusted if you move or change depth ranges. You can also eliminate interference by trying to find a transducer that operates on an alternative, lesser used frequency, say 150 kilohertz instead of the standard 200.

Otherwise, the best way to reduce interference is to go to a smaller cone angle, which concentrates your power into a narrower field. You can also make your signal the "loudest" by using the most powerful transducer and battery, carefully adjusting your sensitivity, and fine-tuning your suppression settings. If interference persists, you'll need to adjust your suppression. The higher you set the suppression, the less interference you'll get, but the harder it will become to mark fish. For best results, adjust your power relatively high and the suppression set low, or when possible, turned off completely.

Strikemaster's "Polar Vision", a compact sonar device that provides a simple, accurate means of obtaining easy to read digital depth readings.

The Sonar Advantage

Now for shooting readings through the ice. The most compact, simple sonar product I'm aware of is made by Strikemaster. Called "Polar Vision," this unit provides a great way to find depth. A hand-held unit about the size and weight of a flashlight, it provides easy-to-read digital depth readings. A similar unit, the LPS-1, is made by Vexilar.

In either case, simply clear away surface snow or slush away from clear, solid ice, squirt down some water—I prefer heated saltwater, it doesn't freeze as easily—and make sure the bottom of your transducer is completely immersed in water. Place the transducer level on the clean surface to establish a seal. Properly sealed, the units will read depth. With repeated readings, you can easily pinpoint fish-holding structure.

Just understand several differences exist between using such technology in summer and winter. First, no transducer will provide a reading if you're shooting through slushy, mottled or air-bubbled ice. Transducers can't obtain signals when interfered with by objects or air. Secondly, when shooting through the ice, your unit will disregard the presence of ice and tell you only how deep the water is. In other words, if the ice is 2 feet thick over 12 feet of water and you shoot through it, the depth will read 10 feet. But if you drill a hole

Readings can be taken through clean, solid ice, but when shooting through, the sonar will disregard the presence of ice and tell you only how deep the water is. In other words, if you're in 12 feet of water and shoot through two feet of ice, the depth will read 10 feet (top). Drill a hole in the same location and repeat the reading, however, and the unit will display a depth reading of 12 feet (bottom).

in the same spot and re-check the depth by placing the transducer in the water-filled hole, the screen will read 12 feet. The difference? Water now occupies the space where two feet of ice once was, and the sonar reads the water where it didn't read the ice previously. This may not seem important, but I've seen many anglers who mark the depth on certain structures in summer become needlessly confused by such discrepancies after the ice forms. Remember to account for them when shooting through the ice.

You can also obtain readings using more complex sonar units like flashers and LCGs. Simply form a seal of water around the transducer, and adjust the sensitivity until you obtain a depth reading. Although the Polar Vision sounds an alarm and flashes the depth when fish move into the cone, the advantage to using standard sonar is the unit reveals not only depth and fish, but bottom content, presence of cover and forage. Like the Polar Vision, however, readings cannot be shot through slushy, mottled, or air-bubbled ice.

Either way, once you've obtained a depth reading, mark the depth next to each hole, and continue this process by taking multiple readings. By marking the depth and moving strategically—all while setting a plotter trail and referencing your

GPS map—the bottom configuration, including structure, will be revealed. Once the structure is outlined, begin looking for unique features or irregular contours in association with each productive structural element. Look for a finger on the edge of a submerged hump, a hook on a point, a weed edge near a drop off, all would be primary fish-holding areas, and all can be revealed simply by using sonar and outlining the feature with icons on your GPS map.

It's always fun to watch a fish strike, something that can be accomplished from within a darkened shelter—or closely monitoring a sonar unit.

Continue taking readings, referencing your map while doing so, and you'll eventually locate various structures and their orientation. Once you've uncovered a good piece of structure, look closely at your readings on those unique features or irregular contours; you should also be able to determine depth, secondary structure, bottom content, presence of cover, forage and fish.

On the sonar, bottom will simply appear as the depth at each reading, and by combining various depth readings with personal knowledge and map interpretation, you'll be able to determine the placement and orientation of various structures and secondary structures. Furthermore, hard bottoms will register thick and dark and feature a "double echo" on a flasher. Soft, thin, dim readings are indicative of a soft bottom. On an LCG, the bar graph for sensitivity will also read high in soft bottom areas, and low over hard bottoms.

If present, weeds, wood and other forms of cover will also appear as batches of fine lines or stacked markings forming columns attached to and rising from the bottom. Plankton and baitfish look similar, but will generally show up as suspended scatterings or "clouds" of fine lines or dots separated from the bottom. When inside your transducer cone, your lure will also appear as a distinctive moving "blip" or line at the depth you're fishing that moves as you lift or drop your lure.

If your pre-determined locations aren't holding fish, simply save them as waypoints for future trials. Make reference notes, so if you wish, you can come back and try them another time. Such areas may hold fish under a different set of conditions.

Once fish are found, accurate depth control often makes the difference between no fish and a limit. So, before you begin jigging, measure how many inches of line your reel picks up per revolution of the handle. Do this by marking the line at your rod tip with a marker, turning the handle 360 degrees, and measuring the distance between

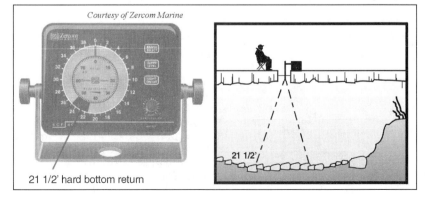

Hard bottoms such as rock or sand will appear as dark, bright signals on a sonar unit. (Illustration Courtesy Zercom Marine)

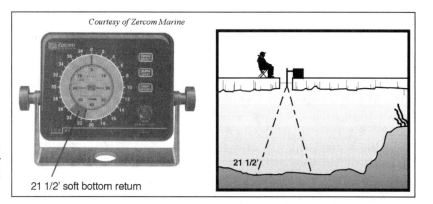

Soft bottoms such as silt or muck will appear as light, pale signals on a sonar unit. (Illustration Courtesy Zercom Marine)

21 1/2' soft bottom return

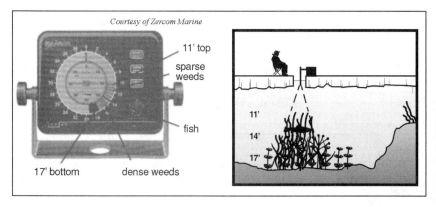

11' top

sparse weeds

fish

17' bottom   dense weeds

If weeds are present they will usually appear as batches of fine lines above the bottom. Sparse weeds will be thin, light and separated, while dense weeds will appear thin, light and batched. Here, a fish, a more dense target, appears as a dark line within the less dense weeds. (Illustration Courtesy Zercom Marine)

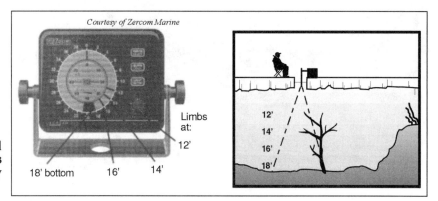

Limbs at:

12'

18' bottom   16'   14'

If submerged wood is present, it will appear as thick, solid, non-moving lines above bottom. (Illustration Courtesy Zercom Marine)

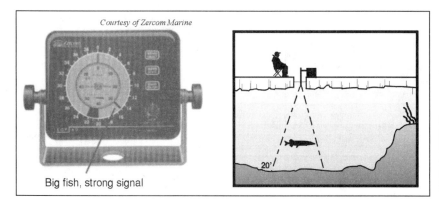

Big fish, strong signal

Suspended fish will appear as a distinct mark at the depth they're swimming through. Big fish or fish directly in the cone will create the strongest signal and appear the darkest. (Illustration Courtesy Zercom Marine)

your mark and the rod tip. Now you'll know precisely what distance every turn of your reel handle will move your lure, and this, combined with what you're sonar shows you, lets you know precisely where your jig is in relation to the bottom. More importantly, this can show you where your lure is positioned in relation to fish. I also use the practice to determine the width of my "dead zone," as described earlier, and you should, too.

Obviously, your lure or bait is most effective when placed near fish. When you work a bait in conjunction with sonar, you can't help but increase your odds of being in the right place at the right time. It's simple. If you can see fish on your screen, you can lower your lure to them, and seeing your lure in relation to the bottom and where fish are coming through is vital to success.

How would an angler fishing in 30 feet of water and not using sonar be able to consistently catch fish suspended 15 feet down? I've had several instances where someone was fishing next to me, I was catching fish and they couldn't get a bite. The reason? Depth. They were fishing near the bottom and the school was suspended. Without sonar, they were at a total disadvantage.

There's no excuse for not seeing fish, as they create obvious marks. If you're using an LCG that features a "Fish ID" readout, fish will register as conspicuous fish shapes, some units will even provide the precise depth the marked fish are holding. Otherwise, single, faint lines suspended off the bottom and away from surface clutter are representative of suspended fish on the outside edge of your transducer cone, while thick, bright lines are fish suspended directly inside the cone. Fish on or near the bottom will appear as thin lines barely separated from the bottom signal.

You can even estimate the size of the fish by the height of the signal. Sonar measures the distance of an object from the transducer, thus large objects closer to the transducer will register smaller in length than objects of the same size located farther away. In addition, you're sitting stationary, which enhances this "lengthening" effect. Thickness, not length, indicates size. It may seem as though I'm dwelling on this point, but that's because I've seen too many ice anglers mistakenly believe that long marks are large fish, when actually they're just marking fish holding high or stationary within the cone. Interestingly, you can even surmise the species being marked on sonar by noting its position. Walleyes often hold near the bottom, while brown trout and salmon tend to suspend.

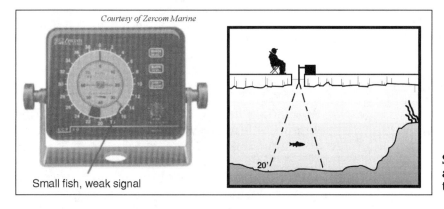

Small fish will create a weaker signal and appear lighter. (Illustration Courtesy Zercom Marine)

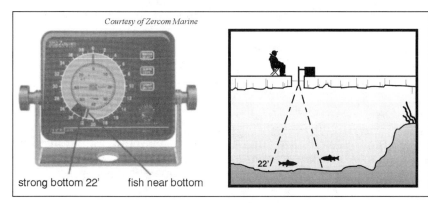

Fish holding near bottom will appear as distinct marks just off bottom. Those holding tight to bottom will simply create a fluctuating depth reading, so be alert for their presence. (Illustration Courtesy Zercom Marine)

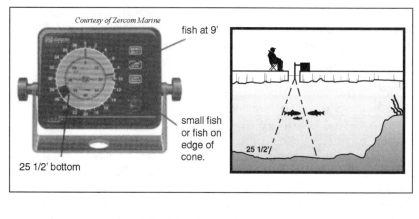

Here, two fish are shown on the screen: one large fish, and one smaller fish below. (Illustration Courtesy Zercom Marine) Note the fish outside the cone does not appear on-screen.

Like a small fish, fish on the outside edge of the transducer cone will create a weak signal and appear lighter. The fish inside the cone registers as a distinct, thick mark. (Illustration Courtesy Zercom Marine)

Of course, where it's legal, placing an underwater camera down a nearby hole could clear up any misconceptions in short order. By closely looking at the depth, bottom content, structure, secondary cover and position of various numbers and sizes of fish, you can begin to pattern them. Consider the consequences of these advantages carefully. Using our understanding of high-percentage winter gamefish locations, lake maps and GPS with mapping capabilities, we can move efficiently to pre-determined high-percentage locations. Once there, sonar allows us to determine depths, locate drop-offs, rises and breaks. By taking multiple readings, we can determine structural layout, bottom content, secondary cover such as weeds, rocks or sunken timber forage. You can even locate fish and determine their relative size, and mark them electronically on our GPS map by establishing plotter trails and icons. From here, it's possible to discern what depths, bottom contents, structures, cover and forage the fish are relating to. If you have an underwater camera to identify specific fish-holding locations, identify forage, and place your bait near marked fish to observe their reactions. Use that information to make changes in lure styles, sizes, colors and actions until a winning combination is found.

Obviously, electronics can do more than just read depth or help you find structure and gamefish. Using this technology, you can actually start piecing location patterns together even before drilling a single hole!

Monitoring Fish Activity Levels

Watching a fish strike is always an interesting experience. It's fun to watch a finicky walleye suck in a minnow-tipped jig, see a lake trout dart out from outside the cone to hit an airplane jig, witness an eelpout kiss a jig and minnow laying on bottom or tense up as a pike crushes a jigging minnow. And whose knees wouldn't shake as they witness a brown trout smash a spoon 10 feet under the ice?

Without a doubt, most anglers enjoy watching fish strike, not only because it's exciting to see and adds to the fishing experience, but also because it's possible to judge the approximate activity level of the fish, based on how hard they strike and how often they hit. In the past, these things were for "sight anglers" watching shallow fish. Today, knowledgeable use of sonar and underwater cameras allow the same thrills, even in deep, clear water.

By now you realize how important it is to understand and use electronics for finding high-percentage locations and winter gamefish. Knowing how you're positioned in relation to fish is of key importance. Yet to fully appreciate the applications of electronics for ice fishing, you must also understand electronics are equally valuable in determining gamefish activity levels and monitoring presentation responses. When properly set, sonar and underwater cameras can accomplish this feat.

When fishing for schooling gamefish species such as walleyes, sauger, brown trout, smallmouth bass or channel catfish, it's best to find tightly clustered schools of fish as opposed to scattered ones. Concentrated schools are more likely to be feeding, active fish. Schools of "squiggly" or "fluttering" marks near suspended forage are especially good indicators, as they designate groups of moving, actively feeding fish moving in and out of our transducer cone. They appear and disappear from your screen as they move. If you run across this situation, quickly drill a couple of holes, lower your underwater camera in one and your sonar and lure down another, then watch to confirm where and how they're feeding.

This can be determined by monitoring how the fish are positioned and how they react to your lure. Are they reacting slowly, spooking easily and short-striking, or are they aggressively chasing your lure and completely swallowing the offering? Do they want the bait moved quickly or slowly?

Once such questions have been answered, you can adjust your specific lures and techniques according to the mood and activity level of the fish. For instance, if the fish spook easily, lighten up and work smaller baits more gingerly. If they're aggressive, work larger, more aggressive flash or jigging lures, and work them hard. Also experiment with lure style, action, color and live bait tippers. Do they show any preferences? If so, make adjustments in your presentation accordingly. Your extra efforts should pay off.

If the fish are producing firm, lone or scattered marks in one suspended position or hugging bottom and won't react to various presentations, they're probably sedentary, non-active fish. Always try fishing them, but if they don't respond within a few minutes, don't get hung up trying to trigger them. Instead, move on, search for active fish, but save the location as a waypoint for future inspection.

Just remember, not all gamefish species are schooling fish. Pike and musky, for example, are often lone fish. When fishing for them, be prepared to modify your techniques accordingly, and spend more time looking for structural features likely to attract them. Yes, large groups of pike may form outside shallow bays during late ice as they stage prior to the spawn. But this is an isolated instance we'll touch on more in the upcoming species-specific chapters. For now, let's stick with the basics.

The only way to consistently and efficiently find productive structures, mark active fish, accurately track their movements and systematically monitor their activity levels–in other words, pattern the fish–is with sonar and underwater cameras. Yet strategic use of sonar is dependent on a working knowledge of how to read lake maps, and how to properly set and interpret what your units are showing you. Without those skills, even the best state-of-the-art electronics will be of little use.

Large pike are often lone fish, so be prepared to modify your techniques, spending more time looking for structural features likely to attract them, then moving often to increase your odds of hooking up.

So next time you ice fish, don't make the mistake of randomly drilling holes. Instead, do your homework. Read up on the species you're seeking and the lake you plan to fish. Carefully review a lake map before you begin searching for primary structures. Mark high-percentage locations and plot waypoints on a GPS unit most effectively, then choose an LCG or flasher best suiting your ice fishing needs. More importantly, learn how to use its features to their fullest capacity, and if you wish, follow up by dunking an underwater camera down a nearby hole to confirm what you see on sonar.

You'll soon discover how proper use of electronics will increase your number of successful "hard water" fishing trips. The culmination of all these efforts means you'll see exactly what's below in terms of structure, cover and forage. This will help you locate a variety of winter gamefish and understand what's happening below you in terms of fish position, movements, activity levels and responses.

Assembling Location and Presentation Patterns: The Total Pattern

Going this far has already placed you among the best ice angling crowd, but you can take this even farther. With an integral knowledge of winter patterns and through the use of electronics, you can establish both location AND presentation patterns: the total pattern.

The best way to determine total winter patterns begins with examining detailed lake maps, then, taking into account how the species you're seeking will instinctively respond to the many variables. You can then pinpoint the best locations using sonar and underwater cameras, and target gamefish in the most productive areas. In effect, you'll be deciphering productive winter patterns.

Following such practices repeatedly, you'll soon realize productive winter gamefish patterns. These patterns will often repeat themselves, winter after winter. Consider the big picture! If you find a large school of active gamefish several years in a row on a gradually sloping shoreline point covered with cabbage weeds stretching from deep to shallow water, there's a good chance you'll find them in similar locations throughout other areas of the lake. You might even find them in similar locations on other lakes.

However, fish will seldom follow the same location patterns from one lake type to another. A shal-

With an integral knowledge of winter patterns and use of electronics, you can establish both location and presentation patterns, or "the total pattern" which can be used to catch fish like this. (Courtesy Northland Tackle)

low, weedy, bowl-shaped lake may not present distinct structural elements like a deep, structurally diverse one. Yet the bowl-shaped lake may feature distinct weed bed pockets or stump field edges which become primary structural locations. To decipher winter patterns consistently, you must note as many details as possible.

Evaluate. What lake type are you fishing? What's the prevalent weather pattern? Predominant bottom content? Cover type? Is there a well-defined "edge" in the form of a weed line, change in bottom content, change in depth, change in cover or other variable that may be causing the fish to hold there? Is there a specific forage fish present? How deep is the forage, and how are the gamefish positioned in relation to it? How deep are the most active biters? Are they holding along a major migration route? Do specific holding points exist that active fish are relating to? When?

Sonar and underwater cameras will allow you to determine these answers. Be thorough and always decipher complete location patterns. Every lake is different, featuring different water clarity, bottom content, prominent vegetation types, nutrient concentrations, oxygen contents and so on. Again, you may find similar lakes, but you'll seldom find two that are identical, because most gamefish won't be doing the same thing at the same time. Even populations of the same species in the same lake won't necessarily follow the same location patterns, because while their needs and natural instincts are the same, various fish are exposed to different conditions, causing them to react differently on a seasonal, daily, or even an hourly basis. A weather change, the movement of forage, an increase in fishing activity or simply the sight of a passing compet-

I'm convinced a major difference between "good" ice anglers and "experts" is experts often spend hours pondering over maps, carefully considering potential hot spots prior to setting out on the ice. (Courtesy Northland Tackle)

ing species can break up established patterns and lead to new ones. This means numerous winter gamefish patterns often exist simultaneously. But frequently one stands out, and it's best to search for clues revealing the most productive one.

BE DETAIL-ORIENTED, It's important! If your goal is a trophy, large lakes generally offer more potential than small ones, because there's a greater amount of water in which gamefish can hide, feed and grow. But because there's so much area to cover, high-percentage hot spots holding active fish can be more difficult to find. Again, the best method for defining specific patterns is to record productive locations on your lake map and GPS. Other pertinent information, including the date, time, weather conditions, prevalent bottom content, forage base and cover should also be noted. Such references will help establish repetitious annual patterns that create degrees of consistency few other anglers can match.

I'm thoroughly convinced a major difference between "good" ice anglers and "experts" is that experts spend hours looking over maps and carefully considering potential hot spots. At times, experts may invest more time looking at maps, thinking about the predominant conditions, and drilling holes than actually fishing. But once they're in the right location, the action is fast, and they often leave the lake with more fish than those who spend all day fishing just a mediocre spot or two. The secret? Spending quality time fishing within the highest-percentage areas with the highest-percentage presentations.

Now, just as you can locate microstructure on several good structural features at the right depth, you can also pinpoint the most productive presentation patterns. Gamefish behave differently in winter. At times, some species like largemouth and smallmouth bass or catfish may even settle into semi-dormant states. Yet these fish must feed, and they bite, aggressively at times, throughout the winter. Ice pros understand this, and realize the secret to consistent winter catches begins with capitalizing on these periods by determining precisely when and where they will occur–in other words, they pattern the fish from a location perspective.

The Presentation Perspective

However, TOTAL winter gamefish patterns are based on two fundamental principles: the locations where these fish will likely be most active—which we've already covered—and the most suitable presentations needed to catch them. Just as

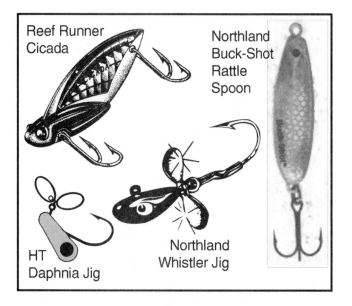

In deep or dark water environments where fish can't see as well and rely more heavily on their sense of hearing and vibration, flashy, noisy or vibrating lures such as blade baits (Reef Runner's Cicada), rattle spoons (Northland's Buck-Shot rattle spoon), prop jigs (Northland's Whistler) or flipper jigs (HT's Daphnia with fins) are excellent choices to help gamefish find your bait.

top ice pros must analyze each situation and decipher the best location patterns, choosing the right presentation isn't a random process, either. Since all gamefish species are unique and respond differently under various conditions, experts must select their presentations based on the fish, the lake being fished, the prevailing weather, depth being fished, water clarity—even the habits, size and color of the target species' primary forage bases.

In deep or dark water environments, for example, gamefish can't see well and instinctively rely on their senses of hearing, smell and the ability to sense vibration. Therefore aggressive jigging presentations with vibrating blade baits and larger, high-profile, brightly colored lures and baits with rattles or fins are often helpful for attracting fish and creating consistent catches. Ditto for phosphorescent colors. You should do everything possible to help the fish find your bait. Adding live bait is often helpful, as this adds natural scent, taste and texture, rounding out the appeal to each of the fish's primary senses. This is especially important during winter.

In clear water, over-sized noisy lures and unnatural color schemes may spook gamefish. In such instances, more subdued, realistically sized, natu-

rally moving, naturally colored baits are more likely to catch them. Because these fish rely on their sense of sight to feed, and since they have ample time to examine your bait, you must make them believe they're looking at something real. Again, a touch of live bait is a plus, and should closely resemble the natural forage.

However, as with location patterns, successful presentation patterns go beyond such basics because you must locate schools, then determine the primary forage of these schools and their activity levels. So when you find a school, start by determining the prey they're likely eating. Then, if applicable, begin fishing larger, more active lures such as swimming and vibrating lures. After all, active fish will strike almost anything, and often, larger, louder, fast-moving "action lures" are the quickest way to attract and catch active biters.

Still, monitor their responses carefully. If the fish spook or strike at the lure halfheartedly, try switching to less active jigging lures, or baits with more subtle actions, styles, sizes and colors to determine which draw the most strikes. To prepare for these situations, it's a good idea to rig several rods and tip-ups with a variety of lures and rigs. Then, like a successful golfer who chooses various clubs given different situations, you'll be able to change quickly to presentations that best suit the situation.

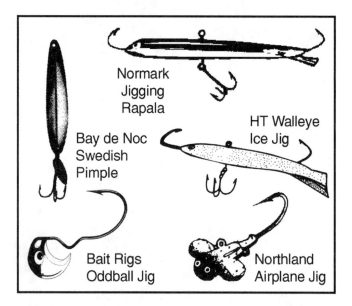

In shallow or clear water, more subdued, realistically sized, naturally colored baits such as Normark's jigging Rapala, HT's walleye ice jig and Northland's airplane jig are good bets. Flashy spoons like Bay de Noc's Swedish Pimple or stand-up, open-gap jigs like Bait Rigs' Odd'ball jigs are also good selections.

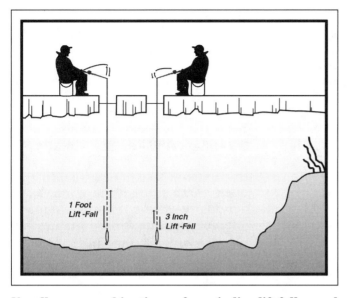

Usually, a combination of periodic lift-falls and finesse style jigging movements are important. The lift-falls attract the fish's attention, and the gentle jigging motion incorporated in-between teases strikes.

This is important because no two plankton, minnow, or insect species look and act exactly the same. Some are short and fat, some are long and skinny. Some rest on the bottom, some swim slowly up then drop in vertical movements, while others make quick darting horizontal movements. These motions may vary given the lake type, time of day and light intensity. So experiment with various lure weights, sizes, colors, designs and jigging actions, trying to "match the hatch," using balanced tackle. The extra effort often pays off and this is where consistently successful anglers stand out. Given such conditions, knowledgeable anglers utilize a mobile approach, take numerous electronic readings and keep open minds while experimenting with a variety of presentations in numerous, high-percentage locations. By sticking it out and analyzing each situation right down to the most minute detail, you'll often discover gamefish feeding on certain prey items or utilizing specific depths, and consequently, be able to piece together viable patterns even under the most agonizingly tough conditions.

Sometimes, combining a gentle, finesse-style teasing approach with a more aggressive "triggering" action is important. This is especially worthwhile during cold fronts, bright conditions, and periods of inactivity. A gentle tease may trigger a few fish, and an aggressive jig may trigger a couple more. I've found the best way to catch numbers consistently is to blend the two techniques, using a basic finesse approach with lures representing the natural forage, then adding periodic aggressive

movements to draw fish or instinctively trigger strikes.

Yes, there will be times you encounter gamefish that just won't bite. When this happens, move along in search of more active fish, but always mark the area so you can return. Remember, the school may be inactive at the moment, but they must eventually feed. This may occur an hour, several hours, even a day or two later. If you remain aware of their changing activity levels, you could end up catching a limit from just such a school.

Whatever the conditions, the challenge is to systematically work out the most productive patterns by carefully and systematically observing groups of location and presentation variables. Then monitor these variables as they change and gamefish responses vary. After all, most gamefish can be found in certain places and are vulnerable to certain presentations much of the time. Don't just randomly drill holes and haphazardly drop your bait down just any hole. Rather, pay attention to location details and be mobile in your approach, until you pinpoint these high-percentage locations for the time and day you're fishing. Then be versatile in your presentation to determine their vulnerability.

Also keep in mind the menu analogy from Chapter Two. You remember: Head to a restaurant and

Whatever the conditions, the challenge is to systematically work out the most productive patterns by carefully observing groups of location and presentation variables, then monitoring them as they change and gamefish responses vary. (photo Courtesy Wil Wegman)

give several people identical menus, and not all are likely to choose the same thing. Since fish aren't much different, I usually start by trying tiny ultra-light presentations, then gradually work larger lures and presentations with more active jigging motions (or vice versa, depending on the conditions and the species being sought) and then a mixture thereof until I determine the fish's activity levels and the most efficient presentation for catching them. This should result in at least a fish or two, especially if you've located a school.

However, if nothing happens after 10 or 15 minutes, try another hole! It's always tempting to fish long and hard when a school is found, but finding fish doesn't mean you'll actually catch them. Many frustrated ice anglers will attest to this. So don't get caught up in this Catch-22, it completely defeats the purpose of this efficient ice fishing approach. Rather, fish wisely and efficiently, stay mobile and whatever you do, always search for the most active fish.

Do this at several high-percentage waypoints, and it's unlikely you'll strike out on each one, but rather, you're likely to find willing fish on some or even most of them. One waypoint may hold no fish, another nothing but inactive fish, while a third is bustling with activity. Or you might simply catch a couple fish from each area on varied presentations. Find the willing fish on each spot, stay with them as long as possible, and when they move or become inactive, move to the next waypoint. Such efficient processes lead to consistency. You'll gain invaluable experience, and over time, learn to consistently pinpoint high-percentage gamefish-producing locations and top producing presentations. That will save you valuable fishing time and make you an increasingly more efficient ice angler learning to better understand winter gamefish location, behavior and activity levels on various lake types given a variety of conditions.

So don't just randomly walk onto the ice and sit in one place waiting for fish, or casually use electronics without fully interpreting what they're telling you. Many ice anglers don't realize it, but we're living in a historic age. We are essentially moving from the stone age to the space age. The present-day ice fishing scene is much like the open-water fishing scene years ago. Think about it. You'd be hard pressed to find a serious walleye tournament angler in today's world of fishing that doesn't attempt to move from spot to spot, trying to determine the predominant location pattern. And these anglers attempt to match the correct presenta-tion—be it a slip bobber and minnow, tube jig, spinner rig, jig and minnow or crankbait—to the particular summer walleye pattern to obtain the best results.

But it's fairly easy to find ice anglers that have never considered winter location patterns. Unfortunately, there aren't a great many frontiers left in open-water fishing, but there are many in ice fishing. Those anglers who capitalize on them now are in for a real treat.

Join in! After all, if you study the gamefish species you're seeking, learn to read the water, interpret lake maps, properly use electronics to pinpoint the primary winter locations of actively feeding winter fish, then top this with the best presentations, you're sure to latch onto some productive patterns—and some awfully nice winter catches as well.

Individual Species

Now having covered basic winter patterns and how to practically apply this knowledge to deciphering general winter gamefish patterns, we need to move ahead by evaluating how individual gamefish species respond given various conditions. So, let's begin covering specifics relating to individual species.

Although practical limitations don't allow intricate detail, we can now apply our system to determine how specific gamefish species respond and relate to various lake types, weather and water conditions. We can then use a mobile, versatile approach for determining their reactions and activity levels to properly match the correct presentations with the conditions to maximize success. Incorporate these strategies at the right time, and the results will lead to more consistent winter gamefish catches, even when many other anglers are coming off the ice empty-handed.

We'll start with walleye and sauger, and begin by summarizing a number of winter location patterns details, many of which are the basis of other patterns that, in modified form, cross over to other gamefish species. Keep this in mind as you read, because we'll build on these gradually more specific location, movement and presentation patterns as we move onto other individual gamefish species sections later in the book.

Put these pieces of the puzzle together, and you'll get more out of each ice fishing outing, simply because you're putting more in. And along the way, you'll experience more consistent winter gamefish action than you've ever dreamed possible.

Chapter 4

Understanding Walleyes and Sauger in Winter

Walleye are identified by their greenish-gold sides, whitish bellies, black spots at the rear of the dorsal fin, white tip on the lower lobe of their tail, and distinctive, large mirrored eyes. (Courtesy Northland Tackle)

The scent of evergreen and faint trace of smoke linger in the icy air. Nothing moves in the stillness, aside from evening shadows cast by radiant winter moonlight glimmering through tall pines, and wispy gray clouds drifting silently past a glowing, full moon. Tranquillity muffles all sound, except desolate whispers of distant breezes sweeping through the pines.

I pause, thankful for the quality of life here, then walk through the backyard to my snowmobile. It seems a shame to shatter pristine winter silence, but holding my breath, I hit the electric start. A sputtering engine catches, and the bright headlight pierces the darkness, revealing a panorama of light snowflakes gently settling to the ground. Smoke billows from under the track and the smell of two-cycle emissions fill the air as I race the motor and rock the machine, attempting to free it from the ground's icy grip. Then, slowly, the snowmobile begins inching forward.

After a short, cold ride I arrive at my waypoint. The motor beats to a stop and the headlight fades; silence and darkness return. My eyes adjust to the dim light and scintillating, bright stars sparkling in the immense blackness above. Peace.

Led by the familiar glow of my sonar, I take readings and enter a plotter trail to outline the structure. Then I repeatedly grasp the throttle on my power auger and listen as the auger slices ice until I feel the blades crack through and icy water swirls over my boots. Before long I have enough holes drilled to cover the point. Satisfied the primary area is covered, I set a few tip-ups and start jigging. Fifteen minutes later, my rod tip bounces. I set the hook and pull a fat, 5-pound walleye from the hole.

Such scenes are common throughout the North American ice fishing belt. A challenge to catch and luscious to eat, walleyes are favored winter targets. All you must do to enjoy walleye fishing is understand primary winter location and presentation patterns. Then you should have a few good recipes for preparing their delicately flavored and delicious fillets.

Walleye

Walleye are identified by their greenish-gold sides, whitish-yellow bellies, black spots at the rear of the dorsal fin, white tip on the lower lobe of the tail and those distinctive, large mirrored eyes that allow them to feed in darkness. They thrive in large, clear, cool bodies of water including rivers, reservoirs and drainage lakes. They will feed on crustaceans, insect larvae and baitfish.

Characteristically, walleyes hold in deeper, darker water during the day, then migrate to shallow shoals to feed under the cover of darkness. They will move with changes in light intensity, forage availability and changing oxygen concentrations.

Sauger

The sauger is the walleye's cousin. Identifying features include brownish-gray sides with irregular dark brown splotches, a brown spotted front dorsal fin, and no white tip on the lower tail. Their eyes are best adapted to feeding in dark or turbid water, and consequently, they survive in large lakes and reservoirs, but are most common in large, turbid river systems and drainage lakes where they feed on invertebrates and baitfish. Like walleye, sauger are most active during twilight. They are also great table fare.

Searching for Walleyes

Consistently locating schools of active walleyes is hardly easy. The process is compounded when cold temperatures and ice inhibit free running mobility and exploration.

But walleyes can be caught through the ice. First, consider lake type. Walleyes may inhabit fertile, dark water lakes, sandy clear mesotrophic waters, or deep, rocky, ultra-clear oligotrophic lakes. While these systems are all capable of supporting tremendous walleye fisheries, each features different combinations of physical, chemical and biological properties.

Walleyes may inhabit a variety of lake types, including fertile, dark water lakes, sandy clear mesotrophic waters or deep, rocky, ultra-clear oligotrophic lakes.

Preparations should begin before you reach the ice. Check various ice fishing records and winter fishing contest results. You'll often discover certain waters produce surprising numbers of good walleyes. Also note the times that the most or biggest fish have been taken. Obtain lake maps and study them, carefully noting the most prominent features. Reefs, rock piles, sunken islands, shoreline points, inside turns, fingers, bars and "saddles" between such structures constitute primary structures. The larger and more diverse, the better.

Large structures featuring gently sloping or tiered contours are better than those with sharp breaks, because moderate, irregular edges harbor more notches and protrusions that attract baitfish. These areas give the walleyes the opportunity to trap baitfish at various depths offering varied temperature, levels of light penetration and oxygen concentration. Walleyes may be relating to hard-bottom reefs, for example, but only those topping out in strata where oxygen is most suitable. The fish will often ignore areas in zones outside their preferred range.

Diversity is important, too. Structures offering microstructure such as steep rock breaks on one side and gradually sloping soft bottoms on the other and secondary changes in bottom configuration such as miniature points, turns, dips or rises are better than those without. In waters where the bottom is mainly sand, rocky features may draw larger concentrations of walleyes. In rocky lakes, sandy, weed-covered structures may produce better.

Large, diverse, elongated structures extending from the shallows into deep water are likely to

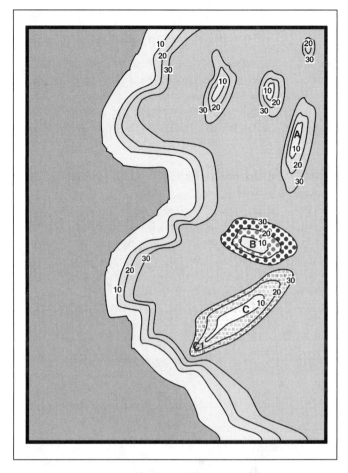

Larger structures offering differing bottom contents from the surrounding terrain (B, C) and miniature points or other microstructure (C1) are even better bets.

draw winter walleyes because fish wandering at various depths are more likely to eventually happen onto these expansive edges. These areas act as convenient migration routes between deep and shallow water. Walleyes seldom cross expansive, featureless flats to reach small, isolated structures.

There is a difference! Large, elongated structural features offering a variety of bottom contents and cover types provide the greatest blend of structural diversity. In doing so, they draw more forage, and in turn, more walleyes. The ideal structure might be a large shoreline point featuring numerous fingers, inside and outside turns. If this area has variety of bottom conditions and is extending toward deeper water in a gradual, stair-step fashion, all the better. Add in a "saddle" area leading to a series of large mid-depth shoals and you've got a tremendous combination of available structure, cover and poten-

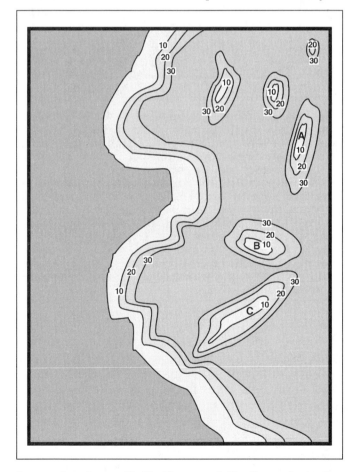

Large structures (A, B, C), especially those featuring gently sloping or tiered contours (B, C) usually attract the most winter walleyes.

tial forage-holding areas that will attract winter walleyes.

However, nothing is etched in stone. When larger, structurally diverse features linking shallow food shelves to main lake breaks don't produce or the best available structure is a small, isolated gradually breaking sand hump, the key to consistently catching fish is in the details.

Watch for Details

Once you start patterning winter walleyes, you'll eventually discover one of the biggest mysteries of winter walleye fishing: why certain spots consistently hold walleyes, but other seemingly identical spots don't. This could be a result of fishing pressure, but the solution is usually in some slight structural variation that might not be

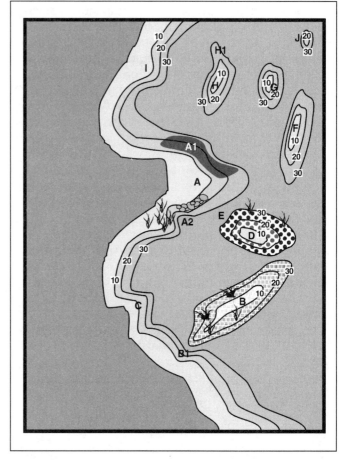

If such large, diverse, elongated features running from shallow to deep water offer differing bottom contents, cover types and good potential migration routes featuring ample holding areas running through several depth, temperature and oxygen strata, the potential for holding winter walleyes is increased several fold (A, B). The best migration routes on these three features would be B1 and A2. Structures F, H and H1 may also be good secondary areas to try, as might reef G and the saddles between bars H and G and bars G and F. Given the amount of structure available here, point I and small, isolated reef J would likely offer only moderate potential.

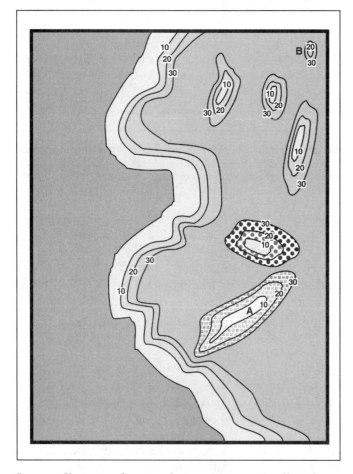

Large, diverse, elongated structures extending from shallow to deep water and offering a variety of bottom conditions extending out in a gradual, stair-step fashion are often the features worth trying first when attempting to narrow down your search (A).

obvious to you but makes a big difference to the walleyes.

Take sunlight for example. Calm, sunny weather on clear lakes may cause walleyes to hold on shaded structures. In more turbid water, however, they might relate to exposed, sunny structures. In shallow, eutrophic lakes where oxygen becomes depleted and carbon dioxide, hydrogen sulfide and methane gas accumulate, walleyes may be forced to vacate some structures in favor of those offering subtle micro climates of suitable oxygen provided by currents or springs. Maintain an open mind!

The Pattern Mix

"Structurally Limited" Waters

Structurally limited waters may offer completely unique sets of patterns. They may support large populations of walleyes, but lack classic structure. Imagine removing major underlying classic structural features you'd look for on more structurally diverse lakes. What's left is a

Once you start patterning winter walleyes, you'll eventually discover one of the biggest mysteries of winter walleye fishing: Why certain spots consistently hold walleyes, but other seemingly identical spots won't. (Courtesy Northland Tackle)

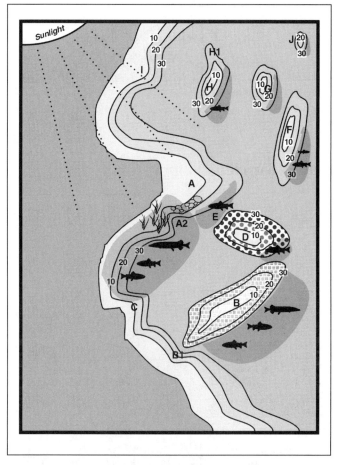

Once on these features, note how the fish are positioning themselves in relation to sunlight, current and other factors. Remember, pattern the fish.

lake bottom with only slight depth changes. Are these barely discernible changes significant? The answer is an emphatic, resounding, yes! All too often, ice anglers equate structure with dramatic lake contours. But there's more to structure than dramatic depth changes.

Structure is any change in lake bottom distinguishing it from surrounding areas. No matter how slight, these changes are likely important. Subtle differences in depth, cover or bottom content can be walleye magnets. Often these areas aren't shown on lake maps, they're something only knowledgeable use of sonar will reveal. Cover such as weeds or submerged timber is often important, too. Just don't make the mistake of fishing directly within expansive flats of indistinguishable cover. Rather, focus your efforts along deep edges or pockets of differing cover. Such places provide variety to attract forage–and the more forage, the more likely the spot is to hold walleyes.

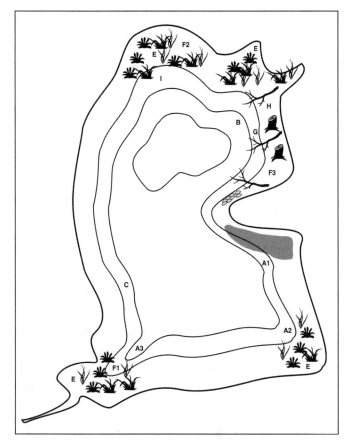

In "structurally limited" waters, subtle structural variations such as holes in vegetated flats (F1, F2), deep weedlines (A2, A3, I), downed trees (H), deep submerged wood (G), pockets in wooded flats (H) or soft-bottomed points surrounded by hard bottom (A1) will attract gamefish.

Weed Walleyes

The best weed walleye locations include weed lines, holes in vegetated flats, vegetated areas bordering hard-bottom rock flats, current-influenced areas near inlets, outlets or springs and soft-bottom weedy points or reefs surrounded by hard-bottoms or vice-versa. The edges of different cover types are good, too. And just as there are distinct differences in the quality of various structures, there's also a difference in the quality of vegetation. The best weeds are tall, healthy broadleaf types, which offer more cover, shade, forage, and at times, more oxygen than short, thin varieties.

"Microstructure" also exists. Differences in vegetation types provide distinguishable edges, as do openings, appreciable differences in density or the height of the vegetation, or any combination

thereof. Since weed-oriented walleyes often hold only temporarily along various segments of these edges, only by systematically working each area will you discover the best patterns.

Wood Walleyes

Some waters may also be conducive to productive wood patterns. This is especially true on dark-water reservoirs without much natural structure, weeds or other forms of cover. Fallen trees, stumps, brush piles, standing timber and submerged timber are all good. Horizontally positioned logs offer more cover than do vertical logs, and usually hold more walleyes. It should also be found near differences in depth, bottom content or cover. Just remember, depth is relative. You may find walleyes holding in wood 10 feet deep on a typical dark, shallow northern Wisconsin flatland flowage, while in a deep,

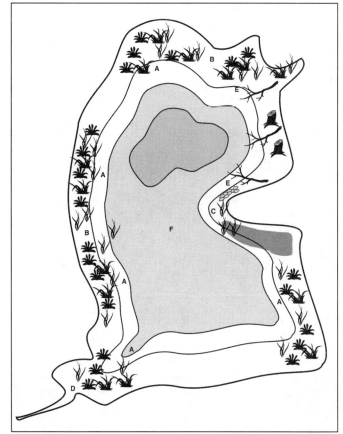

On "weed related" waters, the best weed walleye locations include deeper weed lines and slots (A), holes in vegetated flats (B), vegetated areas surrounding hard bottom rock flats (C), current flushed inlets, outlets or springs (D), the edges of differing cover or bottom content (E) or deep main lake flats (F).

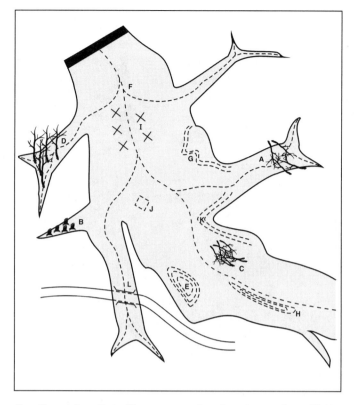

On "wood related" waters, the best wood walleye locations include fallen trees (A), stumps (B), brushpiles (C), or standing timber (D). Find such cover on or along rises (E), channels (F), points (K), turns (G), bars or shoals (H), flats adjoining the river channel (I), building foundations (J) or current graced areas (L), and you've located structures offering excellent walleye holding potential.

clear Canadian Shield reservoir, walleyes may utilize wood in 50 feet of water.

Wood is also a productive winter walleye pattern on lakes where both weeds and wood are available and population of pike and walleye coexist. Pike prefer weeds and being the dominant predator, force walleyes into a different ecological niche—wood. If the weed bed is large and supports enough forage, you may find some walleyes in the weeds. Pike and walleyes may even use the same weed bed simultaneously. But under such conditions, wood patterns typically produce more walleyes than weeds.

Specifically where walleyes will position in the wood and when they'll feed varies with lake type. In clear water, walleyes usually hold deeper, tighter to the cover and bite better during twilight and evening periods. This is often just the opposite of the walleye's response in a dark-water environment. Remember the deadly dozen factors!

High-Percentage Structure

After searching for the largest, high-percentage structures featuring the best possible combination of walleye-attracting features, make concessions for winter walleye positioning and movements. Consider the following checklist:

1. *VARIED BOTTOM COMPOSITION* is important because it adds diversity. Different bottoms grow different vegetation types, which provide differing cover that, in turn, draw varied forage bases. Thus, the greater the bottom mix, the greater the diversity of vegetation and forage and the greater chance the area will draw walleyes.
2. *DEPTH* is important, because gradual slopes tend to draw walleyes early and late in the winter or during twilight and evening hours. Deep breaks are better during mid-winter or mid-day periods.
3. *PRIMARY FORAGE TYPES* heavily influence location patterns and positioning. If the primary forage base is perch, most walleyes will hold near the bottom, along the bases of weedy structures or open flats where perch usually hold. If the forage base is a suspending, open-water species such as cisco, walleyes may suspend over open water adjacent to such features, or perhaps near no structure at all.
4. *THE AMOUNT OF FORAGE AND OTHER FISH SPECIES PRESENT* are also key factors. If forage is abundant, walleyes are less competitive

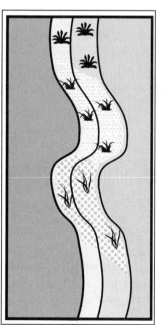

Varied bottom content is important because it adds diversity — and diversity means a greater chance the area will draw a variety of cover, forage and walleyes.

and more difficult to catch. If there is not much to eat walleyes are more competitive and more likely to be aggressive. If other fish compete for this same forage base, walleyes may adapt to a special means of gaining predatory advantage. They could be feeding under the cover of darkness, for example, which can also influence location, positioning, timing and movement patterns.

5. *LIGHT LEVELS AND THEIR INTENSITY* are important. Walleyes are usually most active during low-light periods, or what they perceive to be low-light conditions. These times may vary in turbid water or under thick ice, dictating primary walleye-holding locations positioning and movements.

On calm, sunny days in clear water, walleyes tend to stay deeper, hide in thick cover and remain inactive. Look for points, projections or humps extending into deeper water with

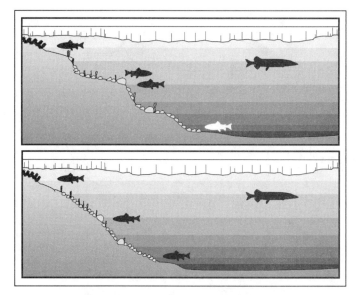

Diverse, stair-stepped breaks leading from shallow to deep water can be either gradual or sharp-dropping. Both will draw walleyes. Gradual breaks are better early and late in the season or day, and deeper ones are better during mid-winter or mid-day periods. Fish will disperse along the break based on lake type, cover, forage and oxygen availability.

Specifically where walleyes will position and when they'll feed varies with lake type. (Courtesy Northland Tackle)

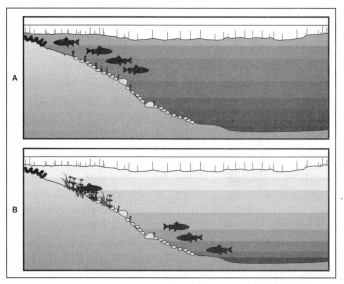

Walleyes are usually most active and move more shallow to feed during low-light periods—or what they perceive to be low light conditions. These could include turbid water or thick ice (A). The fish will hold deeper and feed less often in clear water or brighter conditions (B).

In dark water or overcast conditions, walleyes often feed frequently throughout the day, but usually not intensely. In clear water or bright conditions, walleyes tend to feed in short, but more intense periods during twilight or night periods. (Courtesy Northland Tackle)

heavy cover along the sides or explore adjacent deeper flats. Otherwise, switch your efforts to dark-water lakes or wait until twilight or evening to fish. Given lowered degrees of light intensity, walleyes may become more active and hold shallower, on top of these structures or adjacent food shelves.

6. *LIGHT LEVELS AND WEATHER* also influence how long and intensively walleyes will feed. During high-pressure, bright-light conditions, walleyes hold deeper and tighter to cover. They still feed, but usually in shorter, more zealous sprees during twilight periods or at night. In dark water or during overcast conditions, walleyes often feed longer, but less passionately. In other words, bright light doesn't stop feeding activity, it just slows, shortens and intensifies feeding periods. Timing and presentation are critical. During low-light or overcast conditions, walleyes are in less of a hurry to feed and often bite all day, but intense bites are rare. Rather, strikes tend to be more frequent but less vicious. Consequently,

you're likely to catch more fish, but often just a few here and there.

Yes, there are variations to these general winter patterns. If vulnerable baitfish suddenly show up during bright conditions, for example, an isolated school of walleyes may turn on. This might explain why one isolated location can be good during an offbeat time when no one else can catch a fish. It's up to you to sort these variables and determine the most productive patterns, given the situation.

7. *THE STABILITY OF LOCAL WEATHER PATTERNS* is important, because it dictates how many fish will be active. The greater and longer the weather stability, the more active a greater number of fish will become. Such seasonal and daily factors may also influence where fish hold on particular structural features. Walleyes tend to hold shallow on top of structural features when active and deeper along the sides when inactive. This is another reason graduated breaks with a number of various depth levels generally offer better winter fishing than those dropping off smoothly or abruptly.

8. *FISHING PRESSURE* is especially important in today's world. If good fishing areas have attracted large crowds, you may have to fish deeper or consider other areas. Crowds often turn off winter walleyes. Be prepared to move given such conditions.

9. *ODD FACTORS* such as moon phases also have an effect on walleye activity. Just as tides effect ocean fish, the moon apparently influences winter walleyes. So, strange as it may seem, those solar/lunar tables appear to have some credibility.

After finding major walleye-attracting structures attempt to combine them with the greatest level of structural diversity and a variety of forage. Consider the lake type, depth, time of day, how far the winter has progressed, the current weather conditions and various odd factors before stepping on the ice. Walleyes demonstrate tendencies to hold near specific, diverse structures and orient their location, positioning and movements to these bottom configurations, weeds, wood, currents and other features that can be used to their predatory advantage. Using their ability to see in darkness, walleyes may also time their feeding tactics to surprise their prey. Understand this behavior, and you'll learn to eliminate unproductive water and find active walleyes more consistently.

Setting Up

After reviewing lake maps to identify likely winter walleye holding structures, mark these locations as waypoints on your GPS, head to the lake and begin observing. Arrive early and try to decipher what features seem to be attracting walleyes. Is it the bottom configuration or content, cover, oxygen, forage, current or a combination of the above? Once you establish a theory, punch holes across key areas, focusing on "combination" spots of secondary cover. Be careful not to overlook the potential of shallow water. Some of my best early- and late-winter catches have come less than 5 feet deep during twilight and evening walleye feeding frenzies.

Next, move across the structure, covering as much area as possible before your activity spooks active fish. Mobility now becomes key. Since walleye use particular depths and structures and fol-

Since walleye use discrete depths and structures and often follow specific migration routes, good action can often be found only a few steps away from nonproductive locations. Be mobile!

low specific migration routes, good action can often be found only a few steps away from nonproductive locations. Thousands of hours using two tip-ups and a jigging rod has led me to this conclusion. In Wisconsin where we're allowed three lines, I often drill sets of three holes a couple feet apart across different depths and structures. I'll be jigging one hole while watching tip-ups placed in the second and third. I've often taken limits from one hole, but received few or no bites from the others, even though they're positioned only a few feet away.

Beware. Understanding the deliberate way foraging walleyes move is important. Almost every ice angler has experienced the frustration of being 10 feet away from someone hauling out one fish after another while their own efforts were futile. Under these circumstances, anglers are more likely to question choices of presentation, not believing moving a few feet can make a difference.

But moving can make a difference. Next to microstructure, primary travel lanes are probably the most overlooked factor in winter walleye fishing. Always try to locate combinations of secondary features. Then try to figure out how, when and where fish move through these areas. You can count on walleyes generally moving from deep water to shallow-water food shelves, or in shallower lakes, moving from thicker cover towards openings, pockets and weed line edges during twilight and evening periods. These schools continue moving until they locate prey. The fish then linger in these locations until the prey moves or is scattered. The trick is to identify these travel lanes and times they're used.

Say we're fishing a long, main lake point and some people are catching walleyes. Based on good versus bad holes, I can refer to my map and determine where fish are likely coming from and what direction they're heading. That will help me to figure out their migration routes and primary holding features along these lanes. An angler can often intercept walleyes by making a minor location change.

If you notice fish being caught along a 15-foot contour, that depth will often remain hot as it winds around the structure. If you try the same contour where others are catching fish but action is slow, move farther along the same contour. It's possible your holes are positioned over thick weeds or an obstruction the walleyes are detouring around. This is a situation easily remedied by moving only a few feet.

Establish a plotter trail on your GPS as you work the break. Each time you encounter fish, lock down an icon. This will help you visualize what's happening below. If there's a lot of activity on the ice and the action shuts down, look at your map, and find other locations offering similar features to the one being fished. Often, you'll find almost identical combinations of highly productive structures and cover holding virtually untouched schools of active walleyes away from the crowds.

Often the difference between catching a few walleyes and really scoring big is fishing at the right times in the right areas, then carefully moving along these migration routes or primary holding areas looking for fish. Determining the best structure requires study. After all, every lake is different, and if the pattern you initially choose doesn't pay off you'll need to analyze all the newly collected information and continue repeating this procedure until you're able to assemble a viable pattern for active fish.

If you're marking fish on sonar but they won't bite, drop down an underwater camera to confirm they're walleyes, and if they are, try experimenting with a variety of presentations before moving.

Notice I said active fish. If you're marking fish but they won't bite, try experimenting with a variety of presentations before moving. If you have one, use your underwater camera to see what's going on. Always try different baits and lures, setting or jigging them at different speeds and changing lure sizes and colors. It might pay off. However, don't waste time. If the fish refuse to bite, let them rest. Save the location as a waypoint and return later. In the meantime, move about, fishing various schools, but never spending too much time in one spot. Remember: active walleyes seldom sit in one place nor roam erratically, neither should you.

Timing

With most species of fish, I consider location and movements the most crucial factor in determining consistent winter walleye catches. You can use the most refined presentation in the world, but if you're not on fish, you simply won't catch them. With winter walleyes, however, timing is of equal magnitude. You may be on a great combination of structure, cover and forage and have a huge school of walleyes located, but if your timing isn't right and the fish aren't active, you may as well be jigging a winterkill lake. They simply won't bite.

The key is understanding this unique species. The walleye's light-gathering eyes are adapted to

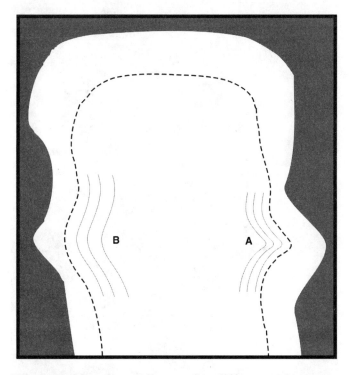

When looking for walleyes, the difference between the beginner and the expert is not only being able to identify irregular, structurally diverse features leading from the shallows to the deepest available water, but also the most distinct turns and irregularities on them. Here, for example, if A and B are both irregular, structurally diverse features separating the shallows from the deepest available water, the distinct contour break shown on the right (A) would be much more likely to hold fish than the break on the left (B).

The walleye's light gathering eyes are adapted to feed under low light conditions when prey species are at a sight disadvantage.

feed under low light conditions when prey species are at a sight disadvantage. Unless you're fishing a dark-water lake or waters covered by a thick layer of ice and snow, you'll often have to focus your efforts during twilight or evening periods.

We must now apply these principles based on how far winter has progressed.

First-Ice Walleyes

Once ice becomes safe, where do you start? Again, consider lake type. While shallower lakes don't always produce the largest fish, they do offer the earliest ice. In fact, during normal winters, you can often begin fishing small, shallow lakes three to four weeks before larger, deeper lakes in the same area have even begun to ice up. This presents a unique situation. Deep-lake first-ice action typically begins about the time the first-ice rush ends on shallow waters. This is good news for enterprising ice anglers, because this means by switching from shallow to deep lakes, it's possible to stay on hot first-ice walleye bites for several weeks.

After choosing a lake, location patterns are relatively easy to decipher with the help of lake maps and electronics. On shallow walleye lakes featuring clear water, good weed growth is generally present. The largest, thickest weed beds and their associated edges will be the primary haunts of first-ice walleyes, because they offer the most cover and forage. These areas are easily located with today's high-powered sonar and underwater cameras. Deep weed pockets are also good at times.

In shallow, dark-water lakes not supporting good weed growth, walleyes often cruise shallow shoreline contours foraging on insect larvae and baitfish along shore and in large, soft-bottom bays. These fish especially like those areas featuring some sort of alternative secondary cover such as rocks or wood. Again, these areas are easily identifiable on good lake maps and can be pinpointed using today's electronics.

When clear, mid-depth lakes offering distinct weed lines begin freezing over focus your efforts in shallow weeds and along mid-depth weed lines, especially on drops near expansive, shallow vegetated flats. Both harbor excellent cover, hold vast

While shallow, protected lakes won't always offer large walleyes like this one, they do offer the earliest ice, and can often be fished three or four weeks before deeper lakes in the same area have even begun to ice up.

quantities of forage and draw tremendous schools of walleye. Hard-bottom bars, humps or points extending from these weed edges are also good producers, as are pockets inside the weeds. Finding such areas may require numerous sonar readings and extensive drilling, but once found, are usually worth the effort.

Finally, deep clear lakes become productive. To be consistently successful, night-fishing is often the key to success. The edges of large, shallow sandbars, flooded wood and stretches of shoreline containing reeds or bulrushes are primary night-fishing areas, where you'll often find groups of active first-ice walleyes cruising just outside shallow structure or cover. Deep weed lines and edges of large, hard-bottom mid-depth "classic" structures, also produce well during twilight periods or at night.

While sometimes difficult to find and fish, small shoreline rock humps, points or bars topping out in the 10- to 20-foot range and located near these larger shoreline points or bars consistently produce first-ice walleyes, especially on heavily pressured lakes. If you can find such structures producing fish and keep your catches secret, these smaller structures sometimes continue to remain hot throughout the winter. Just remember,

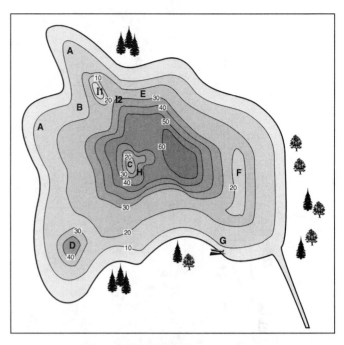

In clear, mid-depth walleye lakes, pockets in shallow vegetation and mid-depth weed lines (A) and hard-bottom points extending from these weed edges (B) are productive first-ice locations. Mid-winter, deep weed lines (E), mid-depth bars (I1, F) reefs (C) and deep holes (D) become better bets. Note important migration routes on these features, too, such as slot (I2) and (H).

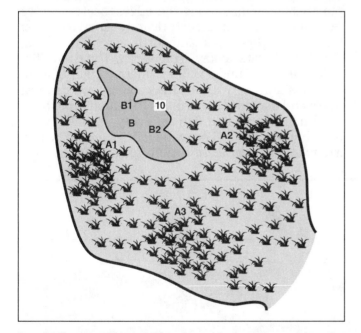

In shallow walleye lakes featuring clear water, the thickest weed beds (A1, A2) and their associated edges and deep pockets (B), especially irregularities along them (B1, B2) will hold the most first-ice cover and forage...and the most first-ice walleyes. Fishing productivity often fades later in the season due to limited forage and oxygen availability.

because they're small, such spots may go dry after producing for only a short time. So, if your catch rate suddenly drops off, get out your electronics and try focusing on similar mid-depth structures or deeper, larger main-lake structures featuring irregular turns, cuts, points, bends and varying bottom content. Such areas provide better cover and offer more diverse varieties of forage that in turn will draw walleyes.

Similar patterns also produce first-ice walleyes in reservoirs, although contrary to typical peak walleye timing, on stained water reservoirs, shallow stump flats and rock piles can also be good bets for daytime fishing.

Mid-Winter

Mid-winter walleyes tend to scatter, so marking main-lake points, then moving around with electronics is a good way to pinpoint active walleyes.

Why points? First, regardless of the pond, lake or reservoir you're fishing, there's usually a point somewhere. Secondly, they're usually obvious, easy to find with electronics and hold forage.

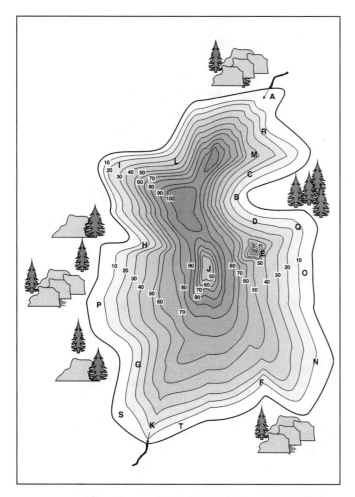

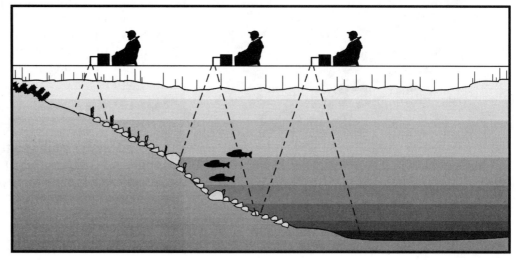

In deep, clear lakes, stretches of shoreline offering reeds or bullrushes (P, S, T, O) and shoreline points (B, F, G, H, L) are good first-ice bets for night fishing. During the day or mid-season, deeper weed lines surrounding shorelines (C, D, I, M, Q, R) and mid-depth shoals, bars and reefs (E) or deep sunken islands (J) are worth checking.

Since mid-winter walleyes often scatter, searching for fish along points is a good bet, because points occupy a wide range of depths and diversified strata, allowing you to pattern walleyes more efficiently.

Because they occupy a wide range of depths, they are one of the easiest places to pinpoint mid-winter location patterns because you can start shallow and gradually progress deeper.

Finding such patterns requires electronics. Years ago, many ice anglers fished mostly first and late ice when shallow walleyes were easily accessible, but declared mid-winter fishing to be difficult. Not that they didn't want to catch fish, many ice anglers figured walleyes went deeper, but since they didn't have any way of easily finding them, they either fished low-percentage shallows, or quit fishing.

Some anglers still follow this old-school thinking, but with today's electronics, there's really no excuse for not finding and catching mid-winter walleyes. Use your GPS to mark large, elongated points, move to them, then use sonar and GPS plotter trails to outline the edges, looking for specific secondary features along the point. You may locate a weed line, turn, finger, stump field edge lining a river channel, or perhaps simply a change in bottom content, whatever. Just remember, the objective is to find fish, and this often requires fishing a secondary irregularity.

If you find the right combination of elements at the right depth, you'll find mid-winter walleyes. The best way to thoroughly work a point is to take multiple sonar readings along the edges, searching systematically for microstructure and secondary cover. I typically work back and forth across the break lines. If I locate a key irregularity, I start drilling holes, using an underwater camera to pinpoint the best positioning. Without the camera, you can drill holes and use your electronics to search for fish.

You'll seldom find fish on every secondary feature, but any natural or man-made object providing irregular structural deviations provide your best

With today's electronics, there is really no excuse for not finding and catching mid-winter walleyes. (photo courtesy Lowrance Electronics)

opportunity. Check them out. More often than not, you'll hook only one or two fish as they move through because points are natural migration routes. If the action stops after you catch a couple fish and fail to mark many fish on your sonar, don't think there are no active fish left. Rather, assume the school is still nearby, and immediately change lures to see if you can come up with something to draw the school back or allow you the opportunity to catch another fish. At times, switching lures will mean an extra fish or two, and by being thorough, you'll often be able to pick up additional fish with each subsequent lure change. This can add up.

If the action continues to slow or stops, the fish have likely moved out, and you'll have to move deeper, shallower or try other prime mid-winter hot spots featuring similar depth ranges and structural characteristics. Experiment to determine the most productive presentation pattern.

Late-Ice Walleyes

Late-ice walleyes. That's a vague term because the ice may go out anywhere from mid-February to the end of March, even April, depending on your location. Furthermore, ice-out can occur fairly rapidly or relatively slowly, depending on the weather.

With ice-out alone dependent on so many factors and varying so greatly on a calendar basis, it's easy to see why late-ice walleye activity is equally effected by so many variables. You've probably heard how fantastic late-ice walleye fishing can be. Many anglers make it sound as though late ice is a magical time when walleyes come easy. Perhaps, late ice walleyes bite better than they do during the mid-winter period. Yet, I've found many ice anglers don't do that well with late-ice walleyes.

Sure, they catch fish—a select few even catch limits—but the fishing isn't necessarily easy. It can be downright tough, and anglers must use specific methods. Talking with numerous successful late-ice walleye enthusiasts and experimenting with various methods, I've pulled together a few tricks that make late-ice a time of superior walleye action.

Start with timing. Fishing talk is filled with references to the benefits of being timely. Some of the clichés include: Timing is everything. Be in the right place at the right time You should have been here yesterday.

All these are particularly applicable when it comes to late-ice walleyes. Simply put, there's no time to waste. Late ice may be short-lived, so every second counts. Consistent late-ice walleye anglers have to find active fish quickly, then stay on them.

Maximum late-ice success generally comes from larger, deeper, bigger lakes that sustain both oxygen and forage in the depths. Yes, exceptions exist, because in years with light snowfalls and relatively mild temperatures, thin ice and little snow allows weeds to stay green and continue to grow under the ice even on shallow lakes and reservoirs. This condition draws forage and sustains oxygen, so walleyes may remain relatively shallow or stay near the bottom. During years with high water, more inlet activity may provide higher oxygen levels in deeper water.

Large hard-bottom points and sunken humps supporting turns or irregular features are favored

Late-ice walleyes constitute a vague term, seeing as the ice may go out anywhere from mid-February to the end of March, or even April, depending on your location. Nonetheless, pre-spawn walleyes are often very active during this period.

spots. However, since oxygen content is an increasingly important factor in late-ice walleye location, it's not uncommon to see fish heavily schooled near springs or inlets providing fresh oxygen. For maximum productivity, these primary features should be located near shallow spawning flats or river mouths and support a combination of bottom types such as sand, gravel and rock, complete with secondary cover such as healthy green weeds or submerged wood.

However, with ice anglers becoming more educated, I'm noticing such areas becoming victimized by fishing pressure. This often forces active late-ice walleyes off these more obvious locations. If this appears to be the case, check around the perimeter of other anglers. Fishing pressure may push the fish slightly in one direction or another, but usually not far. Using your electronics, you may locate walleyes in the immediate vicinity. If you don't find active fish, don't fight it. Instead, try moving to other similar, less-crowded sites. When you find a good spot, drill numerous holes. But do so quietly. Late ice walleyes aren't bold, and it takes a stealthy approach to consistently fool these fish.

One more thing: if you locate a school but they won't bite, cut numerous holes both shallow and deep in the most productive areas, then leave. After resting the area awhile, return approximately two hours before dark, and depending on local regulations and the number of anglers in your group, set tip-ups, then begin jigging while waiting for the twilight bite. You'll likely encounter actively feeding walleyes at dusk. If you wait long enough you'll see them again at dawn and during late morning the following day, because walleyes have that distinct vision advantage over their prey during these times.

Now fish hard. Your productivity should increase.

Very Late Ice

Where the season is still open, this is one of the hottest walleye fishing times of the winter. The process begins as snow starts melting and the ice begins to thaw. As days warm and the sun climbs higher, thawing occurs to the upper ice, creating a thin layer of water, which is further warmed by the sun. Holes in the ice, such as natural pressure cracks or holes drilled by anglers, allow warmer water to enter and merge with the colder water below. This meltwater seems to rejuvenate walleyes, and they gradually begin moving back into many of the same areas they frequented early in the winter. Thus, if the season remains open long

> ### Fish Bottlenecks
>
> *Unless a lake is remotely located or subjected to only light fishing pressure, your best bet for finding winter walleyes is locating what I refer to as "bottlenecks." These are areas that concentrate active, migrating walleyes from an otherwise scattered "big-water" population. Good examples include early-ice movements of walleyes moving into concentrated, shallow bays, mid-winter fish returning from shallow bays into narrow river channels on a large impoundment, and perhaps most importantly, migrations of late-ice, pre-spawn walleyes from large Great Lakes bays moving into adjoining frozen river ways.*

enough, walleye fishing becomes excellent as active walleyes begin congregating near steep breaking drop-offs adjacent to shallow spawning flats. In these areas warming temperatures cause a resurgence in the food chain. Plankton concentrations rebound in the shallows, minnows return to feed, panfish move in to feed on the minnows, and walleyes move in to feed on them.

"Classic" walleye structure such as points, reefs and vegetated flats, especially on clear water lakes, make excellent bets for winter night fishing. (Courtesy Northland Tackle)

Still, while very late ice can be extremely productive, caution is mandatory. Again I emphasize, no fish is worth your life. Be careful. Then consider and weigh these related factors as you attempt to pinpoint key patterns.

Night-Time Walleyes

There's a cycle to winter fish location and feeding activity, yet it's hard to generalize about walleyes in different kinds of lakes, because the rules are never the same. Things can change radically, even on the same lake for the same species during a certain segment of the season because conditions are constantly changing.

However, if you know what to look for, you can greatly improve your chances of success. You've just got to be patient and apply the right techniques in the right places at the right times. With walleyes, that often means fishing under the cover of darkness.

I should clarify I'm not a night person. I like to sleep. Always have. However, I also love to catch big walleyes. A dilemma? Not at all. Fortunately,

Due to their large, specialized eyes, walleyes are well adapted to feeding at night, and anglers willing to sacrifice a few hours sleep are often justly rewarded.

when I say "night" fishing for walleyes, I don't mean fishing at 2:00 a.m. While winter walleyes certainly feed during the wee hours of the morning, I've found twilight periods highly productive times to fish. The reason for such behavior is likely several fold. First, the activity level of baitfish slows during twilight periods, and it doesn't take the class valedictorian to see this affords walleyes big opportunity. Inactive prey provides an easy meal, and walleyes take advantage of the situation.

In addition to their food being easier to catch, walleyes have a vision advantage over their prey, particularly at twilight. Without getting into finer details, suffice to say that prey vulnerability and the walleye's vision advantage are most evident during two major periods: the first couple hours after sunrise, and again from about three hours before sunset until about two hours after dark. The last hour before dark is the best. You may notice a slow period the first hour after dark, I have no conclusions about why, I only speak from experience. It happens. However, if you fish during twilight periods in a good location several times a week, you're likely to ice some nice walleyes.

The Approach

My night-fishing experience has revealed a logical approach to catching winter walleyes, and it's actually quite simple. First, clear-water lakes tend to be the best bets for night fishing. From here, I fish known spots or classic structural elements such as reefs, points, weedy flats, or secondary break lines. I've found even on highly pressured waters, few anglers are fishing before sun-up, and most folks are gone before it gets dark. This leaves good opportunity for walleye anglers willing to tough it out during peak pre-dawn and pre-dusk hours.

Again, fish hard. Be on the water as many days as possible. Make every attempt to get out before work and again after you've got your eight hours in. This way, you'll stay on top of what the walleyes are doing. Sure, you're bound to have good days and some poor ones. But personally, I kind of like the tough days, especially two or three of them in a row. I don't feel this way because I've spent too much time in sub-freezing temperatures. It's because I know walleyes must feed, and given the right location and presentation, two or three days of little or no activity frequently means a "hot" bite is approaching—and no serious ice angler wants to miss out on that.

New moon periods also appear to have some effect on walleye activity levels at night. But, in my opinion, stable, favorable local weather and the physical qualities of the individual lake play larger roles than moon phase. Ice fishing within twilight hours during periods of stable weather or immediately before an approaching winter storm, for example, seems to be a good time to run across good walleye bites.

Once you've found a probable location and have suitable weather conditions, don't waste any time. Get on the ice prior to "prime time." Drill your holes and set a few tip-ups, always leaving extra holes for jigging. Just as twilight periods mean opportunity for smart winter walleyes to take advantage of a situation where they can capitalize on their prey and come out with their bellies full to the limit, smart ice anglers can take advantage of an opportunity to capitalize on some great ice fishing and come out with their buckets full to the limit.

Winter River Walleyes

While limited to certain portions of the country, winter river walleyes can be an abundant resource. Here in the Midwest, blessed with "walleye factory" rivers such as the Fox, Wisconsin, Wolf, Mississippi, Rainy and Saginaw plus thousands of acres of river backwaters, there's no shortage of river winter walleye ice angling opportunities. Backwaters freeze early, and those with current flow to provide oxygen to these cover- and forage-laden areas draw walleyes. Simple as that.

Locks adjoining dams along the Mississippi River channel are also outstanding. I won't guarantee you'll catch a 10-pound walleye, but limits of eating-size walleye and sauger are pulled from these slow-flowing waters each winter. Large Great Lakes tributaries like the Fox and Saginaw produce immense late-ice walleyes from ice capped holes. These fish often achieve double-digit weights.

However, while river currents provide critical oxygen and forage to attract walleyes, they also raise havoc with ice. Since this is moving water, never walk out unless you're sure it's solid, and avoid areas of fast current where the ice may be weak. If fishing near dams, dress as though you're going fishing in -30-degree weather. Then add another layer. The amount of moisture in the cold air on these open waters makes dressing warm very important.

Frozen waters surrounding river locks on the Mississippi River are outstanding winter walleye and sauger hot spots.

Current also causes challenges with fishing lures when you're trying to jig vertically off bottom, so use heavy baits. My favorite is a large Jigging Rapala tipped with a small crappie minnow or minnow head, but large, heavy spoons and heavy leadhead jigs, work too–which brings us to the next section: effective presentation strategies for winter walleye.

Effective Strategies for Winter Walleye

Once prime locations are deciphered, you've determined the best times to fish and strategically drilled your holes over the best looking spots, it's time to start rigging up.

Tip-Ups

I usually start by setting tip-ups. Stationary models such as HT's Polar, Arctic Fisherman's "Beaver Dam," HT's Polar II, Polar Therm, Polar Pop-Up, Frabill's Igloo, the Heritage or Frontier are particularly good. Polar tip-ups are lightweight, low-profile, virtually indestructible tip-ups that are easy to set and guaranteed not to freeze. Polar II's are smooth, also guaranteed not to freeze and feature large wood frames. Igloo and Polar Therm Thermal tip-ups virtually guarantee your holes won't freeze, while the Heritage and Frontier high profile tip-ups are good in deep snow, because they're more easily visible. The Polar Pop-Up offers a light, magnetic trip that can dramatically improve winter walleye catches.

Also carry a selection of wind tip-ups. Since these units automatically jig your bait—a tactic deadly for walleyes—you can experiment with a wider variety of presentations. There's something about keeping your bait moving that attracts and triggers winter walleyes. More than once I've seen wind tip-ups like the Windlass outfish stationary tip-ups 3 to 1. In addition, the jigging action produced by wind tip-ups tires baitfish, especially relative to stationary tip-ups. Although this means your unit will need to be checked more often, since fresh, lively bait is another secret to consistent winter walleye catches, this in itself can mean more walleyes. And don't forget, jigging lures can be used in place of a plain hook or live bait rig.

Reliable tip-up lights also play important roles in many night walleye strategies. HT's Omni Strike

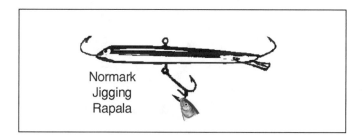

Large, heavy jigging Rapalas tipped with minnow heads are excellent winter river walleye lure because they hold well in current.

Stationary tip-ups like HT's Polar Therm are lightweight, guaranteed not to freeze–and with this model, prevent snow and light from entering the hole thanks to the hole cover design.

Wind tip-ups like HT's Windlass automatically jig your bait using the wind for power.

Lite is my first choice. This is one of the most compact, reliable units on the market. It operates on small lithium batteries, is interchangeable with lighted floats and, weighing just 1/4 ounce, is the most lightweight. The light easily clips to any tip-up flag, and is off in the horizontal position. When the flag trips and the unit is turned vertically, the light comes on. HT's ML-7 Micro Light is my second choice. The unit features a small metal bracket that clips to the base of the tip-up flag wire. Your line fits into a small set of contacts that break the light connection. When a fish strikes and pulls line from between the contacts, the circuit is completed and the light flips on. The unit operates on a lithium battery.

For convenience, some tip-ups also come with built-in lights, so if you're a die-hard night angler,

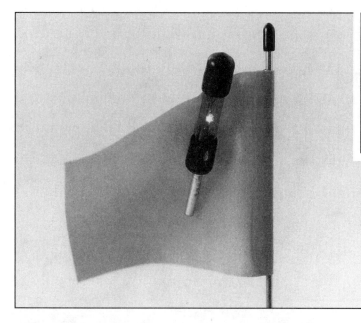

The Omni Strike Lite is powered by a standard lithium battery.

Reliable tip-up lights, such as HT's ML-2 Omni Strike Lite, remain off when tip-up flags are down and in a horizontal position and switch on when the flag trips vertically upon the strike.

these models might be for you–just be sure they come from an established, high-quality tip-up manufacturer. HT Enterprises Polar Pop-Up tip-up, for example, works with a magnet on the spool and magnet on the trip. When the two are lined up, the flag stays down. When a fish strikes and turns the spool, this magnetic force is broken, and the flag trips with minimal resistance. Best of all, the Polar Pop-Up is available with a self-contained light system that automatically goes off when the flag is tripped, and the Polar Therm Mag even comes with a hole cover!

More and more anglers are also finding balance tip-ups and tip-downs are also outstanding walleye tools. Quite simply, when fish strike, the balance arm tips down and line spools from the reel freely, with little or no resistance to light-biting fish. This works like a dream.

Tip-Up Strategies, Placement

Strategically place your tip-ups along productive structures or flats, concentrating within open pockets in thick weeds, along weed lines or structural breaks. In addition to being key fish-holding areas, such placement helps keep your bait free from tangles and offers walleyes easy targets.

Strategic tip-up placement begins with finding the right location and specific areas of secondary cover holding active fish. Say you've moved to a new walleye hot spot, a sunken main-lake rock hump separated from a long, hard-bottom, vege-

The Polar Pop-Up, a magnetic release tip-up offering virtually no resistance to light biting walleye. (Courtesy HT Enterprises, Inc.)

More and more anglers are discovering the minimal resistance offered by balance tip-ups and tip-downs are tremendous walleye tools when walleyes are fussy and bites are light. (Courtesy HT Enterprises, Inc.)

tated shoreline point by a soft-bottom saddle area. This area adjoins an expansive, shallow shoreline food shelf. Carrying a squirt bottle of saltwater, your sonar and a hand-held GPS, you shoot readings through the ice with sonar while recording them on a GPS plotter trail to define the perimeter of the hump, point, and pockets on the flat. Remember, provided your transducer maintains contact with the surface of solid ice, simply pouring a little water down will allow you to shoot readings and determine these boundaries without drilling a single hole.

Drill holes over small projections, turns and pockets along the island and point where the hard-bottom drop ends and the soft-bottomed saddle area begins. If you have an underwater camera, you can watch for schools of baitfish and walleyes. Pay attention to likely migration routes between structures leading from deeper water to the shallows, and pockets of cover likely to attract cruising walleyes. Be sure to allow plenty of time to complete this process prior to peak twilight periods so you don't spook active fish. Then begin setting your units.

Position your tip-ups throughout as many different depth ranges and primary holding areas as allowed. At the above location I'd set units in pockets on the shallow food shelves on top of

both structures, along the edges of the flats adjoining these breaks, over the break itself, along the base of the drop off where bottom content changes, and a couple over the saddle area between the two structures. I always focus my efforts along likely migration routes and holding areas of secondary cover.

Basic Tip-Up Rigging

When it comes to basic tip-up rigging, keep things simple. To make bringing walleyes in easier and prevent freeze-up, start by spooling with premium, 15- to 20-pound test teflon-coated braided dacron such as Gudebrod's Tip-Up line or HT's Polar freeze-resistant tip-up lines. Use #10 ball-bearing swivels to connect a two to 6-foot length of 6- to 12-pound monofilament leader tipped with a split shot and a sharp #8 or #10 treble hook. Attractors such as a strip of colored yarn, plastic or beads threaded on the hook or line can also be helpful. When fishing wind tip-ups, small, lightweight jigging spoons or flash lures can be used, and are also highly effective.

The best hooks are those with "fast setting" ability, such as Mustad 144 wide gaps or Triple Grips. Two- to four-inch fatheads, suckers, golden, blue or gray shiners work wonders and are readily available from bait dealers. Otherwise, chubs or large fatheads will suffice. Just use baits of a similar size, profile and color to the walleye's naturally preferred or most available forage.

Hook your minnow on one tine of the treble, centered in front of the dorsal fin and pointing toward the tail. Centering hooks in front of the dorsal with the points facing the tail places your hook in the walleye's mouth immediately when it grabs the bait, and since walleyes usually strike the head of a minnow, also places your fast set hook in the best hook-setting position. Even with these specialty hooks, however, it's often advisable to allow 30 seconds to one minute for the fish to chew the bait before setting the hook, then gradually pull up to see if the fish is holding on. If not, gently jiggle the bait in an attempt to make them take the hook deeper.

When you're ready, hook sets should be gentle but firm, followed by a steady lifting motion to gradually bring the fish to the hole. Try to keep your line near the center of the hole, taking your time and playing the fish skillfully, giving line whenever the fish runs or surges, especially at the hole, where most walleyes are lost.

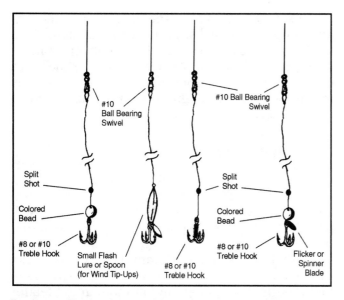

Basic walleye tip-up rigs incorporate teflon-coated braided dacron lines and a barrel swivel separating a treble hook-tipped light line leader. Often, small attractants such as strips of colored yarn, plastic or beads are added to help draw fish. Small flash lures can be used when fishing wind style tip-ups that automatically jig the lure for you.

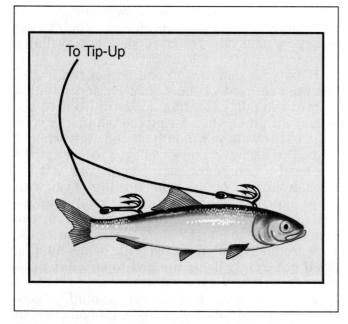

Always hook your tip-up minnows with one tine of a treble, centered in front of the dorsal fin with the hooks pointing toward the tail for better hooking potential. Where legal, a stinger hook rig (shown here) can also be helpful if the walleyes are striking short.

Rigging Tips for Trophy Walleyes

When targeting larger walleyes, spool your tip-ups with 25- to 40-pound test dacron line, such as HT's Ice Line or Gudebrod's braided ice line. Tie a #4 ball-bearing barrel swivel to the end of your tip-up line, run an 8- to 10-pound monofilament leader off it, pinching a light split-shot to your leader. Tip it with a couple colored beads and #6 treble hook.

I keep extra rigs available by pre-tying terminal rigs with various shot and hook sizes, adding a swivel to the end of each one, and storing them on snelled hook holders for easy access. This way if I want to re-rig or if a leader breaks, all I have to do is attach the two snap swivels together, bait up, and I'm ready to fish.

If possible, try different species of minnows and various sizes to see if this makes any difference, leaning toward the larger, 4- to 6-inch size. I've also found cutting back a minnow's tail makes them swim more aggressively to right themselves, while making them easier for finicky walleyes to catch. They also have less swimming power this way, and are less likely to cause "false flags."

Quick-Strike Rigs

Quick-strike, or "quick-set" rigs are special, double-hooked rigs that allow improved and faster hook sets. I usually carry pre-tied quick strike rigs tipped with smaller hooks. You can tie them yourself, or purchase them pre-rigged from companies such as Bait Rigs or HT. With these double-hook rigs, simply slip the trail hook into the minnow just behind the dorsal fin at a slight angle facing the minnow's head, while the hook at the end is slipped just behind the bait's head with the same orientation. Be sure the hook points are fully exposed and pointing towards the minnow's head to improve hook-setting position. A small spinner added to the rig creates additional fish-attracting flash and vibration. This is important if you're fishing in states such as Minnesota, where the spinner effectively makes such rigs a lure, making them legal.

For best results with quick-strike rigs, set the hook as soon as possible after a strike. Such practice vastly increases the odds you'll hook fish in the mouth. That way, if you wish, fish can be released and stand a good chance of survival.

Depth Setting

Typically you'll want to set your rigs within 2 feet of the bottom. Run a couple higher, especially

When targeting larger walleyes, try fishing larger minnows with their tail cut back slightly. This makes them swim irregularly, triggering strikes from these larger, more educated fish.

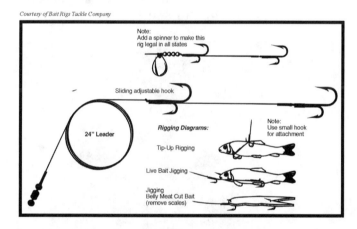

Courtesy of Bait Rigs Tackle Company

Quick-strike, or "quick-set" rigs, are special double-hooked rigs that allow faster and better hook sets. (Courtesy Bait Rigs Tackle Co.)

if the walleyes may be feeding on open-water baitfish or you suspect low oxygen concentrations along the bottom may cause suspension.

After determining the depth you want your minnow placed, set a depth indicator on your line. This makes it easier to determine how much line a fish has taken after a strike and saves time when re-setting your depth after a hit. To accomplish this, clip an HT line marker at the position directly below the spool on stationary tip-ups, or just below the fan on wind tip-ups. Then set your flag and light indicator systems, and check your bait regularly. Unlike some gamefish species, dead minnows don't seem to trigger winter walleyes.

At this point, the wait begins, but eventually certain areas will become obviously better than others. Once a pattern is established, you can move and reset your tip-ups accordingly. In the meantime, be quiet. I see it frequently, the moment a tip-up flag trips, a whole army of anglers run over to see what's happening. This often spooks the fish holding the bait–and sometimes spooks the entire school. It makes me cringe every time I see it.

One of the secrets to catching winter walleyes consistently with tip-ups is, with the exception of checking bait, stay away from the fishing area, keeping noise and movement on the ice to an absolute minimum, especially when fishing shallow water. If a flag pops, carefully approach the hole using patches of snow to conceal your shadows and footsteps. If possible, approach from the opposite direction the fish is running, always keeping the number of helping hands to a minimum. You'll note a difference in your catch ratio.

The only exception to this "quiet" rule is when fishing a large flat. I've found that by WIDELY circling the area SLOWLY with a four-wheeler or vehicle I can get fish moving, helping trigger strikes.

So don't catch yourself ignoring one of ice fishing's oldest, most effective walleye-catching traditions. Instead, contact some willing friends, select a potential lake, combine productive tip-up strategies with the proper knowledge of where and how to fish them. Then modify your specific locations and presentations to match the given situation. Properly placed and rigged strategically, few ice anglers can deny the tip-up's ease of use, fun and effectiveness.

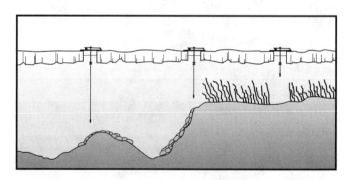

Typically you'll want to place your tip-up rigs close to bottom. But it also pays to experiment with some set higher. Do this if walleyes may be feeding on open-water baitfish or you suspect low oxygen concentrations along the bottom may cause suspension.

Understanding Walleyes and Sauger in Winter ❖ 109

Ice, Twilight, and Tip-ups

There's something special about ice, twilight, tip-ups and walleyes. It's challenging, fun, rewarding and productive. But to make it so, fishing the right location with the right equipment is mandatory. So let's sidestep into this specialized, winter walleye pattern.

General winter twilight walleye patterns aren't difficult to decipher. During this time, depending on lake type, walleyes can be found actively feeding on relatively shallow food shelves, such as flats, coves, bays, points, reefs and weed lines. Deciphering which holds the most active walleyes becomes the challenge separating men from boys. However, good lake maps laid out before knowledgeable biologists, resort operators or bait shop owners narrow down the possibilities. Asking questions should provide enough information to get you started.

Once there, you'll want to cover the area thoroughly with tip-ups. You can try jigging, but, moving around in the dark trying to untangle snarled lines within the dim glow of a sonar screen isn't a tremendous amount of fun. Sure, a mobile approach using a combination of tip-ups and a well-lit portable shelter in which to jig is a good way to cover water. But for twilight walleyes, I prefer to fish tip-ups. While I may not catch fish as fast, using a strategic placement plan, I usually see enough action to match the catches of even the best jigging purists. The best way to accomplish this begins with choosing the proper locations, specifically the best combinations of secondary cover within likely walleye holding locations.

Fishing in large groups to spread out your efforts helps, too. My friends occasionally con me out of a full night's sleep, and we make a night of it, bringing along a couple grills which serve a dual purpose: they provide warmth and they allow us to serve up some hot food and beverages. We gather around these grills, treating them like the social institution they are, and monitor our strategically placed units while visiting and eating.

This also provides good camouflage. Night walleye hot spots are hard to keep secret, simply because once they're located, catching fish really isn't difficult. By standing around a grill acting like we're just fishing nonchalantly, other anglers are more likely to pass up our spots.

Fishing walleyes with tip-ups at twilight is challenging, fun and productive.

When fishing twilight and evening periods, we often make a night of it, using grills to provide warmth...and hot food.

While tip-ups produce numerous walleye each winter, more anglers are discovering the advantages of jigging. (Courtesy Northland Tackle)

Jigging

While tip-ups produce numerous walleye each winter, more anglers are discovering winter walleyes readily strike fluttering spoons and flashy jigging lures. And why not? You can cover more water and catch bonus fish by simply setting a tip-up or two and, depending on your local regulations, work a jigging rod with another line. Besides, jigging winter walleyes is highly effective. It also makes the wait between tripped tip-up flags seem a little shorter.

When it comes to using ice rods, dangling a minnow beneath a slip bobber has probably accounted for more walleyes than any other ice angling method, but there are times other jigging techniques definitely take more fish.

Why? By jigging, you're increasing your mobility and versatility, you can switch holes easily–usually without taking time to change or put on fresh bait. After catching a fish, you can easily drop your lure back down and immediately continue fishing. So if your group cuts plenty of holes in advance to minimize spooking the fish, you're mobile versatility and persistence of carefully evaluating each situation to pattern the fish, will usually lead to success.

Choosing the Ideal Walleye Rod

Longer, stiffer, fast-action graphites allow you to position yourself away from the hole, yet are sensitive enough to detect light strikes. They feature excellent fish-fighting strength and control. Quality ice rods also feature genuine cork handles for sensitivity and comfort, and numerous, well-placed guides for evenly distributing your line along the blank.

For walleyes, I prefer stout, fast-tipped, 24- to 48-inch graphite rods with large guides, stiff butts and sensitive tips. Stiff butt sections provide strength for hook sets and fighting fish. Large guides help prevent freeze-up and, since winter walleyes can be notoriously soft biters, fast tips for increased sensi-

Longer, stiff backboned, fast action graphite ice rods allow you to position yourself away from the hole, yet are sensitive for detecting light strikes and feature excellent fish-fighting strength and control. (Courtesy HT Enterprises, Inc.)

tivity are especially important. Lightweight, medium-light action graphite ice rods like HT's Premium Polar Lite Elites, Arctic Airs or Polar Golds feature strong butt sections and fast tip actions, oversize, lightweight single-foot guides, blank through construction and genuine cork handles. They are among my personal favorites.

Carry Multiple Ice Rods

"There's a reason ice pros carry so many rods," said professional angler Will Wegman. *"Pros realize the more rigged rods they have, the more apt they'll be to change presentations and be more versatile."*

You should carry lots of rods, too. For the same reason.

Outfit your favorite with a high-quality spinning reel properly lubed for cold weather fishing. The reel should preferably be a ball-bearing model featuring brass pinion gearing, a smooth, multiple-washer front drag, free-turning, ceramic bail roller with strong spring tension so your line rides on the bail roller and not the bail itself. Initially spool with premium, 6-pound monofilament, but carry interchangeable spools filled with 4-pound for clear water environments and 8- to 10-pound abrasion-resistant line for fishing large fish or thick cover. Then prepare to determine the best presentation patterns to compliment primary location patterns.

Fluorocarbon Lines

Fluorocarbon lines have been called the most invisible lines because, it's claimed, the refractive index of fluorocarbon is so close to water the line all but disappears when submerged. This makes it worth a try when fishing bright days in clear water. Fluorocarbon is also highly abrasion resistant, doesn't loose strength when wet and isn't damaged by ultraviolet light.

Winter Walleye Jigging Basics

Successful winter walleye jigging requires planning, effort, and strategy. Put the right mix of these factors together, and you can bag those 8-, 9- or even 10-pounders.

Walleyes will seldom drop down for a bait, but instead, tend to feed horizontally or rise to strike.

As with any successful winter outing, you must determine your goal. Do you want to take the kids out to experience action? Catch a limit of "eaters," or target that elusive trophy? Different lakes offer various levels of potential. If you have your goal outlined ahead of time, someone may be able to steer you in the right direction. Many lakes even have specific "hot" patterns. On one lake near my home, fishing shallow, vegetated flats with #5 silver Swedish Pimples tipped with 3-inch shiners during first-ice twilight periods is the ticket. It took me several seasons to decipher this pattern, but if you'd call me prior to heading out to the lake, you could learn this pattern in less than five minutes. Ask around before stepping on the ice.

Otherwise, you'll be left with choosing your own weapon. A myriad of effective winter walleye lures exists. Each design has its own purpose. However, walleye lures basically fall into one of four primary classifications: Blade baits, swimming baits, jigging spoons, plastics and standard lead-heads. The key is learning to apply the right ones, given the situation.

Courtesy of Reef Runner Tackle

Reef Runner Cicada

Reef Runner's Cicada is a blade bait that creates a unique, fish-attracting vibration when lifted and irresistable flashy, darting, fluttering motion on the fall. (Courtesy Reef Runner Tackle Co.)

Blade Baits

Blade baits come under a variety of commercial names, including Reef Runner's Cicada, Blitz Lure's Blitzblade, and Heddon Sonar. Each have a slightly different means of accomplishing essentially the same thing: creating unique, fish-attracting flash and intense vibrations that can't be matched by any other ice lure. The flash and vibration occurs when the bait is lifted, and an irresistible flashy, darting, fluttering motion occurs on the fall. This combination of intense action and flash works great for attracting active walleyes in deep, dark or murky water. It also works for triggering strikes from neutral fish. Available in a variety of sizes and colors, these little gems work well for either panfish or gamefish.

Most blade baits feature thin, oval, blade-like slices of metal attached to elongated, weighted heads. Two double hooks are attached, one aft on the thin slice of metal, and one on the weighted head. Line is attached with a snap slipped through a hole in the top of the metal blade.

They're best fished by dropping them to the desired depth, then snap jigged once or twice by quickly lifting your rod tip to draw fish in. Once fish appear, simply jig upward then let the lure fall, always varying the height and speed of your lifts and drops and watching your line as the lure falls. Since walleyes generally strike on the drop, maintain a tight line as you lower your blade bait.

Moderate the speed of the fall, too, as fish often show definite preferences for particular drop speeds. In response, blade baits will make wide, fluttering circles as they fall, then stop and circle back. This looks a lot like a dying minnow and is a prime target for irritated fish.

Blade Bait Walleye Tricks

For maximum lure action, use the lightest line feasible, 6-pound is best, 8-pound with larger models.

Always use a plain snap–not a snap swivel–for attaching blade baits to your line, or the lure's dramatic wiggling action will likely fray your line at the knot.

Try placing a large barrel swivel 18" up the line from your lure to help prevent line twist.

Keep your hooks sharp, and bend the hook gaps open 10 degrees to enhance the hook angle. Both result in improved hooking percentages.

Try adding the back piece of a plastic curly tail grub to the rear hook for more color, texture and slightly different lure action.

When it comes to color, a general rule is to use silver in clear water on bright days, black chrome in clear water on dark days, and gold in stained or murky water.

Watch your rod tip and line for any deviation in action. Some strikes are very subtle.

Swimming Baits

Swimming baits include jigging minnows such as Normark's Jigging Rapala, HT's Walleye Ice Jig, and swimming jigs like Northland's Airplane Jig or System Tackle's Flyer. Since these lures feature fins or wings that make them swim in partial or full circles when jigged with high lifts followed by quick drops of the rod tip, they work especially well for aggressive walleyes. Just remember: The larger the lift, the larger the circle. Swimming style lures should always be tied directly with a strong knot such as the improved clinch or Trilene knot, and can be modified by adding plastic twist tails or flavor-enhanced plastics to the rear or center treble.

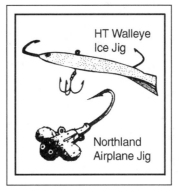

HT Walleye Ice Jig

Northland Airplane Jig

Swimming baits are lures that swing out and glide in partial or full circles when jigged. They work especially well for aggressive walleyes, but will catch walleyes under virtually any condition.

Swimming style baits like these swimming minnows from Normark and HT work especially well for aggressive walleyes. For best results, never do the same thing twice when jigging. If you mix snaps, pops, shakes, lifts and falls of varying height and intensity–you'll increase your percentages.

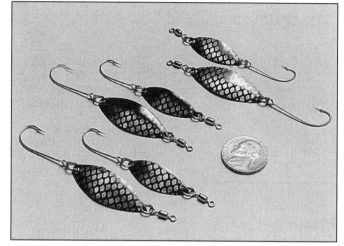

When fishing finicky, shallow water waters, small, lightweight flutter spoons like these Bait Rigs Willospoons create excellent finesse jigging presentations. (Courtesy Bait Rigs Tackle Co.)

Jigging Spoons

Jigging spoons include famous ice lures such as Bay de Noc's Swedish Pimple, Do-Jigger or Vingla, Bait Rigs Deep Willospoons, HT's Marmooska Spoon, Northland's Fire-eye or Bucktail Rattle Spoons, Acme's Kastmaster, Luhr Jensen's Krocodile, Mepps Syclops, Reef Runner's Slender Spoon, the Sutton, Doctor or any number of other models and styles. These baits work well for walleyes in many situations, and are jigged much like swimming lures. Instead of swimming to the side these lures flutter and flash on the fall, producing a close imitation of a wounded minnow. That allows them to work under a variety of conditions. They're best tied using split-ring attachments to facilitate maximum action.

Plastics

Relatively new to the winter walleye scene, plastics include large tube jigs and plastic twist tails. They're most often fished on various jig heads, but can also be tipped on swimming lures or jigging baits. Tube jigs, for example, can be tipped on a swimming airplane jig. A tube body rigged on the rear hook helps slow these wide swimming lures as they fall. This same concept also works with curly tail designs which also adds lure action. The advantage of using a tube is that when a fish bites down on the plastic, the tube flattens against the hook shank, exposing the hook point and providing superior hooking qualities.

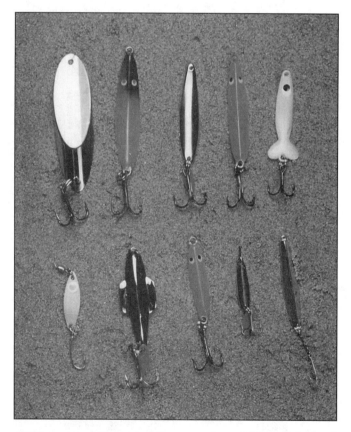

Jigging spoons come in a variety of models and styles, but all basically produce a unique vertical fish attracting flash and fluttering fall imitating a wounded minnow. For best results, fish them with short snaps of the wrist mixed with light shaking motions sprinkled with brief pauses.

Relatively new to the ice fishing scene, large plastics such as this minnow-tipped tube jig have proven highly effective for winter pike.

Tube jigs also make a unique addition to various sizes of jigging spoons such as Bay de Noc's Swedish Pimple, HT's Marmooska Spoon, Bait Rigs Willospoon or Custom Jigs and Spins' Stinger. Many of these spoons actually fit inside some tube designs, allowing the tube to form a sheath around the lure body. Essentially, this adds a slower fall to the spoon, plus a hint of contrasting color, a more natural feel and subdued flash, which can be a powerful combination for walleyes.

Stinger Hooks

Professional angler John Peterson of Northland Tackle recommends adding a small "Sting'r hook" to any walleye jig or jigging spoon. "Stingers will increase your catch by 25 to 40 percent," John claims. "Simply attach them to the tie-eye or hook on jigs, or the split ring on spoons."

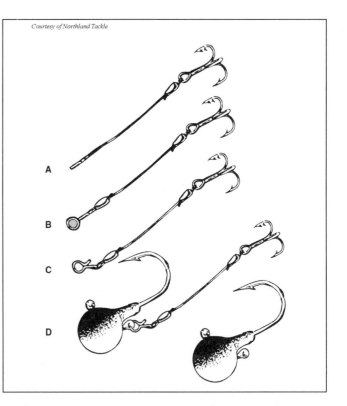

Courtesy of Northland Tackle

Stinger hooks are a great means of hooking fussy, short-biting walleyes. They can be attached with a standard knot or clip to the gap of any hook or split ring. They can be used on a variety of jigs and spoons, or may be tied or clipped on specialized jigs offering a secondary eye for attaching stinger rigs.

Leadheads

Leadheads are simply standard lead-head jigs like Northland's Sink 'n Jigs or HT's Ultralite Lures. Specialty designs like Bait Rigs Odd'Ball improve the hook gap and make it easier to add movement to your presentation. The advantage of using leadheads is you can add as much or little action to them as you want. You can fish light, plain leadheads with just small minnows and gentle jigging motions for the shallowest or fussiest fish, or tempt large, active or deep walleyes by aggressively working larger, heavier, gaudier versions tipped with plastic action tails or large minnows. Leadheads work best when tied with a loop knot to help maximize action. Of course, always experiment with various sizes, styles and colors.

Tipping any of these baits with a touch of fish scent or attractant is also a good idea. My favorite formulas are Berkley's Powerbaits, or Fish Formula's Sparkl'Scales formulas, which not only feature potent fish attractants, but also release metal flake "Sparkl'Scales" into the water that resemble loose scales from an injured baitfish.

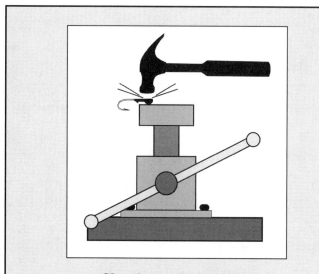

Slowing a Jig's Fall

To slow the fall of a standard lead-head jig for fussy walleyes, flatten the head by placing it in a vice, and striking it with a hammer. The flattened head will now create more water resistance, and fall more slowly.

Tube-U-Lure Lures

Of all the new innovations in ice lures, one of the most unusual is Outdoor Creations "Tube-U-Lure." According to Outdoor Creations Pro Staff member Greg Fisher, the hollow tube design catches water and forces it through the lure as it's jigged. "When you lift up, the result is a shaking, wiggling motion much like a crankbait," Greg explained. "As you lower the bait on a slack line, the bait slowly glides down in a perfectly horizontal position." The result? A perfect mix of intense walleye attracting motion on the lift, followed by a sudden, motionless slow falling drop that triggers strikes on the fall. The lure also glides to the side when dropped, allowing you to cover water efficiently, making a good "search" bait.

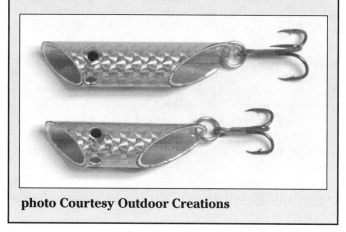

photo Courtesy Outdoor Creations

Jigging Tips

If someone asked me to evaluate jigging motion, I'd say most ice anglers work their baits too hard, too fast, or both. The trick to jigging walleyes is to tease them into striking. Sometimes the slightest motions imaginable prove most effective.

Oh sure, the "classic" lift-fall method works some days, but when it doesn't, try periodic lifts combined with longer periods of gently jiggling the lure an inch or two. Sometimes just holding a spoon in place while making the treble hook wiggle at the base is the ticket. Remember, you can always increase the action of your lure. The point is, find an action to begin with, then speed things up or slow them down. Mix and match, carefully evaluating your level of success at each stage, until you come across a winner.

Also try tipping the lure of your choice with a minnow, piece of pork rind, plastic action tail, or other attractant. Some winter walleye veterans add paint, prism tape or larger trebles with split rings. Some will bend their hook points out slightly, or add stinger hooks to increase hooking percentages. Most sharpen their hooks religiously. Again, these are "extras" that should be experimented with until you find what works best for the given situation.

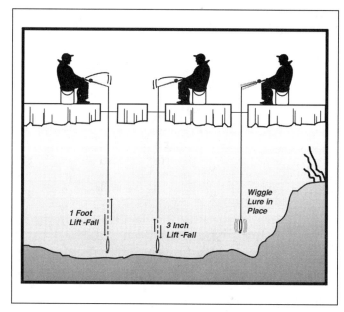

A mixed jigging rhythm incorporating lift/falls of varying height interspersed with slight lifting motions and gentle, in-place wiggling movements will help attract walleyes, then tease strikes once the fish is there.

Finally, strict concentration is helpful when jigging, especially when walleyes aren't super-
aggressive. If you feel a strange sensation, such as
your bait suddenly feeling heavier or different,
more often than not, a fish has struck. This will
often occur while the lure is falling, so establish an
effective rhythm of drop-stop, lift-fall or jiggle-
pause. Should anything change or unexpectedly
interrupt this rhythm, set the hook!

Consider Your Goals

If you want to jig winter walleyes, consider
your goals. Then select your tackle systems and
jigging strategies based on the situation at hand. If
the walleyes are holding near dense concentrations of forage or inhabiting dark water and
appear active, you might want to try jigging
aggressively with a vibrating blade such as Reef
Runner's Cicada, a jigging minnow such as Normark's Jigging Rapala or jigging spoons such as
Bay de Noc's Swedish Pimples, Custom Jigs and
Spins Stinger, HT's Marmooska Spoons, Bait Rigs
Willospoons, Reef Runner's Slender Spoons or
Northland Fire-Eye or Buck-Shot Rattle spoons to
get the walleyes attention.

Color? Be versatile and experiment. Walleyes
may change preference from day to day, even hour
to hour. But as a general rule, in deep or dark
water, stick with gold, copper, glowing or bright
fluorescent colors. In shallow or clear water, try
silver, or natural shades. The more subtle colors
are better in these cases.

Also experiment with different prism tapes,
blade styles, sizes, weights, and natural bait "tippers." Keep your hooks well-sharpened, and try a
variety of speeds and jigging motions. Always
maintain control of your line as the bait drops. If
you drop back rapidly as the bait sinks, slack line
will form and you'll miss strikes, and if you place
tension on the line, you'll often diminish lure
action. Instead, keep your line semi-taut, watch

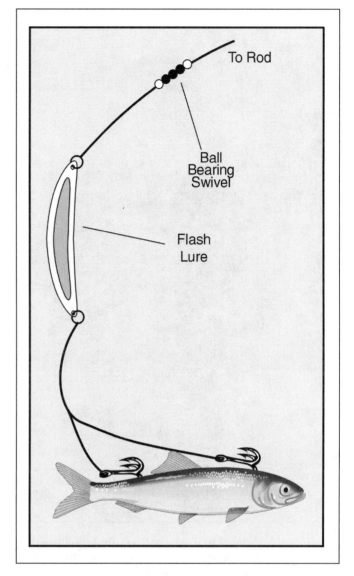

**A dropper rig tied beneath a spoon is a highly pro-
ductive winter walleye technique when the fish are
striking short. Where legal, stinger hooks can also be
incorporated into such rigs, further increasing your
hooking percentages.**

carefully for any indication of movement. If you
see or feel anything unusual, set the hook!

When fishing clear water, suspended or inactive fish try using small, lively minnows fished as
droppers below spoons. They are highly productive winter walleye baits. For best results, squish
a flavor-enhanced plastic or tie a small scrap of
fluorescent yarn around your hook to draw fish
and trigger more strikes. Better yet, replace your
hook with a fluorescent jig such as HT's #6 Marmooska, Custom Jigs and Spins' #6 Rat Finky, System Tackle's #6 Flats or a #8 Northland Sink'n'
Jig. For something really different, try one of

Special Winter Walleye Strategies: Mobility and Versatility

An additional set of keys to winter walleye presentation success include mobility and versatility. On the ice, I often spend several hours reviewing the areas efficiently with sonar and underwater cameras. And another hour to pinpoint the hot presentation.

I've never fished any waters where one magic location is always the hot spot and one magic lure is the only way to catch walleyes all winter. Every lake has its hot locations, productive lures, jigging motions and colors. These may change seasonally,

Every walleye lake has its hot locations, productive lures, jigging motions and colors—and they may change seasonally, daily, hourly.

Don't just bounce around drilling holes like a wayward pinball. Instead strategically search for specific features providing the right combination of depth, bottom type, cover, forage and oxygen. Your winter walleye catch will increase.

Northland's or Hawg Wild's colored hooks baited with a minnow. Walleyes see the target better and strike at the hook or jig, reducing short strikes.

If the walleyes are especially fussy, try attaching a stinger hook to a spoon by tying a length of line tipped with a #10 bronze treble to the bend of the hook eye. Then bend the point of your hook and stinger hook points slightly outward. The extra hook and special bend will improve your hooking percentages. Of course, minnows can also be fished tight line alone, or rigged beneath a neutrally balanced slip bobber.

I also use jig rods in the event a fish is missed on a tip-up. Generally, missed fish will still be cruising the area, and by promptly lowering a lure into the same hole, can often result in a strike while jigging.

daily, hourly. And there will be times when overlooked locations and baits produce better, especially on heavily pressured lakes where walleyes become conditioned to crowd-favored locations and lures. Walleyes are a unique breed, and ice anglers wishing to catch them consistently must learn the odd behavior and habits of this fascinating species. The best way to do this is by utilizing a mobile, versatile approach.

Remember: Choose a lake with a healthy walleye population, combined with moderate amounts of classic structural features such as points, reefs, bars, weed lines and gradually sloping break lines. Waters with large amounts of varied structure have more places for walleyes to relate to, scattering fish and making catches less consistent. Those lakes with little structure have few hot spots to consistently hold fish. Either makes a mobile, versatile approach for patterning winter walleyes difficult.

Lakes with generous, but not excessive, amounts of structure make a mobile approach to searching for high-percentage fish-holding structures a reasonable task. Again, the key to winter walleye success is mobility. Active schools of winter walleyes are usually on the go. Depending on the lake, they may be relating to specific flats, weed lines, depth contours or structures. Yet such features often encompass large areas. If you're not willing to move from structure to structure and hole to hole using electronics, drilling holes and experimenting with various presentations to pinpoint and pattern walleyes, your results are likely to be inconsistent. The easier it is to eliminate unproductive areas and patterns, the easier it is to effectively target locations with the most potential.

Move and keep moving until a school of active fish is located–but move efficiently and wisely. Don't just head onto the lake and bounce around shooting sonar readings and drilling holes on these structures like a wayward pinball. Instead, use carefully planned strategies. Move around on each structure, searching for specific features providing just the right combination of depth, bottom type, cover, forage and oxygen levels. Once in the right area, you'll typically catch a couple fish, just don't get lulled into spending long periods of time in holes yielding only a strike or two.

By the same token, you'll occasionally find a hot hole or two that produce especially well. When you find such holes take a couple fish then rest them momentarily before continuing so you don't spook the school. Always mark these spots

for repeat visits. Such special holes are usually positioned over some type of underwater structure that regularly funnels migrating walleyes within striking distance of your presentation. Remember, walleyes use definite structures and migration routes throughout the winter. To catch them consistently you need a general knowledge of the winter walleye's preferred locations, positions and movements, which vary given the environment and the conditions. But learn them using a mobile approach, and you'll increase your catch.

Secondly, carry a basic selection of tip-up rigs, jigging lure designs, sizes and colors. Given changing circumstances, be willing to try various combinations of them until you determine the best choices, in other words, be versatile.

Once you've located a good hole, versatility in presentation often becomes the secret to taking multiple fish. Do everything possible to enhance your versatility. The first step is to make lure changes quick and easy. A snap swivel rig makes lure changing simple. To make one, place a small barrel swivel on the terminal end of your line and tie a monofilament leader of the desired length and test tipped with a small snap for attaching lures to the opposite end.

Besides making lure changing a simple matter of clipping the snap on instead of tying knots, the swivel eliminates line twist, and the leader can be

When it comes to winter walleye fishing, it pays to be versatile! (photo Courtesy Berkley/OTG, Inc.)

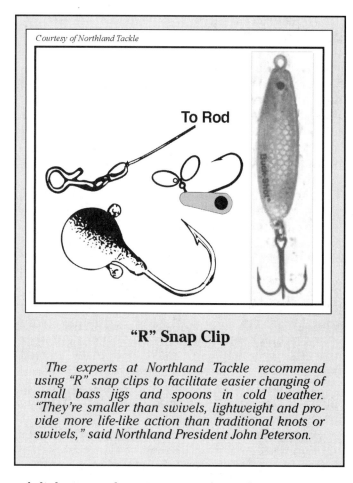

To Rod

"R" Snap Clip

The experts at Northland Tackle recommend using "R" snap clips to facilitate easier changing of small bass jigs and spoons in cold weather. "They're smaller than swivels, lightweight and provide more life-like action than traditional knots or swivels," said Northland President John Peterson.

small? What color? Should they be jigged quickly or slowly? With or without dropper lines or stinger hooks? Tipped with any special bait? The answers to such questions provide clues toward patterning winter walleyes. To be consistent, the ice angler must use a systematic approach to determine answers as efficiently and quickly as possible.

Walleyes recognize movements and flash. They feel vibrations, hear sound, see color and smell and taste food. In order to catch them consistently, you must offer maximum appeal to each of these senses. Thus, using refined, truly versatile jigging methods requires a working knowledge of a variety of jigging presentations.

Most winter walleye jigging spoons have large treble hooks which help you hook fish more easily. But some come with small hooks which only

of lighter or heavier test than the main line. Lighter leaders help increase lure action, and heavier leaders help resist breakage when landing large fish. When pulling fish up the hole, you'll also be able to tell when walleyes are close to the hole when the barrel swivel appears.

More On Lure Selection

Lure selection begins with a good understanding of walleye feeding habits. Like most predators, walleyes are opportunists, eating whatever food nature provides. Yet while walleyes may feed on various forage bases, baitfish comprise most of the walleye's diet. Consequently, lures that represent minnows are typically the most productive. But not just any minnow-imitating bait will work. Winter walleye jigging presentations require determining the fish's activity levels by monitoring their responses to your specific presentations, then adjusting your presentation to tempt the most strikes.

Do the fish want flashy lures, swimming lures, jigs, plastics or blade baits? Large, medium, or

When it comes to winter walleye fishing, it pays to be versatile! Always carry a variety of jig hooks.

cause you to lose walleyes that aren't well-hooked. So, if your lure comes with a small hook, replace it with a larger one and try bending the hook points out slightly. Both tricks increase your hooking percentages. Many anglers are also replacing their hooks with new trebles such as Excaliburs that turn the hook points toward biting fish.

Again, be versatile! Walleyes in different environments demonstrate a range of activity levels given the situation, often preferring different lure styles, sizes and colors–and easily become conditioned to overused presentations. Don't become a one method Joe. In order to create consistent catches, you'll need to be versatile enough to switch lures and find what modifications–and jigging actions–will produce best.

For example, I've found "swimming lures" such as Normark's Jigging Rapala and Northland's Airplane Jig outstanding performers, but not as good in dark water. This is probably because walleyes can't locate these wide-swinging lures in dark water as easily. And plain lead-head jigs tipped

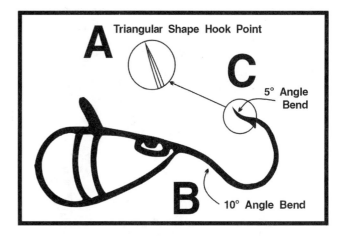

Bending your hook points out 5 degrees and the shank 10 degrees will help increase your hooking percentages.

with a minnow and fished gently are too slow to help you catch fish consistently when the walleyes are active or inactive, but they are good bets given "neutral" activity levels. Try subtly tempting these light-biters to take your slowly worked jig and minnow. Plastics such as tube jigs or twister-type tails tipped on standard leadheads then rigged with a minnow can also be outstanding given tough conditions. Plastics tend to fall slowly, and worked with gentle, twitch, lift-fall motions, even the fussiest walleyes can't seem to resist them.

At the other end of the spectrum, walleyes can sometimes be tempted with an aggressively jigged rattling flash lure or tight-vibrating blade bait. Work these lures aggressively to anger fish into snapping at the bait. Just note walleyes can become conditioned to specific lures. In other words, fish learn not to strike at them. You'll have to be prepared to make concessions. Watch your sonar or, if you have one, keep an eye on your underwater camera monitor carefully, noting fish responses to each lure style, size and color. Let the walleyes tell you what they want.

Also experiment with live bait tippers. With most jigging lures, I prefer small, whole 1 to 3 inch minnows better than minnow heads or large minnows. They not only add realistic motion, scent, texture and taste, but also balance better on most ice jigs. I generally use small to medium sized shiners or where available, rosy red minnows. Shiners provide a great deal of flash, but unfortunately, aren't very hearty and must be replaced fairly often. Rosy reds resemble fatheads, except for their highly visible orange coloration. Hardy rosy reds also outlive and wiggle better than most minnows. They make excellent ice fishing baits.

Almost invariably, jigging winter walleyes requires precision technique. (photo Courtesy Tom Neustrom)

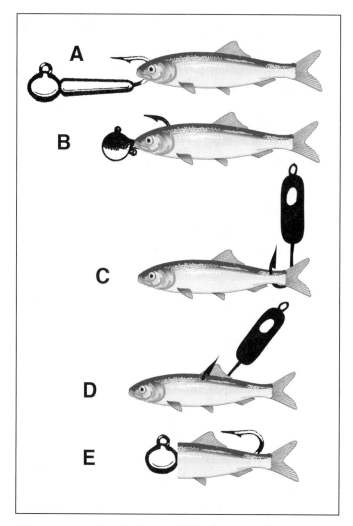

Minnows can be lip-hooked (A), head-hooked (B), tail-hooked (C), reverse-hooked (D), even cut and horizontally positioned (E). This might seem obvious, but it's amazing how often just a different way of hooking a minnow will be the difference between catching a limit of walleyes and catching none. Many winter anglers never experiment with such presentation details.

Minnows can be lip-hooked, head-hooked or tail-hooked depending on the mood of the walleyes. Generally, lively head-hooked baits with stingers draw positive strikes from neutral fish. When the bite is on and walleyes are slamming lures, lip-hooked or tail-hooked minnows provide better hook sets. Another tactic growing in popularity for light-biting fish is "reverse hooking"– hooking minnows by the tail. Rigged this way, minnows continually fight the downward pull of the jighead, and the struggling action attracts hungry walleyes. As you experiment with each lure design, size, color, live bait tippers and hooking methods, carefully monitor their response to pat-

tern the fish. Many anglers don't think small details are important. They're not only important, but critical. Such things have often made the difference between a good catch and none.

Such monitoring is easy if you're fishing visible walleyes in shallow, clear water. But this is a rare situation. With typical winter walleye fishing occurring in deeper water or during low-light conditions where you can't see the fish or your lure, sonar and underwater cameras become your eyes. Using these electronic tools, you'll not only see structure and cover for determining location patterns, but also the fish, the depth at which they're holding and your lure. Furthermore, you'll be able to observe their reactions to your specific presentations by watching their responses.

At times, walleyes will dart forward to smack your lure immediately upon sight. Sometimes they'll swim out and look it over carefully before striking, other times, they'll swim out, look the bait over, and choose not to hit. Either way, the obvious advantage to the electronics approach is that you can watch such behavior, then try different hooks and baits, jigs and lures in a variety of styles, sizes, colors and actions to determine what the fish are most interested in when trying to tempt a strike.

Almost invariably, jigging winter walleyes requires precision technique. If the fish are neutral, fast jigging actions will likely spook them. But jig too slow, and the fish may not get excited into striking. Use your electronics to determine the key mix of lure design, size, color and jigging action. Remember, every lake, every day, every situation is different. To be consistently successful, you must be mobile and versatile.

Summary

The secret to consistently catching winter walleyes is dictated by proper deciphering of location patterns and fine-tuned presentation methodology. After finding the right location, you must learn to place tip-ups strategically and feel every movement of your presentation. Work at developing your own productive jigging style by experimenting with various lure styles, sizes, colors and actions. Then try to anticipate strikes; always monitoring your electronics to fine-tune your presentations to get the best response.

Keep an open mind. Carefully research the proper lakes and lake types given the existing conditions, always having backups in mind in case the first doesn't produce. Then use lake maps and electronics to properly locate high-percentage areas. Set up prior to twilight and evening peak periods with high-quality equipment and strategically set rigs, baits and lures. Always experiment with different potential hot spots with various presentations until, using the process of elimination, you determine a winning combination.

Yes, this takes time and effort. But if you want to catch more and larger walleyes, you'll soon discover these organized, mobile, versatile approaches and strategies are the key to accomplishing your goal.

Understanding Sauger In Winter

In many environments, anglers mistake sauger for walleye, even though they have a distinctly different coloration. Remember, saugers have a black

In many environments, anglers mistake saugers for walleyes, even though their mottled, grayish-brown coloration and absence of a white tip on the lower lobe of the tail distinguishes them from the walleye. (Courtesy Northland Tackle)

dotted dorsal fin and feature a gray or mottled brown appearance, not green; and their tails feature no prominent white spot. Saugers are also generally smaller in size–a three pound fish would be considered a good catch by most anglers. In terms of habits and behavior, saugers usually hold somewhat deeper and can withstand more turbid waters than walleyes.

Still, many anglers don't know the difference between walleye and saugers. A January 28, 1961 creel census showed that 2,813 of the "walleye" anglers checked had taken 3,998 saugers, which constituted 75% of all fish taken. While this population has since mysteriously dwindled, saugers are still often mistaken for walleye catches on these frozen waters and many others throughout the North American ice fishing belt.

Primary Winter Sauger Location Patterns

Winter fishing patterns for sauger are very similar to walleye. Both fish are often caught in precisely the same areas. Points, bars, reefs and their associated edges are commonly "hot" sauger fishing areas. Those featuring secondary cover such as rock or vegetation and supporting a readily available source of forage are especially productive. Since saugers tend to be mobile and move often, mobility is critical to consistent catches.

The major location difference between winter walleye and sauger is the sauger's love for slightly deeper water, and the fact sauger tend to more often be found in moving water. Often, when fish-

Fishing frozen river holes beneath large river dams and locks is a highly effective means of catching winter sauger.

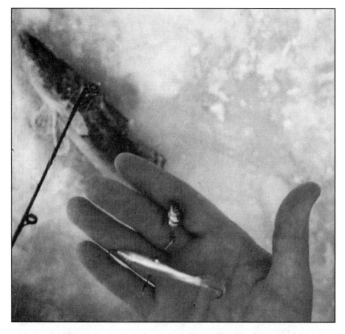

Working jigging minnows like this Normark Jigging Rapala tipped with a minnow head is a great method for catching winter sauger. This works especially well when fishing in current because the heavy, streamlined body design is easy to position and fish just off bottom, the river saugers' primary strike zone.

ing frozen river holes or pockets beneath Mississippi River locks, for example, sauger constitute the bulk of the catch.

Effective Winter Fishing Strategies

Fixed position tip-ups rigged with light leaders and small to mid-size minnows work wonders. As with walleyes, when the weather cooperates, wind tip-ups baited with small minnows are a highly effective means of catching saugers.

Jigging can be highly productive, too. Jigging minnows, jigging spoons, blade baits, rattle baits, plastics, lead-head jigs, slip bobbers—virtually any winter walleye lure will attract and catch saugers. While smaller versions seem to be more productive, saugers are aggressive and aren't afraid to strike larger baits and lures. So, as with walleyes, experiment to see what lure styles, sizes, weights, colors and action result in the most consistent catches.

In terms of timing, sauger are much like walleyes and become most active during twilight periods, although they may be more active during the day than walleyes.

Chapter 5

Understanding Pike and Pickerel in Winter

(photo Courtesy Berkley/OTG, Inc.)

I take a deep breath, exhale, and watch as wisps of my breath hang momentarily in the early morning darkness, then vanish in the frigid stillness.

In the glowing light of a lantern, I reach for the padlock on my shanty door. Stinging cold metal immediately penetrates my insulated gloves, drawing heat from my fingertips. Hurriedly I press the key into the lock. When it sticks, I force it back and forth until the frozen mechanism finally turns and clicks. I crack a smile at Terry. He smiles back. After all, if the pike are biting this morning as well as they have been during the past few days, we don't want to miss out because of a frozen padlock.

Grabbing my sonar, minnow bucket and 5-gallon pail of tip-ups, I stumble into the frosty darkness. Using the moonlit shadows of my old holes as reference points, I kick snow away from a new spot, dump a puddle of water from the minnow

bucket onto the ice, flip on my flasher and place the transducer down. The glowing screen indicates a soft bottom covered by thick weeds. Moving out, I mark a semi-soft bottom with sparse weeds. A few steps farther, hard bottom with no vegetation. I've found the outer edge of the weed line. Perfect.

I mark an icon on the GPS, then continue forming a plotter trail while taking additional readings. I now have a pretty good idea where the weed line runs and have plotted several cuts and projections along the break.

As the morning sun stretches over the horizon, painting the sky deep shades of purple and royal blue, I fire up my auger, cut holes in strategic spots, and begin anxiously setting tip-ups. When they are all in place I walk back to the shanty where Terry is laying bacon into a heavy frying pan. However, since the pan isn't hot enough to cook, the strips just sit there. We look at each other, then reach for the bottled juice and donuts.

After a few satisfying drinks, we begin studying our lake map, reviewing previous notes beneath the white light and soft hiss of the lantern. Suddenly, Terry jumps and his chair topples, and I turn to see a tip-up flag snapping to vertical. Bursting out the door, I notice the trip shaft spinning—fast. Quickly I grasp the line, and set the hook.

Weight. Heavy weight. The fish begins burning line from my fingers.

"Could be a big walleye," Terry blurts.

But the deep, wide head shakes and powerful runs indicate we're dealing with a 10-15 pound fish, likely a pike. Carefully, I work the fish to the hole, then watch as a thrashing 36" pike emerges from the icy water.

Why the action? Each year, three peak periods occur providing good opportunity for catching big pike, or lots of pike if you prefer quantity over quality. Two of them occur during the ice fishing season. Hit key locations during these periods, and you'll increase your catch. But first, the fish.

Northern Pike

Northern pike can be identified by their large, toothy mouths and greenish-gold flanks spattered with rows of pale, cream-colored spots. Their rounded, reddish-orange fins form a backdrop for irregular black markings. Pike are known for their voracious appetite for bait fish, and many anglers believe pike feed more beneath the ice than during the open water season. While pike fillets are filled with numerous "Y-bones," properly cut, these can be minimized. In terms of eating quality, pike rate high.

Northern pike can be identified by their large, toothy mouths and greenish-gold flanks spattered with rows of pale cream colored spots and rounded, reddish orange fins with irregular black markings.

Pickerel are smaller than pike and distinguished from northern pike by their light pale greenish-yellow sides and dark, chain-shaped markings. (photo Courtesy Frank Fischer)

Pickerel

Pickerel are typically smaller than pike. The most common species taken through the ice is the chain pickerel, distinguished from northern pike by their light yellow-green colored sides prominently marked with dark, chain-shaped markings.

Pickerel are especially popular ice fishing quarry throughout the eastern United States, particularly in the shallow ponds of New Jersey and New York. Their preferred habitat consists of cool, clear waters featuring moderate vegetation growth. Since their feeding habits are similar to pike, we'll cover basic winter patterns for them together, then point out some of the pickerel's unique facets at the end of the chapter.

Primary Winter Pike/Pickerel Location Patterns

Since pike and pickerel inhabit a wide geographical portion of the North American ice fishing belt and feed actively during winter, ice anglers catch them readily. The trick is to catch quality fish consistently. So, before getting into seasonal patterns, let's divide patterns for pike into two categories—those primarily productive for small pike, and those more effective for consistent catches of larger fish.

The common denominator in virtually any winter pike location pattern is vegetation. It's no secret that winter pike and pickerel are caught from shallow weed beds, but this has proven to be a rudimentary winter pattern for meager fish. Most pike are taken from shallow vegetation because that's where most smaller, competitive fish hold. This is where most ice anglers focus their efforts. But other than the pre-spawn late-ice period, the key to successful trophy winter pike is fishing deeper water.

For Big Pike, Fish Deep

Mid-sized to monster pike often hold along deep weeds, and some huge trophies suspend over deep holes. Understand that these often lone, suspended fish are difficult to locate, and usually not worth pursuing. For now, unless your goal is smaller pike, it doesn't pay to concentrate your efforts in weeds on stagnant, shallow flats. These can be great places if you want fast action, but they aren't likely to produce many big fish.

Note I said "aren't likely to produce many big fish." Stagnant, shallow-water flats may draw good fish, they just aren't consistently good bets. Also, don't confuse stagnant flats with shallow, vegetated flats and structures at the mouths of lightly current-swept spawning creeks and marshes. These can provide fabulous late-ice action for

"Stagnant" shallow flats will often attract smaller pike, especially at first ice. These areas aren't good bets for consistent catches of larger fish.

For big pike, fish deep, away from "stagnant" shallow, weedy flats.

monstrous pre-spawn pike. The concern here is spending too much time fishing shallow, densely vegetated, vast stagnant flats isolated from water flow and deep water.

Instead, start by choosing seldom-fished or underpressured bodies of water. Such waters are influenced by current, which maintains oxygen, cover and forage. Such waters also draw migratory fish, and if you work areas offering the best combination of oxygen, cover and food—namely the edges of deep, fresh weeds lining large structures protruding within zones of well-oxygenated water near concentrated forage—you'll likely find more and larger pike.

Then you'll be faced with the challenge of finding these prowling pike—yet there's no need to worry. If you know how to read hydrographic maps, understand pike fishing patterns and have a working knowledge of electronics and power augers, you're on your way to eliminating unproductive water—and well on your way to catching more and bigger pike.

Just make efficient use of your time. High-percentage structural features and their associated breaks must be identified and marked prior to fishing. Remember, large structures are better than small ones because larger predators demand more

Many winter pike anglers focus their efforts in shallow weeds. The fish they catch are often small.

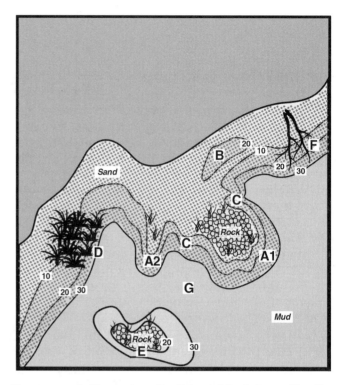

Deep weed lines, productive mid-winter pike hot spots, may extend for miles on big water. The key to finding pike is to focus your efforts on irregularities such as fingers (A1, A2), pockets and turns (C), deep weed lines with bottom content transitions (D), deep weed lines lining sunken islands (E), or areas of varying cover such as wood (F). Deep holes (B) along inside weed lines may also be good.

space. Still, these larger, pre-marked spots are only starting points. You might mark the best-looking spots on your target waters, but if adequate cover and food isn't found when you get there, it's unlikely any pike will be found either. You must examine these features more closely.

Fish Large Flats and Structural Features

You'll improve your odds of catching bigger pike by concentrating your time on large, prominent, vegetated mid-depth flats and structural features, especially those adjacent to expansive, forage-rich feeding flats offering diverse depth breaks with various bottom content changes and cover types. Such areas offer a quality mix of cover, access to shallow forage, and quick routes into the stable environment of deep water. This is where you'll find the good-sized pike.

These breaks may extend for miles on some deep natural lakes and reservoirs, so to focus your efforts, search for irregularities along these edges. The best areas include pockets and inside turns or protrusions such as fingers, points and outside turns. I recommend "running" your lake during the open water season, and using an accurate lake map and sonar, to locate these high-percentage locations. Enter them into a hand-held GPS unit as waypoints; jot down each location with its associated number, name and coordinates in a logbook;...and wait.

Once safe ice forms, you can use the map, logbook and GPS to relocate these spots efficiently, then use sonar and underwater cameras to pinpoint primary locations featuring the best combinations of secondary cover, forage and fish for the time you're fishing.

Look for Deep, Green, Broad-leaf Vegetation of Varying Height

Weeds are primary winter pike attractants, but must be located in structurally diverse areas. The weeds must also be deep, green, and have broad leaves. Pike seem to prefer weeds of varying

Deep, green, broadleaf vegetation such as cabbage—especially cabbage of varying height and mixed with other shorter, branchy weeds—provides diverse cover options for forage. This attracts winter pike.

height. Large, tall, broad-leaf weeds interspersed with shorter, branchy weeds provide diverse cover to harbor forage. They also provide numerous ambush points pike may use for attacking unwary prey. The best strike zones are not only the deep edges of well-defined weed lines, but those separating large, weed-covered flats or structures from relatively deep holes.

Use your sonar to find them. Recollections of weeds from summer are rarely adequate. More often than not, ice formation causes reduced sunlight penetration, causing weed lines to recede, or worse yet, change areas of lush summer vegetation into aquatic deserts. These dying weeds also use oxygen, and although pike are able to withstand periods of time in low oxygen waters, such areas provide little chance of holding pike consistently.

Scattered stands of healthy green weeds survive throughout winter in many lakes. Finding these spots are the keys to success. They may be a challenge to pinpoint, but if the job was easy, everyone would be doing it. Just be assured that once you identify deep, green, broad-leaf, vegetation, you can bet they'll be magnets for first-ice pike.

Fish the Deepest Outside Edges

There is also a subtle sub-pattern I've stumbled onto, based, I believe, on intra-species competition. While the best winter pike action tends to occur on the edges of large, vegetated mid-depth shoreline flats and structures, I've noticed most catches of larger pike occur near the deepest outside edges of this weed growth. Apparently, larger "alpha" fish take up residence in the best feeding locations along these outside edges. They then push smaller fish into shallower, secondary feeding areas. Typically, distinct outside weed edges formed by deeper breaks, bottom content change or turns in creek channels—anything to produce changes in weed type or height—are high-percentage locations for larger pike.

Again, let me emphasize: Fishing pockets in vegetated shallows often provides more action. Deep outside weed lines or smaller, deeper weed beds usually hold fewer fish, but usually offer the most potential for catching larger fish. Best of all, this pattern may persist well into mid-winter during years with low snowfalls and relatively high temperatures when more sunlight penetrates the

While the best winter pike action tends to occur along the edges of large, vegetated mid-depth shoreline flats and structures, most catches of larger pike come from the deepest outside edges of the weed line.

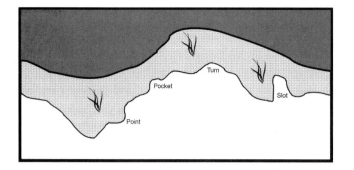

Weed line irregularities such as points, fingers, pockets, turns and slots are places featuring deep, green, broadleaf vegetation and lining the deepest outside edges. These are places to focus your efforts for larger pike.

ice. Weeds stay green and healthy, maintaining oxygen and keeping the food chain active. This draws pike. Combine this with an inlet, outlet or spring providing some current flow and consistent supplies of oxygen and food, and you've got a primary winter pike area.

Lack of fishing pressure may be another reason pike remain along mid-depth weed lines later into the season. Given suitable conditions on a private or geographically isolated, seldom-fished lake, large pike may even hold shallow. And with that, we're ready to discuss specific seasonal movements.

First-Ice Pike

To fully understand the first-ice pike period, it's important to understand the habits of pike during late fall, because this is when it all starts. As the bright summer sun begins losing its sizzle, shallows begin cooling. This generates temperatures more agreeable with pike, which love cool water. Big fish that just spent a season restricted to deeper, colder lake bottoms are free to migrate shallower.

These movements aren't random. Big pike don't just wander into any shallow area and stay there. The fall period typically demonstrates a food shortage in most bodies of water, because bait fish numbers are significantly reduced thanks to predation throughout the open water months. Bottom line? Big first-ice pike are hungry, and often search mid-depth, vegetated flats and shoreline structures for food. They simply continue searching until they find something to eat. While they are going about their business, unhampered by fishing pressure or recreational boating, ice

begins forming over their heads. If anything, they become even more active.

Why? By nature, larger female pike must spend a period of time in water gradually decreasing in temperature, followed by an extended length of time in cool water so their eggs develop properly. Maybe it doesn't seem important, but this little tidbit of trivia is one of the keys to understanding why big pike can be caught so consistently first ice. Developing eggs demands a certain amount of nutrition beyond the female pikes' already healthy winter appetite. Sure, the fish's metabolism is slowed by the cooler water, but being cool-water fish, they still

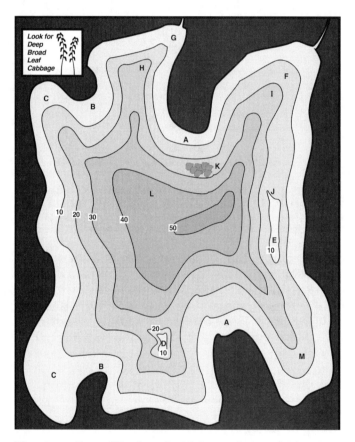

First-ice pike will often hold in pockets within shallow vegetation and mid-depth weed lines. Shallow, stagnant flats like area (C) will hold mostly small pike, while deeper turns and weed lines such as areas (A, F and M) and shoals such as (E) and migration route (J) will be more likely to support big fish. Such mid-depth weed lines lining mid-depth bars like area (D) can also be productive. Mid-winter, deeper weed lines such as areas (H) and (I) become better, as do mid-lake rock piles (K). Some mid-winter pike may also suspend over deep water, too (L). Late ice, shallow, current-graced weed flats and spawning bays (G) are the place to begin your search. And remember, always look for deep, green broadleaf cabbage.

feed relatively aggressively. This offers ice anglers unique opportunities to catch big, actively feeding females. This is also a time when environmental conditions stabilize and become more consistent than the turbulent fall period. As many anglers know, periods of environmental stability often mean good fishing, particularly if the conditions meet the specific needs of the fish. Well, pike don't mind cold water in the least; in fact, they thrive in it.

Yes, cold temperatures cause the lake's ecosystem to slow down, and the crop of bait fish yielded from the spring spawn has usually been dramatically decreased. But this is a bonus for serious winter pike anglers. With baitfish often in relatively short supply, food is more difficult to locate, and hungry pike actively search for prey which is often slowed down and featuring slowed reaction times thanks to the cold. So, while baitfish move at a slower pace, don't move often and feed less, pike are active. This gives the pike a distinct feeding advantage. Be there, and you can get in on the action.

Mid-Winter

Many winter pike anglers mistakenly believe pike relate to shallow and mid-depth weeds all winter. Some fish may hold back, depending on the lake and conditions, but most demonstrate a progressive movement toward deeper water. Anglers continuing to fish shallow often think mid-winter pike fishing is poor. Don't buy into this. If action slows in the shallows and along mid-depth weed lines, don't waste your time there. Begin searching deeper, hard-bottom edges and breaks adjacent to prominent, hard-bottom main-lake bars, points and humps.

Why do the pike move deeper? Think back to those significant mid-winter panfish movements from the second book of the *"Hooked On Ice Fishing"* Series. As the season progresses into mid-winter, shallow cover often recedes, and the forage base of plankton drops deeper. Panfish follow. Since pike feed on panfish, they drop down, too.

Sure, if conditions allow, some smaller bluegills and perch may remain shallow. Likewise, so will a few smaller pike, leaving just enough remaining action to keep mediocre ice anglers fishing shallow, and leading to the common misconception that quality pike catches deteriorate mid-winter. Truth is, most anglers are simply fishing the wrong location.

Many pike anglers believe winter pike relate to shallow and mid-depth weeds all winter. This may be true with smaller fish, but often, deeper weed lines and hard-bottom breaks are the keys to catching bigger winter pike. (photo Courtesy Wil Wegman)

Think Cabbage

After finding the deepest, greenest broadleaf vegetation of varying height you can find lining large, main lake structural features, seek pockets of cabbage. I've noticed when vegetated structures contain various weed types, pike tend to prefer scattered pockets of green cabbage. This is a good example of "microstructure" that we discussed earlier.

Secondary projections off these weed edges are the "best of the best," especially if they support thick, healthy patches of cabbage that vary in height. I usually look for classic inside or outside turns off long, vegetated shoreline points or bars extending toward deeper water. Such places funnel schools of bait fish into concentrated areas. These areas also often support the best remaining green weeds mid-winter. When cruising pike come upon them, they stop to feed, and as long as the cover and a consistent food supply remains, so will the pike.

Deeper, elongated main-lake hard-bottom areas such as gravel points, main creek channels or rock piles can also produce exceptional mid-season pike action, especially if prime areas of mid-depth weed growth are depleted or intensive fishing pressure has spooked shallower fish. These areas are often good mid-season walleye spots as well, so don't pass them up if you're interested in mixed bag catches.

In river backwater areas, reservoir creek arms or main-lake creek channels, deeper, hard-bottom features offering wood for cover and located just outside shallow, soft-bottom food shelves featuring current flow constitute another hot mid-winter pattern. I've found these areas most productive during tough weather conditions, or after vegetation begins dying off.

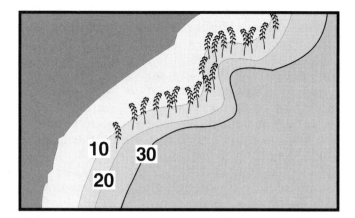

A good example of mid-winter "micro-structure." These sharp, deep vegetated inside and outside turns could be lining a shoreline weed line, or be positioned along a point, shoal or sunken island. Regardless, this would be a spot likely to corral schools of baitfish into concentrated areas, thus attracting pike.

Open-Water Loners

Another prominent mid-winter pattern involves open-water, pelagic pike. These fish can sometimes be found in deep, open-water areas. They are often difficult to find, so begin taking multiple sonar readings, watching carefully for schools of suspended bait fish with large, thick, solitary marks positioned beneath them. These large marks are often pike. Here, the combination of understanding winter pike movements, map-reading skills, and knowledgeable use of sonar allows you to find bait fish and deep, roaming open-water pike without drilling a single hole.

Late-Ice Pike

In many areas, the season for pike is closed by late-ice to protect pike moving shallow to spawn. But in areas where the season remains open, late-ice action can be fabulous.

As mid-winter gives way to late-ice, begin checking deep weed edges on sections of bars or points breaking from deep water into mid-depth ranges, and eventually, into shallow spawning bays and marshes. Find such structures featuring sharp-breaking drops adjacent to wide, shallow shoreline flats or bays offering a variety of secondary cover. Especially good areas include those offering weeds and being fed by inlets, outlets or springs. Find these areas and you'll have likely discovered a classic spawning bay—and a potential late-winter trophy pike Utopia.

Pike can be caught from many forms of remaining vegetation, but broadleaf cabbage is typically best.

This is an ideal situation and you'll rarely find it, but the more of these features you discover in one place, the greater the chance of finding late-season pike. Remember, late winter is a transition period between mid-winter and the spawn. You can expect pike to begin migrating from deeper water structures toward their spawning areas at this time. Any features offering food and cover and acting as migration routes between mid-winter depths and shallow, vegetated spawning flats are always possible late-ice fish holding areas.

There are also some odd forage situations that may draw late-ice pike into the shallows and create viable patterns. Frogs emerging from their dormant winter state is one of these. I've seen mud bottoms appear to come alive as hundreds of frogs break hibernation. Being relatively slow-moving in the cold water, they're vulnerable. Late-season pike recognize the opportunity and often take advantage of the situation.

Hard to find, deep, open-water suspended pike are available on many lakes, and knowledgeable anglers well versed in the use of electronics can find and catch these fish.

Tracking Trophy Pike

While the above methods will lead to better than average catches, true trophy pike can be the challenge of a lifetime. Catching trophies over 20 pounds gets more difficult every year. But you can increase your odds of catching these fish by thinking strategically.

Pike are highly adaptive. They can survive in a diverse array of waters from the cold, clear Canadian Shield lakes and "big water" areas of Europe, to the warm, muddy backwaters of the Mississippi River. They are also found in thousands of small eutrophic lakes, ponds and rivers scattered across Scandinavia, Europe, and North America. While

After finding high-percentage locations, you'll want to cover them with precise presentations efficiently. Efficiency demands mobility.

pike may survive in waters featuring low oxygen levels, warmer water temperatures, poor forage bases, intense competition and excessive fishing pressure, these limiting factors also shorten their life spans and impede "normal" growth. Environments exhibiting these qualities seldom produce trophy pike.

This is why so many serious winter pike enthusiasts fantasize about the opportunity to fish monstrous European pike or catch a thrashing trophy within the deep, remote wilds of northern Canada. In Europe, superior growing conditions produce pike of gigantic proportions. In Canada, minimal fishing pressure allows pike the opportunity to grow, making catches of trophy fish more common.

Yet there's no need to travel in search of trophy pike. Sections of many lakes, reservoirs and Great Lakes shorelines and bays meet the pike's ideal habitat requirements: They are oxygen-rich, cool water environments allowing pike to remain active virtually all year. The best of these are found on the large, deep cool bodies of water. Given an abundance of high-protein, soft-bodied forage consisting of smelt, alewives, shiners, ciscoes, shad or emerald shiners readily available, these shorelines present virtually optimum growing conditions.

Species like emerald shiners and smelt often suspend in deep, main-lake areas and expansive bays making the pike relating to them difficult to find. But, these bait fish do make shallow-water migrations. The spring Great Lakes smelt run, for example, brings massive schools into shallow bays, marshes, harbors and river mouths, and if these movements coincide with late ice in an area offering an open season on pike, the action can be phenomenal.

Finally, an additional word about suspended, trophy pike location patterns. Catching these trophy pike involves searching deep, open-water areas for suspended loners. These pike may appear almost impossible to find, but if you're a mobile angler well-versed in knowledgeable use of sonar, catches are possible.

Cutting multiple holes and "leap-frogging" tip-ups along them is often an effective means of catching winter pike.

Most of these pike relate to suspended schools of forage, such as shad, cisco or smelt. Learn to identify them on your sonar, and you can work around the school, searching for large marks indicating the presence of pike. These predators are usually suspended below the baitfish. While this process can be a challenge, the rewards come when the head of a 20-pound fish thrashes from the hole.

Effective Winter Pike Fishing Strategies

After finding high-percentage locations, you'll want to cover them with precise presentations. To be efficient demands mobility.

Good pike presentation begins with power augers to minimize the work of drilling multiple holes. Keep your power heads maintained and the blades sharp. Remember, mobility along lengthy, deep weed lines is often the key to finding and catching pike consistently. A dull or poor-quality auger can make this a difficult proposition. Studies have also indicated power augers are quieter than chisels or hand drills. This is another important factor to consider, particularly when fishing shallow or mid-depth, first-ice and late-season pike.

When you're ready to drill, stagger your holes across primary areas. Cut holes directly over breaks surrounding primary structures. Scatter a few atop vegetated flats several feet inside the weed line, and place one or two several yards off the weed line to search for any "loner" fish that might be suspended off the break. But don't stop there. Holes placed on deep weed edges should not only follow the contour of the weed line, but should have special emphasis placed on points or projections that might concentrate active fish. Extend these for a distance along elongated features.

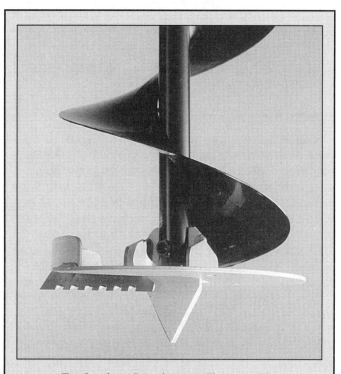

Reducing Ice Auger Freeze Up

A common problem with ice augers is frozen blades impeding cutting capability. Jiffy has helped change this by using D-Ice'r ARMOR™. A coating made with DuPont Teflon® is applied to the entire bottom end of the drill assembly, providing a smoother, slicker cutting edge.

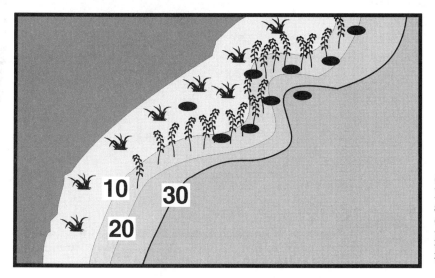

Once you're ready to drill, stagger your holes across breaks surrounding primary structures, focusing along the deep edges, but placing a few in shallower pockets and over sharp, deep vegetated points, turns or slots that adjoin deep water.

Since active pike usually strike within 10 minutes of lowering a bait or lure, it doesn't take long to cover water. Cut numerous holes right away. If you only drill a couple holes at a time, you'll be constantly drilling. Such activity is not only tiring, it can scatter active pike, rendering the standard use of "search" baits and lines ineffective.

By drilling a number of holes over a large area at once, you may stir up a few pike, but by covering long sections of deep breaks, you can easily return to fish the first holes you drilled first, then proceed down the line. This allows pike ample time to settle down before you fish. The strategy works, and I've found rather than starting and stopping the drill repeatedly, I can quietly and efficiently move from hole to hole in search of active fish. Once the area is covered, you can move onto other structures using similar strategies. Or, if you wish, retrace your steps, covering the best areas more thoroughly.

Depending on the amount of fishing pressure, keep cutting holes in this fashion every 20 or 30 yards along the weed line beyond your "spot on the spot." The extra holes allow you to leap-frog tip-ups as you search the weed line for active fish. This brings us to one of the most important parts of winter pike presentation.

Tip-Ups

For many ice anglers, the thrill of hooking a big pike on a tip-up is what ice fishing is all about. This becomes rather obvious when you scan frozen lakes and notice hundreds of tip-ups being watched by an even larger number of ice fishing enthusiasts. Winter pike and tip-ups go together like cookies and milk.

Yet ask most ice fishing folks what patterns they're fishing for tip-up consistency, and you're likely to get some pretty funny looks, because many anglers aren't considering such things when

For many anglers, the thrill of hooking big pike o tip-ups is what ice fishing is all about.

The odds of catching winter pike can be increased by following a few general patterns, then modifying them to the time and waters being fished.

they set up. Most set tip-ups and pray for the best, or quickly set a tip-up or two while jigging for panfish. Not that there's anything wrong with this. It's just the odds of catching pike can be increased by following a few general patterns, then adapting and modifying them to the time and waters being fished. In other words, you can make your tip-ups work for you.

Choose Quality

Choose high-quality, smooth-operating tip-ups such as HT's Polar, Arctic Fisherman's Beaver Dam, HT's Polar Therm, Polar Pop-Ups, or on warmer days, Windlass. Time-proven models like the Polar not only offer smooth tripping and multiple settings, but come in various spool sizes, so if

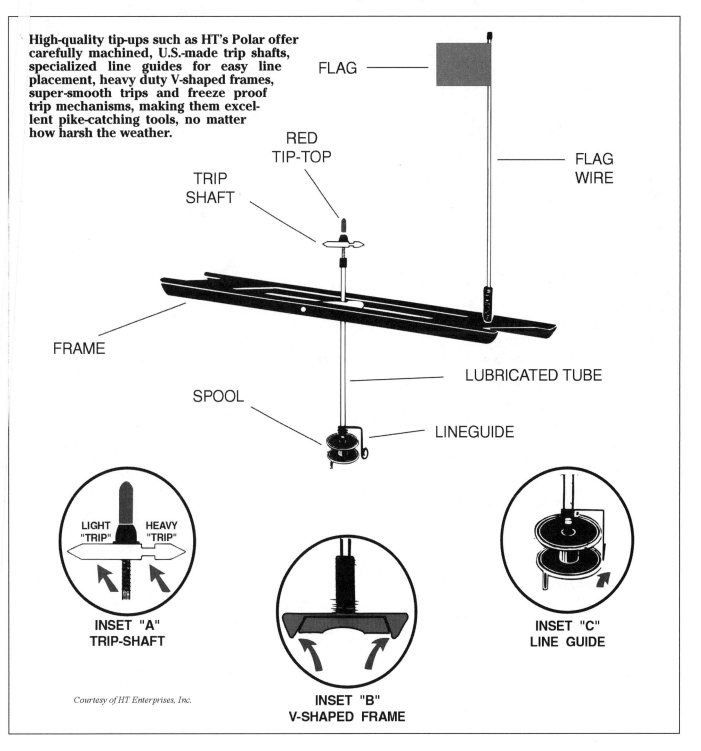

High-quality tip-ups such as HT's Polar offer carefully machined, U.S.-made trip shafts, specialized line guides for easy line placement, heavy duty V-shaped frames, super-smooth trips and freeze proof trip mechanisms, making them excellent pike-catching tools, no matter how harsh the weather.

FLAG

FLAG WIRE

RED TIP-TOP

TRIP SHAFT

FRAME

LUBRICATED TUBE

SPOOL

LINEGUIDE

LIGHT "TRIP"   HEAVY "TRIP"

INSET "A"
TRIP-SHAFT

INSET "B"
V-SHAPED FRAME

INSET "C"
LINE GUIDE

Courtesy of HT Enterprises, Inc.

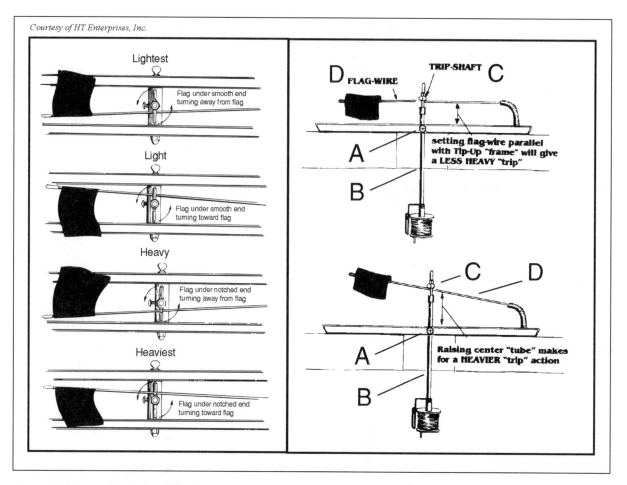

A special benefit of the Polar tip-up is its unique trip setting adjustments. The flag wire can be placed under the smooth or notched side of the trip shaft, thereby allowing the trip to slide either up or slip down the wire changing the amount of force needed to trip the flag. The Polar's "drag" setting feature can also be set for larger pike minnows by loosening the set screw and raising tube mechanism (B) up in frame (A). This increases the angle of the flag wire against the trip shaft, increasing the pressure necessary to release the trip and minimizing inadvertent minnow trips from larger baits.

you're fishing large, hard-running pike in deeper water, you'll have enough line. Polar tip-ups are guaranteed against freeze up, the frames feature a special "V" shape that eliminates freeze down, and with a multiple-setting, fine-tuned drag-adjustable trip set, you can fish even the largest minnows without the concern of wind trips.

When fishing shallow water, especially during bright, cold or snow-blowing conditions, you'll appreciate the benefit of quality thermal units, such as Frabill's Igloo or HT's Polar Therm. Both block light, keep snow out and prevent holes from freezing. With HT's Polar Therms, a choice of small or large spools is again available when fishing larger or deeper pike.

Finally, don't ignore the jigging action of the Windlass. When conditions permit, the adjustable movement offered by these units will catch more pike than any standard tip-up. With the movement properly set, use of colorful minnow-tipped jigs and spoons can increase their effectiveness even more.

Basic Rigging

Basic rigging consists of a strong, pliable teflon-coated 25- to 40-pound dacron backing tipped with heavy, 12- to 17-pound monofilament, fluorocarbon or thin-diameter wire leaders. Tip them with a #8 to 1/0 hook, depending on the size of the bait you're using and the size of your target fish. Add a wiggling minnow (I've had good success with fresh, 3- to 5-inch golden shiners, suckers and chubs), hooked lightly behind the dorsal fin, and you're ready to fish. Just lower the bait and let it work its magic.

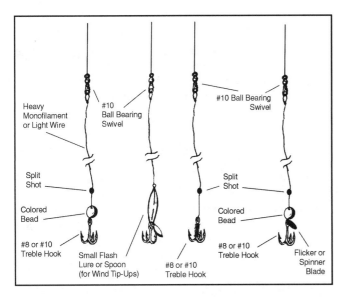

Basic tip-up pike riggings use Teflon-coated Dacron backing tipped with a 12 to 17-pound monofilament or thin-diameter wire leader via a barrel swivel. Typically, a #8 or #10 treble hook pressed lightly behind the dorsal fin of a lively minnow will attract winter pike.

Consider Your Minnow's Hardiness

There's a difference among minnows in hardiness. Emerald shiners, for example, are not a hardy species. Fatheads, however, can withstand dramatic changes in temperature, low oxygen levels and rough handling. Generally, the hardiest species are liveliest on a hook—and this can make a difference in success rates. Since active fish often prefer more lively bait, fatheads might be better choices for active fish. If the pike aren't as active, an emerald shiner might be best.

The only exception to this general rule is when pike are finicky–you know, those days when flags are rare, and when hits finally occur, fish pull out a few feet of line and drop the bait before you can set the hook. On these frustrating days, try lighter, 8# monofilament leaders, 2 -inchemerald shiner minnow with a #10 or #12 treble. These changes will often make dramatic differences in your results, and with smaller trebles, you won't injure the minnow the way large ones can, yet the hook is still large enough to hook and hold pike.

Consider Size, Shape, Flash and Smell

Effective anglers also consider minnow size, shape, flash and smell. Golden shiners have a different profile than fatheads. Shiners give off a great deal of flash. Smelt and other oily baitfish give off a stronger odor than lean-fleshed fish. Experiment to see if the fish show a preference for a particular species or quality—and more importantly, try to determine why.

Inspect Your Bait Often

To improve your chances of attracting a fish's attention, inspect your bait often. If it's not producing as you had hoped, replace it or modify it. Many ice anglers use special live-bait modification techniques. Some clip a small portion of a bait fish's tail, causing it to swim erratically. Others hook their minnows upside down, so as the minnow struggles to right itself, it attracts fish that might otherwise ignore the bait. A few even dye their minnows different colors!

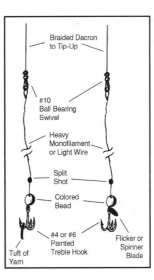

These basic pike tip-up rigs can be modified by painting the hooks bright colors, adding colorful beads, yarn or sponge, ripple rind or flashy flicker blades to draw pike and help trigger more strikes.

For added attraction, many anglers paint their hooks bright colors, add colorful beads and flicker blades, place flashy, plated spinners on the leader, or hook bits of colorful yarn or sponge soaked in fish scent to the hooks. As the minnow swims, the subtle flash, vibration and movement of these additions draws pike and helps trigger strikes.

Specialized Rigging

As for specialty tip-up rigging, it's safe to assume typical pike in today's world weigh between 3 and 7 pounds, so good standard rigs consist of low-stretch, 25- or 30-pound test, Teflon-coated braided Dacron backing. Green/white mix is good because it's difficult for fish to see. Many anglers prefer black because it's easier to watch the direction your fish is running after being hooked. Teflon-impregnated lines are my line of choice because they resist freezing. They also remain limp and won't remain coiled after sitting on a spool for a while. Some tip-up anglers spool on more expensive sinking fly lines for their quality, high visibility and smoother release from the spool. In clear or heavily fished waters, heavy monofilament might reduce visibility to the fish. The choice is yours.

To keep tip-up line from icing up, vinyl-coated or Teflon-impregnated lines are the choices of most ice pros. (Courtesy HT Enterprises, Inc.)

Whatever you choose, your backing line should be tipped with a barrel swivel and followed by a length of heavy, 12- to 25-pound monofilament or light Sevenstrand wire tipped with a #6-8 treble hook. A ball-bearing swivel is recommended for attaching these lines, as this makes tying the two different diameter lines together easier, prevents line twist and causes the leader to hang straight. The light leader and small treble hook increases hits and hooking percentages.

Specialized rigs such as HT's quick-strike rigs or Southway's Flagel rigs, which help improve hooking percentages and provide more realistic presentations, can also be used. Again, quick-strike rigs are two hook rigs with an adjustable hook that accommodates minnows of various sizes. With one hook placed in the minnow's head and the second under the dorsal, you don't have to wait long to set the hook on a running pike. If the trip shaft is moving when you get there, hit 'em. Another advantage is because these hooks usually catch in the mouth or jaw instead of the gills, pike caught on them can be released.

Quick-strike rigs should feature thin, yet strong, wire leaders such as those produced by Bait Rigs or HT Enterprises. Both incorporate two-hook systems, and the rigs are adjustable to fit any size bait. With Bait Rigs' models, the minnows themselves are held by means of smaller, single hook tines, leaving a larger tine completely exposed for hooking the pike.

You can also make your own rigs, just use quality single-strand wire and the sharpest, highest quality hooks available. If larger pike are the target, use larger hooks, and a 9- to 12-inch 20-pound test braided wire leader. You can also look into Bait Rigs' or HT's pre-tied pike tip-up rigs. When fishing "snake lakes" rig with lighter backing and leaders, and try smaller, #10 hooks. The smaller, sharper shafts and points better penetrate the bony mouth of pike.

Another specialized rig, Flagel rigs, are designed for use with dead bait, such as smelt, bloaters or cisco, and feature special wires that run the length of the minnow to hold it horizontally, while positioning the hook in the minnow's mouth for maximum hooking efficiency. More on that shortly.

Trophy Rigging

For trophy fish, go heavier and practice what I call "selective targeting." Start by fishing heavier Dacron backing, wire leaders and larger baits.

Flagel rigs are an effective means of rigging dead bait for winter pike. (courtesy Southway Bait, Inc.)

When trying for trophies, start with heavier Dacron backing, wire leaders and larger baits. The results will speak for themselves. (courtesy Northland Tackle)

Smaller winter pike normally won't mess with larger 10- or 12-inch minnows, but true trophies of 10 pounds or more seldom hesitate. Expect fewer hits and less action when using big baits but when a bite occurs, get nervous. You'll likely have a monster taking your bait!

Just be sure to use the heavy trip settings on your tip-up and properly set your drag. Big fish offer another good set of reasons for using high-quality, multiple-setting Polar tip-ups. With their multiple-setting trip shafts and adjustable, freeze-proof tube mechanisms, they can be adjusted to fish even the largest pike minnows. Clipping the bait fish's tail also reduces false flags.

Dead Bait

Dead, frozen or partially decayed baits work for pike, but must imitate the major forage fish in your lake. Because they must be suspended below your tip-up horizontally, they can be difficult to rig. Another disadvantage of dead bait is that hooks tend to tear out at the slightest nudge from a big fish—or more often, the hard pull of a hook set.

With most dead baits, quick strike rigs facilitate such rigging. By placing one hook in the middle of

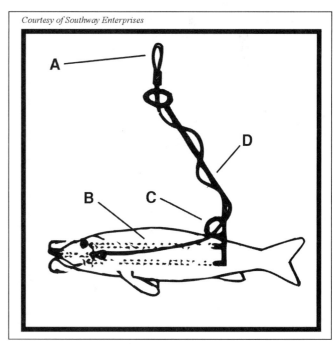

Courtesy of Southway Enterprises

Flagel rigs are used to rig dead minnows for winter pike. The stainless steel tines help sink the presentation and hold the bait horizontally. With the forward positioned hook it offers instantaneous hook sets, reducing lost fish caused by dead bait tearing off the hook on short-biting pike. (Courtesy Southway Enterprises)

the back and one in the lips, you've got the situation covered. The only exception to this rule would be in the case of baits more than a foot long—which may require a third hook placed somewhere in the front half.

Southway's Flagel rigs are another good way to rig dead minnows. These easy-to-set rigs feature a special hook and a wire system that runs through the minnow, positioning the bait horizontally every time. The design allows for fabulous hook-setting percentages. Why are such rigs so good? First, they feature stainless steel harnesses to help sink the bait. The harness also reduces the chance of a fish dropping the bait before you can get a solid hook set. And, since they allow almost instantaneous hook sets, they offer convenient hook removal. This is important, because large pike are highly vulnerable to tip-up fishing. These big fish are generally females playing critical roles in maintaining pike populations. For this reason, catch and release is important. Since quick-strike and Flagel rigs are seldom swallowed, they cause less damage to the fish, paving the way for quick and efficient releases.

I don't use Swedish Hooks, and don't advocate anyone using them on a regular basis. While being an excellent means of presenting a dead bait and a reasonable means of attaining high hooking percentages, pike tend to swallow them, meaning reduced chance of successful release. Studies in Wisconsin have demonstrated this hook's deadly

effect on pike, and this research may eventually lead to the banning of their use. However, if they're legal in your area, there's no size limit on pike and you want to fish dead baits for pike that will be kept, Swedish hooks are a highly effective means of hooking pike.

Depth Settings

Regardless of the rig being used, I'm often asked what depth is best to set a pike minnow beneath tip-ups. That's a tricky question. At times, the best action occurs with the bait swimming just off bottom. But I've had great days with minnows set just below the ice. So what's best?

You should always experiment, but I've discovered a few general rules. In clear water, I've experienced my best success using minnows set close to bottom. This is especially true on bright, sunny days. In dark water, during overcast conditions, or in years with thick ice or heavy snow, minnows set just under the ice seem to produce the most consistently. Under these conditions, try setting your minnows down about 1/3 of the overall depth. In other words, if you're in 9 feet of water, set your minnow 3 feet under the ice. If the water is especially deep, you might want to try varying the depth setting until you find the depth at which pike are holding. Otherwise, be sure your minnow is set above any vegetation, or your minnow will dive down and hide, becoming inaccessible to pike.

To attract fish, try grinding up minnows, mix them in water and pour the mixture into ice cube trays with some form of weight in each cubicle. Once on the ice, sink partially thawed cubes down the hole alongside your tip-ups to draw pike. Kulis, Incorporated of Bedford, Ohio, even commercially produces such a product. I've also heard of anglers using corn, salmon eggs, or even oatmeal to attract fish. I've frozen ground minnows and fish attractant inside ice cubes with a hole through the center. I then run my line through it to help attract fish. Just note that if you plan to use any of these tricks, be sure to check the legalities in your area. Chumming is a highly effective practice, but it is not legal in all areas.

If you don't see a flag within a half hour, adjust your depth or move to the next set of pre-drilled holes, spreading your group's tip-ups over the structure. Watch your tip-ups carefully, noting the ones producing the most hits. This is the best

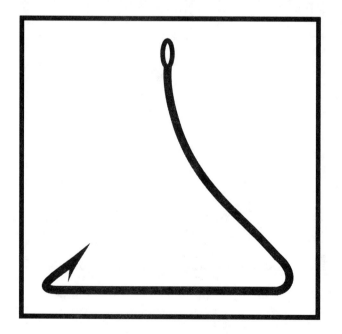

The swedish or "pike" hook traditionally used for rigging dead minnows on a tip-up.

Always watch your tip-ups carefully, noting the ones that produce the most action and evaluating why. Patterns will often emerge.

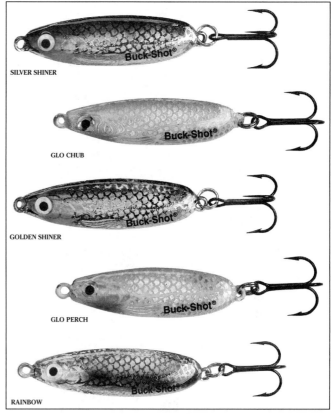

SILVER SHINER

GLO CHUB

GOLDEN SHINER

GLO PERCH

RAINBOW

The Northland buck-shot rattle spoon, an excellent winter pike spoon that can be jigged or rigged on a wind tip-up. (courtesy Northland Tackle)

way to pinpoint patterns. If pike move into shallow weeds atop the break, your tip-ups on top of the flat will indicate how shallow the fish have moved and when they arrived. If pike are using the weed edge or suspending just off the break, tip-ups placed in these areas will let you know exactly where. And if any active pike wander beyond the weed line, tip-ups set off the weed line will cover them. If the fish are biting high or low, adjust your lines accordingly.

Keep presentation subtleties in mind here, too. Remember, pike almost always relate to forage. Understanding the relationship between predator and prey is an important part of consistent presentation success. In lakes supporting good perch populations, you'll often find these panfish number one on the pike's winter menu. Find them and you'll often find pike. Using minnows of similar size and profile to these preferred baits will generally help as well.

This can be taken even farther. Many anglers have noticed they rarely find good pike action within a school of active perch, so they watch perch anglers closely. If there's a lot of arm jerking

among perch anglers, the pike-hunters avoid them. But if they suddenly notice things slowing down in the perch camp, the pikers move in quickly with heavy artillery, trying one of two options.

First, provided other anglers don't mind—try placing tip-ups in the formerly producing perch holes, or concentrate on a nearby weed line if one is available. If weed lines aren't producing or none exists, look for open pockets within the weeds, and aggressively jig with a stout jig rod rigged with a jig 'n' minnow, flashy spoon like Bay de Noc's Do-Jigger or Vingla, Mepps Syclops or a Northland Rattlin' Bucktail spoon.

Jig from the bottom to just under the ice. You might get some funny looks at first, but if you haul a pike or two out within 15 minutes you might be the talk of the town. If you leave and the perch suddenly resume biting—as often happens—you'll be a hero. Best of all, if you are successful, most perch anglers will welcome you back repeatedly. By the second or third time around you may be the subject of local newspaper outdoor columns.

Productive Holes

Once productive holes have been found, don't forget where they are. Good pike holes often contain something special you may or may not recognize right away. You might be fishing an open feeding pocket right next to a thick weed patch, a rise in the bottom, an area near a stump or fallen log providing a holding spot along a migration route—whatever. The important thing is it's a producer, and should somehow be marked for future use.

If you figure out why pike are relating to a particular area, look for other similar areas. They'll often produce well throughout the winter. Unproductive holes, on the other hand, usually remain dead and should only be fished occasionally, such as when fluctuating water levels or serious weather changes cause dramatic changes in fish location.

Additional Tips and Pointers

Unfortunately, you can follow this key general pattern to a tee and still not be successful. If there isn't much snow cover, for example, you'll have to

When setting the hooks on a tip-up pike, try to set up when the initial run begins to slow—especially in shallow weeds. Waiting too long may allow the fish to feel resistance of weights or weeds and drop the bait.

fish cautiously. Pike can see shadows through clear ice, and can easily spook when you walk over them. This is especially true if you're fishing shallow-water flats or river backwaters. If you have to drill holes in snow-free sections of ice, avoid the area as much as possible, only approaching the hole to check your bait or respond to a flag.

There is also technique involved when approaching a flag. First, move slowly on the approach, using patches of snow to shade your movements below the ice. When you near the tip-up, note what direction the fish is running, and try approaching from the opposite direction, then softly kneel beside the hole. If you're using a unit with an exposed trip shaft or spool, you'll see it spinning as fish take out line. If it's turning fast, carefully lift the unit from the water, being careful not to bump the spool or spindle and upset the pike's motion. Whatever you do, never set during the initial portion of the run, you're liable to break your leader or rip the hook out of the minnow without sticking the fish. Rather, set the hook when the run begins to slow. You'll hook a high percentage of your hits if you're able to reach the tip-up by this time and set up.

I've found setting the hook on "second runs" isn't reliable, because pike often burn out several yards of line on the initial hit, feel weight or weeds and drop the bait, or turn and backtrack toward the tip-up, thus the second run is never indicated to the angler. However, if you don't approach the tip-up in time to use this method, patiently wait for the fish to move again before setting the hook. If the spindle doesn't move within a few minutes, start hauling in line and set the hook when you feel weight. By the way, always bring your minnow bucket when going to set the hook. You'll have minnows handy for rebaiting, and perhaps more importantly, you can place the tip-up spool in the minnow bucket, keeping the line from freezing while you're re-setting.

One more thing: if you miss a pike on a tip-up, quickly grab a heavy action pike rod such as HT's Trout/Pike System rigged with a flashy jigging spoon and work the hole aggressively for several seconds. Follow this by a pause at the depth the fish struck. Often the pike will still be nearby and clobber the spoon; hard. And believe me, fighting big pike on an ice rod is an experience you'll never forget—which brings us to the final section of this chapter, jigging pike.

Jigging Pike: The Tip-Up Alternative

Tip-up fishing for pike has become an ice angling tradition, and for good reason. It's a highly productive method. Few things in ice fishing are certainties, but a vulnerable minnow set in the right location and easily visible to active, hungry pike is almost sure to get hit.

However, the key terms here are active pike, proper location and visibility. By now you should realize vegetated flats and weed lines are high-percentage active winter pike locations, and set accordingly, tip-ups will cover them. The problem is that vegetated flats and weed lines are often lengthy, expansive areas that cannot be adequately covered with just a few scattered tip-ups—and even the most strategically set minnows can be difficult for pike to see when hidden among thick weeds.

The answer? Jigging.

Don't get me wrong, I'm not saying you shouldn't use tip-ups. Since most states allow at least two lines, anglers should take advantage of the extra presentations allowed them; after all, the

On waters overpopulated with small pike, jigging them with light tackle can create fun ice fishing action.

more lines you have, the better the odds of encountering pike. But using tip-ups in conjunction with a strategically planned jigging approach enhances your effectiveness. First, it keeps you moving while you're waiting for a flag. Secondly, it's easier to cover water. Simply drill holes over these key areas and, walking quietly from hole to hole, search for the most active pike. With tip-ups, your baits largely remain in one place—at basically one depth, which is fine once you're on active fish and sure of the best strike zones. When searching expansive flats and lengthy weed lines to locate active pike, mobility and versatility are the keys to efficiency. Jigging allows both.

Jigging also allows control. A minnow swimming beneath a tip-up basically swims in small circles at the same depth, and unless a predator approaches, doesn't abruptly change depth, direction or speed. These are all things that trigger pike. By jigging you can raise and lower your lure to cover various depths, plus change lure direc-

Jigging winter pike: The tip-up alternative.

tion, speed, style, size and color. All the while you'll be trying to create just the amount of action and flash you feel will trigger strikes. Using sonar or an underwater camera as integral parts of your approach, you can also watch for pike moving through above or below your lure. You can then respond to these sightings, monitor the fish's responses to your presentations, and adjust to whatever seems to trigger the most fish.

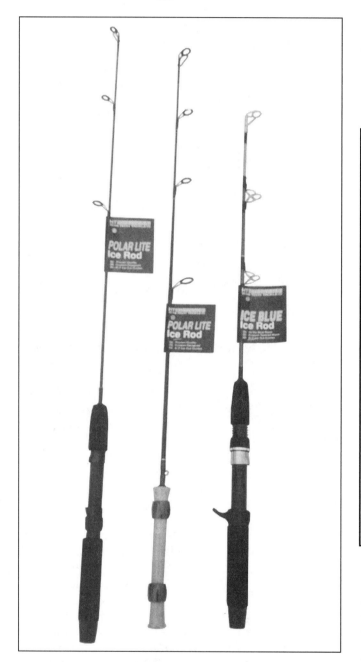

A good pike rod should be a 30- to 48-inch medium to medium heavy casting or spinning rod featuring strong backbone, slight tip action and relatively large guides.

Finally, jigging pike is a thrill. Sure, you've got to be mobile, drill numerous holes and experiment with various lures and techniques to determine the most efficient way of triggering fish, then set your drag carefully and fight thrashing pike with skill. More work? Perhaps. But more excitement and challenge, too!

In terms of ice rods, you'll need a 30-48" medium or medium-heavy action casting or spinning rod featuring strong backbone, slight tip action and large guides. HT's PLC-32 Polar Lite fits the bill. Strength is necessary for hook-setting and fish-fighting power; tip action provides sensitivity and helps keep your line tight while fighting fish, and large guides help prevent ice build-up.

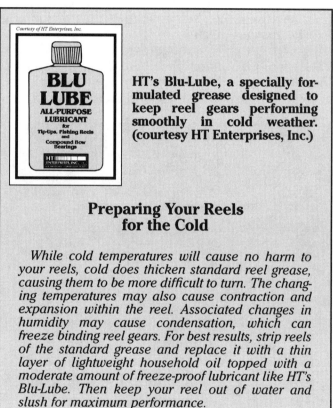

HT's Blu-Lube, a specially formulated grease designed to keep reel gears performing smoothly in cold weather. (courtesy HT Enterprises, Inc.)

Preparing Your Reels for the Cold

While cold temperatures will cause no harm to your reels, cold does thicken standard reel grease, causing them to be more difficult to turn. The changing temperatures may also cause contraction and expansion within the reel. Associated changes in humidity may cause condensation, which can freeze binding reel gears. For best results, strip reels of the standard grease and replace it with a thin layer of lightweight household oil topped with a moderate amount of freeze-proof lubricant like HT's Blu-Lube. Then keep your reel out of water and slush for maximum performance.

Team your rod with a premium quality baitcast or heavy duty spinning reel. You'll need a superstrong, extra-reliable drag system to land these fighting monsters consistently. Most baitcasting reels with quality star drags are adequate. In spinning, something along the order of Shimano's Fightin' Drag Systems are perfect, because you can easily adjust your drag from super light to super strong or vice versa with just one short, convenient motion.

When selecting line, spool with no less than 8-pound test monofilament. My personal preference is 12-pound test on spinning gear and 17-pound on baitcasting equipment–just remember, the thicker the line, the less natural your lure action will be and the slower your bait will drop. A short, single-strand wire leader and snap swivel also comes highly recommended to prevent bite-offs and line twist. But, go with high quality, thin wire leaders and make sure you use strong, high quality ball-bearing swivels.

Lures

Fast-moving, brightly colored baits such as Northland's Airplane jigs, Normark's Jigging Rapalas, large flash lures such as the Mepps Syclops, Bay de Noc Swedish Pimple, Do-Jigger or Vingla, Northland's Buck-Shot Rattle Spoon, vibrating blades such as Reef Runner's Cicada, or large tube jigs such as Creme's Super Tube tipped with a minnow are effective. Just be sure your hooks are needle sharp to maximize hooking percentages.

Keep in mind that choosing the proper lure isn't an easy task. Numerous effective lures exist in innumerable styles, sizes and a rainbow of colors with a variety of dressings and attractants. Some include wings, plastic strips, propellers, even sound chambers. All will catch pike. However, like walleye lures, pike lures basically fall into one of four primary classifications: swimming style baits, jigging spoons, plastics and standard leadheads. The key is learning to apply the right ones under the given situation.

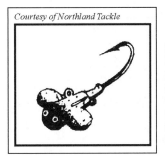

Courtesy of Northland Tackle

Swimming baits like Northland's Air Plane jig feature wings that cause them to swim in partial circles when jigged, allowing you to cover more water and attract more pike. (Courtesy Northland Tackle)

Swimming Minnows

Swimming style baits include jigging minnows like Normark's Jigging Rapala, Bad Dog's Humpback or Northland's Airplane Jig. These lures feature fins or wings that make them swing out and swim in a partial or full circle when jigged with high lifts followed by quick drops of the rod tip. They work well for especially aggressive pike. Just remember: the larger the lift, the larger the circle. Swimming style lures should always be tied directly with a strong knot such as the improved clinch or Trilene knot. Tip the center hook with a minnow head, or try a small plastic twist tail on the rear hook for added attraction. Pike love 'em.

Jigging Spoons

Jigging spoons include famous ice lures such as Bay de Noc's Swedish Pimple, Do-Jigger or Vingla, HT's Marmooska Spoon, Northland's Buck-Shot Rattle spoon, Acme's Kastmaster, Luhr Jensen's Krocodile and Mepps Syclops. These baits are jigged much like swimming lures, but instead of swimming to the side these lures flutter and flash as they fall vertically, producing a close imitation of a wounded minnow. They're best tied using a split ring attachment to facilitate maximum action. Just be sure to polish these to a spiffy shine, and don't hesitate to add reflector, glow or prism tape to add contrast. A shot of fish attractant never hurts either.

Plastics

Plastics are relatively new to the winter pike fishing scene. They include large tube jigs, plastic twist tails, creatures and worms. All are most often fished on various jigheads, but can also be tipped on a variety of swimming style lures or jigging baits. Tube jigs, for example, can be tipped on

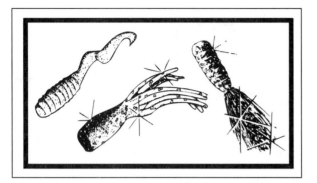

Plastics such as large tube jigs, plastic twist tails and bodies are relatively new to the winter pike scene. They are highly productive when fished on a variety of swimming lures, spoons and jigs, because they help slow the lure's fall, add natural texture and are available in a variety of colors.

a swimming style airplane jig. A tube body rigged on the rear hook helps slow these wide-swimming lures as they fall, plus it won't come off the hook nearly as easily as live bait when jigged.

This same concept also works with curly tail designs. The advantage of using a tube is that when a fish bites down on the plastic, the tube flattens against the hook shank, exposing the hook point and providing superior hooking qualities. To enhance this effect, try carefully bending your hook point up about five degrees. It helps! I even know some ice anglers who pack the tubes with pasty fish attractants or crushed minnows to add flavor pike can't seem to resist.

Tube jigs also make a unique addition to various sizes of jigging spoons such as Bay de Noc's Swedish Pimple, HT's Marmooska Spoon, Bait Rigs' Willow Spoon or Custom Jigs and Spins' Stinger. Many of these spoons actually fit inside some tube designs, allowing the tube to form a sheath around the lure body. Essentially, this slows the fall of the spoon, plus adds a hint of contrasting color, a more natural feel and subdued flash, which can be a powerful combination for pike.

Securing Plastics

When fishing plastics for pike, grasp your lure or hook with a long nose pliers and heat it with a match or lighter before slipping the plastic on. The plastic will melt and conform to the hook, resulting in a firmer hold.

Leadheads

Leadheads are simply standard lead-head jigs. The advantage of using leadheads is you can add as much or little action as you want. You can fish light, plain leadheads with just small minnows and a gentle jigging motion for fussy, shallow water "snake" pike, or tempt large, deep-water trophies with larger, heavier, gaudier swimming versions tipped with plastic action tails or large minnows worked aggressively. Leadheads work best when tied with loop knots to help maximize action.

Other jigging options include dead bait rigs, where a double-hook rig is inserted into a dead minnow. The hook farthest up your leader is hooked just behind the bait's dorsal fin, the other just behind the head. This method is best used after a pike strikes a jigging lure and is missed. In such cases, if the fish is still present, it will often strike the minnow.

Regardless of which lure you choose, cover all water in the vertical spectrum, starting just beneath the ice and working right down to bottom in intervals, allowing each hole 10 or 15 minutes to

When securing plastics to your lure or hook, heat the hook before adding the plastic. The plastic will melt down resulting in a firmer hold.

be sure the area is covered. Experiment with a variety of lures, sizes, colors and motions. If you don't get a hit after 15 minutes, try another hole. Active pike usually don't mess around. Mobility is the primary benefit of jigging, so take advantage of the opportunity being presented. Often, the action will be fast when you're on pike. Then, after an hour or so, things will calm down. At this point, move to another area and return later, after the spot has settled down.

Other Considerations

Style, size, weight and color are all primary considerations when fishing any lure, so always experiment. Each of the above lures work wonders given specific conditions, and it pays to try a variety of combinations—but try to choose lure sizes, profiles and actions that best simulate the primary forage of the pike in your waters under the given conditions. In deeper or darker waters, for example, heavier, larger, gaudier baits sink faster, offer larger profiles and more visible colors pike can use to track your lure, while in clear or shallow water, smaller, slower falling, more natural colors seem to produce best.

If you're getting short strikes, try stinger hooks. Stinger hooks, rigged by running a short length of heavy monofilament to a smaller treble hook pinned near the tail of your minnow, can be helpful for turning short strikes into hooked fish. One trick here: if using dead bait, try using a small, sharp knife to scale the bait and remove its backbone. This allows the bait to "swim" and flutter with a more natural, life-like motion. Tipping your

Style, size, weight and color are all primary considerations when fishing any lure for pike, so always experiment.

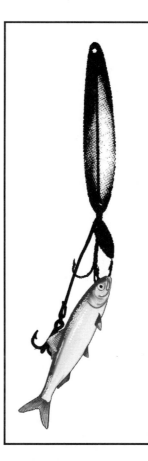

Where legal, stinger hooks, rigged by running a short length of heavy monofilament to a small treble hook pinned near the tail of your minnow, can be helpful for turning short strikes into hooked fish.

jigs with a touch of fish scent or attractant is also a good idea. Some anglers add a touch of pork rind to their plastic presentation for enhanced natural texture, taste, scent and action.

Also be sure to spend some time considering what you're trying to imitate. If you discover the pike's primary prey on your lake is comprised of 3-inch perch, fish with lures and jigs that look like 3-inch perch. If their primary forage is 6-inch ciscoes, fish with 6-inch silver or white lures, or use jigs with white or light-colored plastic tippers. And remember, if aggressively worked larger lures aren't producing, try smaller ones and work them more gingerly. No matter what presentation you choose, frequently inspect your line, leaders and knots for kinks or frays and keep your hooks ultra-sharp. You'll be glad you did when a pike strikes.

Setting the Hook

When you feel a strike, set the hook solidly, and keep your rod positioned high. This will allow you more time to react should the fish make a long, sudden run. Secondly, be prepared to tighten your drag and control runs by "back reeling." Never hurry a pike at the hole. Rather, maintain firm pressure to guide the fish up as it tires, then turn its head into the hole and let it swim up to you.

Selective Jigging

Jigging for pike is a definite winter thrill. One of the nicest things about it is that you can be somewhat selective about the size of the fish you catch. When tip-up fishing selectively, you can use larger minnows for larger pike. You'll catch fewer fish overall, but quality will replace quantity.

Likewise when jigging. Use a larger lure, and you'll likely replace quantity with quality.

But if you'd like to catch lots of pike, those cooperative, overabundant "hammer-handle" pike are very accommodating to smaller jigging minnows and flash lures. These fish can be terrific fun on light tackle. Light-action panfish or walleye ice rods function well. Combined with a light graphite spinning reel spooled with 4- to 6-pound monofilament and a small jigging spoon, you'll find no greater winter challenge. It's also not a bad idea to cut the first 12 inches of line off after every fish to avoid line breakage. Also, carry an extra spool wound with fresh line, so that if your line twists or is damaged extensively, your fishing can continue with little interruption.

Trophy-minded individuals should use larger lures and heavier tackle. A longer, 4- or 5- foot heavy power, medium-heavy action spinning combo rigged with 12-pound test is adequate, and stiff casting rods with slight tip action, rigged with a reliable baitcast reel and 14- to 20-pound test would not be impractical, unless you're fishing from a portable shelter. In deep water, non-stretch lines such as Fireline help fit the bill with this type of fishing, but you'll have to go with a medium action, medium power rod or you'll hear line snapping echoes akin to thunder. Either way, jigging for pike is pure sport and something few ice anglers seem to be capitalizing on.

One last note: Where legal, live bait rigs can also be jigged—smaller minnows for small and average sized pike, larger minnows for larger fish. A dead smelt, cisco, sucker or shiner set on special "quick-strike" rigs or "quick-set" harnesses are also effective, and help promote mouth-hooking for proponents of catch and release.

Jigging pike is a definite winter thrill.

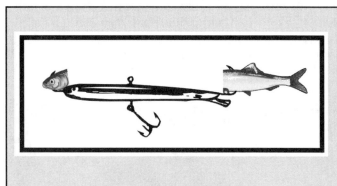

The Cut Sucker Trick

Professional ice angler Wil Wegman says jigging minnows are great lures for pike, but insists that (where legal) cutting a semi-frozen sucker, chub, smelt or cisco in half and placing the head over the front of a large jigging minnow and tail over the rear hook works wonders. "Just work this with a natural, lifelike presentation somewhat slower than you normally would, even letting it sit on bottom once in awhile, pausing frequently. Pike love it," claims Wegman.

Catch and Release

Recent studies have shown large pike are especially vulnerable during winter. Using effective techniques such as those discussed here can harm pike populations when too many fish are taken. However, recent studies have also indicated that lip-hooked winter pike are excellent candidates for release. Since 90 percent of the pike caught while jigging aren't seriously hooked, selective catch and release is a reliable means of selective harvest.

Gently handle fish to be released. Don't touch them with dry hands or gloves as this removes the fish's layer of protective slime. Instead, use wet hands or dampened neoprene gloves. Hold pike carefully behind the head, while keeping as much of its body in the hole as possible to avoid slime removal or damage to the fish. While maintaining a firm grip, gently remove the hooks with a long nose pliers or hook remover. Lift the fish carefully for a photo if you like—by the belly is best—then immediately return the fish, head first, back into the hole, letting the fish swim away under its own power.

One more note: If the weather is extremely cold, make this process fast. A pike's eyes are susceptible to freezing, causing blindness; and frozen gill tissue results in a loss of surface area for the fish to obtain oxygen. Both of these reduce the fish's chance for survival.

Studies have shown lip-hooked winter pike are excellent candidates for release, just be sure to handle the fish carefully and don't subject their eyes and gills to prolonged periods of extreme cold.

Understanding Pickerel During the Winter

This smaller cousin of the northern pike sports similar habits to Northern Pike, but are a different species and may be found occupying different ecological niches in most bodies of water.

For the most part, pickerel are a shallow, quiet water, weed-oriented species thriving in moderately vegetated lakes and sloughs. Chain pickerel—the most commonly caught winter pickerel—are the smallest member of the pike family. Like pike, they have flat, beak-like jaws and feed primary on minnows. Unlike pike, they are thin, slender fish seldom attaining double digit weights. I've never seen a 10-pound pickerel. Such a fish would be a trophy of record status. A 5- or 6-pounder would be considered a trophy by many, although pickerel averaging 20 to 30 inches aren't uncommon catches in some environments.

The chain pickerel, a smaller cousin of the northern pike, sports similar habits to the northern pike, but is often found shallower and isn't as likely to move as much or as often. (photo courtesy Frank Fischer)

Primary Winter Location Patterns

For the most part, pickerel hold shallower than pike. Finding fish in more than 10 feet of water is rare, but finding them holding in less than 5 feet is fairly common. Pickerel also tend to move very little throughout the season. If they do, it is only for short distances to hunt for food or shelter. So, if you find a good hole, stick it out and fish it repeatedly throughout the season. Unless some dramatic change occurs in the environment or weather it will mostly likely continue to produce. The only exception to this would be in lakes or ponds in which the shallows reach very low oxygen counts. In such cases, pickerel may move into deeper water, say 12 to 15 feet. But again, they seldom move farther than they have to.

Like pike, pickerel tend to be most active during the day.

Effective Winter Fishing Strategies

Since pickerel are so closely related to pike, fishing methods are similar. Tip-ups rigged with minnows are highly effective. Since pickerel are smaller, you can go lighter. This is a good idea anyway, as I've found pickerel to be more fussy than their larger relatives, so simple things such as using lighter leaders can be good practice. Most ice anglers also use smaller minnows, although pickerel are certainly capable of ingesting larger baits if you wish to pursue a trophy.

My preference for catching pickerel, however, is jigging. Because of their generally small size, they aren't very exciting to catch on tip-ups, but the challenge of jigging these fish with relatively light tackle, small to mid-sized jigging spoons, plastics, bladebaits and larger teardrops can provide hours of fun and challenge.

Try a fast action, medium power ice rod rigged with a spinning reel and 6-pound monofilament. You'll have the time of your life experiencing true sport, especially if you're fortunate enough to hook into a 6- or 7-pound fish.

Since pickerel are so closely related to northern pike, fishing methods are similar. (photo courtesy Frank Fischer)

Chapter 6
Understanding Lake Trout/Splake in Winter

At 6 a.m. on a dark, frigid December morning I cast frosty shadows in the glow of a Coleman lantern. The sharp blades of my power auger shave away at ice covering 150 feet of water. The loud drone shatters the early morning silence.

As I make sure the hole in a long series is cleared I kill the engine. Immediately, silence consumes the last echo of the motor. I stand alone, enveloped in dark, quiet shadows on a vast, frozen lake. In the distance, I see two tiny beams of light. One is Mike, holding a flashlight as he is busy skimming ice shards from my long trail of holes. The other is Terry, setting tip-ups by lantern. With time to spare, I pour a cup of hot chocolate and sip the smooth, sweet liquid, shivers tingling down my spine with each draw. Patience doesn't come easy. These waters are known for producing trophy lake trout, and an anxious twinge of anticipation aches at my insides.

I live for this. Why? Lake trout offer it all. Mystery. Adventure. Challenge. Excitement. The chance for trophy fish. For these reasons and more, ice fishing lakers has become a legend rich with deep-rooted tradition. This heritage has also led to established, age-old tactics and techniques. While many of these methods are as effective now as they were then, new generations, learning from the basics taught them by their forefathers, are rebelling and trying something new. They are different. Innovative, if you will. And their methods have proven effective. Although time-proven tactics still work, they aren't always best. Today, more effective methods exist.

But first, the fish. If you read the preface to this book, you may remember the story about my Swedish friend. He became anxious when I told him about North America's giant lake trout, and I invited him to come fish these monsters that often attained double-digit weights. Getting off the plane in Toronto, his eyes blazed with enthusiasm. He wanted to catch one of these huge mystery fish. He'd never seen a lake trout and was curious about this "exotic" species.

The next day as I iced my first laker, his jaw dropped. "That's a char!" he exclaimed, surprised. Right he was. The fish we commonly call lake trout are really char, not a trout. Even so, this fine winter sport fish is worthy foe. They grow slow, but big. Double-digit fish aren't unusual, and fish of 30, 40, even 50 pounds have been caught through the ice.

Lake Trout

While most people believe lake trout are fish residing only in deep, cold, dark bottoms of seemingly bottomless oligotrophic lakes, this is a stereotype largely created by summer anglers. It's true lakers live near the bottom of these lakes. They hold deep in summer when temperatures in the shallows and upper strata are too warm for their liking. In winter, temperature and oxygen counts are more uniform, and given the right conditions involving cover and forage, lakers often hold much shallower.

Lake trout can be identified by light spots on greenish light to dark steel gray sides and a deeply forked tail. They feed on crustaceans, insects and baitfish, and while oily, lake trout meat is highly regarded as a good table fare.

Lake trout feature light spots on a greenish to light gray background and a deeply forked tail.

Splake feature worm-like markings along the top side of their body and usually lack the lake trout's deeply forked tail. (courtesy Wisconsin D.N.R.)

Splake

Splake, a cross between a female lake trout and male brook trout, grow much more quickly comparatively, but are less fertile. They feature light spots, distinct worm-like markings on top and usually lack the lake trout's characteristically deeply forked tail. Splake are mainly stocked with "put and take" fishing in mind and will inhabit virtually the same waters as lake trout. Splake are often confused for lake trout by unknowing anglers as lakers.

Like lake trout, splake are predominantly deep-water fish but are more likely to suspend. They feed primarily on insect larvae, crustaceans and baitfish, and are regarded as good table fare.

Primary Winter Lake Trout Location Patterns

Since lake trout and splake feature such similar location preferences and tendencies, we'll treat them as one when referring to specific patterns. I'll use the term lake trout to describe both species.

While winter lake trout are typically active, they can be downright fussy. No matter their mood, they tend to move—often and far. They may hold deep or in mid-depth regions. In waters where forage is abundant, competition from other fish is nil and fishing pressure negligible, they may even hold relatively shallow.

However, let's begin with location basics learned from our mentors: Lakers roam in deep, cold waters and open spaces. Most of us were also taught that lakers inhabit the deepest parts of a lake, holding on the bottom near steep, sharp breaks. While I agree that lakers have an inherently strong desire to be near the bottom and a tendency to roam, it has been my experience, the deep, sharp breaks and open space characteristics don't always apply, especially with splake,

Since lake trout roam, locating them can be challenging. Using a strategic plan, they provide excellent winter action.

channels between these features act as migration routes trout follow from deep to mid-depth water, where lakers forage on perch, smelt, ciscos, whitefish or other baitfish.

As for sunken islands, sharp-breaking main lake structures aren't nearly as productive as many anglers believe. Rather, gradually breaking reefs close to deep water are more likely to hold baitfish and consequently, trout. This is why tapering saddles and channels between mid-depth breaks, reefs and points are so important. They're natural four-lane baitfish migration routes which are sud-

that may hold shallow or suspend. Yes, lakers prefer cold water and are easily forced toward the bottom and the deep, cold climes during summer. In winter, however, cold temperatures dominate the entire lake. Lakers are free. Loving to roam, and given the opportunity to leave restricted areas in search of food, they take advantage of the situation. I know, because I've iced winter lakers from water less than 35 feet deep.

This isn't to say winter lakers never go deep. They do. But they also suspend, inhabit classic mid-depth structural features and even roam mid-depth flats where few ice anglers fish. Innovative anglers not locked into stereotypical mind sets can experience fabulous catches in just such areas.

Why? Again, winter water temperatures aren't restrictive. Furthermore, plankton counts are higher in shallower water, consequently, schools of concentrated baitfish feeding on plankton are there and you can bet lakers won't be far away. Since lakers feed actively, getting them to bite usually isn't a problem.

Still, because lakers roam, locating them can be challenging. To achieve consistent catches, anglers must use systematic, organized approaches and focus their efforts in high-percentage areas.

The System

Start by reviewing hydrographic maps of your water, looking for productive structure. Expansive, mid-depth, hard-bottom flats. Points, sunken islands and any tapering saddles, troughs and turns adjoining them are all prime. Deep, lengthy

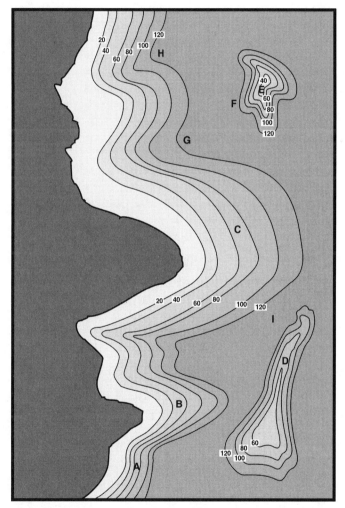

During first ice, mid-depth humps (E), points (C) and bars (D) offering a migration route or saddle running shallow to deep are highly productive lake trout locations. The same areas will produce mid-winter, although deeper, main-lake saddles (I) and shoreline or structural turns near main-lake flats (G, H), and steep walls (A) are normally better. Lakers may also scatter on deep, mid-depth flats. Finding them consistently requires a combination of skilled sonar use and mobility.

denly narrowed to two-way traffic. This constriction concentrates baitfish and trout. The more of these features you find together, the better. Long, gradually sloping mid-depth points separating deep water from expansive, mid-depth flats are especially good. The same feature adjoining a sunken hump or reef connected by deep, tapering saddles extending from these features to deep water would offer even better potential, because the combination provides good structure, natural migration routes and gathering areas for forage.

Just remember, the term "mid-depth" is relative. Lakers and their preferred forage bases are traditionally deep-water fish, often occupying depths of 200 feet or more. The most productive "mid-depth" lake trout structures typically range from 25 to 85 feet. You may have to go deeper or shallower, depending where the largest concentrations of baitfish are holding. Move in search of them.

After you've marked high-percentage areas on your map, use sonar to pinpoint the secondary structural features lakers are using, and precisely where active fish are holding. If you find fish and have a GPS, save these locations as waypoints, and outline them with saved plotter trails. This way, you can return to the exact same spots with just the press of a button.

Unfortunately, many lake trout anglers, relying on tradition, head for steep walls, drill a hole or two and sit there. Granted, steep banks are potential hot spots. But in today's world of increased fishing pressure, these traditional areas typically hold large numbers of anglers, and smaller numbers of trout. Don't spend too much time fishing one deep, highly pressured area. Move around, exploring other high-percentage structures for secondary features. Now, onto seasonal movements.

First-Ice

Lake trout are typically active at first ice. They move a lot and often. Consequently, mobility and cutting a lot of holes is a key to consistent catches.

Start by fishing mid-depth humps, points and large, hard-bottom flats. If you are on Great Lakes bays, the edges of dredged shipping channels ranging from about 25-50 feet deep. Find a grouping of such structures in one area with a deep migration route leading from deep water toward these mid-depth structures, and you're even better off. A large, shoreline point running from a

large, 15- to 35-foot shoal into a 60-foot trough is perfect. Add an extra hump and an island or two all separated by this deep channel, and you've really got something. Not only can you fish a variety of structure efficiently here, but you can do it without the challenges of working excessively deep water. Fishing 25- to 50-feet deep, you can drop reasonably weighted lures or baits down faster and work each hole in half the time of anglers fishing 50 to 100 feet.

Again: The biggest mistake most first-ice lake trout anglers make is fishing too deep, too fast, and not using a mobile enough approach. On relatively quiet, waters with less pressure, anglers should look for places where 25- to 50-foot depths intercept main-lake basin structures such as points, humps, bars off mid-lake islands and even flats. Then gradually move shallower until fish are found. Often, anglers are surprised when they catch big lakers this "shallow." Don't be. With perch, ciscos, sculpin, crayfish and other forage available, lakers will move in to feed. And remember, since fishing these mid-depth ranges doesn't pose the difficulty of fishing hundreds of feet deep,

The biggest mistake most first-ice lake trout anglers make is fishing too deep, too fast, and not using a mobile approach.

By mid-winter, expect lake trout to move toward deeper, main-lake saddles and troughs, especially those leading from mid-depth structures toward deep, main-lake basins.

you can fish more easily, cover water more efficiently and use somewhat lighter gear.

Why do lakers hold shallow at first ice? Again, water temperatures and oxygen concentrations are more conducive to freer movement. Provided food and cover are available, inter-species competition isn't great and fishing pressure isn't heavy, there's no reason for lake trout not to move shallow. Drill lots of holes and cover water. You'll eventually find fish.

Mid-Winter

By mid-winter, these same multi-structural areas will continue to produce if forage remains available. Otherwise, expect a movement of fish towards deeper, main-lake saddles and troughs, especially those leading from mid-depth structures toward deep, main-lake basins. Sloping drops leading from mid-depth structures into deep holes are also good. Even traditional, steep-breaking walls will hold mid-winter fish, but these fish are likely to suspend. Some lake trout

will also spread over deep, mid-lake flats, but they're more difficult to locate and harder to work efficiently. I recommend trying mid-depth options and channels first, before moving in search of suspended fish on steep breaks or scattered fish of the flats.

This isn't to say most active mid-season lakers won't relate to mid-depth structures. It's just that they tend to relate more to traditional deep, main-lake flats, breaks, bluffs, steep shoreline walls and holes, especially on heavily fished waters. I'll usually start around 50 feet and work down, fishing more traditionally in terms of depth, but still spending time looking for structure, bottom configurations, secondary cover and forage that may hold fish. Obviously, whether fishing shallow or deep, using lake maps and electronics will help pattern mid-winter lakers. Electronics will play increasingly important roles the deeper you go.

Just don't forget, seldom, if ever, will you find an entire population of fish relating to the same pattern at the same time. This is especially true when dealing with roaming species like lake trout. As a smart angler, your goal should be to identify the best combination of depth, structure, cover and forage. Often, on lakes not receiving excessive pressure, even mid-winter, this will be in mid-depth ranges of 25 to 85 feet. Experiment, be mobile, be versatile, and above all, be patient. You'll catch fish.

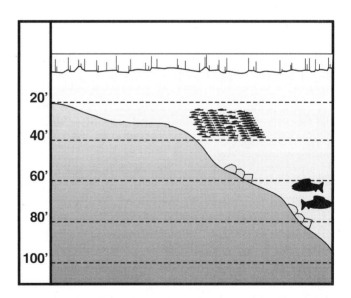

During late-ice, as baitfish move shallow, lake trout often follow, moving up migration routes leading from deep saddles onto mid-depth and shallow structural features and flats.

Late-Ice

Late in the winter, as ciscos, smelt, perch and other baitfish start to move shallow, lake trout often follow. They begin moving up deep troughs and saddles onto mid-depth and shallow structural features and flats, making them somewhat easier to find. Where the season remains open, work the edges of these areas using a mobile, fast-moving approach to search for concentrations of baitfish and active, willing biters.

Timing

As with any species, lakers have their most active times. While first-ice tends to offer the best lake trout action, they bite throughout the winter. On a daily basis, early mornings are typically the most productive, with the first three hours of light being my favorite time to fish. I like to arrive in potential areas well before sun-up, ready to fish by first light—especially during periods of relatively warm, stable, clear weather. Late afternoon may also offer secondary flurries of activity. Depending on water clarity and how deep you're fishing lakers can be caught all day long.

Effective Winter Fishing Strategies

Historically, winter lake trout presentation has been comprised largely of bobbing—a primitive, but highly effective tactic for catching deep-water lakers. Anglers saunter out in traditional fishing areas, drill a couple holes, plunk down, and drop 1-ounce lures on lengths of dacron wrapped around short bobbing sticks. Then they wait for fish. In my home state of Wisconsin, bobbing on Lake Superior near the Apostle Islands has accounted for thousands of lakers over the years, and the tradition continues today. But anglers on the cutting edge have broke tradition and brought some innovations.

Traditional equipment for ice fishing lakers, like location patterns, is largely outdated. Workable, but outdated. Don't get me wrong, bobbing sticks wrapped with dacron catch lake trout. It's just that modern rods ranging from 18- to 60-inches long are better. They offer flexibility and versatility, so you can present and work a wider variety of lures with more control. Plus, with new technology in line development, they help provide more sensitivity, better lure control and help keep tight lines when setting the hook and bringing thrashing lakers to the ice. But first, today's tip-ups.

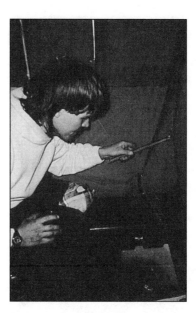

In my home state of Wisconsin, bobbing on Lake Superior has accounted for thousands of lakers over the years. This tradition continues today.

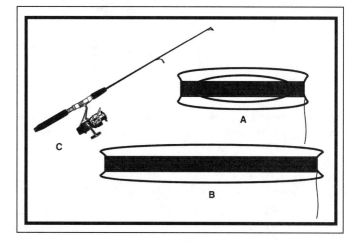

Traditionally, lake trout have been fished with "bobbing sticks" wrapped with dacron line. While these are still used, today's heavy-power spinning ice rods ranging from 18 to 60 inches featuring quality spinning reels and low-stretch lines are seeing increased popularity.

Tip-Ups

Where multiple lines and the use of minnows for lake trout are legal, "Deep-Lake" underwater tip-ups with large spools, like HT's PTU-5 or PTU-10 Polar make good additional lines and increase your chances of catching finicky fish. Set your rigs on the bottom over flats to catch bottom cruisers. Or suspend them just below the ice to catch high-riders. Either way, play "leap frog" with your tip-ups as you move. Don't allow tip-ups to jeopardize your mobility.

Where multiple lines and the use of minnows for lake trout are legal practices, large-spooled tip-ups like HT's PTU-10 "Deep Lake" Polar make good additional lines for increasing your chances of catching finicky fish.

Courtesy of HT Enterprises, Inc.

Where multiple lines and the use of minnows are legal, large-spooled tip-ups such as HT's "Deep Lake" Polar make good additional lines for increasing winter lake trout catches. (courtesy HT Enterprises, Inc.)

Remember, the keys to consistent success are mobility, drilling lots of holes in high-percentage locations, then quickly trying to locate active fish by thoroughly fishing depths from bottom to top. Covering water is the name of the game, and while deep water and currents often make using anything but traditional bobbing sticks difficult, fishing large live or dead minnows suspended beneath large-spooled, tip-ups creates effective secondary lines for many bobbers.

Rigging

Underwater Polars or large-spooled thermal tip-ups like HT's PTT-50 Polar Therm rigged with 30-pound dacron and a length of spectra or heavy monofilament will do. Large, 6- or 8-inch lake shiners, chubs or suckers—large, tough, lively baits—lowered with a great deal of weight rigged in a slip-weight fashion, help reach the depths and draw fish in the deep, dark waters. While underwater currents may occasionally lift baits out of the pro-

Where legal, fishing minnows beneath large-spooled tip-ups creates an effective series of secondary lines for many bobbers.

ductive fishing zone, when currents slow or change direction during the day, these baits will drop, allowing fish to be caught.

When conditions allow, maggot-packed or minnow belly-tipped spoons fished below Windlass tip-ups can also be productive. You'll need to use hole covers, or ice and blowing snow will likely plug up holes and ruin the jigging action.

While neither tip-up method produces unusually fast action, because wandering lakers tend to scatter on immense, deep structures and flats, the chance for a trophy and enough action with intermediate fish offers enough action to keep people coming back for more. The rest of the time, most people try bobbing or jigging.

Jigging

While tip-ups and traditional bobbing methods catch fish, a revolution is occurring that's rocking this world of tradition. You'll now see modern anglers jigging in portable shacks hole-hopping every 15 minutes to half hour, using lake

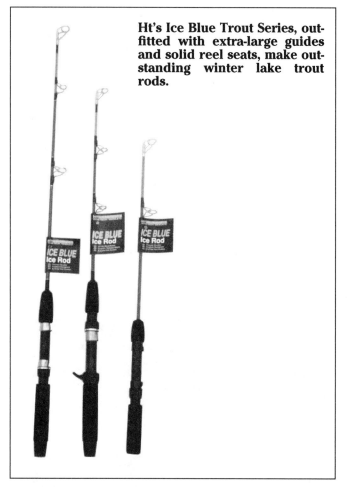

Ht's Ice Blue Trout Series, outfitted with extra-large guides and solid reel seats, make outstanding winter lake trout rods.

Jigging with modern spinning combos and low-stretch lines is becoming more popular each year. Many traditional bobbers are trying these new deep-water methods with outstanding success.

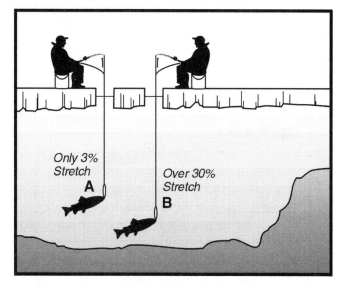

Standard monofilament stretches approximately 30%, while today's low-stretch Spectra, Kevlar and Micro Dyneema lines stretch only about 3%. This results in less of a "rubber band" effect, allowing greater sensitivity for feeling hits and transfer of more power for solid hook sets.

maps and sonar to search for structural features funneling baitfish, and hence lakers, into specific areas.

Start with medium-heavy action rods and quality reels spooled with braided dacron, Kevlar, Spectra (TM) and Micro-Dyneema style lines, or you'll end up with a lot of missed fish, broken lines, perhaps even a broken rod. This system requires exactness in order to be efficient.

Most "outside" anglers jig with 3-foot to 5-foot heavy-action, medium-power, fiberglass or graphite composite ice rods such as HT's IBT-34 or IBT-44 Ice Blues. These are outfitted with special, extra-large, durable guides to resist the Spectra (TM) and large, baitcast reels spooled with an 8-pound to 12-pound Kevlar (TM), Spectra (TM) or Micro Dyneema (TM), which all offer very thin diameter for their strength. This allows anglers to get deep fast without compromising strength. They also have a minimal amount of stretch. This allows plenty of control over a large, heavy presentation. "Inside" shanty anglers usually fish 18-28" heavy action rods like HT's IBT-24 Ice Blue teamed with a large-spooled spinning or baitcast reel and the same lines,

Berkley Fireline, a small diameter, low-stretch line, is perfect for improving sensitivity and hook-setting power when jigging deep water lake trout. (Courtesy Berkley/OTG)

Berkley Fireline

Fireline is a small-diameter, no-stretch line made of Micro Dyneema (R). The material more than 25 percent stronger than Spectra offering little memory when stretched and fabulous knot strength even with standard knots. It is easier to handle than Spectra and is perfect for improving sensitivity in deep-water lake trout jigging applications. Fireline won't absorb water, reducing freeze-up.

Kevlar, Spectra, Dyneema Lines

These small-diameter, low-stretch lines are great for deep lake trout jigging applications, but can be hard to spool because they tend to slip around reel hubs. To prevent this problem, consider taping your line to the reel arbor before you begin spooling, and wrap your line tightly when spooling.

In terms of reels, bait casting reels offer more leverage when fishing for trophy lakers, but they do fish heavy and can be tiresome if you jig with them all day. (Courtesy JWA)

although no-stretch leadcore is a great bet with baitcast systems, too.

In terms of reels, baitcasting reels offer leverage when fighting trophy fish. However, they're heavy, and their bulkiness may catch up with you by day's end. Spinning reels feature less leverage, but are lighter and more comfortable to fish. The choice is yours, but for most applications, I prefer level-wind baitcast reels spooled with no-stretch Fireline or leadcore line and monofilament leaders. Leadcore helps get baits down and allows solid hook sets. On spinning reels, Berkley's Micro Dyneema Fireline performs very well—just make sure your rod has enough bend to absorb the shock of hard hits. Fireline features little stretch. It's a good idea to use leaders of 8- to 10-pound monofilament "shock absorbers" attached via a #10 ball-bearing swivel. If you're in water offering a shot at trophy fish or you want your lure to work more slowly, try 12- or 14-pound monofilament leaders.

Lake Trout Lures

As for lures, you won't need a massive selection. Since you'll be fishing mostly from 20 to 80 feet in heavy current, heavy lures that sink fast are most efficient. Larger blade baits, such as Reef Runner's - ounce Cicada, are good options, but perform best when fish are exceptionally active. Work them with periodic, short upward thrusts—just be careful not to overwork them. Too much action may spook your quarry. I recommend frequent pauses and gentle jigging motions between lifts. A touch of phosphorescent color or live bait on the center hook is also recommended.

Heavy jigging spoons like larger Swedish Pimples or Stingers can also be effective, provided current is minimal. Tip them with your favorite bait, drop the rig to bottom, slowly raise it a foot, pause, drop and repeat. Use occasional sharp lifting motions, then drop your rod tip abruptly, allowing the bait to settle. After a pause, shimmer the lure by gently shaking your rod tip. Your mission is to draw the fish's attention, then provoke it to strike. Concentrate now. If at anytime you feel a strike, tap or line hesitation, set the hook.

When lake trout are fussy, you'll receive lighter strikes. In such cases, work your baits gingerly, pausing longer and more often between lifts. Always

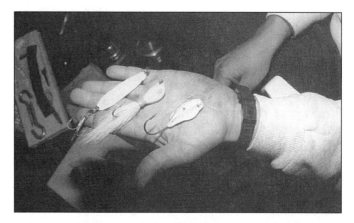

Three outstanding lake trout lures, the Lake Superior "Beetle," Northland's Sting'r Bucktail, and a large, heavy, Bay de Noc Swedish Pimple.

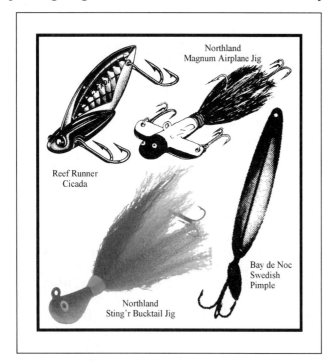

Popular lake trout lures include Reef Runner's -ounce Cicada, Northland's 1- or 2- ounce Sting'r Bucktails, or 1 -ounce Air Plane jigs, and Bay de Noc's 1 5/8- or 2- ounce Swedish Pimples.

Too many lake trout anglers spend too much time fishing directly on the bottom. Raise your bait several feet off the bottom and work your way up. Active lakers will often follow the lure and strike high. (Courtesy Northland Tackle)

To jig lakers, drop your lure to the bottom and pump it several times, pausing between lifts. If nothing happens, raise the lure 15 feet and repeat. Do this all the way to the surface, then work the jig back down in 10-foot intervals to bottom. Lake trout may strike at any depth from bottom to directly under the ice.

When lake trout are striking light, try fishing slightly smaller lures and baits, working them slowly at various depths.

be alert for changes in "feel" before repeating the action—a fish may be mouthing your lure. If this is the case, allow the fish to move off at a slight angle before setting the hook. Hooks are set deeper and more solidly if you set as light-striking fish are moving away.

Large, heavy bucktail or flat-bottom swimming jigs tipped with cut bait are also excellent—just make sure your hooks are sharp or you'll miss fish. Ditto for heavy airplane jigs, especially if you're marking suspended, active fish on your sonar. Tip these baits with plastic twist tails or tubes, a strip of sucker belly or flat-sided shiner—all of which cause the lure to fall slowly and swim in wider circles. Drop the jig down, free-lining it under slight tension, allowing the jig to circle as it falls. Concentrate now, lakers have a tendency to nab these baits on the drop.

If there is no strike, wait until your jig hits bottom, then lift and slowly pump it a few times, pausing between lifts, reeling up 10 to 15 feet and repeating the motion until you mark fish or discover a strike zone. If nothing happens, pause at the surface and repeat the procedure, this time dropping the jig down in 10-foot intervals, then repeating the same pattern.

Large tube jigs have merit, too. Just be sure to leave the head of the plastic stretched beyond the concealed jig head. This way, the lure will work with the swimming motion lakers love when gently jigged. You can also fill the tube with fish attractant or cut bait for extra power. Or, if you wish, use a flavor-enhanced plastic tube.

For even better results, try combining two of these methods. Slip a tube body on an airplane jig, for example, and start by working your lure to the bottom of one hole, then let it sit. Often, lakers will pick the motionless bait right off the bottom. If not, freespool the reel and go to a second hole with another rod to do the same thing before returning to check the first. You'll be surprised how often you'll see your line gliding away.

While lake trout are typically aggressive winter fish, like any species, they have fussy moments. At times, you can try a variety of traditional lake trout lures and come up empty handed—meaning you'll have to try something different. Start by going lighter. A sensitive spinning combo spooled with 10-pound test Fireline is good for starters. To maximize success, try fishing slightly smaller lures and baits, working them slowly at various depths.

If this doesn't work, you'll have to go even lighter—say 8-pound test—and be innovative. First, shatter the illusion lakers feed strictly on minnows. Yes, baitfish are primary targets, but lake trout also feed on crustaceans. Freshwater shrimp, for example, are an important part of the laker's diet. They love 'em. And when trout are fussy, placing a shrimp in front of their face will often trigger strikes when nothing else will.

A simple rig that effectively imitates shrimp—and consistently catches lakers in tough conditions—consists of a #5 ball-bearing swivel with a 2-foot monofilament leader tipped with a #8 three-way swivel. Tie a 3-foot monofilament leader tipped with a 1-ounce bell sinker to the bottom ring, and to the middle, an 18-inch leader of 8-pound test leading to a large-hooked light-weight ice jig tipped with live bait—or better yet, a shrimp-imitating streamer. The rig can be worked at any depth, and provided it's worked slowly to avoid tangles, is highly effective because light striking lakers can easily suck the virtually weightless streamer into their mouths

without a great deal of effort. Odds are you can drop down to them and get bit fairly quickly. If you don't, move. A mobile approach stacks the odds in your favor.

A good method with this system is to take turns, having one member of your party check for fish with sonar, another following to cut holes, and three others fishing different rigs, working efficiently from hole to hole. Favored lures for the first angler include heavy airplane jigs, jigging spoons, blade baits, large, heavy bucktail swimming jigs, tube jigs, or rattle baits—these will nab active fish. Hooks should be sharpened with the care of a muskie addict preparing to catch the trophy of a lifetime. Even though you're fishing deep with heavy tackle and no-stretch lines, your line is likely to bow in deep, under-ice currents, and you'll need

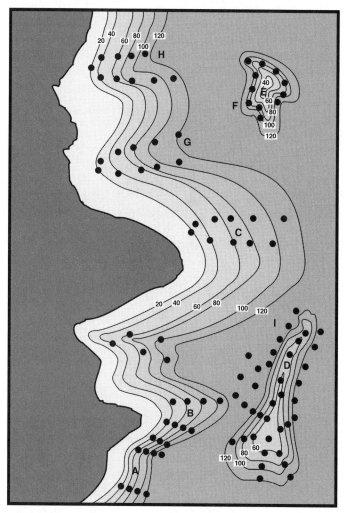

When fishing lakers on big water, focus your hole-drilling along the edges of structure. Try to drill directly over potential migration routes along primary structures in order to pattern the fish.

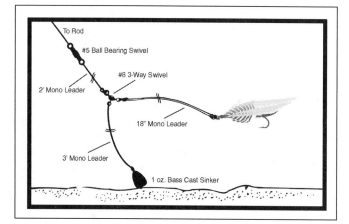

The shrimp rig: A good design for light-striking lakers that can easily inhale the almost weightless streamer.

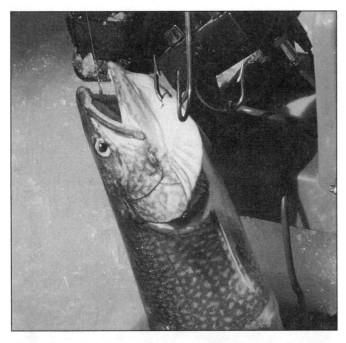

There's a special, mystical quality about ice fishing Great Lakes lake trout that intrigues many winter anglers.

all the help you can get. These lures can be tipped with live minnows, pork rind or carefully cut strips of minnow belly. The second angler should then follow with a soft plastic presentation, and a third with the streamer presentation.

Once set up, move often, taking turns drilling holes and fishing in fresh holes to cover water, leap-frogging from spot to spot along primary locations. In each hole it's best to drop your lure down being mindful that lakers may pick up the bait as it's dropping. If the lure makes it down without a strike, start fishing on bottom, then gradually fish upward in 5- or 10-foot intervals until you reach the ice. Lake trout will often follow a lure right up to the hole. If nothing happens, lower the lure again in the same manner as before.

If a fish strikes but misses, pull your lure away fast and start reeling. Lakers will often chase it down and strike. If not, repeat the process two or three times, but no more than a half hour per hole in an attempt to draw strikes. If you have nothing after 30 minutes, move along. When someone eventually hooks a fish, one person should help land the fish, while another gets a second lure or minnow down quickly. Often, one thrashing lake trout will draw another, turning one catch into a quick double. Just be sure to check your local regulations regarding use of live minnows. The practice is restricted in many lake trout waters.

Finally, since winter lake trout are primarily caught from Great Lakes bays or deep, inland oligotrophic lakes and pits, location and presentation patterns are distinct. Trying to capture the feeling of winter lake trout adventures on these waters is challenging, but let me try taking you there.

Ice Fishing Great Lakes Lakers on Lake Superior

There's a special, mystical quality about ice fishing for Great Lakes lake trout that intrigues me. Superficially, it's the thrill of knowing large, hard-fighting fish are swimming past my lures with each drop of the bait. But the enchantment of Great Lakes fishing—particularly Lake Superior—goes far beyond such rudimentary thoughts. It's the immensity of it all—the realization I'm standing on ice coating water that's more than 200 feet deep. When I'm fishing on Lake Superior, I'm standing on one of the largest concentrations of freshwater on the planet. I fish these waters and feel rejuvenated after each experience.

Wisconsin guide Tim Duffy displays a Lake Superior lake trout.

This is precisely how I felt after completing a last-ice trip to Lake Superior's Chequamegon Bay with guide Tim Duffy of Hayward, Wisconsin. Tim is truly gifted. While mother nature throws curve balls from time to time, Tim's pretty consistent. Ask nicely, and he may drive sixty miles north of Hayward to Lake Superior, and let you try jigging giant lake trout.

"I've been ice fishing Lake Superior 10 years," Tim commented. "I know its dangers—and its potential. Depending how far winter has progressed, Lake Superior kicks out good numbers of nice lake trout and splake. Fishing from sunup until mid-day is generally most productive, but since most winter fishing on Lake Superior, particularly Chequamegon Bay, centers around lake trout and splake which come through in groups, good catches can be made all day."

Tim doesn't leave shore until after sunup and returns with plenty of light left at the end of the day. "If there's one thing I've learned about Lake Superior, it's respect," Tim said. "As with any outdoor situation, each day is different. Some winters are cold and the whole lake gets good ice. Other years, ice forms, but heavy snow will push the ice down and create hazardous slush conditions."

Pack ice, caused by chunks of broken ice of various thickness blowing into areas of open water then freezing, is another phenomenon common on Chequamegon Bay. This must be watched, because one block might be a couple feet thick, while the next is only a couple inches. Compound such condi-

Modern lake trout anglers are finding spinning combos with low-stretch lines a highly effective means of jigging winter lakers.

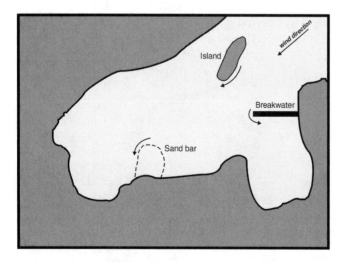

On big-water lakes, projections such as points, submerged and emergent sandbars, breakwaters and extensions of islands gather current and deflect it, often causing thin ice. Be cautious when traversing or fishing near such areas.

tions with heavy snow, and the thin spots can create "boils"—pockets of deep slush among good ice.

"Projections extending into the lake must also be watched," warns Tim. "This is big water, and below-ice currents exist. Projections such as points, submerged and emergent sandbars, pilings, and extensions of islands gather this current and deflect it, causing thin ice.

"Pressure cracks must be carefully navigated, and inlets should be avoided. Furthermore, darkness comes fast and whiteouts aren't unusual, so be sure you've got at least a good map and compass, or better yet, a GPS to ensure you can find shore in the event of bad weather."

My point here isn't to scare anglers away, only to emphasize respect. You must know these waters, be up to date on changing ice conditions, and carry all necessary safety items, including life jackets, ice cleats, picks, rope, spare snowmobile parts and tools. Otherwise, book a guide. Someone like Tim can arrange to meet your party, load the snowmobiles and necessary gear, provide necessary safety instructions or precautions, and drive you to safe access. If the ice is slick, they have cleats. If there's an ice hazard or even the slightest risk of crossing a pressure crack or boil, they'll let you know. These are forms of comfortable insurance coming from being with a professional winter guide. Just dress warm, it gets downright cold in the midst of powerful Lake Superior winds during the long ride out to deep shipping channels, flats and breaks, where lakers roam in search of forage.

Once there, someone like Tim will show you how to fish. "This is a traditional Lake Superior bobbing stick," Tim says handing me a short, light-weight piece of cedar wrapped with heavy dacron line. "Since you're fishing so deep, you need a solid stick that won't bend, and line that won't stretch like monofilament. Bobbing sticks fit the bill perfectly."

When fishing with Tim, I used the stick for awhile, then switched to my spinning combo spooled with Berkley Fireline—not monofilament. The main problem with standard jigging equipment is rods bend and monofilaments stretch. In fact, monofilament stretches up to 30%. When fishing monstrous Great Lakes' depths, if you get a subtle hit, monofilament acts like a long rubber band. Strikes never even register to your hand, instead, they're entirely absorbed by the line. You can see the problem with establishing good hook sets using monofilament. In 200 feet of water a line that stretches 30 percent will give 60 feet!

However, with the development of low-stretch lines like Fireline, you can fish ice rods such as HT's IBT-34 and IBT-44 heavy action trout sticks, spinning reels with fightin' drag style systems. The only catch is weight. A cedar bobbing stick weighs next to nothing, but a rod and reel is somewhat heavy, and jigging with extra weight like this can be quite tiring.

But these new systems are working out. The trick is to use lighter weight, faster-tipped rods so there's not so much weight and at least some give when you set the hook. You'll also need to set your drag correctly. Also be sure to use round or oval-shaped lines if you use Kevlar. Flat Kevlar lines don't work on spinning tackle because they'll twist as they're wound onto the spool. When fishing in 100 to 200 feet of Great Lakes water, this has the potential to create a real mess. When using Kevlar, you're best off to stick with baitcast reels. Spectra or Fireline-type lines work best on spinning gear, provided they're tied securely to the spool hub.

When jigging deep-water lake trout, set the hook hard. Many fish are missed because anglers only half-heartedly lift their rod tips and the hooks are never sunk securely into the fish.

I asked Tim about his favorite lures. "When it comes to lures, make them large, heavy, and sharp," Tim emphasized. "My favorite jigs include Northland's Bucktail Jigs, Large Swedish Pimples, and our locally favored Beetles, a modified swimming jig, in sizes from 1 to 2 ounces. These weights are necessary to get your bait to the bottom and keep them there where most lakers and splake are caught. Lake Superior's waters feature currents of varying strengths beneath the ice, and lighter lures, even if you get them down to the bottom, would soon lift off in these currents. When currents are light or negligible, Swedish Pimples work well, and are fairly easy to fish. Beetles also work in reduced current situations, but are heavier and more tiring to work."

In stronger currents, however, these lures tend to drift and are difficult to fish. Given such conditions, about the only thing that will cut the current and hold are Northland Bucktail Jigs.

"Regardless of lure choice, these baits are then tipped with smelt, lake shiners, or carefully cut strips of belly meat that swim seductively when jigged with long lift-drops," Tim continued. "The

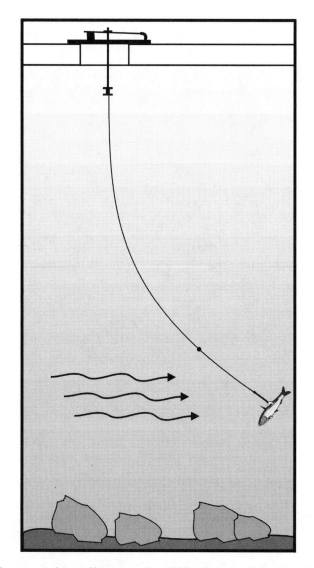

Deep-set tip-up lines can be difficult to position in the strike zone, especially in current. Where multiple lines are legal, however, additional tip-up lines may settle when current lessens or changes direction — which happens to be primary fish movement time — allowing tip-ups to help increase your catch.

main thing is to experiment with how high you lift the lure—trout often show preferences. Also keep a semi-taut line when lowering your lure back down by following your line down with your rod or bobbing stick. Lake trout strikes can vary from a hard yank to just a slight touch, and if you allow slack to form, lighter bites are difficult to detect."

Also remember to stay alert. Jigging trout on Lake Superior is akin to fishing muskies with big jerkbaits. Jigging these heavy lures hour after hour can be downright tiring, and if you fall asleep at the wheel, you'll inevitably miss that important strike. So remain fully alert. Once you get a strike, set the

hook—hard. I'm of the opinion that in these depths, you can't set up hard enough. Often, trout will just "swat" at the bait, and a quick, hard hook set will stick these light-biting fish. If a fish is missed, others should all be on alert. Often when a trout is missed, the fish will swing over and strike another line. Better yet, it could be a part of a large school, and when this happens, things can turn into a fun spurt of temporary chaos.

I asked Tim about tip-ups. "Quality, large spooled tip-ups like the Polar Deep Lake model can be used on Lake Superior and set while you're jigging, but if the currents are strong, lines are difficult to keep on the bottom in the trout's main strike zone," Tim pointed out. "However, since you can really only jig with one rod at a time and you're allowed three lines, you might as well sink a tip-up line. Even if the currents get strong and drift your bait out of the strike zone, their velocity generally fluctuates periodically, and when they slow or change direction, your minnow will drift back down—and often be struck. I like to use lead-core line and attach leaders with a ball-bearing swivel—with this much line out and the presence of currents, lines and baits roll and twist, and if you're not using a swivel you'll be amazed at the resulting tangle."

If you're curious, most Great Lakes lakers and splake average between 5 and 10 pounds, although 10- to 15-pound fish aren't uncommon. Given conditions where cold temperatures freeze the entire lake, huge main-basin lake trout called "fats" are also accessible. These fish can range between 20 and 30 pounds.

"I've had these fish break 20-pound leaders," claims Tim.

In short, anything can happen on these massive waters, so dream big. You'll soon discover why Lake Superior is called a Great Lake.

The "Inland" Lake Trout Adventure

While this first adventure dealt with tactics applied largely to vast oligotrophic Canadian Shield waters and Great Lakes, there's another winter lake trout adventure available on what I call "inland" lake trout waters. These large, deep inland lakes of the Canadian Shield and northern United States, along with other stocked "two-story" lakes and abandoned mine pits provide fabulous trophy potential.

Each winter, about the time the first-ice blitz is coming to a close on smaller, shallower lakes and fish are starting to move into their mid-season patterns, safe ice begins forming on these deep, clear waters—and lake trout will be active. Many anglers fear this first-ice, and with good reason. The staggering depths of these seemingly bottomless lakes means it takes some mighty cold weather for an extended period to cap them with ice. But when solid ice forms, ice anglers have access to some unbelievable action. You just have to learn the lake.

Watch the ice conditions. Be careful when crossing pressure cracks, and always check with local bait shops regarding ice conditions and seasonal movements of fish on your lake. Remember, most inland lake trout waters are highly diverse environments offering clear water, an abundance of dissolved oxygen and high-protein forage. The combination provides an environment conducive to growing some quality lake trout, but it creates challenging fishing, too.

Since these fish see well they may spook easily, and the good water quality, uniform cold water temperatures and a variety of abundant forage allows lake trout the opportunity to move almost anywhere throughout the winter. This means fish can

Many deep, "inland" Canadian Shield and northern United States' lakes offer excellent winter lake trout action. (photo courtesy Mr. Walleye Specialities/Arctic Cat Snowmobiles)

Abandoned iron ore mine pits offer deep, cold environments well-stocked with lake trout. They offer excellent "inland" winter lake trout fishing opportunities.

usually find safe havens away from heavy traffic areas. Given the proper combination of forage and time to grow, it also means if you know how to approach these lakes you've got a good chance at a trophy.

Just be prepared to use your sonar to find primary fish-holding areas, including hard-bottom drop-offs, and the edges of classic deep-water points, humps, bars, walls, turns and other structures that will likely concentrate the most fish. A high-quality, accurate hydrographic map and sonar are a must for locating these high-percentage structures, and don't forget to consider inter-species competition, which can have an effect on productive inland lake trout patterns.

Another good "inland" lake trout opportunity is abandoned iron ore mine pits. Often dug with steep drops leading into water that's 500 feet deep, these cold environments are often stocked and offer some excellent winter lake trout opportunities. Like Great Lakes bays, these fish often roam deep flats, but may suspend over deep water. While most inland lake trout don't grow as large as Great Lakes' fats, they certainly have the potential. Often, anglers seeking other species hook into a surprise. A 26-pound lake trout was taken a couple years ago on a deep inland lake trout water near my home, by an angler light-line fishing for cisco!

That's part of the fun. You never know what you'll catch from the depths of deep, productive inland trout waters. Given a few strong year classes, many inland lake trout fisheries can boom, offering thrashing, trophy fish weighing well into the double-digit range. That's enough to tempt just about anybody onto the ice.

So, if you have a hankering to experience a unique winter adventure offering serious potential to catch a trophy, you might want to consider lake trout. After all, the fish of a lifetime might just await.

Chapter 7

Understanding Great Lakes Browns and Steelhead

A Great Lakes brown pushing 15 pounds is enough to make any winter angler smile!

In the dim moonlight, dark silhouettes of gnarled, brushy pines and cedars cast mysterious shadows. The shaded dolomite banks are steep and rocky along this undeveloped Great Lakes shoreline. The faint scent of pine tints the frigid air, mixing with the distinctive, sodden smell of distant, open water beyond the frozen bay.

The arctic stillness is silent aside from the sound of soft, crunching snow beneath my boots, the gentle etching sound of my plastic sled dragging behind me, and the deep, rhythmic breaths I expel into the frigid early morning air.

Arriving near the intended area, I flip on my sonar to verify the depth. The lighted screen illuminates the darkness. Eighteen feet. Perfect.

I lift my power auger, flip the switch and push the primer bulb. As I pull the starter cord, the dependable motor fires, and the powerful sound of the engine echoes through the tranquil morning. Gaseous traces of two-cycle exhaust drift into the air as the loud, droning whine of the auger whirls and slices through two feet of ice. After drilling a dozen holes stretching from the 18-foot break back into about 2 feet of water, I hit the kill switch, and the stillness returns. I begin setting tip-ups, leaving plenty of holes for jigging. I don't know it yet, but by day's end, each of these holes will produce at least one brown trout—one of which will weigh almost 15 pounds.

We're talking Great Lakes trout. This isn't the typical stocked-trout fishing discussed in Hooked On Ice Fishing II: Panfish. These are Great Lakes browns and steelhead that easily meet our definition of gamefish. Many ice anglers are missing out on these opportunities. I know, because I've seen passersby shaking their heads at our shivering torsos hunched over holes on snowy, windswept Great Lakes bays. Such gawkers often appear rather humored, yet we always get the last laugh as we smirk smugly under our frost-covered face masks, concealing a spectacular, well-kept secret.

Sound intriguing? It should. After all, Great Lakes brown trout and steelhead are plentiful, powerful, hard-fighting fish that bite well throughout the winter. They are some of the most colorful of winter species, and they taste great. Best of all, they're often huge! Many Great Lakes anglers are icing double-digit browns and steelhead—and I don't hesitate to say Great Lakes bays offer some of the most consistent, exciting, and productive ice fishing adventures anywhere in the world.

I should also mention that ice anglers in parts of western and eastern North America catch some pretty hefty inland browns and rainbows, too. High-elevation waters out west and deep, cold man-made and natural lakes of the northeast United States are good examples of waters producing trophy browns each winter.

There is one catch, however. To consistently ice these fish, you must understand their winter feeding habits, movements, preferred forage and, most importantly, location patterns. Since patterns for catching trophy, inland trout are similar to many of the tactics used on the Great Lakes, I'll focus on Great Lakes patterns here, mentioning "inland" specifics only when necessary.

But first, the species.

Great Lakes Steelhead

Great Lakes steelhead are rainbow trout spending most of their time in the open water of the Great Lakes. They migrate up tributary streams to spawn. Most spawning migrations are made early each spring. But to me, the most exciting habit of these fish is a somewhat less known fact: Some strains move into shallow areas in fall, and remain there until the spring spawn. This provides opportunity for ice anglers. A couple strains even make runs into rivers under the ice, holding in or near river mouths, harbors and deep pools of Great Lakes tributaries.

Unlike the more deeply colored inland rainbows, Great Lakes steelhead have long, bluish green backs and silvery flanks often featuring a pale pink line down the center. They also have small, faint spots above the lateral line, and a white belly. (photo Courtesy Wisconsin D.N.R.)

Unlike the more deeply colored inland rainbows, Great Lakes steelhead feature long, bluish-green backs, silvery flanks accented with small, faint black spots above the lateral line. They often feature a faint pink stripe down the center, and a white belly. They eat plankton, aquatic insect larvae, crustaceans, fish eggs and baitfish. Great Lakes steelhead are less wary than browns and typically average 3 to 8 pounds, but may reach twice that size. Big or small, they put up spectacular fights and taste great baked, fried or smoked.

Check with knowledgeable sources to find what strains have been stocked in your target waters and when primary runs occur. Catch one, and if you're like me, you may well find icing steelhead addicting.

Great Lakes Browns

Aside from the fact Great Lakes browns don't make upriver spawning migrations, they often demonstrate patterns similar to winter steelhead. Like Great Lakes steelhead, a couple strains cruise iced-over bays, flats, harbors and rivers in search of food. Some are caught by anglers targeting steelhead—and smart steelhead anglers regularly switch their attention to the browns.

Why? Because these fish aren't small! Two- to 6 pound fish are fairly common, and they get even bigger. Last February on a Lake Michigan bay, I landed a 14-pounder on a Swedish Pimple. Proud of my catch, I returned to a local sport shop to

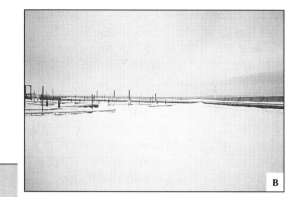

Great Lakes browns are often found cruising harbors (a), marina docks (b) and breakwaters (c) lining Great Lakes shores.

weigh the fish, only to find another angler bringing in a 10-pounder! This isn't surprising. Great Lakes river mouths, harbors, flats and bays offer excellent brown trout fishing. While fish average 3 to 5 pounds, rumors of 20-, 25-, even 30-pound fish being iced have also circulated.

To make such catches reality, however, ice anglers wishing to pursue winter Great Lakes browns must take their fishing seriously. Like steelhead anglers, they must understand the best locations to focus their efforts. They must also understand the baits primarily used to fish them, and the best times to try their hand at this unique opportunity.

Unlike their darker inland cousins, Great Lakes browns feature a gray-silvery sheen, and a pattern of irregular dark crosses and checks along the back and sides that gradually fade toward the belly. They also sport some familiar, but very faint, light brownish-orange or yellow markings. They live in relatively shallow Great Lakes waters, seldom dropping

to more than 60 feet deep. They are often caught much shallower. I've commonly caught them in 15 to 20 feet and have taken them as shallow as 3 feet, where they feed on invertebrates or baitfish. They're highly esteemed as table fare, with a delicate, flaky consistency and smooth taste.

Primary Great Lakes Steelhead and Brown Trout Location Patterns

While all browns and steelhead demonstrate many location pattern similarities and are often caught from similar areas throughout the winter, there are some differences. Inland rainbows and browns typically relate to classic, mid-depth rocky structures such as points, reefs, islands and channels. Steelhead, or Great Lakes run rainbows, are often taken from deep, frozen river holes, or at river mouths and harbors in front of these spawning rivers. Great Lakes browns can be caught in

During late ice, browns and steelhead are caught along in-shore structures, harbors and river mouths.

these same areas, or bays lining the main-lake basins. Since inland trout patterns were covered back in the second book of this series, we'll focus primarily on Great Lakes patterns here, citing specific inland tactics only when clarity is necessary.

Most Great Lakes steelhead and brown trout ice fishing opportunities can be divided into three categories: river hole fishing, near shore shallow harbor and bay fishing, and deep-water bay fishing.

River holes and near shore, shallow and mid-depth harbors and bays offering wind protecting breakwaters or points where ice can form are primary targets. Although some steelhead and browns may hold in deeper or shallower water, because of the variety of species in most Great Lakes bays, fish are distributed into somewhat distinct ecological niches: Warm-water species such as walleyes, pike and perch frequent shallow, weedy flats and bays. Lakers and splake lurk deep on the bottom. While there is some overlap with the lakers and splake, the majority of Great Lakes browns and steelhead relate to deep river pools, mid-depth, hard-bottom river mouth structures and the harbors in-between.

Fishing river holes is simply a matter of finding deep, iced over holes and fishing quietly. Since these opportunities are limited, most Great Lakes ice fishing for browns and steelhead takes place within harbor mouths and shoreline structure in bays less than 40 feet deep, because two major Great Lakes forage species, smelt and alewives, relate to these shallow and mid-depth areas during winter. These fish, in turn, draw concentra-

Most Great Lakes browns and steelhead are caught from protected rivermouths (a) and harbors (d), where ice formation allows access to these species. Top fishing locations include deep, frozen river holes (f), the inside edges of breakwaters (b, c) and the deep, dredged harbor access (e).

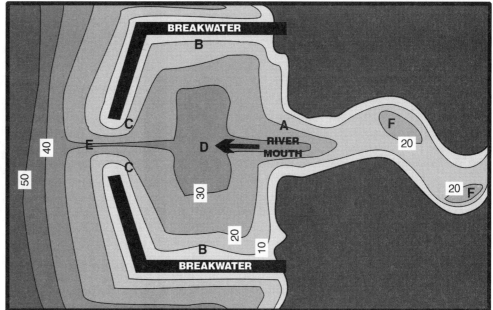

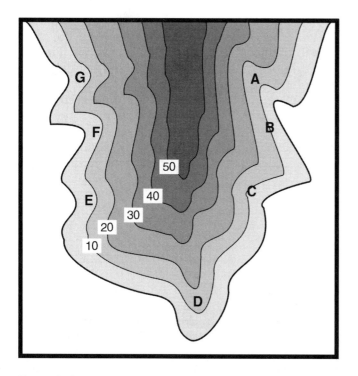

Great Lakes bays can also be productive. While they may be large, shoreline irregularities such as points (a, f, g) deep shorelines (b, c) and turns (d, e) are good locations.

tions of browns and steelhead. In fact, many good winter Great Lakes trout catches come from less than 25 feet of water, where active steelhead and browns frequently cruise.

Movement toward such areas begins in late fall. As water temperatures cool, active browns and steelhead cruise shoreline structures, breakwaters, contours and points searching for food. These schools often stay together and feed several weeks after freeze up, making them relatively easy to find. The schools may be large, and if conditions are right, these fish may remain active along these breaks and flats most of the winter.

Great Lakes bays can also be expansive, and many anglers wonder where to begin. Fortunately, many large and mid-size Great Lakes bays feature a shipping channel or deep contours extending into the bay from the main lake. Breaks formed along these deeper contours are primary target points of fish activity. Any points and projections—particularly in areas where they cut tight to shore—are the best structures on which to focus your efforts. But remember, any adjacent flats, breakwaters, harbors or river mouths featuring cover or holding baitfish can also be good.

Often, deep breaks lining dredged shipping lanes within Great Lakes bays are the primary target of winter trout anglers, who know these lanes act as migration routes from deep to shallow water.

The deep slots surrounding harbor breakwaters are often excellent places to catch early season browns.

In terms of specific location along these contours, current is a major factor. When present, current from incoming rivers and feeder streams brings relatively warm runoff and food, making steelhead and brown trout slightly more active. However, keep in mind such locations can form poor ice, especially in shallow water, so be cautious. Great Lakes trout also tend to spook easily when they're suspended within shallow water. Avoid high-traffic areas. Rather, fish out-of-the-way areas, or at times when activity is minimal. In deeper water, use sonar.

Early Ice

Just before ice-up, steelhead and browns begin hunting. Since deep, main-lake contours seldom assemble large concentrations of baitfish, these schools are often mobile, moving until they come across a reliable food source. Fully 90 percent of the time this means you'll find the largest schools of trout in river mouths, harbors and mid-sized bays. Wait until the ice forms, then use a stealthy, twilight approach on this clear, shallow-water ice. Drill holes along breakwaters, tapering contours or channels. Move from shallow to deep water trying to intercept these schools. In some river holes, harbors or small bays, I've even seen anglers spread blankets across the ice adjacent to their holes, using them to conceal their presence and reduce spooky shadows.

Mid-Winter

By mid-winter, many of these fish move onto deeper flats adjoining these river mouths and harbors, or out into the expanses of larger bays. Like most harbor and small to mid-size bay areas, many large Great Lakes bays have deep contours or shipping lanes extending in from the main-lake basin. These depth breaks act as migration routes funneling baitfish and trout in from their deep water haunts. They also provide a route for shallow-water fish to follow when moving deeper. Use sonar to find these troughs, then focus your efforts where the greatest numbers of fish will likely assemble—along banks, turns or deeper holes lining the trough. Cut your holes along these edges, and be prepared to move. Browns and steelhead simply hold where the most forage is found, and without temperature or oxygen limitations, they aren't afraid to be mobile.

You shouldn't be, either.

Late Ice

If your primary target is steelhead, late ice is prime-time, because this is when most steelhead strains make their annual pilgrimage into spawning rivers. Many ice anglers intercept these fish in Great Lakes harbors adjoining spawning rivers, or fish them in deeper, frozen upstream river holes.

During cold winters when ice is safe and forage is available, I've also experienced positive results fishing browns during the beginning of the smelt run. I found them in deep river holes and pockets near the heads of these channels. Both steelhead

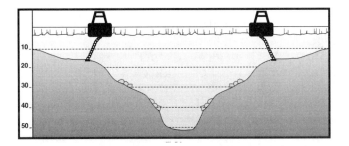

In large Great Lakes bays near port cites, dredged shipping channels or lanes running in from deep water funnel baitfish shallow and act as migration routes for browns and steelhead. They're easily identified by the shipping lane markers frozen in the ice, but use your sonar to find any irregularities along these edges that might act as holding areas.

During late ice, browns and steelhead are caught along in-shore structures, harbors and river mouths.

and brown trout move through these areas regularly as the ice goes out. You'll have to use a stealthy approach, but sit tight. This can be the best time of the winter to consistently ice numbers of Great Lakes steelhead and browns.

There are exceptions, however. A shallow harbor bay featuring a relatively shallow break extending in from the main lake may support forage and draw trout towards the lake, away from the harbor. So it's always a good idea to carefully study a map of the area you intend to fish, and speak with knowledgeable local anglers for up-to-date information before venturing out. Otherwise, most Great Lakes channels and holes are highly productive, as hungry late-ice browns and steelhead often cruise along these channels and their edges in search of forage.

Just don't neglect deeper rocky drop-offs, breaks, points or shoals adjacent to these areas. Baitfish such as smelt often stage on deeper flats, preparing to move in for their upstream spawning runs. You'll often find trout holding near or suspended off the edges of distinct breaks ranging from 3 to 35 feet deep. Such fish are not always

If you move into a shallow harbor or river area, move slowly and quietly, trying not to disturb the fish.

easy to find and demand the use of maps and sonar. Provided the ice is safe, these trout can provide some outstanding late-ice action, especially when late-ice browns begin feeding heavily on smelt.

But again, be quiet. If you move into a shallow harbor or river area, move slow and be stealthy. In the event you spook fish as you approach, just set up and wait quietly. These areas often act as funnels corralling fish as they approach from deeper water. By simply waiting them out you are likely to get some strikes.

Timing

The best Great Lakes ice fishing for browns and steelhead occurs throughout late December and early January, slows going into February, then picks up again from early March until ice-out. However, good weather in February occasionally brings good fishing, so don't be disappointed if your schedule only permits you to make a trip during this period. It can pay off, especially for browns.

On a daily basis, the best inland brown trout fishing is traditionally considered to be the first couple hours after daybreak and again shortly before dark, but I haven't necessarily found this to be the case with winter Great Lakes browns. If anything, I've found the opposite to be true. I've

The rubble and bottom content transitions surrounding ore docks in Great Lakes bays are often worth checking, as they will draw a variety of species, including brown trout.

Great Lakes browns can be caught virtually any time of day. During overcast conditions I've experienced some of my best action between 11 a.m. and 3 p.m.

erally most favorable, although sunny days have been good when the ice is thick and snow cover is deep. Just remember, consistency depends on a quiet approach and versatility. If you're able to sneak up on the fish, changing your location and presentation strategies to match the situation, you'll likely come off the ice with some fat, trophy Great Lakes trout.

Trophy Inland Rainbows and Browns

With all this Great Lakes discussion, I want to again emphasize: Don't neglect the inland trophy rainbows and browns of western and eastern North America. Like the Great Lakes, large, mid-depth rocky drop-offs, breaks, points or shoals holding forage on deep, cold-water lakes and reservoirs will draw trophy rainbows and browns,

caught the majority of my fish between 11 a.m. and 3 p.m., especially when conditions are overcast and feeding activity tends to be more sustained throughout the day. Still, if you're willing, I recommend spending the entire day on the ice. It's fun, exciting, well worth the time and regardless of when a school of browns travels through, you know you'll be there waiting for them.

Steelhead are more particular, with the best action often occurring from daybreak until approximately 8 a.m., then again from mid-through late-afternoon. However, Great Lakes anglers in some areas claim to experience short spurts of action just before sundown, so don't pack up too soon after the mid-afternoon bite ends. Great Lakes trout are a funny breed, and depending where you're fishing, productive times may vary.

Finally, weather is another important consideration. Calm, stable, cloudy conditions are gen-

Although the focus of this chapter is Great Lakes browns, keep in mind some pretty nice fish are caught "inland," too. Try the deep, cold lakes of the northeast United States, or as shown here, the high elevation areas of western North America.

particularly during early and late ice, and they shouldn't be ignored.

Late winter on larger waters is particularly productive, when baitfish often stage on mid-depth flats. You'll often find trout holding near or suspended off the edges of distinct breaks ranging from 10 to 30 feet deep. These fish are not always easy to find and demand the use of maps and sonar to find consistently. Provided the ice is safe and you use a strategic approach, these waters can provide some outstanding winter action.

Effective Winter Fishing Strategies

Once you've located good structures and fish, presentation isn't difficult. The water is clear on most inland and Great Lakes trout waters throughout the winter, and neither steelhead nor browns will experience problems seeing your bait. If they want it, they'll get it.

Since tactics for both inland and Great Lakes trout are similar, we'll again focus on Great Lakes methods. Yes, some inland tactics might differ slightly from those used by Great Lakes trout anglers, but not by much. Slightly modified Great Lakes presentations will catch inland trout, too, so again, let's stick with Great Lakes tactics.

To begin with, the foremost rule is to stay mobile and move frequently when starting out. Browns and steelhead are movers and seldom stay in one place, often relating to nothing more than the depth at which they're suspended. Most of the time, both species cruise in schools searching for food at a specific depth. Until you locate a precise structure or area holding trout and pinpoint the primary strike zone where you can slow down and carefully set your lines, you'll want to keep moving.

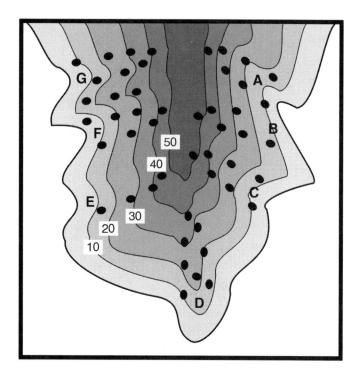

On larger Great Lakes bays, focus your hole drilling along contour irregularities and potential migration routes.

Once fish are found, you'll face a decision: Be mobile or sit still. Being mobile generally works best on larger waters because trout typically cruise constantly. If you carefully follow these schools using a mobile approach, limits aren't difficult. On deep river holes and in smaller shipping lanes, harbors or bay areas, sitting may work—provided you're sitting on a known migration route or staging area and you have your bait in the right strike zone. Nonetheless, there will often be long gaps in-between bites while waiting for schools to return. Sometimes they won't

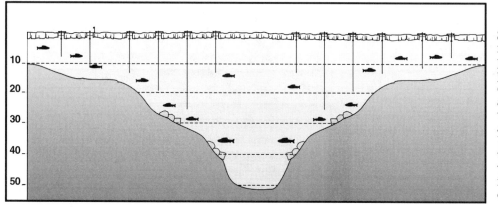

Since Great Lakes trout are movers, a mobile approach pays. When fishing a shipping channel, either set up over a likely holding area and wait for them to move through, or use a mobile approach to cover a long break line. Either way, set tip-ups at various depths while jigging various strata in-between to thoroughly cover the area.

return. Hence, while you can often take fish by sitting still, I feel a mobile, versatile approach is the most consistent method for catching Great Lakes steelhead and browns through the ice. Even when fishing smaller river holes, channels and bays, moving from hole to hole—or in areas blessed with numerous bays, harbors and streams—moving from river to river may help put you on fish. Don't be lazy! The difference between a mover and a sitter can be a few huge trout.

In a normal day of fishing—the exception being smaller river hole fishing—it's not unusual for me to drill anywhere from 20 to 100 holes while in search of and following an active school of trout. My reasoning? Simple. I want to be able to cover channels and their associated structures, as well as shoreline flats adjacent to these potential areas thoroughly—yet quickly—and stay on active fish. Once you mark fish, lower your bait. You'll likely catch a fish or two, then the action will come to an abrupt halt as the school moves on or spooks. Catch as many fish as possible, then try to follow the school.

I should note that thanks to all this moving, I have, over time, identified some small and mid-sized bays that consistently attract schools throughout the winter. In these areas, I've learned

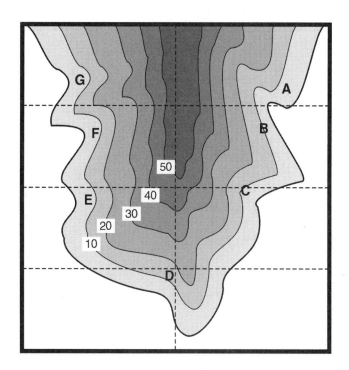

To make locating productive areas an easier process, fish in large groups, then break the bay into sections and spread out, assigning members of your group to each section.

When searching for Great Lakes trout, it's not unusual for me to drill between 20 and 100 holes in search of an active school.

that spreading a line of holes from shallow to deep water, setting tip-ups and jigging throughout the day results in pretty consistent action without constant movement. This is nice when fishing with a group of anglers new to the sport, or at times when ice conditions are a concern.

Presentation is a relatively easy proposition, especially on deep river holes and harbors, where simply spreading a few holes and setting lines at various depths makes covering water easy. The biggest challenge is often current, and the key to success is simply using the least amount of weight necessary to hold your lure or bait within the primary strike zone.

When fishing larger Great Lakes bays, I recommend fishing in large groups, mostly for safety, but also because as a group, you'll be able to use an effective combination of tip-ups and jigging methods to thoroughly cover deeper flats, channels and their respective banks. To make locating productive holes a more efficient process, break these larger areas into sections, and after using sonar to pinpoint the channel boundaries and any productive structures or contours on or within them, assign a section to each angler in your group.

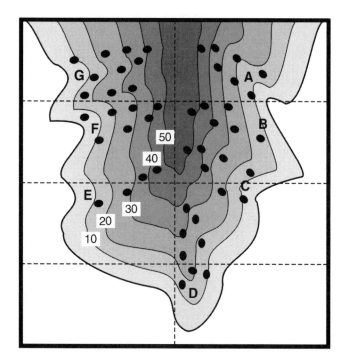

Tip-ups can help you cover water when fishing elongated structures such as harbor breakwaters.

Next, cut holes in the productive areas in your section, fish for a while, then compare notes via radio or cellular phone, arranging to meet in the most productive section(s).

Next, cut numerous holes within each section to cover water, and begin setting tip-ups. Place them strategically along structural edges or contours and cover a depth range from the base to the top of the break. Also be sure to stagger a couple tip-ups high over deeper water, setting them about half way down—this covers you in the event that a deeper, suspended school tries slipping by. If you don't catch a fish within 30 minutes, try moving along the channel or contour in 20- or 30-yard intervals, repeating the process until you contact fish. By sticking with this plan, you're likely to find an active school. Now for the tackle.

Tip-Ups

Let's start with tip-ups. Remember, if multiple lines are legal in your area and current isn't a major factor, tip-ups help you cover more water. The best unit I've found for Great Lakes brown trout and steelhead is the PTU-5 deep-lake Polar. The larger spool on this unit provides more backing when a large trout make a long run.

To rig your tip-up, use premium dacron such as Gudebrod, HT, or Mason's for backing, and tie the

Courtesy of HT Enterprises, Inc.

HT's PTU-5 Polar tip-up features a large spool capacity for fishing deep–and ample backing in case a large brown or steelhead makes a hard, long run.

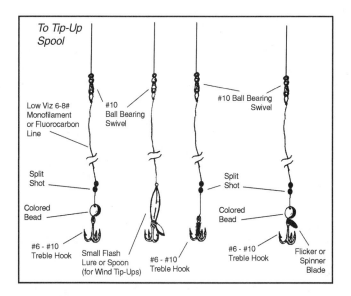

Tip-up rigging for browns and steelhead consists of using premium dacron for backing, and a long length of low-visibility monofilament or fluorocarbon leader tipped with a super-sharp hook. Modified rigs featuring yarn, beads, flicker blades or even spoons for rigs to be used on wind tip-ups can also be incorporated into the presentation.

tag end to one side of a barrel swivel. To the opposite end, tie a 6-foot leader of low-visibility 6- or 8-pound test monofilament or fluorocarbon, and terminate the rig with a super-sharp #6 treble hook. Unless current is present, a couple of split shot will usually be sufficient to properly secure your presentation. In current, use a slip-sinker of suitable weight to hold your bait in place. No matter what you're fishing for, in current or not, set the tip-up as lightly as possible so fish won't feel resistance when the bait is taken. With only slight modification, this rig will cover most trophy Great Lake or inland trout situations.

Spool With Lighter, Thinner Diameter, Low-Memory Line

When tip-up fishing, try thinner tip-up leaders, especially when fishing shallow, clear water. Dropping to a lengthy, 6-foot leader made of 6-pound monofilament in place of a 10-inch leader of say, 10 to 12-pound, might well be the key to increasing your catch. These lighter, thinner lines are less visible and less stiff, thereby allowing freer movement of your bait.

Live emerald shiners, lake shiners and smelt are popular baits on fixed position tip-ups like the Polar. Golden shiners are good, too. I prefer to use bait, but I've seen anglers using dead ciscos or egg sacs come home with heavy pails, too. Still, 2- to 4-inch golden shiners, lake shiners or suckers—in that

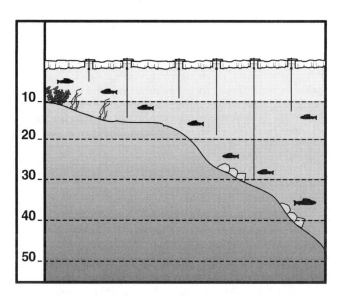

Stagger the depths of your tip-up sets to try pinpointing the main "strike zone," or depth at which trout seem to be feeding.

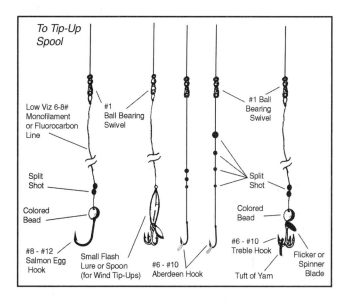

Additional modified tip-up rigs for Great Lakes trout include using salmon egg hooks baited with salmon eggs or insect larvae, small flash lures on wind tip-ups, small Aberdeen hooks with grubs or insect larvae, or adding a tuft of yarn soaked in fish attractant to the hook before baiting. (Courtesy HT Enterprises, Inc.)

order—seem to get the nod of most Great Lakes winter trout experts. I like to set two tip-ups—a Polar rigged with a shiner, and the other a Windlass set with a flash lure or rocker style jig tipped with a minnow head, wax worm or large wiggler.

Either way, hook your bait to keep it alive and hold it level. Stagger the depth at which you set your units, and don't be afraid to play leapfrog with them as you work down a channel, over a flat or around a harbor, break, contour, or structural feature. If one unit begins seeing more action than others, switch the other tip-ups to the same depth. Often, one depth signals the primary "strike zone," and by uniformly setting your baits, you'll increase your catch.

Depth settings can be very particular. Great Lakes steelhead and browns tend to suspend and move through anywhere from just off the bottom to just under the ice. They often won't bite if your bait isn't presented at that precise depth. Fortunately, pinpointing depth patterns isn't that difficult because trout often move through continually at the same depth each day. Yet inattentive anglers who don't use sonar and pay attention to such matters rarely come home with fish, so don't make this mistake.

When a school moves through, try having someone in your group raise and "jiggle" your tip-up baits slightly. This action often triggers hits if they're not set at precisely the right strike zone. Just be warned, tip-ups create a slight drag effect when line is peeled from them—spooky winter trout can be quick to drop baits offering

any resistance—so always position your units close by so you can "jig" them when fish come through. When you get a strike, never waste time setting the hook. If the spool or trip shaft is turning when you arrive, don't be shy. Set the hook immediately, before the fish has the opportunity to drop your bait. Both browns and steelhead seem to grab a minnow, run, then let it go, seemingly enjoying watching the minnow struggle before moving in for the final kill. Consequently, the trick to catching them consistently is often setting the hook on the first run.

This is another reason wind tip-ups are an excellent choice. Great Lakes trout love the jigging motion imparted by these units and because the spool and rocker arm are located above the ice, it's easier to grab lines and set hooks more effectively when a fish strikes. Besides, it's fun to watch fish strike, drop the rocker arm and spin line from the spool. Again, I emphasize, however: position your tip-ups close by. Remember, steelhead and browns have that frustrating habit of hitting and dropping baits within a matter of seconds. If you're too far away, you'll miss fish. If a flag trips, waste no time, and don't be shy. Just

Courtesy of HT Enterprises, Inc.

Great Lakes trout love the jigging motion imparted by wind tip-ups, such as HT's large spooled TU-3 windlass. It's also easier to grab lines and set the hooks more quickly because these models have the spools positioned above the ice. (Courtesy HT Enterprises, Inc.)

set the hook quickly, then try to remain patient. It's easy to become overexcited at the sight of a double-digit fish thrashing beneath your hole. But a hasty response often means a lost fish. Give the fish time to tire before trying to slide it onto the ice.

Jigging

Jigging for large trout poses many unique challenges and requires special tackle. A solid, 3- to 4-foot, medium action graphite ice rod with a flexible tip such as HT's Intrigue, Polar Lite or Polar Gold medium-heavy action rods, or, if you prefer, 5- to 6-foot one-piece medium-light action summer graphite rods provide strength, give and power—qualities that are a must when fishing large Great Lakes trout through the ice. Sensitive rods with a fast tip, strong butt and large guides are the best bets. The strong backbone allows for solid hook sets. The fast tip action helps keep your line tight while fighting fish—counteracting the characteristic run-and-roll escape tactics of Great Lakes trout—and large guides helping prevent freeze-up. Longer rods also position you further away from the hole, reducing fish-spooking shadows in shallow water.

Taping Reels

When using ice rods without reel seats for powerful Great Lakes trout, secure the reel base with a few wraps of reinforced "strapping" tape overlaid with several overlapped wraps of black electrical tape. This provides a secure, warm, durable and waterproof hold.

A warning of the dangers of reducing budget dollars to control the lamprey in the Great Lakes. This brown was iced with a lamprey attached. Without control, the Great Lakes trout and salmon fishery would be in serious jeopardy.

Combine your rod with a large spinning or bait-casting reel. Either way, be sure to coat the gears with a lightweight oil that won't get stiff in chilly Great Lakes weather. An ultra-smooth drag is also important—especially when fishing only 6- to 8-pound test line, as many anglers do. Just be sure to select reels which feature reliable drag systems, smooth-turning bail rollers or level winds, and retrieve ratios that pick up line quickly.

Finally, no matter what you're fishing with—don't overlook using premium, thin low-memory lines like Stren or Berkley Trilene. After putting so much effort into finding and catching these fish, it's ridiculous to skimp on line. I know 6- to 8-pound test sounds light, but lighter tackle is recommended for browns and steelhead, especially when fishing shallow, where these fish tend to be spooky. Just remember, you may hook an occasional monster, and one of these critters hooked 10 feet under the ice can really become a tackle buster. Be prepared. Check your knots and line frequently for abrasion, and either have the drag on your reel set properly, or better yet, flip the anti-reverse off and backreel your fish to prevent line twist.

Lures

If the fish are active, try action lures such as Normark's Jigging Rapala, System's Flyers, Acme's Kastmaster, HT's Marmooska, Bay de Noc's Swedish Pimples, Mepps Syclops Spoons, Reef Runner's Slender Spoons or Northland's Airplane Jigs tipped with minnows. My favorite plated colors include silver, followed by hammered silver, gold and hammered copper. For painted lures I'd go with orange, lime, watermelon or chartreuse. I also recommend using a ball-bearing snap swivel a foot or so up the line to prevent line twist when fishing these fluttering action lures, especially in current.

Again, sharpen your hooks, then work the entire vertical strata from bottom to just under the ice, experimenting with various jigging actions. Many beginning anglers seem surprised when big trout strike just under the ice as they're bringing lures up. What's even more perplexing is most anglers don't catch on and fail to utilize this as a regular method of consistently catching big Great Lakes trout. Both steelhead and browns are cold-water species, and consequently, are some of the most active fish under the ice. They aren't afraid to chase baits, and when aggressive 5- to 10-pound fish are following lures up to strike; well, suffice to say you won't see many more exciting hits beneath the ice. Remember, cover all vertical strata.

With fish this size cruising beneath the ice, one is well-advised to check knots and line frequently for abrasion.

If the fish are striking light, try free-lining a minnow-tipped lead-head jig to the bottom, and remembering Great Lakes trout may bite as the lure drops, maintain slight tension during the drop. If nothing happens, wait until the jig hits bottom, lift, slowly pump it up and down several times, pause, then reel up five feet or so and repeat the procedure until the jig gets to the surface. You'll be surprised by the number of fish that will strike high.

Recently, plastics have also moved onto the scene. Large tube jigs, for example, are becoming

Don't Over-Jig!

Most Great Lakes trout anglers have a tendency to fish too aggressively, which often spooks the fish. Periodic aggressive lifts are good for attracting distant trout, but overdone, may scare them away. Experiment carefully, mixing your jigging motions to see what best triggers fish.

popular. Just be sure to choose colors and jigging styles that closely resemble or imitate the principle baitfish trout are feeding on. Accurate depth control often makes the difference between no fish and a limit when trout are fussy, so try various levels.

If this doesn't work, try fishing a spoon and dropper rig tied to a #4 minnow-tipped jig head. Open your bail or engage your free spool, and allow the lure to drop to the bottom. When the line becomes slack, you're there. Engage the reel and begin fishing about a foot above bottom. Then gradually work upward, always being sure to work the entire vertical spectrum from top to bottom—slowly. These fish will often follow jigs up and hit just beneath the ice. If nothing happens, however, simply repeat this sequence as you move from hole to hole until you locate more active fish. Simply wiggle the jig and minnow dropper gently right in front of their face, then pause. Great Lakes trout usually strike on the pause. When you get a strike, set the hook, be patient, keep your rod high and your line tight, adjust your drag carefully, and play the fish gently against your rod, allowing the pull of the rod and your reel's drag or backreeled spool pressure to perform their respective functions. It won't be an experience you'll soon forget.

When fishing clear, shallow harbors or rivers where trout often become excessively fussy or spooky, you'll need to carefully select the right

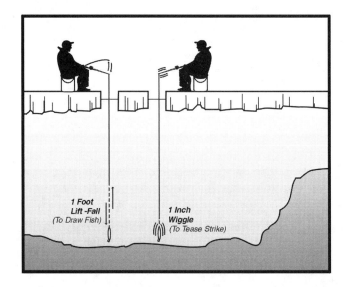

Most Great Lakes trout anglers have a tendency to fish too aggressively, which often spooks the fish. Periodic, aggressive lifts are good for attracting distant trout but, if overdone, may scare them away. Experiment with a combination of 1-foot lift-falls to attract fish, interspersed with only slight, 1-inch wiggles to tease strikes.

lure and proper jigging motion—and this often requires a great deal of consideration. After all, lure size, shape, and color all play critical roles in winter jigging success. Flat bottom or lightweight ice jigs, for example, fall more slowly than traditional Great Lakes trout lures, resulting in a slower presentation for neutral or inactive fish.

Keep Your Hooks Sharp!

Hook sharpness is another critical factor. Examine your hooks frequently. If they require sharpening, shave the outside edge of the point using a hook file, filing toward the hook point. Remove enough metal so the edge is flat and angled slightly toward the inside of the point. Next, turn the hook over and repeat the process, then smooth a third edge the same way, ultimately creating a three-sided point.

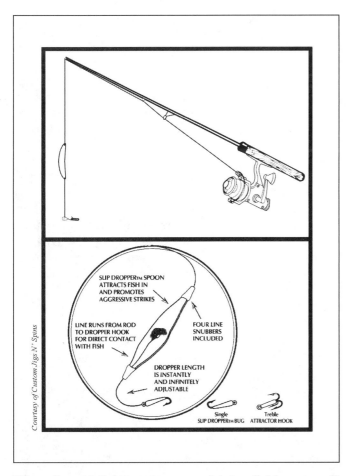

Courtesy of Custom Jigs N' Spins

When Great Lakes trout are spooky, try fishing a small minnow, mealworm, wax worm, nymph or slice of spawn sac rigged on a small ice jig. Attach this to a dropper line below a flash bait. Finesse jigging the bait is the rule, but using occasional lifts to flash the spoon will help attract fish. (Courtesy Custom Jigs and Spins)

If the trout are really spooky, a small minnow, mealworm, waxworm, nymph or slice of spawn sac rigged on a small ice jig and fished as a dropper lure below a flash bait are other popular options. Smaller horizontal baits such as #6 Custom Jigs and Spins Rat Finkees, HT's Marmooska Jigs, Bait Rigs Odd'Ball Jigs or Northland's Sink'N'Jigs are good bets for just such applications. Provided current isn't strong, they can also be fished as droppers off tiny, lightweight spoons such as Bait Rigs Willow Spoons, or fished alone. For best results, tip your favorite with a single salmon egg, waxworm, mealworm, mousie, grub, maggot or insect larvae such as a wiggler—and let the bait dangle from the hook, allowing it to wriggle seductively to attract fish, occasionally jigging gently to tease fish, and adding occasional "jumps" to attract distant fish.

Try Insect Larvae

Insect larvae are often the ideal ice fishing baits, especially when tipped on ice flies, jigs or teardrops. Another good method is to just barely nip a fine wire hook through the tip of a single larvae. Clear liquid will ooze out, but their internal organs won't be injured and they'll stay alive and wiggling. Just remember, use the smallest, sharpest hook you can. I often pinch the barbs on my hooks down slightly if they seem too big for the size and style bait being used. I am careful to hook the baits so they remain alive, longer. In addition, I'm convinced the cold, dense water of winter tends to suspend the scents of these natural juices, helping excite positive response from interested fish.

By the way, when ultra-light rigging with a nymph—or any insect larvae for that matter—run the point of your hook through the middle of the insect's back, then slide it gently underneath the shell or skin until the barb comes out near the head. This causes the bait to be positioned naturally in a horizontal manner, and the compact design of this presentation combined with a subtle jigging approach is a tremendous attraction advantage during periods of slowed feeding activity.

Where live bait isn't legal, soft plastic bodies in black, brown or green rigged on a jig head and dipped in fish attractant may closely match the trout's preferred forage. I've even seen some folks experiencing success by hiding tiny hooks within

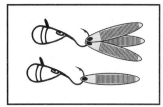

When fishing grubs or maggots, always gently nip the tip of the hook through the skin, allowing the grubs to wiggle attractively.

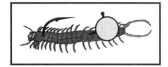

When fishing insect larvae, run the point of your hook through the middle of the insect's back, then slide it gently underneath the shell or skin until the barb comes out near the head. This will position the larvae in a natural, horizontal position.

Uncle Josh's pork rind Ice Flecks, Johnson's Ice Magic Baits and Berkley Power Baits.

Once you've selected a bait and a fish appears, you'll have to convince it to bite. I've experienced most success fishing "tightline" on sensitive, light-action ice rods like HT's Premium Polar Lights. By gently raising and lowering the bait with short, subtle twitches before dropping it to the bottom, or with the help of a super-sensitive balsa slip-float, such as Thill Tackle's Center Slider, I can stabilize movement, barely "quivering" the bait in place to tease fish into striking.

When you receive a strike on an ultra-light rig, pause briefly, then set the hook with a firm, upward movement. Adjust your drag or backreel and hold your rod high while fighting the fish. This allows more control and extra play should your trophy make a fast, hard run. Often trout are lost within just a few inches of the hole simply because overzealous anglers aren't able to react quickly enough when fish make long, last-ditch head shaking runs for freedom.

For really spooky trout, some anglers drop down to 2-pound line and simply tip a #4 salmon egg or circle hook with tiny minnows, spawn sacs or chunks, waxworms, corn or wigglers, then barely jig the bait. If you try this approach, it's a good idea to stagger various sized micro-splitshot up the line to help keep your bait down, especially if there's current present, and be prepared for a long fight.

Incidentally, for proponents of catch and release, winter trout are releasable, provided they're handled gently, not deeply hooked or taken from excessively deep water.

A Final Note

If you're an avid inland trophy rainbow or brown angler, by this time you've probably realized Great Lakes trophy trout tactics don't vary much from those used inland. The only major differences include monitoring the individual lake for differentiating factors such as water clarity, structure, cover and forage availability, and the effect of inter-species relationships. By recognizing these factors, then simply modifying your presentation to meet the conditions—you might be deeply rewarded. Remember, some chunky inland rainbows and browns meeting our definition of "game fish" are out there, and if available in your area, they are certainly worth fishing.

Safety First

One last thought, and that's safety. Whether you're fishing large inland waters or the Great Lakes, safety can't be emphasized enough. Always travel in pairs, be particularly cautious when traversing river channels and river mouths featuring ice-eroding currents. Avoid ice heaves and cracks—given big water, currents and winds can open these from a few inches to a few feet in relatively short time periods—and always carry safety equipment such as ice cleats, picks and rope.

Be careful, but if you're up for trying a new, exciting challenge this winter, why not try a big inland water, Great Lakes river, harbor or bay near you? After all, if you've been itching to try something new, innovative and challenging, the trophy winter rainbow, brown or steelhead experience might just scratch your itch.

For really spooky trout, some anglers drop down to 2-pound line and simply tip a small salmon egg or circle hook with tiny minnows, spawn sacs, wax worms or wigglers, then finesse jig these fussy, light-biters.

Chapter 8

Understanding Largemouth and Smallmouth Bass in Winter

Everything I'd ever heard about largemouth and smallmouth bass in winter seemed to indicate they were almost impossible to catch. Throughout my childhood, no ice angler ever mentioned targeting largemouth or smallmouth bass during the frozen water period. That remains essentially true today.

This always intrigued me. Being an avid summer bass angler, I started asking others why they don't fish for bass through the ice. No one seemed to know. Most simply hadn't tried it. Others said catches were incidental, and of the two good anglers who said they had seriously tried targeting winter bass, both indicated their consistency was minimal.

I started asking myself why ice anglers have so much trouble consistently hooking bass, and why a somewhat stable pattern couldn't be found. Although I didn't know it at the time, this simple, self-directed question set me on a quest that eventually led me to some working winter patterns. I found these through trial, error—and a touch of luck.

But first, the fish. Let's start with largemouth.

Largemouth Bass

Largemouth bass are one of the most widely distributed and popular game fish in North America. They cruise ice-crusted waters throughout much of the ice fishing belt, feeding on insect larvae, crustaceans and small baitfish. They're easy to identify by their golden-green sides and a dark band of black blotches lining the lateral line.

Largemouth bass are one of the most widely distributed, popular gamefish in North America for open-water fishing. But when it comes to winter, few anglers seem to know much about their sub-ice habits.

But most photos of anglers holding bass are taken in bass boats. You simply won't see many on-ice photos, because few people know much about winter largemouth habits. Let's change that.

General Winter Largemouth Location Patterns

I ran across the first hints of a stable winter largemouth pattern coincidentally while crappie fishing. Knowing most first-ice crappies congregate around areas supporting forage, I began studying the habits and movements of the crappie's favorite prey items, small minnows. I figured if I could understand their prey, crappies wouldn't be far away. The idea worked.

I had also noted first-ice winter largemouth feed on the same basic prey items that winter crappies do—principally small baitfish. So while jigging specific target areas for crappies, I started to notice fairly consistent catches of largemouth, even though I wasn't pursuing them. But my success wasn't consistent enough to call a pattern.

This brought me back to why ice anglers have so much trouble consistently catching largemouth. I began focusing on largemouth, experimenting with the various details of location and presentation, keeping everything as constant in my strategies as I could—lake type, structure, depth, cover, jigging speed, lure color, size and style—everything was changed only one variable

at a time until I finally started to find the right combination and consistently hooked them. A tedious process, yes, but gradually, the answers started to become more clear.

Don't get me wrong. I'm certainly not saying winter largemouth are an easy proposition. There simply aren't many such circumstances in the rather intricate, obscure world of ice fishing largemouth. But the systematic pattern I've discovered offers a fair amount of consistency—the foundation of any successful ice fishing pattern.

The Basis

The basis of any winter largemouth pattern begins with a few facts: The fish either tend to school closely in relatively small areas surrounding structure, or hold in loose schools over mid-depth, soft-bottom mud flats. Secondly, although largemouth generally move deeper than smallmouth during the winter, they are also typically more active.

Early in the winter and just before ice out, bass will usually hold over deeper pockets on shallow to mid-depth flats and weed lines in smaller ponds and natural lakes. During mid-winter they can be found along the edges of deep weed lines surrounding main lake points or on deep mud flats. Since these fish can be difficult to find, it is wise to focus on relatively smaller ponds and natural lakes featuring limited structure. That's because there's less deep water and structure to choose from making patterns easier to pinpoint.

Start by identifying the largest, deepest, vegetated main-lake points and turns, then search for the steepest breaks leading into the deepest available water. Begin looking deep, fishing the deepest flat. Then gradually work your way up the point searching for bass. Focus your efforts during low-light, early-morning and late-evening periods, or during long periods of mild, stable, overcast weather when most feeding activity occurs.

This all might be hard for summer anglers to understand. Summer largemouth in most waters focus their activity around primary drop-offs and any associated shallow-water flats. But this is winter, and this is also just a general pattern. Now

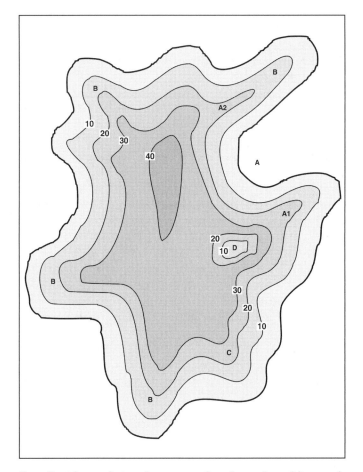

For first-ice winter largemouth, sharp-breaking primary drop-offs (b) lining shallow bays and flats are primary areas, especially if they feature healthy green vegetation. During mid-winter, bass will drop deeper along these edges, but often hold along turns lining main lake points (a1,a2). Other turns, distant from points, (c) may attract fish, but not in the numbers associated with main-lake points. Rises (d) may also draw mid-winter fish, but again, to a much lesser degree than points.

First ice, flats and sharp-breaking drop-offs supporting healthy, green vegetation or wood are one of the largemouth's favorite hangouts. (Courtesy Northland Tackle)

let's look at largemouth movement through the winter more closely.

First Ice

Flats and sharp-breaking primary drop-offs supporting healthy, green vegetation or wood are one of the largemouth's favorite hangouts when the ice first arrives. Healthy green weeds or wood extending from the base of the primary drop all the way into the farthest reaches of shallow water bays; coves and flats offer the most cover and forage. Early ice bass may move freely throughout these shallows, making first ice bassin' a fairly easy proposition. This is also when most ice anglers hook a few bass. But the period is short-lived.

Mid-Winter

As the season progresses, ice anglers lose touch with largemouth, because as shallow weed

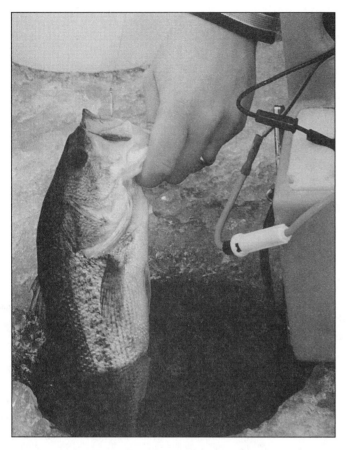

Most mid-winter largemouth are taken from areas offering healthy, green broadleaf cabbage or deep, main lake mud flats.

growth deteriorates, largemouth holding within these weeds gradually begin moving down the primary drop-off. On shallow lakes or ponds without a well-defined primary break, bass may still relate to any available shallow vegetation. Otherwise, look for schools to begin congregating along vegetated primary drop-offs, especially steep breaks near points featuring good inside turns, mid-depth, soft-bottom flats. Secondly, look along mid-lake humps, bars or shoals.

But there's more to the weed line pattern. After fishing several frozen lakes for a number of years, I took this basic pattern even farther. I knew almost every time I found green weeds on a steep break with an inside turn lining a deep main-lake point I'd catch some largemouth. But also noted I caught more and bigger bass at two specific turns on my favorite lake. Just knowing bass were there wasn't good enough. I wanted to know why.

My first observation was when my jig fouled weeds in these hot spots, I always hauled up thick masses of cabbage or coontail weeds. Other less productive areas yielded different vegetation types, or at best, sparse cabbage. Since then, I've experimented extensively on several more natural lakes, fishing various vegetation types, and discovered I usually catch more mid-winter bass in cabbage and coontail.

Another piece of the puzzle. But it still wasn't consistent enough to establish what I would call a definite pattern. However, I eventually discovered another variable, and it's this dimension that makes the major difference in consistently successful winter largemouth bass fishing.

Finalizing a Mid-Winter Pattern

It all began one morning on the way to my favorite lake for some mid-winter bassin'. The thought crossed my mind that being a largemouth during winter must be pretty tough. Temperatures are cold, oxygen and pH levels unstable, and small baitfish are not only difficult to locate and catch, but rarely available this time of year. Obviously, such a forbidding environment is far from the largemouth's preferred conditions. This would make their activity levels low and feeding activity slow.

However, if there's one thing I've learned in all my years of ice fishing, it's that almost every seemingly impossible situation has an answer if we just use the brains God gave us. And after a great deal of thought, an idea struck me. If I could find a deep, inside turn where a relatively stable temperature, pH level and oxygen count could be found along with cabbage or coontail weeds and a stable food source, the bass would not only be present, but probably concentrated as well. It would be some sort of underwater bass oasis.

And then, it struck me. What about springs? Springs not only offer uniform water temperatures, these temperatures remain nearly 50 degrees all year. That's 10 to 15 degrees warmer

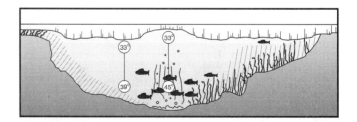

Due to the warmer water, more stable oxygen and higher pH concentrations, springs are primary mid-winter largemouth attractors.

Fishing springs has turned out to be the basis for a series of hot mid-winter largemouth patterns that start just after the first-ice period ends, and often continue right through ice-out.

than the surrounding water. Springs would offer high, stable oxygen and pH counts, and assuming adequate sunlight penetrated the ice, would support green vegetation. With forage available, this situation would be somewhat akin to walking into a warm kitchen with a hot meal waiting. And this has turned out to be the basis for a series of hot mid-winter largemouth patterns that start just after the first-ice period ends, and often continue right through ice-out.

Are springs hard to find? Not really. Since spring water remains in the low 50's all year, springs can be located by scouting a lake's primary breaks in summer with temperature probes. You'll be searching for 50-degree water. If you don't have a temperature probe you can simply watch the lake freeze to see which spots freeze last. Sure, this takes time, but once you've identified a spring on a deep, cabbage vegetated supporting inside turn near a deep point, hump, bar or shoal, you've likely located a winter bass gold mine. On many waters this will also provide potential for good mixed-bag catches including walleye and pike as well.

I've also been made aware of a secondary mid-winter largemouth pattern by expert angler and friend Duane Peterson of Northland Tackle. He has found numbers of good size largemouth holding on mid-depth, soft-bottom flats running 21 to 25 feet deep which happen to often be far removed from any hard-bottom or structure. Apparently, these fish eat worms, insects, crustaceans and other forage holdings in the thick bottom silt suspended in the dense water at lake bottom.

On many reservoirs and flowages deeper springs in mid-depth mud flats among standing timber, stump fields or other forms of wood can be just as productive as green weeds on natural lakes. Don't ignore these alternative forms of cover. Secondly, always be careful when fishing around springs. Remember, the relatively warm, moving water can soften ice and make conditions dangerous, particularly during first and last ice.

Expert angler and friend Duane Peterson of Northland Tackle, has discovered that some winter largemouth hold on mid-depth, soft-bottom main-lake mud flats far removed from any real "structure." (Courtesy Northland Tackle)

Late Ice

Late winter largemouth often hold deep around mid-winter holes along steep breaks and springs. They will gradually rise up these breaks into shallower water as ice-out approaches, light penetration increases, oxygen counts improve, shallow-water weeds develop and forage rebounds. Watch for these movements, because where the season for largemouth is open, late ice action can be tremendous.

Winter Largemouth Bass Activity and Location: Yet Another Twist

For some unknown reason, I've found river backwaters more productive for winter bass fishing than lakes. Not that this is easy fishing—backwater largemouth concentrate thickly in areas near springs on vegetated or timber-strewn holes. So if you're not on the exact spot, you probably won't catch many largemouth bass.

Ice fishing for largemouth poses many challenges and requires special tackle and lures, such as this Northland Buck-Shot rattle spoon, used to attract bass. (Courtesy Northland Tackle)

Even on the right spot, after you've caught a couple from the school, other fish may spook and refuse to bite. But if you can locate several springs, you'll probably be able to catch a couple fish from each location and accumulate a respectable catch. Of course, accomplishing this consistently requires a great deal of mobility, finesse and versatility. Using the right equipment and techniques is imperative.

Timing

Largemouth are most active at first-ice and during late ice. The morning and evening twilight periods are the best, although periods of mild, stable, overcast weather may cause them to bite later into the morning or begin earlier in the afternoon.

During late ice, largemouth bass action often increases as these fish gradually move shallower and feed more actively.

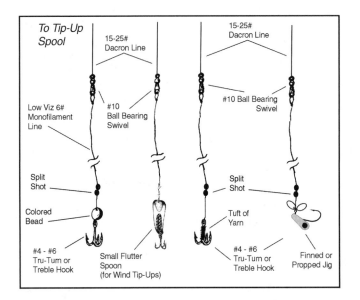

Tip-up rigs for largemouth should be long and light. Eighteen to twenty-four inch leaders of six pound monofilament or fluorocarbon line hooked to a #4-6 treble hook and a small, two or three inch fathead lowered with a minimal amount of weight is the preferred rig. Small, lightweight flutter spoons work well on wind tip-ups, as will small prop or finned jigs.

Effective Winter Largemouth Fishing Strategies

Ice fishing for largemouth poses many challenges and requires special tackle. My favorite method for catching wary largemouth is jigging, but I usually set a few tip-ups as well. Stick, stationary, or thermal models placed along deep breaks work fine, but because largemouth bite so lightly, balance, tip-down or wind tip-ups are even better. To rig them, keep things simple—and light. Start with 15- to 25-pound dacron, and connect an 18- to 24-inch length of 6-pound monofilament with a #10 black barrel swivel. Tie a #4 or #6 Tru-Turn or treble hook to the end, baiting it with a 2- or 3-inch fathead minnow, using a minimal amount of splitshot to hold the bait in place.

With wind tip-ups, you can also tie small, lightweight flutter spoons like Bait Rigs Willospoons or Reef Runner Slender Spoons to the terminal end of the line. Remove the hook and attach a short length of monofilament to the split ring, ending the rig with a #6 teardrop jig tipped with a 2-inch fathead. Just be sure to experiment with various depth settings. If your bait isn't set in the primary strike zone, it's unlikely to get hit. Standard, finned

teardrop such as HT's Helicopter and finned Daphnia Lures or prop jigs such as Northland's Whistler packed with grubs, are also excellent wind tip-up baits for largemouth; just keep them small and light.

Consider Grub Type

Maggots come in different sizes, shapes, actions, textures and scents. Each may generate different responses from fish. I've seen times where bass snubbed their noses at waxworms, but inhaled lively red wigglers or nightcrawlers. I'm not saying you must carry two dozen different types of live bait on the ice. I only want to make you aware that doing so might provide a distinct edge. So always try traditional waxworms, spikes and mousees—they'll often produce. But don't ignore specialty baits, they can increase your winter bass catch!

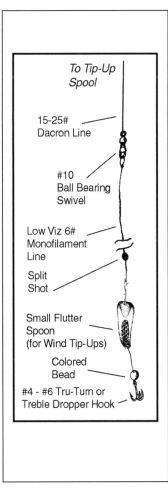

A highly effective modified wind tip-up rig for largemouth involves a small, lightweight flutter spoon outfitted with a short dropper line leading to a small, supersharp stinger hook.

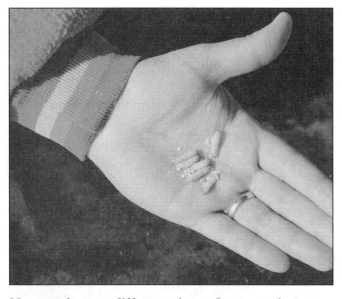

Maggots feature different sizes, shapes, actions, textures and scents, and each may generate different responses.

Jigging

Since winter largemouth are often so fussy, I've found precision jigging approaches to be the most effective way to catch them. A medium, medium-light or light action graphite ice rod such as Berkley's Lightning Rod, HT's Premium Polar Lites, Intrigues or Polar Golds rigged with a high-quality spinning reel spooled with thin, low-memory 4- to 6-pound test monofilament like Berkley Trilene XL works beautifully. Keep it light, though, or you'll be decreasing your presentation potency.

During the early season when the bass are still actively feeding, small jigging minnow lures like Jigging Rapalas, System Tackle Flyers, Nils-Master Jigger Shad and Bad Dog Humpbacks are good choices. Tip them with a minnow head or grub,

---

Spool with Thinner Diameter, Low-Memory Line

When jigging, lighter lines hang straight, even with light lures, allowing close contact between the lure and your strike sensing equipment. Done correctly, this is so sensitive, you may even see the slight quiver of a minnow registering on your float or rod tip as it swims gently on your jig below. Now, should a fussy bass so much as nip the lure, your line will move, registering a strike on your spring bobber, float or rod tip. Then you can set the hook. Results? Increased hooking percentages.

---

and work them off the bottom a foot or two. Pump-jig the lure up 6 to 8 inches two or three times, allowing it to fall, then pausing briefly before continuing to simply wiggle the lure with a gentle jiggle before repeating the pump-jigging motion.

Jigging Spoon Tips

"When fishing bass with jigging spoons like Bad Dog's Crippled Willow, a common mistake is jigging too hard," said Bad Dog pro staff member Steve Felegy. *"Instead of jerking the spoon, pump the bait with three consecutive, gradual 10- to 12-inch pumps, drop the lure gently, and pause 15 or 20 seconds. Most strikes will come on the pause or, when fish are aggressive, on the fall."*

The experts at Northland Tackle have experienced excellent catches of mid-winter largemouth on mid-depth, soft-bottomed, main-lake basin mud flats far removed from any "structure." They have done very well fishing Buck-Shot rattle spoons with short, quick snaps mixed with shaking motions. The snaps draw fish in and brief pauses instigate strikes. (Courtesy Northland Tackle)

Light, low-diameter, low-memory lines, like this specially formulated Berkley Trilene cold-weather line will provide greater presentation control and sensitivity when fishing light-biting fish.

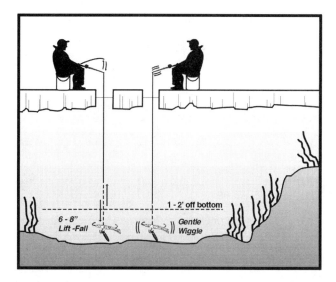

At first ice, when largemouth may still be actively feeding, small jigging minnow-style lures tipped with a minnow head or large grub can be effective. Try pump jigging them two or three times, allow them to fall, then pause several seconds before simply wiggling the lure in place, and repeating the motion.

Small jigging spoons, large teardrops or small plastic tube jigs tipped with a small minnow or scent enhanced plastic can also be productive. To jig, lift the bait a foot or so three times, and quickly return the rod tip to its original position, allowing the lure to slowly flutter down as it settles. Next, wait 15 seconds before gently jiggling the lure. Then repeat lifting the rod to a different height. If the bass are fussy and won't hit, switch to a standard lead-head jig tipped with a small shiner or fathead and work it with an ultra-slow, jiggling motion.

During the early season when largemouth are still actively feeding, small jigging minnow lures like jigging Rapalas are good presentation choices.

Tip with Scent

In winter when water is colder and denser, scent tends to suspend and stay in the bass' strike zone longer, so live bait and fish scents can give a definite advantage.

In either case, pause several seconds between lifts, allowing bass plenty of time to strike. Largemouth usually aren't very active, and here you're using a jigging motion to attract them; the pause is to tempt them into flaring their gills and sucking in the easy meal. Fish slowly.

In winter when water is colder and denser, fish attractants tend to dissipate slower and suspend in the bass' strike zone longer, making them a definite presentation advantage. (Courtesy Berkley/OTG)

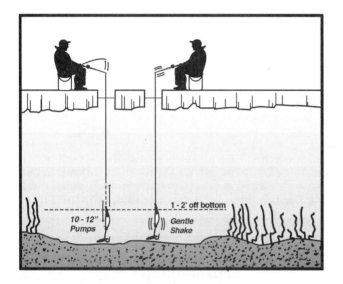

When using jigging spoons for winter largemouth, gently pump the bait with three consecutive, 10- to 12-inch pumps, drop the lure near bottom and pause for 15-20 seconds. Most strikes will come on the pause.

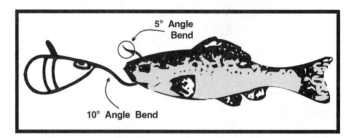

When fishing minnow-tipped jigs for winter largemouth, bend the hook point out slightly so it will stick through the minnow and leave plenty of the point and barb exposed to better hook the fish.

For added hooking potential, bend the hook out slightly so it will stick through the minnow and leave plenty of the point and barb exposed to stick the target fish. Always use fresh bait—healthy minnows react to the approach of a big bass in subtle ways that trigger the bass to hit. That's something you simply can't accomplish alone. And no matter what, make sure your hook is sharp to ensure solid, efficient hook sets into the tough cartilage surrounding the jaw.

If bass are present but still not striking, switch to a light or ultra-light rod combo spooled with 2- to 4-pound test Trilene XL or Stren Easy Cast, and try a small, delicately balanced slip float and minnow rig. Or you can tie on a smaller #8 or #10 horizontal ice jig packed with maggots. Work these baits with a slight, continuous jiggle while gradually raising or lowering the lure. Again, use fresh bait, and hook them carefully so they stay alive and wriggling. Most strikes will occur as you lower the jig.

Still, don't expect to catch a pile of winter largemouth in short order—except perhaps at first ice. If it's a great deal of ice fishing action you're looking for, largemouth probably won't be your bag. If you want to socialize and play cards while you fish, set up some tip-ups and do so.

But if you want to try something new, something on the cutting edge of the ice fishing revolution, bass fishing is a full-bore challenge calling

When fishing winter largemouth, it's important to always be able to feel the weight of your lure to maintain constant contact with the bait, or you'll miss these often light-biting fish. (Courtesy Northland Tackle)

As in summer, largemouth appear to find a wiggling nightcrawler and irresistible temptation.

you to boldly go where few ice anglers have gone before, try using the basics presented here to establish some working winter largemouth patterns on your target waters. Like me, you might find catching five or six big bass is more rewarding than a limit of pike.

Understanding Smallmouth Bass in Winter

Like largemouth bass, smallmouth aren't pulled through the ice by many. This is likely the result of three factors:

1) They may hold deeper than most anglers like to fish on many lake types,
2) They concentrate heavily, so if you're not in the right area, you're unlikely to do well,
3) They typically aren't very active throughout most of the winter.

However, smallmouth can be caught, and because they concentrate, if you enjoy the challenge of using your knowledge, maps and electron-

Smallmouth aren't considered a winter-sought species by many ice anglers, but given the right conditions, they can be caught. (Courtesy Anglers' All Roger Lepenter)

Smallmouth bass aren't a commonly sought winter species, but some are taken.

ics to find fish, smallmouth may just whet your appetite for a wonderful winter challenge paying big rewards.

Smallmouth bass are native to the Great Lakes and a few river systems of the eastern and central United States and Canada. Today, however, smallmouth are widely distributed and have become a popular game fish throughout the North American ice fishing belt, where they feed on insect larvae, crustaceans and baitfish. They're easy to identify by their golden-bronze sides and dark vertical bars.

Although smallmouth usually don't attain the size of their larger cousin and are rarely active in winter, they tend to congregate even more tightly than largemouth. They can typically be found around the bases of steep rock breaks (or in the Great Lakes at breakwaters or ore docks) surrounding soft bottom, mid-depth flats. Find them, and they can be caught.

Primary Winter Smallmouth Locations

The secret to catching winter smallmouth begins with finding lakes or Great Lakes bays supporting good populations of smallmouth and, more importantly, relatively low populations of directly competing species such as walleyes, largemouth bass or crappies. This reduces interspecies competition, making potential locations that may be holding concentrations of smallmouth easier to pinpoint.

In some respects, finding primary winter smallmouth locations is easy, because they virtually always relate to specific areas and group tightly, winter after winter. However, wintering locations are often so small and specific, they can be like finding the proverbial needle in a haystack.

Beginning in late fall, smallmouth usually begin migrating along deep or mid-depth, hard-bottom reefs, points or breakwaters leading from shallow to mid-depth water. As ice forms, smallmouth drop close to the bottom and congregate in the deepest available water nearest the base of these structures or along mid-depth shelves (25 to 35 feet) off the edges of deep, hard-bottom flats, often right where

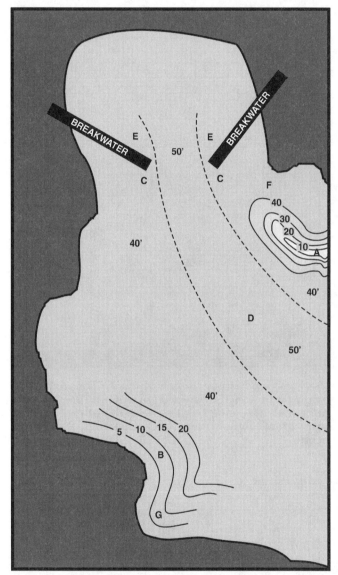

First ice, smallmouth can be caught along deep or mid-depth hard-bottom reefs (a), points (b) or on Great Lakes bays, along breakwaters (c, e). During mid and late-winter, smallmouth often simply position along the deepest edges of these same features, although deep turns (g) lining bottom content transitions are primary targets. The edges of deep shipping lanes (d) rubble-strewn shorelines, contours or features such as breakwaters or ore docks on Great Lakes bays are also productive.

they meet soft bottom flats or basins. In many waters, this is where smallmouth often remain until near ice-out, when they may begin moving closer to shallower spawning grounds. Essentially, wintering smallmouths relate largely to mid-depth, hard-bottom or rip-rapped reefs, points, rock bars, breakwaters and shelves bordering mid-depth water or sand/rubble spawning flats supplying a consistent supply of forage. If you can identify such areas using lake maps and sonar, you've likely accomplished a big part of establishing a viable, winter-long pattern.

But now for the pinpointing. From here, look for diverse mixtures of bottom contours and content including sand, gravel, rubble or rock bordering soft bottoms and good secondary cover, Or, better yet, combinations of secondary cover holding forage. Again, the best combinations are those located near steep drop-offs, breaks and contour turns where hard-bottom structure edges out and meets soft bottom. Provided there isn't much inter-species competition chasing the smallmouths into some unique ecological niche, you'll usually find winter smallmouths gathered in specific areas fairly heavily.

In deep lakes or Great Lakes bays supporting competitive species such as lake trout, splake or walleyes, you may discover smallmouths pushed onto shallower structures, because the dominant trout patrol the deep water and walleyes are king of the hill on mid-depth structures. This leaves smallmouth no choice but to move shallower where forage is more readily available. Either way, you'll usually find smallmouth congregated in specific areas. Locate one or two of these spots where they likely winter, use sonar and underwater cameras, if you can, to positively identify these concentrated, bottom-hugging schools, and you'll be able to catch winter smallmouth with some consistency.

Since this leaves winter smallmouths so vulnerable, however, try to keep such places to yourself, and release any fish you catch. Winter smallmouths are sporting to catch and worthy of release. Since they don't move much and usually concentrate so heavily in winter, if you're irresponsible and spread the word, too many anglers fishing these schools could ultimately harm the fishery.

Remember, most ice anglers don't pursue winter smallmouths because most don't possess the knowledge to do so. If they're not right on them, they're not likely to catch many fish and won't harm the population. But if someone finds the exact spot, the opportunity to catch a lot of smallmouth is possible. A couple good anglers fishing a tightly concentrated school and starting a chain reaction where anglers start hauling in 5-gallon pails full of smallies could seriously hurt a smallmouth fishery. So please, respect the resource. With knowledge comes responsibility.

Timing

Winter smallmouths are most easily caught through early ice, although anglers catch them during the mid and late winter periods, particularly on Great Lakes bays or waters supporting large populations. On a daily basis, winter smallmouth may bite all day, but like most winter species, you're most likely to get bites early and late in the day.

Effective Winter Smallmouth Fishing Strategies

Winter smallmouth presentation basically boils down to one important factor: Precision. Fish even a few feet from a school, and you're not likely to get a bite. Find them and drop a bait on top of them however, and the action can be quite consistent, simply due to the sheer number of fish available.

Wind tip-ups such as HT's Windlass, tipped with small, flashy jigging spoons can be the ticket to catch winter smallmouth. They are much better than fixed position tip-ups on many occasions.

Smallies usually feed best early and late in the day during first ice, and this is when fixed-position underwater tip-ups set on a light trip and rigged with small, 2- or 3-inch shiners or chubs will catch them. Wind tip-ups, if the weather is cooperating, will work well, too. In fact, wind tip-ups tipped with small, flashy jigging spoons can be the ticket, taking even more fish than fixed-position units on many occasions.

Jigging with 24- to 42-inch medium-action spinning combos, 6-pound monofilament, smaller jigging minnows or jigging spoons tipped with tiny minnows, lead-head jigs tipped with small minnows, even still set balsa slip-float rigs and 2- to 3-inch minnows can be highly effective winter smallmouth presentations. For best results, fish with slow, methodical lift-drop motions directly on bottom, or just above the level of a marked school. At times, especially in clear water, light-action graphite ice rods, smaller spinning reels spooled with 2- to 4-pound line and rigged with heavy, small-profile jigs such as Northland's Jig-A-Bits or HT's Marmooskas, and "stand up" models like Bait Rigs Odd'Ball Jigs tipped with grubs, maggots or wigglers and jiggled gently on bottom can have good results as well. Bites are usually firm and solid, but gradual. Give the fish a little time with the bait before setting the hook—then hang on!

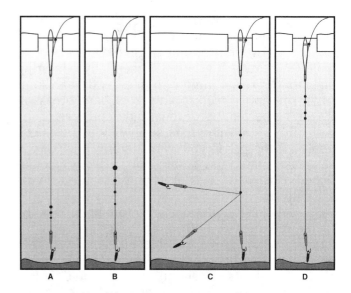

Working smaller jigging minnows, spoons or jigs tipped with minnows or grubs are all effective for winter smallmouth, but slip bobber rigs consisting of a tiny, grub-tipped rocker jig may be the most effective of all. Rig the slip bobber neutrally buoyant. In deeper water or current, positioning a split shot or two closer to the lure (a, b) will help keep your presentation in the strike zone, in shallow or still water areas, spreading the shot higher still maintains the float's neutral buoyancy, but also results in a slower fall (c, d).

Try Alternative Grub-Tipping Methods

You can also hook grubs with light wire hooks threaded through the tail and out through the head. Then turned inside out to release body juices. This will attract bass. Sometimes, rather than removing larvae mangled by nipping fish, leave them on when you add fresh bait. Often, the additional movement and scent filtering through the water attracts smallmouth.

Just remember, when icing smallmouths, take a couple pictures and quickly release them. The challenge of winter smallmouths is locating them and getting them to bite. They should not be considered "catch and kill" table fare. Be careful with the fish, smile with pride over your skill reading difficult winter fishing patterns, but don't abuse the resource. Remember, with knowledge comes responsibility and respect. I'm sharing this information hoping that you will, in good faith, be a true sportsman and not abuse our precious smallmouth fisheries.

Pass it on.

When fishing winter smallmouth, experiment with different baits, tipping and hooking methods. Usually, lightly nipped, lively, wiggly grubs, maggots, nymphs, red worms or night crawlers work especially well.

Chapter 9

Understanding Whitefish in Winter

Canada's Lake Simcoe ice fishing guide Leon Maloney displays a nice whitefish. (photo Courtesy Wil Wegman)

My first winter whitefish outing took place on the famed waters of Ontario's Lake Simcoe, where I met two die-hard winter whitefish anglers. Both were showing enthusiasm over the exceptionally large whitefish of Lake Simcoe, explaining that the fishery draws anglers from all over Canada each winter. After hearing more about this unique fishery, I became intrigued, and sensing my interest, these gentlemen not only began showing me their equipment and tactics, but also invited me to accompany them fishing the following day.

So early the next morning in a cold, pre-dawn Canadian snowfall, we met, loaded up our four-wheelers and headed to their hut positioned over a deep, mid-lake mud flat. After setting a couple of tip-ups, we went inside and rigged three special, delicately balanced tip-downs with four hook spreader rigs. Laid directly on the bottom, the rigs were baited with small minnows at each corner. Arms on the tip-downs were precariously bal-

anced pointing down, and occasionally jigged to move the spreaders below. I was told to simply watch for subtle, upward movements of the arm, because when whitefish strike they lift the spreader, and consequently, the weight holding the arm down is released, tipping them up and indicating a strike.

While waiting, we jigged small, flashy spoons, and, whenever time allowed, we'd grab a minnow or two from the bucket, break their backbones so they couldn't swim away, and pop their air bladders so they'd sink into the depths. Then we'd drop them down our holes. The goal was simply to draw scattered whitefish toward our baited hooks, using the minnows as an incentive.

Fifteen minutes later, an arm on the outside tip-down rose a quarter inch. One of my alert friends jumped, set the hook and started pulling in the line, hand-over-hand. I quickly cleared other lines, then watched as a 4-pound whitefish struggled as it was pulled up from the depths of the clear, green-tinted water. Later that morning we cleaned and baked four fresh whitefish. Seasoned to perfection and dipped in drawn butter, few meals I've experienced have tasted better.

The Fish

Whitefish have long been important to residents of northern North America. Tales have been told of the importance of whitefish to North American Indians. When whitefish moved to shallow waters to spawn in late fall and early winter, natives would gather to trade furs, make maple sugar, and eat whitefish. Even as late as the 1950s and 1960s, catches of 35 or 40 fish a day were not unusual for Canadian ice anglers fishing the prime, early-ice period.

Today's regulations often limit anglers to just a couple fish per day, but today's whitefish spawn can be equally as significant to modern, first-ice anglers. The whitefish spawn in late fall and early winter which is an event that may last several weeks. In winters featuring early cold snaps, ice

Canadian fishing guide and tackle expert Steve Chenier with a typical lake Nipissing whitefish, caught on a Blue Fox Tingler spoon with a stinger hook. (photo Courtesy Steve Chenier)

may form over gravel or rock spawning grounds along the shore, shoreline reefs and the mouths of small tributaries. This provides ice anglers access to concentrated groups of whitefish. Since this occurs primarily at night, fishing twilight and evening periods provides good action.

Throughout the lakes of northern Ontario, Canada, bountiful quantities of these delicious fish can be taken. In Lake Simcoe, about 20,000 whitefish are still iced annually, and studies have indicated more anglers fish whitefish than any other species here. This is not surprising, considering Lake Simcoe has supported one of the largest winter whitefish sport fisheries in Ontario since the early 1900s. Modern anglers know this, too. On the second day of the 1992 World Ice Fishing Championships, 132 competing anglers confined to a mid-depth area caught 158 whitefish.

Whitefish are a member of the trout and salmon family. They love relatively deep, cold, clear, oxygen-rich water and are often found roaming the same deep, cold flats as lake trout. They can best be described as having silvery, bluish-

Canada's Lake Simcoe has supported one of the largest winter whitefish sport fisheries in North America since the early 1900s.

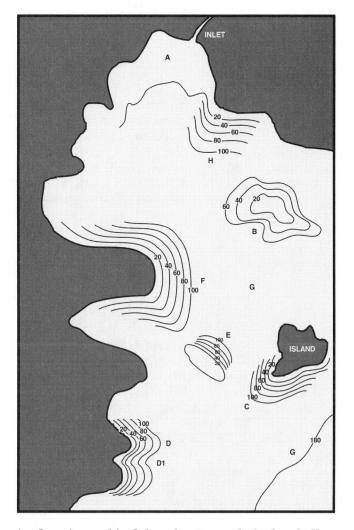

At first ice, whitefish relate to relatively shallow, hard-bottom shoals and tributary mouths (a), but often, they relate to hard-bottom mid-depth shoals (e, h) as well. This is especially true as mid-season approaches, when flats adjoining the deep bases of main-lake points (d, f) also become increasingly productive. The bases along points extending from main-lake islands (c) are good mid-season locations, and often, whitefish will scatter over deep, main-lake flats (g). Late season, the bases of structures lining main-lake flats (b, c, d, e, and f) are especially good. Those offering solid migration routes such as (b) or (d1) would justify the most effort. Just before ice-out, more gradual breaks leading from deep water to shallow shoals (h) and the shallow shoals themselves (a) may also be worth checking.

white sides and a pale green top section, white bellies and distinct, down-turned, sucker-like mouths. The mouth is what differentiates them from the closely colored cisco, a species with which they are often confused. Whitefish typically average about 15 to 20 inches and weigh from 2 to 5 pounds. The world record weighs over 14 pounds, and many experts predict this record will be broken by a Simcoe angler in the near future.

Throughout winter, whitefish feed on small fish, crustaceans, plankton, insects and invertebrates and with their turned down, vacuum cleaner-like mouths, are best adapted to feeding directly on bottom. When hooked, they put up respectable fights. Whitefish fillets are an oily, but great-tasting meat highly regarded for their quality table fare when smoked, baked, blackened in the pan or broiled.

Primary Winter Whitefish Patterns

In terms of location, the worst mistake most winter whitefish anglers make is sitting in one place too long. Whitefish are a wandering, roaming species that's usually on the move throughout the winter. Mobility is a key to success. A second mistake many winter whitefish anglers make is fishing too deep. While often found on deep flats during the mid-season, mid-depth flats running 40 to 60 feet deep are much more productive early and late in the winter.

Another location error is spending too much time on structures such as points or reefs. It's a known fact that winter whitefish relate to these structures, but they primarily use them as migration routes. Fishing these areas means you're targeting moving fish, and you're likely to intercept fish only once or twice a day, even if you're fishing the perfect depth. Most winter whitefish concentrate and feed on flats; specifically, flats supporting light grass or "moss beds" where concentrations of invertebrates offer forage. Find such areas near a major migration route, and you'll likely find whitefish.

Early Ice

Since whitefish spawn in late fall and early winter, they relate to relatively shallow, hard-bottom shoals and tributary mouths during first ice. In many areas, they're protected during this period of vulnerability, but where the season is open and the weather cooperates by creating ice, winter fishing action can be tremendous.

Mid-depth to deep clay, sand, gravel and rock shoals running between 20 to 100 feet deep comprise the most commonly used habitat. The bases of steep drops surrounding long points, fingers, bars and mid-lake islands can also be good. When post-spawn, first-ice whitefish are relating to tribu-

Once you've located first-ice whitefish in shallow water, move in to drill your holes, then be quiet and minimize movement to allow the fish to return. If you don't, whitefish are likely to see your shadow and scatter.

tary mouths, they often hold quite shallow. Since this typically happens early in the winter during thin, clear-ice conditions, whitefish can easily see approaching anglers and commonly scatter, especially when anglers drill holes.

Don't let this bother you. Just choose your favorite location, cut a number of holes, organize your gear, then sit still so you don't make additional noise or cast shadows. Some twilight anglers even spread blankets over the ice to conceal their presence. The main thing is to be patient and stealthy from this point forward. If you are, whitefish usually return. With an organized approach, you should be able to catch plenty of fish.

Also note that tributary whites seldom migrate into deeper water during this period. Instead, they make parallel movements up and down the shoreline. So if you have a difficult time finding a concentration of fish after they've been spooked, try moving down the shoreline. You should be able to find the school.

Mid-Season

As winter progresses, whitefish move from these tributaries and shoals into deep, main-lake points, using them as migration routes to access mid-depth or deep water flats. These mobile schools can be tough to find consistently, but with knowledgeable use of sonar, they can be found holding along lengthy secondary sand, gravel or rock fingers lining these points where they drop into deeper water.

Later in the winter, migrating fish can also be intercepted along the edges of large, main-lake structures and islands. My favorite mid-season structure consists of long points extending from mid-lake islands and dropping quickly into 60 to 90 feet of water, where whitefish can be found as they move into deep, main-lake flats. While mid-winter whitefish often school, they are fairly mobile, congregating around food sources. If a preferred or readily available food source remains in a general area, so will the whitefish. Look for areas on the flats supporting light grass, invertebrates and smaller bait fish to produce most consistently.

In forage scarce winters, whitefish may make significant movements and finding them can be difficult, especially when they roam loosely in deep, open-water flats. For best results, gather information from reliable sources regarding where recent catches have been made, then move in search of these schools. Where legal, many mid-season anglers chum with egg shells, oatmeal, fish scales or minnows to attract roaming fish and improve their catches.

Late Ice

Late in the winter, you'll find whitefish scattered across deep-water flats before they gradually move back onto shallower hard-bottom shoals and structures toward ice-out. Using a mobile approach, work the edges of elongated main-lake points extending from mid-season, deep-water flats towards shore. These structures provide migration routes for whitefish to follow towards shallow water, and provide guidance for mobile anglers searching for these transient schools and trying to identify the depth at which whitefish are most active. Spend most of your time on the flats

During forage-scarce winters, whitefish may make significant movements. Finding them can be difficult, especially when they roam loosely over deep, open-water flats.

at the bases of these structures, but if you don't encounter fish, move up the migration route trying to intercept groups of moving fish.

Timing

Whitefish are usually most active during twilight periods, with morning and evening bites being most prominent. Anglers situated over a school may catch fish throughout the day. Evening bites can be especially good during first ice, when schools of active, post-spawn whites may feed heavily.

Effective Winter Whitefish Strategies

In terms of winter fishing strategies, whitefish techniques are very similar to traditional lake trout tactics, as the fish feed directly on the bottom along deep-water flats, using their downturned mouths to peck invertebrates off the bottom. One Canadian biologist said feeding whitefish look like "barnyard chickens" pecking the ground as they feed along the bottom, often with their tails pointing straight up.

Tip-Ups

In Canada, where winter whitefish fishing has a strong following, long-time anglers use small, precision-balanced tip-downs. Comprised of L-shaped wooden stands with removable rocker arms placed on frames, they're rigged with dacron line and monofilament leaders. Lines are tipped with weighted wire spreader rigs, equipped with single, fixed-position hooks, each hooked with an emerald shiner. The bait is usually tail-hooked so it struggles upward attractively. Most anglers use baits of varying size to determine if whitefish are demonstrating size preference. This is then lowered and fished on the bottom.

To attract fish, anglers periodically tap the back of the rocker arms to drop and lift the minnows, fishing with long pauses in-between. When a whitefish picks up the bait or moves off with it, the freely placed, fulcrum-like rocker arm tips up, and is quickly lifted to set the hook before the fish feels weight and drops the spreader. Fish are then pulled to the surface.

To help draw fish while awaiting strikes, chumming—where legal— is often done by pinching minnows until the backbone is cracked and the air bladder is ruptured, then sending the wriggling critters skittering toward bottom. Wounded minnows, while often carried away by deep underwa-

Comprised of L-shaped wooden stands with removable rocker arms, small, precisely balanced tip-downs have been popularized for fishing winter whitefish in Canada.

Many quality winter whitefish are taken on tip-downs, quality underwater tip-ups like the polar, or wind tip-ups.

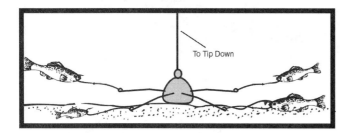

To Tip Down

Tip-downs in Canada are often baited with 2- or 4-hook wire spreader rigs fished directly on the bottom. Spreaders are often baited with minnows of varying size to see if whitefish show any preference.

ter currents, help draw roaming, deep-water whitefish into the area.

Many modern anglers also use quality underwater tip-ups such as the Polar or wind tip-ups like the Windlass, which excel with winter whitefish. With the option to add a tip-up light for twilight or night fishing, these rigs are not only highly effec-

tive, but easy to use. When whitefish prefer a stoic, motionless presentation, rigging underwater tip-ups with standard, small minnow rigs positioned just off the bottom is a combination that's hard to beat. Just set the unit lightly and keep it nearby so you can set the hook quickly before a fussy whitefish drops the bait.

When some presentation movement appears necessary, wind tip-ups can be rigged similarly to underwater or traditional tip-downs, and allowed to let the jigging action and minnows work their magic. The addition of a small flicker blade or lightweight, flashy spoon body can also be productive to help draw fish to your bait.

Don't ignore specialty riggings. Adding yarn soaked with fish scent, tiny colored and phosphorescent beads or pearls to spreader rigs or standard tip-up rigs is always a good idea, and because whitefish are usually found in deep water, hook sharpening is of utmost importance. Also note whitefish have very tender mouth tissues, so simply a firm lift of the rig and consequent constant pressure on the line is all you want to achieve when setting the hook and pulling up on these fish. Sharp hooks help accomplish this goal. Dull hooks, on the other hand, have accounted for many lost whitefish over the years.

Some anglers will also drop small weighted cups down their tip-up holes prior to setting a line. The cups feature a spring loaded top, with a line attached. Anglers fill these cups with fish eggs, oatmeal or ground up minnows, lower them to the bottom, and with a firm pull on the line, spill the contents on the bottom as chum. Another common technique is to freeze ground minnows in ice cubes; frozen with a hole in the center. Cubes are slipped over the tip-up line before the hooks are rigged, and lowered. They gradually melt in the water, dispersing the attractant. Just be sure to check the legality of chumming in your area before practicing such tactics.

Jigging

Fishing deep whitefish with bobbing sticks wrapped with dacron backing tipped with a monofilament leader and a jigging lure is the traditional method of jigging deep-water whites. Short, stiff poles with a little give at the tip, spooled with low-stretch braided dacron, Spectra or Micro Dyneema lines work, too. However, since whitefish feature small, curved mouths, you'll need to use small, carefully sharpened hooks and fish directly on the bottom. Many anglers simply use tiny, sharpened, colorful, beaded hooks tipped with a minnow. Using a gentle jigging motion, they do well.

When whitefish are shallow and spooky during first ice, light-action spinning rods rigged with 2- to 4-pound monofilament or Micro Dyneema and smaller, grub-tipped jigs can be effective. Salmon eggs may also be substituted for grubs; some anglers even strip eggs from recently caught female whitefish and have good luck using them as jig tippers.

Use Fresh Line

Using fresh line results in a strong, smooth, low memory connection between your lure and rod. This gives optimum strength, sensitivity and presentation control.

Fishing deep whitefish with bobbing sticks is the traditional method for hooking these fish. When whitefish are shallow and spooky during first ice, experts know that light action spinning rods and light lines account for more fish.

As for unique lures, I prefer a 2- to 3-inch, 1/8-ounce tube jig for fussy, shallow first-ice whitefish. Try dunking them in fish attractant, and tipping them with a small, 1- to 2-inch minnow or flavor-enhanced plastic. Work the lure with gentle lift-drops right off the bottom. Then hang on. Whitefish suck tube jigs up readily. Heavier versions work in deep water as well.

If shallow-water whitefish are more active, tie up a small, relatively lightweight flashy jigging minnow. Or, better yet, a small profile, flashy blue and silver spoon. Such spoons rigged with long dropper lines leading to painted treble hooks work well. The treble should be graced with a twist of colored yarn soaked in fish scent and tipped with a salmon egg, power bait, minnow head, slice of minnow belly, or whole minnow. To modify this rig, try adding various colored prism tapes or paint colors. Don't underestimate the importance of color. Sometimes silver will produce and gold will be a zero. Other days, just the opposite is true. Experiment!

As winter progresses and whitefish move deeper, I prefer a 30- to 36-inch medium-light walleye-style spinning ice rod combo with 4- to 6-pound monofilament. When fishing in areas that may be holding lake trout, longer, stiffer rods rigged with low-stretch 6- to 8-pound Spectra or Micro Dyneema lines are better bets. Either way,

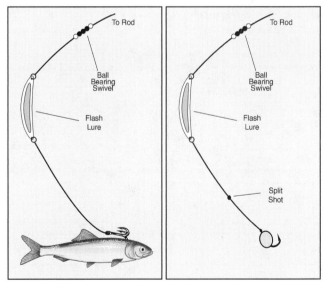

Spoons rigged with long dropper lines leading to painted treble hooks graced with a minnow or salmon egg are highly effective winter whitefish rigs. A twist of colored yarn soaked in fish attractant can be added to the hook to help draw whitefish, especially when anglers are fishing deep, expansive flats.

try fishing with larger, heavier jigging minnows or heavy spoons in white, hot pink, chartreuse, hot orange and bright green. If these are graced with a shiny, finished gold or silver backside, whitefish can't help but take notice.

If currents aren't strong, monofilament dropper lines from these flashy spoons to plain hooks or light jig heads are also effective. Once you've chosen a color, work these baits with gentle bouncing motions, letting the dropper fall to the bottom. Pause and periodically bang the bottom with your spoon to stir up silt and attract curious fish. The tufts of silt are signs that other whitefish are feeding. Whitefish usually pick the bait off the bottom during the pause. Just remember, since the key to successful presentation for whites revolves around attracting fish, triggering strikes and consequently setting the hook quickly, periodic movement and maintaining a close watch on your lines is of utmost importance.

One reminder: Whitefish have very thin mouth tissues, so don't set the hook too hard, or you'll

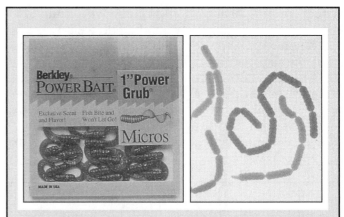

Using flavor-enhanced plastics such as Berkley's Power Baits can dramatically increase your number of whitefish strikes. (Courtesy Berkley/OTG)

Flavor-Enhanced Plastics

In shallow, clear water, whitefish feed primarily by sight. In deep, dark water, they use smell and taste. In either case, today's scent-emitting flavor-enhanced plastics can increase strikes. Most feature natural-looking shapes imitating insect larvae or grubs. Since they're available in many sizes, colors and styles, they're versatile. Action-tail grubs, for example, slow a lure's fall, add action in clear water and sound in dark water. Combine this with a variety of fish-attracting colors and their natural scent, taste and texture, and you'll see why these baits help stimulate whitefish feeding.

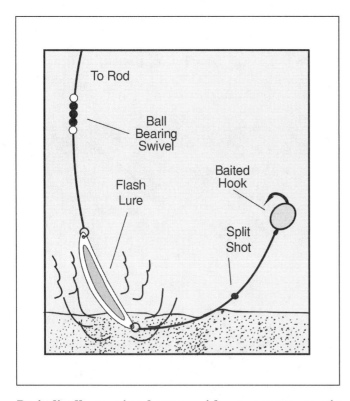

Periodically tapping bottom with your spoon to stir up silt helps attract curious whitefish, who likely see the disturbed bottom as a sign of other whitefish feeding, and move in to capitalize on the situation.

simply tear hooks loose. A quick, firm, steady upward motion is enough to set the hook. Keep the line tight and allow the rod to gently guide the fish up. Do this properly, and you'll experience the thrill of watching thrashing whitefish fight their way up from the clear, icy waters below. Once you're home, you'll enjoy some of the finest fish fillets you've ever tasted.

In many areas, whitefish command a high price, and I can see why. If told to name my favorite fish, I would consider blackened whitefish fillets set on a bed of wild rice second only to perfectly fried, golden-brown walleye. I've even heard that when sprinkled generously with salt, pepper and paprika then baked in a wrapping of thick, hickory-smoked bacon, whitefish have a flavor similar to smoked ham.

Now that's something I'll have to try.

Chapter 10
Understanding Salmon in Winter

Kokanee salmon, a landlocked, dwarfed version of the sockeye salmon, are limited to primarily a few high-country lakes and reservoirs. Although they may grow large enough to be defined as gamefish—the world record exceeds six pounds—they seldom grow over a foot long.

Ice fishing for salmon is a spectacular thrill. There's something intriguing about knowing a chunky, powerful, tackle-smashing salmon may strike at any moment.

Standing on a coating of fresh ice separating me from 60 feet of icy water, this thrill is mixed with fear. It's not really the depth or temperature, but the fact this fresh, clear ice measures 5 inches thick. Yes, it's enough to hold us, as long as we don't find a weak patch.

But as I begin scanning distant tip-ups while focusing on jigging, I realize that salmon rank among the largest, hardest-fighting, most power-ful-running, brute-strength magnum trophy species of any taken through the ice. Twenty minute fights aren't unusual, and I know winter salmon fanatics who have tangled with stubborn monsters for 45 minutes. That's sheer power and excitement. Knowing that at any moment I could set the hook to start such a battle, is enough to keep me on the ice.

An hour passes as I gradually work along fresh ice coating a steep, main-lake point. Nothing.

We pack up and head for another pre-marked, main-lake point, and begin repeating the process. Twenty minutes later my sonar lights up, revealing a huge cloud of suspended forage, most likely smelt, the primary forage for winter salmon. I feel a rush of adrenaline as my partner moves in and notes some large marks holding beneath the school, providing mounting evidence of salmon.

We drill a couple dozen holes and pull out underwater cameras, which reveal what appear to be smelt. Nabbing our ultralight ice rods, we lower tiny, grub-hooked jigs trying to hook a smelt to confirm our suspicions. Affirmation comes as a narrow, silvery, toothy torpedo-shaped smelt soon flops at my feet. Acting quickly, everybody joins in, and soon, we're hooking the smelt as bait on tip-ups and lowering them just below the school of baitfish.

These lines set, we start preparing to jig, but never get the first lure down. A tip-up flag trips, and the rapidly spinning trip shaft indicates a salmon. Knowing winter salmon usually take the bait quickly, I waste no time setting the hook. Dacron burns through my cold, wet fingers as the powerful fish surges with several long, hard, run-and-roll escape tactics. I do my best to keep the line tight as I gain on the fish. Almost 15 minutes later, the thrashing, powerful body of a salmon smashes her muscular tail upon fresh ice. With shaking, numbing hands I hoist the fish while yelling jubilant screams of victory, which quickly dissipate into the blustery, frigid winter air. Nothing compares to this.

If you're surprised to see a chapter in an ice fishing book dedicated to salmon, don't feel bad. You're not alone. Geographically, the ability to ice fish for salmon is limited. With their strict demands for deep, cold, highly oxygenated water, most salmon waters are resistant to freezing. Throughout much of their distribution along western and eastern North America, ice formation is limited. Unless you fish the Great Lakes or live near one of a handful of natural high-elevation lakes or cold-water reservoirs that freeze well enough to make winter salmon angling possible, you may never have been aware these opportunities exist.

Even where ice fishing for salmon is possible, opportunities are limited. Great Lakes salmon, for example, spend most winters in deep, open water. They are seldom accessible to ice anglers. Even in shallow and mid-depth bays where they can be reached, numbers are often limited and, with their tendency to suspend, can be almost impossible to find. Add the fact that ice conditions are often treacherous, and few anglers are willing to take the risk.

As for "inland salmon lakes"—my term for salmon stocked lakes and reservoirs that freeze outside the Great Lakes—many have only recently been stocked and those few ice anglers who have seriously tried fishing these salmon haven't been doing so for long. Thus, complete winter patterns haven't been realized, and little material has been assembled about these mysterious winter salmon and their patterns.

Let's break the ice.

Kokanee Salmon

If you read *Hooked On Ice Fishing II: Panfish*, you've already been introduced to the most common salmon taken through the ice: kokanee. "Kokes" as those who ice fish have lovingly deemed this incredibly feisty little tackle-buster, are basically a landlocked, dwarfed version of the sockeye salmon. They are limited primarily to just a few high-country lakes and reservoirs. While they may grow large—the world record is a tremendous 6-pound fish caught in the 1970s—kokes are really a stunted salmon rarely growing more than a foot long. They aren't considered game fish by our definition, so I've classified them as "panfish" and covered them in book II.

Instead, we'll focus on the three trophy winter salmon game fish species: Landlocked Salmon, Coho Salmon and Chinook Salmon.

Landlocked Salmon

Landlocked salmon are an Atlantic salmon and certainly one of the prettiest of all winter-caught salmon. They usually feature a silvery-gray to light yellowish-brown color covered with large, dark spots and white borders. Their range is very limited and they are primarily caught from just a few

Landlocked salmon are a variety of the Atlantic salmon, shown here, and look similar but feature dark spots throughout the entire body. (Photo courtesy Wisconsin D.N.R.)

select, cold lakes in the northeastern United States and Eastern Canada. Their diet consists of insect larvae and baitfish. Like most salmon, they taste great baked, grilled or smoked.

Coho Salmon

Coho salmon are fat, silvery-sided Pacific salmon accented with brilliant steel blue to light green topsides. They have small, dark spots along the back, upper sides, base of the dorsal fin and upper lobe of the caudal fin. They feature white bellies and unique, very distinguishable white gums. The primary winter diet consists almost entirely of baitfish, which accounts for their typically rapid growth and tremendous size. Coho of more than 20 pounds have reportedly been taken through the ice.

To reach this tremendous size, however, forage must be adequate for them to grow normally throughout their young, insect larvae-based diet stage and begin eating the larger, high-protein baitfish which results in this rapid growth. Inland stockings in some smaller, deep, cold-water lakes have established populations, but there is little quality growth. For all practical ice fishing purposes, the best opportunity to catch trophy cohos through the ice comes from Great Lakes bays.

Coho are usually caught incidentally during the mid-winter when they are found suspended over deep, pelagic inshore areas. Anglers usually catch coho when they are fishing for other more commonly caught Great Lakes species, such as lake trout, splake or browns. Coho can be taken regularly during early, or better yet, late ice.

Thanks to intensive, repeated stocking, coho are found throughout the Great Lakes, but are usually taken by ice anglers targeting the frozen bays of Lake Superior and Lake Michigan, where ice anglers have found them a superb fighting fish with tremendous eating qualities.

Chinook Salmon

Like cohos, chinook can grow to be thick-bodied, immense fish. These silvery-sided Pacific salmon feature an iridescent green to blue-green back and upper sides with a few black spots scattered on the back, top of head, upper sides and all fins. They have a silvery-white belly, and can be distinguished from the coho by black lower gums. Young chinooks feed primarily on insect larvae, while larger fish demonstrate a preference for large baitfish.

Great Lakes chinooks are the king of all winter salmon. They reach the largest size, and therefore make a better trophy species than coho. However, they're often inaccessible in winter because they frequent mid-depth to deep-water regions—areas that rarely freeze—but are occasionally taken from Great Lakes bays, where they suspend and are caught incidentally by lake trout, splake, brown and coho anglers as they pass through.

Another opportunity for icing winter chinooks comes from cold-water lakes and reservoirs of the Canadian Shield and deep, high-country lakes and reservoirs of western and eastern North America. These are waters where annual ice formation is common and chinook have been stocked with moderate success. A few of these cold-water "inland" North American lakes and reservoirs, or portions of them, support suitable numbers of winter salmon. Provided large enough areas of cold, highly oxygenated water are sustained all year, some "two-story" lakes can maintain stocked salmon populations, as can the deeper, lower portions of some reservoirs like Lake Oahe in South Dakota or North Dakota's Lake Sakakawea, where a large enough region of cold water may maintain schools that are accessible during the winter. While the total outcome of such stocking efforts have yet to be determined, the Dakota chinook populations appear to be holding their own and, although they may not grow as large as their Great Lakes counterparts, they still offer viable winter fisheries.

Chinook are considered a delicacy in terms of food value, and can be prepared any number of ways. Baked, smoked, cut into steaks or grilled over an open fire, most anglers agree you can't go wrong.

Primary Winter Salmon Location Habits, Patterns and Movements

Since we aren't covering kokanee salmon, which often demonstrate somewhat different general winter patterns than landlocked, coho and chinook salmon, we can cover the remaining three species' primary winter location patterns and movements in basically two large groupings: Great Lakes salmon, and "inland" stocked salmon. So for this chapter, I will simply refer to landlocked, coho and chinook salmon as "salmon." Where specific pattern characteristics or qualities of an individual species require special attention, I will note them, listing the species by proper name.

Ice fishing the Great Lakes usually means lake trout and splake, but mixed bag catches including occasional coho or chinook salmon aren't uncommon.

Great Lakes Patterns

Ice fishing on the Great Lakes usually means lake trout and splake but, over the years, coho and chinook have been caught by these Great Lakes enthusiasts with increasing frequency. And why not? If a large fish suddenly showed up 10 feet beneath the ice on your sonar, you'd be tempted to raise your bait and give it a try, too. Ice anglers specifically targeting these fish, however, are rare.

Most Great Lakes salmon fishing takes place for cohos later in the year within or along protected bays, harbor channels, and at times, within securely frozen deep holes of incoming tributaries. Cohos usually hold in main-lake basin areas, but these areas are difficult or even treacherous to access, so anglers usually fish in-shore bays.

First Ice

Movement towards in-shore areas begins in fall, as water temperatures cool. Note, however, many of these coho and chinook will be four-year-old upstream spawners. They are of no consequence for ice fishing because they die soon after spawning, prior to ice-up. But younger fish may form large schools and are often active as they cruise river holes, harbors, shoreline contours and points searching for food. If the conditions are right, these schools may remain active as the ice forms. Some may even feed in these areas throughout the winter, moving in and out of shallow river mouths, harbors and bays. In shallow water, this is the most exciting, ultimate "sight fishing" thrill you'll ever experience; just watch for suspended fish. In deeper bays, use sonar to pinpoint fish and the depth at which they're holding.

Of course, Great Lakes bays can be large, and many anglers often wonder where to begin. Start by locating large, deep, in-shore points, shoals, breaks, channels or shipping lanes. Then target the steepest contours separating classic shallow river mouths and harbor flats from the deepest available water. Be alert for any secondary indentations, turns and fingers along these deep breaks, as these are primary first-ice salmon-holding locations. Search them out.

Mid-Winter

As winter progresses, salmon usually move into deeper water. You have two basic strategic approaches for catching fish: Be mobile or sit still. Being mobile generally works best because Great Lakes structures can be immense; plus, salmon typically cruise incessantly, and if you carefully try to find these fish using a mobile approach, it's easier to create consistent catches. However, sitting still may work too, provided you're positioned on top of a known migration route, trough, shipping lane or staging area. Just watch your sonar and fish the strike zone where salmon are most actively feeding.

Either way, there will often be long gaps between bites while waiting for the school to return—if it ever does. Hence, while you can often catch Great Lakes salmon using a still fish-

Great Lakes salmon are known to move in and out of Great Lakes bays, often using deep shoreline contours, troughs and shipping lanes as migration routes between deep and shallow water when searching for food. Be there at the right time, and you may intercept them.

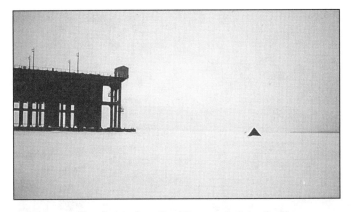

During early ice, the breaks and break lines surrounding Great Lakes ore docks may attract occasional salmon.

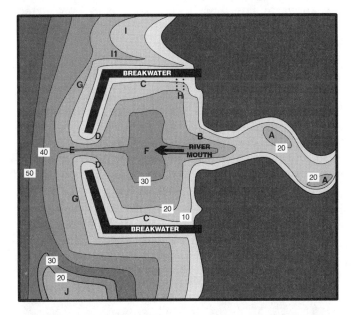

Most first ice Great Lakes salmon are caught where they suspend along inshore reefs and points (i,j), harbors (f) and river holes (a). Primary fishing areas include the river mouth (b), inside edges of breakwaters (c,d), the outside edges of breakwaters (g), pilings within harbor marinas lining summer boat docking areas (h), harbor openings (e), and turns and projections (i1) along main bay points and reefs.

ing approach, I feel a mobile jigging approach is the most consistent method during mid-winter. In a normal day of fishing—with the exception of river hole fishing—it's not unusual for me to drill 50 or 60 holes while searching for an active school. I simply begin by fishing frozen Great Lakes harbor channels and their associated structures. These structures might be any deep, adjoining river holes and the shallower sides of the largest in-shore breakwaters or structures adjoining these river mouths. These are locations where perch and shiners provide adequate forage. Anglers can then gradually move to steeper breaks and deeper, open-water areas surrounding them, where alewives and smelt provide the main forage.

Again, winter Great Lakes salmon patterns are a difficult proposition, and probably one of the least understood of all winter gamefish patterns, for two reasons: First, salmon are often scattered in deep, unfrozen waters. Secondly, fish scattered near in-shore areas can be difficult to find and even more difficult to accurately present a bait. If your presentation isn't right on, second chances are few and far between, which doesn't allow much time for experimentation. I can only recommend hard work and meticulous watching of your sonar. If large, suspended fish come into view, get a bait to them fast.

Late Ice

Late in the season salmon tend to suspend higher, then gradually return to the shallower ends of in-shore structures or back into harbors, marina pilings and river mouths when smelt begin running inshore to spawn. With forage concen-

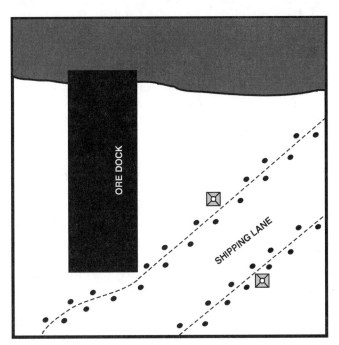

Leap-frogging tip-ups while jigging along the edges of dredged Great Lakes shipping lanes is a good way to find irregularities along these break lines, helping locate mid-winter salmon.

During late ice, Great Lakes salmon tend to return to the shallower ends of in-shore structures, harbors and river mouths when smelt begin their spring spawning run. During this time, mixed bag catches of lake trout, splake, browns, steelhead—and yes, salmon—are not unusual.

trated and more accessible, nice days in late March and early April can bring excellent winter salmon catches. Hit them right, and you can catch quite a few in a day.

Inland Lake And Reservoir Patterns

If you haven't already realized that winter salmon fishing is more of a hunt than a fishing trip, you will. This is not only true of Great Lakes salmon, but "inland" winter salmon fisheries as well. Salmon are an intrinsically wandering species, which means the search is on for serious ice anglers desiring consistent catches.

It's this very reason why there is some advantage to targeting what I call "inland" lakes—those deep, cold natural lakes and reservoirs outside the Great Lakes. They've been stocked with winter accessible salmon. I like fishing these waters for two primary reasons: First, the smaller size of

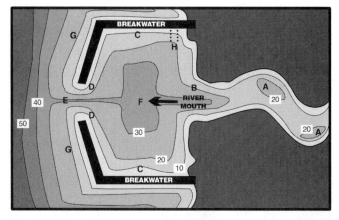

During late ice, Great Lakes salmon return to shallower in-shore structures, harbors and river mouths as baitfish, such as smelt, move in-shore to spawn. Nice days in late March and early April can bring some of the best winter salmon catches of the year.

Like winter Great Lakes salmon fishing, "inland" winter salmon fishing is a relatively new undertaking. There is still much to learn, but the rewards can be tremendous. Photo by South Dakota Tourism.

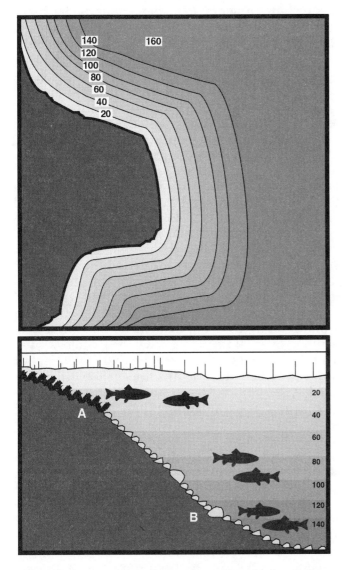

"Inland" lake salmon are often found along deep, large main-lake points which hold large schools of baitfish such as smelt. It's widely believed schools of salmon hold in these areas, only moving as the baitfish do. They will be generally shallow early and late in the winter (a), and deeper mid-season (b).

not a fish-a-minute experience. But there are ways to improve your odds.

According to my ice fishing friends in Pierre, South Dakota, a city stationed on the expansive inland salmon waters of Lake Oahe, the key to catching winter salmon is homing in on the largest concentrations of the chinook's preferred forage: smelt. Find smelt, and you'll usually find salmon.

These salmon school, too. They may be loosely formed schools, but compared to the scattered, suspended fish you find moving through wide expanses of a Great Lakes bay, at least your odds of multiple fish improve. Local biologists familiar with this winter fishery even suspect these loose schools don't move much, but rather establish home areas near deep, steep breaking, main-lake structures such as points and reefs holding concentrations of smelt. These fish may remain in such an area all winter. Biologists believe these schools may move shallower or deeper throughout the season, primarily depending on forage movements. But the theory is that these fish use

When ice fishing for salmon, go out of your way to avoid noise and on-ice traffic. You'll spend more time probing, but less time trying to trigger spooked, semiactive or negative fish.

these waters helps concentrate salmon and make them more accessible. Secondly, inland salmon appear to school more tightly than those in the Great Lakes. So, if you can find them and start fishing before crowds develop, action can be consistent.

Don't get me wrong, these are still large bodies of water and, salmon being the roaming species they are, finding fish is seldom easy. Plus, with inland winter salmon fishing on most of these waters being a relatively new undertaking, there is still much to learn. Inland winter salmon action is the same structures and stay in the same general vicinities all winter long.

Fishing evidence supports this theory. Once a school is located, action can be pretty good, with a fish caught once every half hour, maybe even three or four fish in an hour. Further proof comes from what usually follows. When these schools are located, word usually spreads and anglers move in on the schools. As this occurs, the action starts off great with a couple fish an hour common. This is gradually reduced to a few fish per day, and eventually slows dramatically until only occasional fish

When an "inland" school of salmon is located during first-ice, the action can be pretty consistent. (Photo by South Dakota Tourism.)

are caught. Anglers focusing regularly in these same areas may still take fish periodically throughout the winter, but the action really slows.

The point? Quite likely, as is common with other schooling gamefish, the most aggressive salmon are caught early, and the remainder become spooky. Combine this with the mid-season doldrums of less available forage, thicker ice and deeper snow reducing light penetration and oxygen, and you can understand why. However, ice anglers moving away from these "old" schools and locking onto fresh ones on other structures or newly frozen parts of the lake often find respectable action—until word gets out and things slow down again.

The same pattern follows from freeze-up until ice-out on most inland salmon waters. The only significant difference is these various schools tend to make gradual, subtle depth movements as they follow their forage and respond to local water and weather conditions. At first ice these fish are often found relating to deep, main-lake points, but suspending over 20 to 30 feet of water. By mid-winter, it's not unusual to find them over 60 to 120 feet of water provided such depths are available. Toward late-ice, these schools gradually move up vertically, then start migrating into bays featuring water flow as smelt begin moving in to stage for their spring spawning movements.

The trick to consistently finding these schools is to pre-fish, using sonar to identify primary, main-lake humps and points bordering some of the deepest water in the lake during the open-water season. Mark such areas with your GPS, paying special attention to secondary "microstructure" offering steep, sharp breaks into the deepest available water. Once ice forms, use a mobile approach and your GPS to target these locations. Then use sonar and underwater cameras to locate and identify groups of forage and the salmon relating to them. Always be prepared to drill lots of holes as you search for fresh, active schools.

Timing

The best time to fish winter salmon on inland waters is early ice, before crowds spook schools and ice and snow get thick, causing salmon to become lethargic. On the Great Lakes, late ice offers the best action, when chinook and coho move in to feed on shallow-schooling smelt that are preparing to make their spring upstream spawning migrations. In both areas, action can be good throughout the day, but is usually best during twilight.

Effective Winter Salmon Fishing Strategies

Winter salmon are commonly caught on live minnow tip-up rigs, and a variety of jigging techniques. Let's start with tip-ups.

Tip-Ups

Setting tip-ups not only increases the number of lines you have, improving your odds of dropping your bait in front of active salmon, but can also help identify productive structures, migration routes and strike zones while you jig the periphery searching for fish. Whether fishing the Great Lakes or "inland" waters, because salmon are nomadic and may be scattered, spreading tip-ups over a large holding area can be a good way to pick up distant fish you might otherwise miss.

However, because salmon often hold deep and run hard and long, the first rule is to use only premium, smooth-tripping underwater tip-ups with large line capacity and drag adjustable spools. HT's ETU-10D Deep Water Fisherman or PTU-10 Deep Water Polar work great. The strong, solid frames, carefully machined trip and freeze-proof tube mechanisms ensure nothing will go wrong when large salmon strike hard. The large-capacity

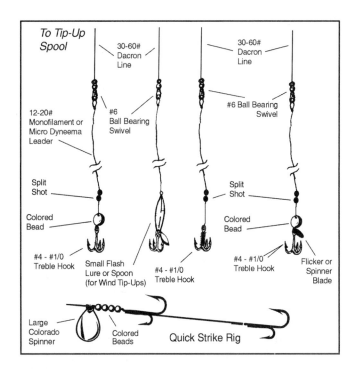

Heavy dacron tip-up lines, large ball-bearing swivels and heavy 12- to 20-pound leaders leading to large, carefully sharpened hooks or quick-strike rigs are primary winter salmon tip-up riggings. Flashy, shiny spoons, spinners, yarn, flicker or spinner blades may also be added for more attraction.

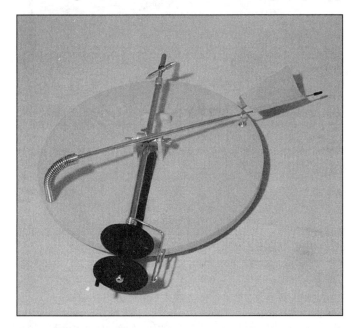

HT's PTT-50 Polar Therm tip-ups prevent hole freeze up, keep snow from blowing into the hole and stop light from entering the water. The Polar Therm also features a large spool for deep, hard-running salmon.

spools ensure adequate line backing when salmon make their long, fast, powerful runs. The drag mechanisms prevent spool backlash during strong runs. Use anything less, and salmon will rip the hook from their mouths, break your line or backlash your spool. Lesser models sometimes break in half.

When salmon are shallower, mid-size spools such as those offered on HT's ETU-5D Fisherman or PTU-5 Polar will usually be adequate. Large-spooled hole covering models like HT's PTT-50 also help block light from penetrating holes. Otherwise, using a homemade or commercially available hole cover is a good idea, as they help prevent snow from entering the hole and ice from forming. Until another quality, larger spooled thermal model becomes available, anything else is destined to fail.

Spooling with strong, teflon coated, low-stretch 30- to 60-pound dacron such as HT's Polar Tip-Up line provides the strength necessary to set the hook and fight these powerful fish. The teflon won't be subject to freeze-up like an uncoated line. A large, #6 ball-bearing swivel should be used to tie the dacron to a long, strong, heavy, 12- to 20-

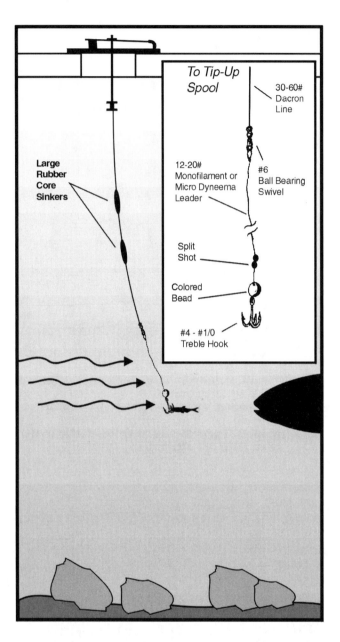

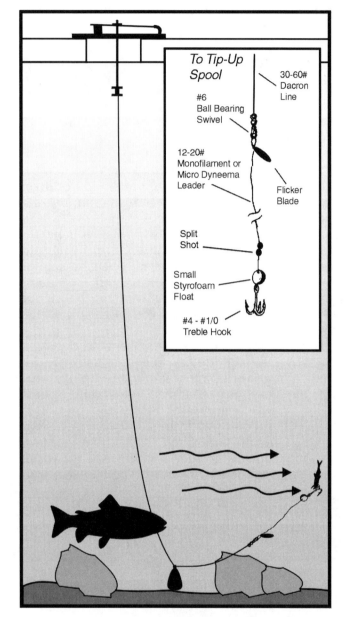

When deep-water salmon are suspended, especially in current, a number of heavy rubber-core sinkers may be necessary to position your bait in the strike zone.

When salmon are suspending just off the bottom, slip-sinker rigs with floating jig heads or foam floats may be used to properly position your bait at the correct depth.

pound monofilament or Micro Dyneema (TM) leader. Some anglers even opt for thin, single-strand, 20-pound wire leaders leading to good sized, carefully sharpened 1/0 treble hooks or 1/0 treble quick-strike rigs.

If fish are suspended, large rubber-core sinkers should be used to fix the bait at the proper depth. In current, several may be necessary to pin the bait down or your line may simply drift up, out of the strike zone. If fishing on the bottom, large bass cast-

ing sinkers or egg sinkers can be rigged as slip-sinkers to eliminate resistance to soft-biting fish.

When salmon are suspending within a few feet of the bottom, slip-sinker rigs with floating jig heads or small Styrofoam bobbers are a great way to rig deep, heavy finesse-style tip-up presentations. Simply lower the weight to bottom, release the amount of line desired to float up to the fish, and set the flag. When a fish bites, the line slides through the slip-sinker rig without resistance, and the flag is tripped. Just remember, current can push a floating rig, too. You may have to take this into consideration when using such rigs. Of course, when fishing deep current, it's important to help salmon find your bait. You may find a flashy, fish-attracting spoon or spinner blade incorporated into the rig may help improve your catches. Just allow the current to work the attractant.

Without question, however, the best live bait is a large, lively smelt caught from the same waters you're fishing. Use ultra-light tackle to catch fresh smelt and bait up, if this practice is legal in your area. Few if any states allow transport of live smelt, so they must be caught from your home waters. Because they are so effective, some states don't allow the use of live smelt at all. Be sure to check the laws in your area. If you're not allowed to use live smelt, you'll have to substitute a large sucker or shiner. When using live smelt is legal,

bait-up and hang on. This is unquestionably the most deadly way to ice winter salmon, Great Lakes or inland lakes, deep or shallow, early or late, for active or inactive fish.

Properly Hook Your Minnows

Always hook your minnow so the hook points face the tail. Game fish usually eat prey head first, and by facing hook points toward the tail, your hooks are always in the optimum hooking position. Also, keep your hook points ultra-sharp, positioning them carefully so your bait balances properly and allows the baitfish freedom of movement.

Some anglers also substitute fresh, brightly colored salmon roe or salmon eggs for minnows, especially when fishing early and late ice in Great Lakes river mouths or river holes. Simply rig the bait so it remains near the bottom and let the current move the bait.

More on Using Tip-Ups for Salmon

Again, if multiple lines are legal in your area and fast current isn't a major factor, tip-ups will help you cover ice. Large-spooled, deep lake tip-ups like the PTU-10 Polar, rigged with live smelt or

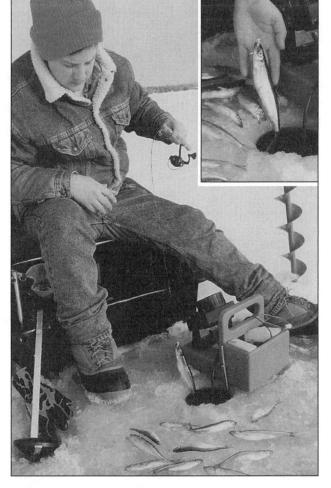

If the practice is legal in your area, use ultra-light tackle to catch fresh smelt and bait up—they're winter's number one salmon bait!

Setting tip-ups along deep breakwaters can be a great way to catch Great Lakes salmon when they move into in-shore areas.

emerald shiners are effective. As an alternative, use large golden shiners. Stagger the depth at which you set your units, and play "leapfrog" with them as you work down a breakwater, channel, shipping lane, over a river mouth area, flat or structural feature. If one unit begins seeing more action than others, switch the other tip-ups to the same depth setting. Often, one particular depth constitutes the primary "strike zone." By uniformly setting your baits at this depth, you'll

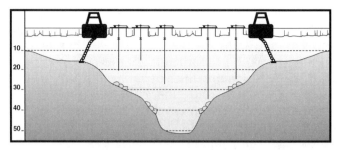

Using sonar in combination with varying the depth settings of your tip-up lines along Great Lakes shipping channels or main-lake break lines will help you pinpoint the most productive "strike zones."

increase your catch. Also, position your units close by, and never waste time setting the hook after a strike. If the spool or trip shaft is turning when you arrive, set the hook immediately before the fish has an opportunity to drop your bait or backlash the spool.

Finally, since winds on expansive salmon waters are often harsh, I recommend using a small, portable shelter that cuts the wind but doesn't hamper your tip-up mobility. USL's fold down Fish Trap or Frabill's Ranger style models make terrific wind blocks while setting up, lowering or reeling up wet line from deep water. And don't forget to bring a gaff. When you attempt to bring your first giant salmon onto the ice, you'll be glad you did.

Jigging

Many winter anglers consider jigging salmon the ultimate winter fishing experience. When hooked, their fast, hard, head-shaking runs are a challenge for even the toughest ice tackle. When these fights last up to 40 minutes, it's not only your tackle that will be tested, but your patience and endurance as well. Believe me, a 10- or 20-pound salmon fought for a half hour through the ice can make even the strongest man beg for a break.

While deep water Polars make tip-up fishing relatively easy, jigging winter salmon poses many unique challenges and requires special tackle. If you're fishing outside, use stout, 3- to 4-foot graphite rods such as HT's Ice Blues trout series with large guides to help prevent freeze-up. Their moderately fast action and flexible tip for sensitivity will function well. In truly deep water that calls for deep-water tactics, models with roller guides also allow the use of wire line. More on that in a minute.

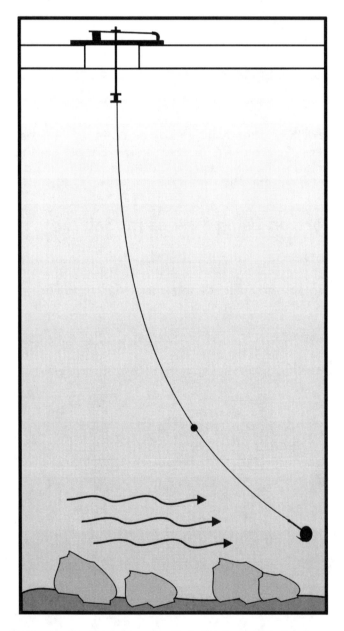

Some anglers may use fresh, brightly colored salmon roe or eggs instead of minnows on their tip-up lines. These work well to attract salmon, especially when fishing early and late ice in Great Lakes river mouths or river holes.

Single "station" type portable shelters are excellent wind blocks while setting tip-ups on blustery Great Lakes bays or inland salmon waters. (Photo courtesy Frabill, Inc.)

If you prefer, standard, 5- to 6-foot one-piece medium-action summer graphite jigging rods provide the strength, give and power necessary to land salmon through the ice. If you're fishing inside a shanty, an 18- to 24-inch ice model will be better suited to your situation. Longer rods are impossible to fish efficiently inside a shanty.

Combine your rod with a quality spinning or baitcast reel. Either way, coat the gears with lightweight oil that won't get stiff in frigid weather. An ultra-smooth drag is also important, especially when fishing lighter, 6-8 pound monofilament lines, as some anglers do.

Still, no matter where you're fishing, don't overlook using premium lines. After putting so much effort into finding and catching these fish, it's ridiculous to skimp on line. Since winter salmon tend to suspend in deep, open water away from cover, you can get by with 6- or 8-pound line, but most anglers feel more comfortable with 10- to 17-pound. Salmon have teeth that can nick lighter lines. Since they often swallow the hook, you are at risk of a "bite off" if you fish too light.

Also keep in mind that monofilament stretches. This is an especially important consideration when fishing deep water because of the demands for hard, affirmative hooksets. Consequently, many winter salmon anglers opt to use the thin

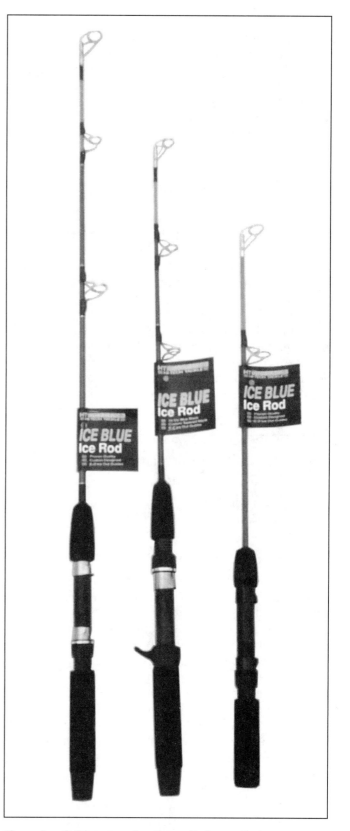

If you're fishing trophy Great Lakes salmon, a stout, stiff, large-guided ice rod is an important part of any jigging system.

diameter, Kevlar (TM), Spectra (TM) or Micro Dyneema (TM) style lines over monofilament. The low-stretch, thin qualities of these materials are the characteristics many deep-water salmon anglers are looking for. A few deep water Great Lakes salmon anglers even use rods fitted with roller guides and tips to accommodate single-strand or braided wire lines. These also eliminate line stretch. The choice is yours.

Lures for Winter Salmon

As for lures, jigging minnows such as Normark's Jigging Rapala, Nils-Master Jigger or Bad Dog's Humpback are all good when salmon are active, and currents and depth aren't restrictive. Tip them with a strip of carefully cut minnow belly to create fish attracting undulations. Or you can simply use a minnow head comparably sized to your lure, then jig with a constant jiggling motion interspersed with periodic, 12- to 18-inch snap jigs and you're set. Heavy swimming jigs such as Northland Airplane Jigs tipped with a minnow or wiggly belly strip and fished in a similar manner are popular, too.

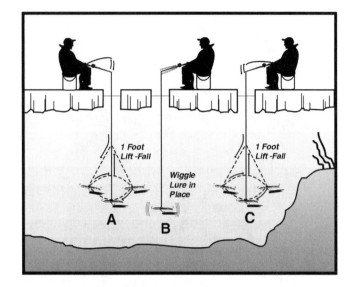

Flashy swimming minnows are good bets when salmon are active, and currents and depth aren't restrictive. Tip them with a slice of minnow belly, and begin jigging with a 12- to 18-inch snap jig (a). Continue with a constant, gentle wiggle (b), pause, and finish with a snap jig to draw fish in. Continue repeating this motion at various depths to determine the primary strike zone. Shiny spoons can also be effectively worked with a similar jigging motion.

Don't Overdo It!

Most salmon anglers have a tendency to fish too aggressively, which often spooks the fish. Periodic aggressive lifts are good for attracting distant fish but, overdone, may scare them away.

Trusted spoons such as Bay de Noc's Swedish Pimple or Do Jigger, Acme Kastmasters, Northland's Fire Eye or HT's Marmooska Spoon shined to a sparkling, silver finish and tipped with a minnow or belly strip are also excellent choices when salmon are active and current isn't a major factor. Again, periodic snap-lifts combined with a constant jigging motion to keep the lure moving should be sufficient to attract and trigger salmon. Be sure to experiment with various colors, prism tapes and spoon styles. Salmon often demonstrate distinct preferences. Try various combinations, always keeping them shiny and colorful, and your efforts should pay off.

For slow-reacting fish, depending on the depth and current, try standard, heavy-bodied lead-head jigs tipped with smaller minnows. They can either be fished at the precise depth you're marking fish or just beneath a school of suspended baitfish. Jig-

For slower salmon, try standard, heavy-bodied lead-head jigs tipped with smaller minnows and jig at the depth you're marking fish, or just beneath a marked school of baitfish, with a gentle lift-drop motion.

ging with a gentle, lift-drop motion is the best. If smelt are legal in your area and you can catch a fresh one or two, these should be your primary jig tippers. Otherwise, a shiner, sucker or minnow belly strip will have to suffice.

Recently, plastics have also moved onto the scene. Large tube jigs are becoming popular because of their soft, natural texture, huge color selection, ability to be packed with fish attractant and capability to be slipped over a spoon or the base of a swimming jig. Just choose colors and use jigging styles that closely resemble or imitate the principle baitfish salmon are feeding on and experiment with color.

Open your bail or engage your free spool, and allow the tube to drop to the depth at which your target fish are holding. Engage the reel, and start fishing about a foot above the fish or the bottom of the forage. Then gradually work downward, jig-

Large tube jigs are becoming a popular winter salmon lure because of their soft natural texture, huge color selection and ability to catch a variety of other Great Lakes species. Fish commonly caught along with winter salmon include lake trout, splake, browns or steelhead.

ging slowly, always being sure to work past the fish before moving upward again. You should be experimenting with different jigging motions all the while. Salmon will often follow jigs upward and hit. This sometimes happens as high as just beneath the ice. If nothing happens, however, simply repeat this sequence as you move from hole to hole until you locate active fish.

Deep-Water Jigging

Deep-water jigging presents a unique set of conditions. Stiffer, fast-tipped rods and lead-core, low-stretch or wire lines are mandatory. Accurate depth control often makes the difference between no fish and a successful day. Before fishing, it's a good idea to see how many inches of line your reel picks up per revolution of the handle. Do this by marking the line at your rod tip, turning the handle 360 degrees, and measuring the distance between your mark and the rod tip.

Say, for example, one revolution equals 24 inches. Now you'll know every half turn of your reel handle brings your lure up one foot. Of course, you can watch your sonar for active depth control, but when fishing deep with gliding or swimming lures, these baits can temporarily slip outside a transducer cone. Even heavy jigs can move to the side on the fall, especially in current, making this simple manual system an asset when attempting to jig various depths.

Jigging technique? Simple. Watch how the fish are moving by peering down the hole or watching your sonar. If they appear active, gently twitch the lure in place, pause briefly before quickly "snapping" or "ripping" the lure upward 2 to 3 feet. Then repeat the sequence. Salmon usually strike on the pause and fall. You must be ready. These powerful fish are all muscle and they've been known to pull ice rods right from people's hands.

If the salmon aren't aggressive, which can happen, especially during the mid-season when ice thickens, try a jig and minnow (preferably smelt) rocked slowly and gently right in front of their face—which means right at the depth the fish are suspending. Salmon roe may also be a good jig tipper. If fish activity slows because of crowding, fish the outside edge of the school to stay on fresh fish. Some salmon anglers also turn their extra rods into modified tip-ups by placing them in firmly secured, weighted rod holders, baiting them with live smelt, setting the drag and placing the reel in free spool. When a fish bites and the reel sings with action, they run over to set the hook.

Painstakingly and meticulously sharpen your hook. The more factors you can tip in your favor, the better.

Safety First

As always, safety can't be emphasized enough. Winter salmon fishing is fun, but fishing them can be dangerous on the big water. Utilize a guide on unfamiliar waters and always carry a GPS with at least one access point entered as a waypoint. This is especially important when venturing more than a half-mile out. If you plan to drive on the ice, use extreme caution. Large cracks and ice heaves often develop on these large waters. Always follow roads if they're available, and never travel alone.

One more thing: As winter salmon fishing becomes more popular, I fully expect increased fishing pressure will bring new fishing regulations. Ice fishing for salmon can be very productive, and as new, productive patterns continue to emerge, state and federal biologists are likely to become increasingly concerned about the ever-intensifying affect of winter harvest on salmon fisheries. I strongly recommend checking the rules and regulations for the area you intend to fish before drilling any holes.

If you're up for trying a new, exciting challenge this winter, why not leave the walleyes and pike behind for awhile. Check the ice conditions and local regulations, pack up your vehicle and head for a salmon fishery near you.

If you love ice fishing adventure and trophy game fish, I doubt you'll be disappointed.

Chapter 11

Understanding Eelpout in Winter

No other winter-caught species has more common names than the eelpout. It is often called burbot, ling, lawyer, loach, lingcod, lush, cusk maria, mud shark and others. Many of these names are usually uttered with anger or frustration by somewhat less-than-elated ice anglers.

I caught my first eelpout several winters ago. While fishing late-ice along a steep, hard-bottom break in 40 feet of water, my sonar revealed two fish moving through just off the bottom. Thinking they were walleyes, I responded by lowering a minnow-tipped jig, and immediately, felt a soft take. Setting the hook, my graphite rod nearly bent to its limit. I clambered to loosen the drag, but didn't make it in time. The line snapped faster than a rubber band in a schoolboy's hands. Disappointed, I reeled up and re-tied, carefully considering the position and motion of my jig at the time of the strike. After all, if a school of large walleyes was moving through, I didn't want to miss out.

Quickly I tipped a mid-size, silver Swedish Pimple with a fresh minnow head, lowered it to the bottom and repeated the same motion. Within seconds, my rod tip bounced, but this time I was ready. Soon, a strange, curled up yellowish brown fish with mottled black markings, a tapering tail

and a long dorsal fin sloshed from the hole. Eelpout!

Don't recognize the name? That's understandable. With few exceptions, no other freshwater species has more nicknames. Depending who catches them and where, eelpout have been called burbot, ling, lawyer, loach, lingcod, lush, cusk, maria, or mud shark. These names are often uttered with anger or frustration by ice anglers who simply don't like the fish.

Burbot inhabit northern lakes, rivers and even brackish estuaries, especially the cool waters of large rivers, the lower reaches of their tributaries and associated lakes. They're often caught by anglers throughout the North American ice fishing belt seeking walleyes and pike. Yet even with its extensive range and relatively high populations, this somewhat mysterious species is overlooked by most ice anglers. Because of its bad reputation, even where it's known, it is seldom a select target.

Eelpout are easily distinguished by their elongated tapering yellow-brown mottled bodies, rounded tails, continuous dorsal fins and large powerful jaws. (courtesy Strikemaster Ice Augers)

Too bad. Not only are eelpout worthy game fish and fun to pattern, but they bite readily, grow fairly substantial in size, fight hard, and, properly prepared, make a fine meal. Furthermore, since eelpout are found at the top of the food chain and consume virtually all species of baitfish, they're predators monitored carefully by fishery professionals. This is done primarily to help prevent competition with more desirable species such as walleyes, but they've also been considered for controlling the stunting of other species in a few select lakes.

Eelpout are easily distinguished by their elongated, tapering, yellow-brown mottled bodies rounded tails, distinct, continuous dorsal fins and large, powerful jaws designed to hold and crush their prey. Young eelpout feed primarily on inver-

tebrates such as immature aquatic insects, crayfish and freshwater shrimp. Consequently, they are found primarily on shallow, hard-bottom vegetated flats. Adult eelpout often put their powerful jaws to work pursuing a minnow diet comprised of sculpins, smelts, chubs, sticklebacks, even small perch or walleyes. Deeper areas over substrates of sand, gravel, rubble or mud are most likely to hold fish.

Voracious feeders, adult eelpout are very opportunistic and feed on just about anything. Pieces of tin, plastic, rocks and wood have been found in their stomachs, demonstrating the depth of their indiscriminate feeding habits. In fact, eelpout seldom stop feeding throughout the winter until there's no room for a single morsel more. The exception is perhaps during the actual spawning period, which uniquely takes place beneath the ice sometime between January and March. Like other species, they feed heavily during prespawn, and are often active throughout the winter.

Still, these fish are often scorned, occasionally even hated by many ice anglers. When incidentally

Voracious feeders, adult eelpout are very opportunistic and will feed on just about anything. (photo courtesy Mr. Walleye Specialties)

caught while fishing for other species, they are often left to become frozen carcasses on the ice. Consequently, management officials have kept eelpout at the bottom of their list of priorities. Despite wide distribution and sporting qualities, relatively few scientific studies have been conducted, so few winter eelpout patterns have been established.

But this is changing. The more eelpout are being fished, the more they're becoming understood. Despite the eelpout's preference for deep water and their mysterious winter movement patterns, anglers have discovered the average Midwestern eelpout weighs a respectable three pounds. It's also true that 7- to 10-pound fish aren't unusual and trophies up to 18 pounds are available. Consequently, some dedicated winter anglers have noted the worthiness of this respectable gamefish. Many of these select anglers have managed to keep their target quarry and their most productive patterns under their hats by disguising themselves as unsuccessful walleye or pike anglers. As the worthiness of pursuing these highly powerful, respect deserving fish is being discovered, their secret is slowly slipping out.

In-depth studies of the eelpout's winter habits have yet to be undertaken, but given their increasing popularity, more is being learned each year.

Effective Winter Location Patterns

In-depth studies of the eelpout's winter habitat, habits and movements have yet to be undertaken. Those searching for the fish have found winter eelpout patterns difficult to decipher primarily because little preliminary information has been assembled. It is also true that patterns vary greatly between lake types. Furthermore, eelpout tend to move and feed most actively under the cover of darkness.

Eelpout also feature the unique quality of spawning during the mid-to-late winter period, which leads to some interesting winter patterns. In fact, I've opted to scrap the first-ice, mid-season and late-ice location pattern distinctions used for every other winter panfish and gamefish covered in the Hooked On Ice Fishing series. Instead, I've opted to assemble basic winter eelpout patterns using a unique winter classification system broken into three categories: pre-spawn, spawn and post-spawn.

Pre-Spawn

On large, shallow lakes, eelpout are most active during pre-spawn feeding modes just as the lakes begin freezing. Large schools of eelpout often begin congregating on large, shallow, offshore rock, sand or gravel areas in less than 10 feet of water. They will often hold along deeper breaks during the day, then move up at night to feed. The most active feeding takes place just after sundown and right before sunrise. During these times, you can expect relatively shallow, main-lake structural features to offer the most productive fishing.

In larger, deeper lakes, similar pre-spawn movements often take place on offshore spawning structures, but not until sometime between mid-January and mid-February. The key to finding these pre-spawn eelpout is to locate massive, main lake humps, reefs, bars and points extending from deep water but topping out shallow. Those offering huge expanses of 2 to 20 feet of water on top and offering sharp breaks leading into deep water are favored locations. The best spots on these structures are points or fingers extending into the deep basin—especially those featuring irregular features like inside turns or rock piles on an otherwise flat, gravel or sandy bottom. The bigger, longer and steeper the break, the better.

As pre-spawn eelpout move up these breaks, they pass through quickly in large schools. Don't

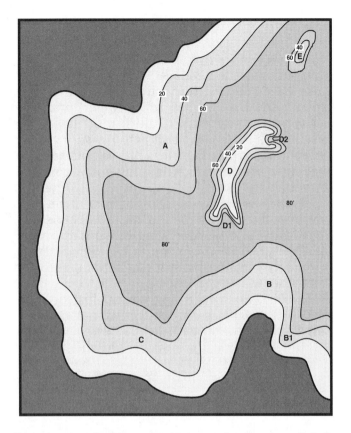

Pre-spawn eelpout congregate on large, steep-breaking, hard-bottom offshore reefs (E), bars (D) and points (A, B) lining shallow water, where they often position deep during the day and rise higher at night. Steep-breaking turns (B-1, D-1 and D-2) are primary fishing areas. During the spawn, eelpout cruise at night across the tops of shallow spawning shoals (D, E) and retreat into adjoining deeper water during the day. Post-spawn eelpout move back into deeper water along the bases of deep, main-lake structures (A, B and D). Area (C) and the slot alongside it would be a possible secondary location to try, but isn't as well defined and probably wouldn't hold as many fish.

Eelpout are unique in that they spawn beneath the ice. Their winter patterns revolve around three periods: The pre-spawn, spawn and post-spawn. During the spawn, eelpout congregate in huge, swirling slithering masses on shallow sand and gravel shoals under the cover of darkness. (courtesy Strikemaster Ice Augers)

stop to eat a candy bar or drink a soda after catching a fish. You may catch a half dozen fish in 15 minutes, then not have another bite for three or four hours. Don't waste time. Ice your fish, re-bait and get back down fast. The action is likely to be intense, but short.

The Spawn

The spawn begins with smaller males cruising the tops of shallow, sand and gravel spawning shoals at night and retreating into deeper holes during the day. Spawning sites are often completely deserted during the day. Some limited feeding activity may take place among smaller pre-spawn males, usually during the classic eelpout primary activity periods at twilight or just as the fish move from deep to shallow water. Several days later, however, as larger females begin joining these daily movements, focus is placed increasingly on spawning activities. Feeding wanes, then virtually ceases during the spawn. The actual spawn takes place at night, with eelpout often congregating in huge, swirling, slithering masses.

Post Spawn

After spawning, eelpout begin moving back into deep water. They can be caught during twilight and evening periods along steep-breaking drops adjoining spawning structures. They are tired from the spawning ordeal and apparently sapped of energy. They tend to move less and feeding activity is usually limited for a day or two. Soon after, however, they resume feeding on shallow water baitfish at night.

Once you find a productive eelpout structure, mark the location, it will often produce eelpout winter after winter.

Timing

Although eelpout remain fairly active all season, the two or three weeks prior to the spawn provide the best eelpout action of the winter.

Once you find a productive eelpout structure, mark the location, it will often produce eelpout winter after winter. (photo courtesy Mr. Walleye Specialties)

Daily, the first few hours of evening and about an hour before sunrise usually produce best as eelpout move between the shallows and deep water along specific migration routes. Some fish, however, may be taken throughout the evening along the tops of steep breaks.

Effective Winter Fishing Strategies

The process of locating winter eelpout begins with taking numerous sonar readings over steep-breaking structures suspected of drawing eelpout. Readings should be taken during the day or early afternoon prior to the start of their movement in an effort to identify migration routes and pinpoint locations likely to draw fish.

This should be followed up by drilling a series of staggered holes over the break at various depths. Eelpout tend to travel up these breaks in tightly held paths that often vary from night to night. You'll need to move around to determine just where to find the fish. By having numerous holes drilled early and covering the entire drop,

you'll be ready to undertake an effective, mobile, quiet approach once the fish begin moving.

Ninety percent of the time, these schools will become active just after dark, so get out there early. If you attempt to drill as the fish start coming in they'll spook. Properly set up, however, you should be able to take advantage of the prime-time bite.

Anglers caught up on their sleep may also experience short bursts of action throughout the evening as stragglers periodically move up and down the drop. If you're up for the experience, sticking it out until morning may pay off.

Tip-Up Techniques

Once in the right location with your holes drilled, setting effective tip-up presentations is relatively simple.

A few quality, standard stick tip-ups like HT's Fisherman with drag, or underwater Polars with mid-size spools work well. When they are combined with hole covers to help prevent freeze-up they provide plenty of trouble-free action. Thermal style tip-ups, such as Frabill's Igloo or HT's Polar Therm rigged with medium-sized, live minnows suspended just off the bottom work wonders, particularly during cold or blustery, snowy nights.

On milder evenings, wind tip-ups such as HT's Windlass rigged with rocker style jigheads tipped with minnow heads or small minnows and set to jig gently just off or directly on bottom work nicely. The use of phosphorescent beads, painted

The process of locating winter eelpout begins with taking numerous sonar readings over steep-breaking structures suspected of drawing eelpout. (courtesy Strikemaster Ice Augers)

hooks or small chemi-lightsticks also help eelpout find your presentations in the dark. They often improve catches dramatically. To help you see on the surface, adhering reflector or phosphorescent tape to your tip-up flags can be helpful. Quality tip-up lights like the Omni Strike Lite or lighted tip-ups like the lighted Polar Pop-Up or Polar Therm Mag can also be winners.

Remember, the Polar Pop-Up and Polar Therm Pop-Up are magnetic release tip-ups, meaning the spool and trip mechanism are held by only a magnetic field. When a light-biting eelpout strikes and turns the spool, they can almost effortlessly break this magnetic field, and feeling next to no resistance, eelpout are more likely to hang on longer.

Some anglers also use ice house rattle reels and wheels rigged with bottom-set minnow rigs to catch eelpout as they cruise through. These rigs are especially good when fishing throughout the night, when constant monitoring and tending of lines is difficult.

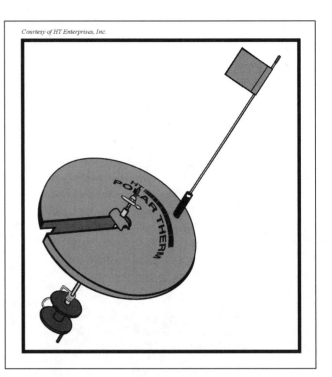
Courtesy of HT Enterprises, Inc.

HT's large spooled PTT-50 Polar Therm tip-ups work wonders when fishing eelpout on cold, blustery nights because they prevent hole freeze-up and eliminate snow from blowing into tip-up holes. (Courtesy HT Enterprises, Inc.)

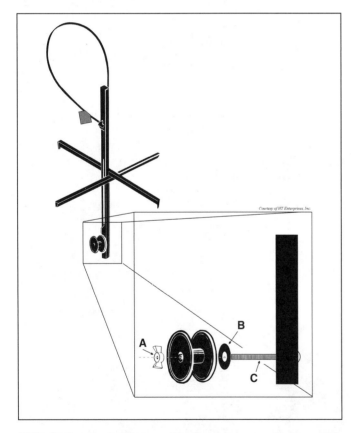
Courtesy of HT Enterprises, Inc.

HT's Fisherman tip-up with drag is a good, economical choice for fishing winter eelpout. If necessary, larger-spooled models are available, and interchangeable larger spools can also be purchased to convert smaller-spooled models into units capable of effectively fishing deeper water. (Courtesy HT Enterprises, Inc.)

HT's Polar pop-up features a magnetic release trip, which minimizes resistance to fussy, light-biting eelpout. (Courtesy HT Enterprises, Inc.)

Jigging

Eelpout are especially fun to jig with ice rods. Medium-action walleye-style outfits of 24 to 32 inches should be rigged with quality spinning reels. Since you're fishing at night and the fish can't see very well, slightly heavier monofilament of 8- to 10-pound test is fine. In deeper water, low stretch Berkley Sensi-Thin or Fireline is okay and helps prevent bite-offs from this fish's toothy, powerful jaws. Just be sure to set your drag properly. Better yet, flip off the anti-reverse and back-reel. Eelpout often make powerful runs. Running against a drag they tend to twist line, making night fishing frustrating. By turning off the anti-reverse and back reeling, you can avoid twisting while minimizing line breakage and maintaining control of these strong fish. Be ready for an interesting fight. Eelpout usually dive straight down when hooked, and again as they approach the hole.

For best results, try rigging a minnow below a slip-bobber positioned just off the bottom. You can also try jigging the same areas with a minnow hooked on a carefully sharpened, glow-in-the-dark jig head, a small phosphorescent jigging minnow or jigging spoon. A 1/8- to 1/4-ounce lure with #6 or larger hooks generally functions well—unless you're fishing exceptionally deep water or current, when 3/8- to 1/2-ounce baits may be necessary.

Use Fresh Bait

Hundreds of hours of eelpout observation have shown fresh minnows and grubs trigger more strikes. As a rule of thumb, change your bait every 10-15 minutes when jigging, every half hour on tip-ups.

Since your holes should be drilled prior to the onset of darkness and most eelpout will still be deep, start by fishing the base of your structural break and the adjoining flat with heavy jigs and spoons. At about sundown, focus directly on the base of the break, and gradually move up as the fish begin moving in. Constantly switch holes in a frantic search for fish. As sun-up nears, backtrack to the base of the break and onto the flat.

Again, regardless of your presentation style, work your bait gently, and don't lift it more than a couple inches off bottom. In some instances, you may actually mark fish moving through directly on the bottom, and be required to work your bait right on bottom to maximize your catch. Other than that,

presentation methods for consistent fishing are relatively cut and dried. The rules are simple: Fish near or on bottom. Work the jig or spoon with only subtle rocking actions. Allow the lure to provide the attraction and the subtle movements of the min-

Watch Hook Style

Hook styles and qualities are also important. Your hook should be large enough so the point protrudes slightly from your minnow, but no larger than is needed for the bait and method of hooking. Proper wire thickness depends on the size of the bait. When using smaller baits for smaller fish, thin, small-barbed light wire hooks are your best bets because they help keep your bait lively and best produce a slow falling, natural presentation. However, light wire hooks aren't practical when fishing with larger minnows. Here, heavier, larger-barbed hooks are better bets, because they're stronger and hold more securely. Circle hooks, a more rounded, saltwater design known to improve hooking, are also becoming more popular among winter eelpout anglers.

Furthermore, hooks with short points penetrate more easily. The long points hold better. Spear points are stronger, hollow points are thinner and sink better. And turned down eyes and bent shank designs like the Tru-Turn improve hooking because they direct the point into fish upon the hook set. Even hook color can be important. At times, red, silver or gold help attract fish, while bronze or green hooks are less visible.

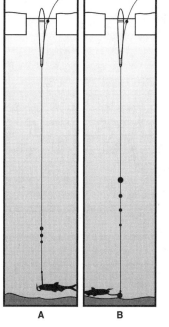

Popular eelpout rigs include minnows fished just off bottom and rigged beneath neutrally buoyant, carefully weighted and balanced slip floats (A). Very sharp, glow in the dark jigs can also be fished effectively in a similar manner (B), or a variety of phosphorescent spoons or jigging minnows can be fished "tightline" right on bottom.

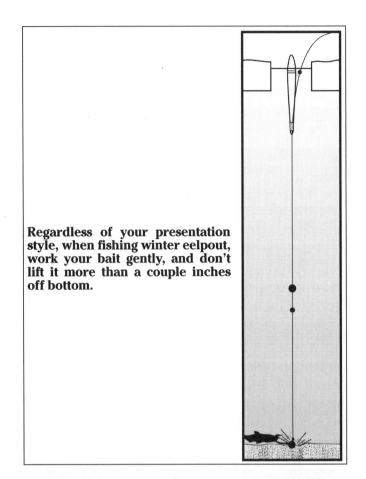

Regardless of your presentation style, when fishing winter eelpout, work your bait gently, and don't lift it more than a couple inches off bottom.

now to prompt strikes. And again, phosphorescent beads, plastic strips, tape or tiny cyalume sticks can be helpful for attracting fish to your bait. As a bonus, fishing these shallow-water, hard-bottom structures at night often means picking up a few bonus walleyes or saugers in the process.

The Eelpout Festival

Eelpout excitement has really caught on in the small northern town of Walker, Minnesota on the famed Leech Lake. Besides the interest in walleyes, eelpout have become a major draw. Each year, Walker sponsors an "Eelpout Festival" the second weekend in February. The annual get-together has become such an attraction that typically, seasonal businesses reopen for the weekend, just to accommodate the rush of eelpout enthusiasts from all over the country.

Eelpout Edibility

I'm often able to convince fellow avid ice anglers eelpout are valuable winter gamefish, but not always so successful arguing they're highly nutritious as well. I'm not sure why. Eelpout are a member of the cod family, a species commonly consumed throughout North America. The belief eelpout make poor food has probably taken hold because anglers stereotype this fish as a "rough" species and aren't open-minded enough to try it.

Fishing shallow-water, hard-bottom structures and their associated steep break lines at night is a highly productive means of catching winter eelpout.

The eelpout has been publicized by the "Eelpout Festival," an eelpout ice fishing tournament started as a joke by a group of ice anglers in the small northern Minnesota town of Walker. Hundreds of pounds of these fish have been caught throughout the several years this event has taken place. (Courtesy Strikemaster Ice Augers)

Since eelpout are a member of the cod family, their food value can be tremendous when taken from winter's cold waters—but they must be prepared and stored properly for optimum quality. (photo courtesy North American Fisherman)

Despite common misconceptions, eelpout are another winter gamefish worthy of the ice angler's respect. (courtesy Strikemaster Ice Augers)

Or maybe it's because most people don't know how to prepare them.

The food value of eelpout was realized in the early 1900s, when the former United States Bureau of Fisheries made an attempt to promote use of eelpout for food through extensive publicity. These efforts were largely futile and the project was scrapped. More recently, Canada initiated a more successful program to promote eelpout. Filleted and distributed to various restaurants in Toronto, chefs were asked to prepare the meat and provide their feelings about the burbot's qualities. Responses included comments such as "excellent" and "compare favorably with any fish which I have received from top wholesalers."

Some excellent recipes evolved through this effort, too. Among the best is filleting eelpout just as you would a walleye. Be sure to remove the tough skin and bones. Fortunately, since the ribs are thick and the tail section has no bones beyond the spine, the entire skinning and de-boning process is simple. When you start filleting an eelpout, however, you'll notice the meat is somewhat oily. Don't let this bother you. Rather, simply boil the fillets in salt water to remove the oil and enhance their flavor. Most people drop the fillets into a pot of boiling saltwater for one minute, then flavor the water with lemon juice, lemon pepper, a bay leaf or two, celery, black pepper, chopped onions and onion salt and a pinch of garlic, parboil them for a couple minutes, and drain.

The meat will now resemble cod or haddock. This is not really surprising, considering eelpout are members of the cod family. These can then be served with a touch of seasoning salt and melted butter, or you can bake or fry them in your favorite seasonings or batter. While the preparation time is slightly longer than traditional fillets, the consistency and flavor is terrific. In my opinion, it actually tastes similar to lobster, a food item which also happens to require slightly more preparation time than standard fillets.

There are drawbacks, however. Not properly prepared, eelpout fillets don't store well in a freezer. Apparently, enzymatic reactions occur when the meat is frozen, causing the meat to toughen. To avoid this problem, cook it prior to freezing. The cooking process breaks down these enzymes. Still, while eelpout fillets can be stored, they may turn a harmless but undesirable brown color. Thus, I feel eelpout is best when prepared fresh. For those interested, eelpout roe is also considered a delicacy in some areas, where it's often seasoned and served on toast.

So despite what some people may think of eelpout, they are positively another game fish worthy of respect—and in my opinion, ice anglers not taking advantage of them are missing out on yet another exciting opportunity within the realms of one of winter's most exciting sports.

Chapter 12
The Allure of Sturgeon Spearing

To some, sturgeon spearing might seem like an unsportsmanlike way of taking fish. Those who don't like the sport might question why I would cover it in the Hooked On Ice Fishing Series.

But sturgeon spearing is special to an entire group of people. It is something unique, an exclusive outdoor experience falling into the likes of elk hunting in the mountains out west, tarpon fishing in the Florida's Keys, or successfully landing an honest 50-pound musky. For many, sturgeon spearing is more than that. In Wisconsin, the practice is as much a part of ice fishing as is using tip-ups for northern pike. So here's exclusive coverage, beginning with one gentleman who feels sturgeon spearing is more than just a unique fishing practice.

"I'm an avid sportsman and enjoy all sorts of outdoor activities," said James Patt, a veteran Wisconsin sturgeon enthusiast. "But sturgeon spearing is special. Not only does it provide an opportunity to spend quality time with family and friends, it's a tradition I've enjoyed since I was a boy. You sit there staring into the lake through a small window into this giant underwater world and, all of sudden, a monster fish appears. Success hinges on split-second decisions, so there's always that anticipation, that brief moment of instant tension and thrill."

Such enthusiasm is easy to understand. First, consider the sturgeon. It is a huge, prehistoric fish with a long, flat nose. It has barbels on the lower snout and an angular, rudder-like tail. A sturgeon can attain weights exceeding 200 pounds. Such trophies have been speared in the only place in North America that still offers an annual winter spearing harvest: Lake Winnebago, Wisconsin. The largest sturgeon taken in recent history was a 180-pound fish speared from Winnebago in 1953. Old-timers from the Oshkosh area still talk of a 187.5 pound fish caught, not speared, August 6, 1913.

Today, the lake sturgeon population in these waters comprises the largest remaining population in the North American range. This population

Sturgeon are huge, prehistoric fish and popular winter quarry on Wisconsin's Lake Winnebago.

Lake sturgeon—huge, prehistoric fish featuring long, flat noses with barbels on the lower snout and angular, rudder like tails—can attain weights exceeding 200 pounds.

is closely managed by the Wisconsin DNR to eliminate the possibility of over-harvest and help preserve the number of larger fish. In fact, it's specifically managed to ensure a continuous, naturally spawning sturgeon fishery and sustain the annual sturgeon spearing season.

Like so many other parts of our outdoor heritage, a conservation-minded group of sturgeon spearers has helped ensure this crucial management. Spanning nearly a century, a continuous series of studies on Lake Winnebago's sturgeon fishery has contributed to its maintenance, perhaps even preserved this magnificent, prehistoric fish population. Without the attention generated by this group of spearing enthusiasts, it's unlikely these studies would have been conducted with such intensity. The absence of such information would likely have dramatically changed the present status of this unique fishery and its related ice fishing opportunity.

Other than Lake Winnebago, the only other sturgeon spearing season in North America existed in some isolated waters of northern Michigan. Not as carefully monitored over the years as the Lake Winnebago fishery, officials in this region became increasingly concerned about annual harvest, and as of 1999, the Michigan spearing season folded into history, leaving the Lake Winnebago fishery the only one of its kind left in North America. The Lake Winnebago season in 1999 was cut short by an emergency rule which closed spearing after a predetermined harvest cap was reached. At first there was a public outcry from anglers who thought their tradition was about to disappear. Later public hearings showed broad-based support for protecting the fish with such a cap.

Today's biologists estimate these mysterious, slow-growing, long-living fish must live more than 80 years to reach the coveted triple-digit weights

This 180-pound, 79-inch sturgeon nabbed by Elroy Schroeder, February 17, 1953, featured a 37-inch girth. (photo courtesy Wisconsin D.N.R.)

which lead to more than just the excitement of bagging a trophy, but the wonder of knowing your trophy has been swimming your waters longer than most of us have lived. The sturgeon's prehistoric ancestors likely roamed these waters long before anyone ever thought to spear them through the ice. That's part of the reason the rich history of this spearing tradition is so deep.

"The sturgeon spearing tradition on Lake Winnebago dates back more than half a century," said Bill Casper of Fond du Lac, Wisconsin, a lifetime sturgeon spearer and founder of a conservation organization called "Sturgeon For Tomorrow." SFT is a group dedicated to preserving sturgeon populations. "I remember when we cut holes by hand. And once set up, we rarely moved. Four-wheel drives weren't available until after World War II, and the Model A Ford we used had its limitations."

At that time, the limit on sturgeon was three, and Bill remembers one year when he took his limit. "They weren't that big," Bill admitted, "but I had one fish of 53 pounds and two in the 40-pound range."

Back then, these were relatively new, progressive regulations. "Prior to 1915, there were no restrictions on sturgeon harvest, and for a time after that, the limit was five," Bill pointed out. "In an effort to preserve this majestic fish, however, sturgeon harvest became illegal from 1915 until 1931, when their excellent recovery allowed a revived spearing and short-lived set line season." Today, the winter spearing season is the only legal means of harvesting sturgeon on Lake Winnebago, and currently, the limit is one fish per licensed spearer, with a minimum length of 45 inches.

The System for Locating Winter Sturgeon

In many respects modern sturgeon spearing hasn't changed much from historical practices. But today's innovative practitioners have used years of experience to tip the odds in their favor. Take Larry Smith of Berlin, Wisconsin. Larry is an experienced lifetime angler, sanctioned member of the MWC and dedicated sturgeon spearer.

"I get a queasy stomach the night before the spearing opener," Larry smiled. "I've been fortunate. I've had the opportunity to successfully participate in big game hunts and fish a variety of species throughout North America. But nothing gets me going like sturgeon spearing."

Judging by the number of spearing shacks on the ice of Lake Winnebago last season, others agree. And with high success rates among spearers in recent years, even more spearers are likely to need an antacid. Yet spearing requires technique and lots of patience.

"It took me five years to get my first fish, and I'll never forget it. I sat there in the shanty staring through a glowing green hole with nothing hap-

Larry Smith is a lifetime angler, tournament competitor, guide and dedicated sturgeon spearer.

pening," Larry explained. "I was starting to think it would never happen. Then, all of a sudden, there he was. My heart jumped into my throat as I threw the spear, and when it hit home, I became so overanxious my partner was worried I'd hyperventilate," he laughed. "But the experience was worth the wait."

Since then, Smith, along with other die-hard spearers, have learned techniques for increasing their odds. One such factor is watching for signs of sturgeon while fishing open water in the fall. "You'll often see sturgeon surfacing," Larry pointed out. "They do this to remove parasites obtained while digging through bottom substrates searching for snails and redworms, which comprise their main diet. Since these same redworm beds often persist through winter, noting places sturgeon jump may help you locate primary sturgeon feeding areas and increase your odds of success in winter."

Smith, well-equipped, carefully marks these areas on his hand-held GPS for future reference. Two weeks before the season, he prepares by checking ice conditions and drilling holes at his best waypoints, searching for primary feeding locations offering the best water clarity. Once he finds such locations, he throws a blanket over his head, allows his eyes to adjust and peers down, looking for signs of sturgeon. Often, like the markings of a moving clam but much larger, trails where sturgeon have foraged along bottom appear. To make sure forage is still available, Larry drops a heavy, open-ended pipe into the bottom muck, retrieves a sample, and filters through it looking for redworms.

"This may sound like a lot of work, but the extra time is well invested," Larry insisted. "Like anything, the more time you spend early, the more dividends you'll likely get later."

Spearing Equipment

When it comes to equipment, the first thing you'll need is something to cut a spearing hole. A standard chain saw with a 36 or 48" bar is best–otherwise, repeated hole cutting with an ice drill in a continuous line shaped to a rectangle also works. Either way, Larry advises cutting holes so they face west.

"This way, holes collect light during late afternoon, a time sturgeon are often moving...and many spearers are leaving thinking it's too dark to see. Yet those who know sturgeon understand they're night feeders. When things quiet down toward the end of the day, they become active. By cutting your hole to maximize twilight spearing time, you'll be able to focus your efforts during these high-percentage times." Once cut, the resulting ice block can either be pushed beneath the ice, or two holes can be drilled in the center for attaching a chain and subsequently removing the block.

With a hole opened, you'll need a permanent dark house. Dark houses are much like any other "permanent" fish house, except they have no windows, one large hole in the floor, and typically, a bar running from wall to wall high over the hole, rigged with special hooks to hang spears. Some spearers also place "leaning bars" over the hole at sitting level. These bars provide additional support as spearers wait for fish. Some spearers will tie themselves to the shanty with a safety rope, just in case. Most importantly, be sure to have proper ventilation for air exchange, especially if using a stove or portable heater.

When it comes to equipment, the first thing you'll need is something to cut a spearing hole. A chain saw with a 36-48" bar works best. (photo courtesy Sturgeon for Tomorrow)

After the spearing hole is cut, the chunk is forced under the ice to safely remove the ice block. (photo courtesy Larry Smith)

As for the shanty, Larry recommends an average-sized shanty that's durable but lightweight. This is important for two reasons. First, you'll likely want to move your shack periodically—plus, since late season ice can get poor, heavy shanties cause more problems than they're worth. Drop axles are a good idea because they tow better, and since you don't have to tip the shanty, your equipment can remain inside during transport. Of course, don't forget to clearly mark your house with your complete name, address and phone number as required by law.

Once your house is positioned, you'll need to choose a spear. Good quality spears with large tines are important. Small tines pull out of fish too easily, resulting in no catch and injury or death to the missed fish. Flying barbs help too, as they penetrate well without sacrificing solid hits. Handles should be weighted at the head to facilitate rapid propulsion toward the target.

A detachable head tied to 100-125 feet of line is another good idea. The detachable spearhead allows you to remove the stem and fight the fish free of the cumbersome handle, providing less leverage for the fish to free itself. Longer lines allow ample room to fight your fish without applying excessive pressure, which is a common cause of lost fish. Smith also advises having a second spear readily accessible, so in the event of a bad hit, the spare can provide a second chance at the fish, instead of leaving it wounded, or worse, to die and be wasted.

Larry also insists upon regular spear maintenance. "Although there's no reason quality spears won't last a lifetime, maintenance is important,"

Sturgeon Decoys

Sturgeon decoys have been around for years. In fact, traditional wooden models haven't changed much, and "modern" plastic decoys are even being replaced with wood again by some manufacturers. "Decoys come in a variety of sizes, shapes, styles and colors," said Jim Sprague of K&E Tackle, "but the most popular are 8- to 10-inch, naturally painted models imitating perch, pike or suckers."

Larry advised. "If using flying barbs, lube them with petroleum jelly prior to the season—and always sharpen your points with a good file." Spears should also have a safety cap to prevent dulling or injury when not in use.

Your next task is choosing sturgeon decoys, which come in a unique variety of forms, shapes, sizes, styles and colors. Traditional decoys are colored wooden blocks shaped like fish and offered commercially by companies such as Lakco and K&E Tackle, but spearers have found sturgeon are attracted to a number of unusual items, including bowling pins, stuffed animals, dolls—even porcelain.

That's right, porcelain. "There's something about the white color that consistently draws a sturgeon's attention," Larry smiled, "although most objects colored white work well. The past couple years, I've used two 10-foot lengths of white PVC tubing joined together with a bolt and a huge washer on top, then I turn them 45 degrees, forming an 'X'. When lowered to bottom, this pro-

For sturgeon spearing, good quality spears with large tines are important tools, as are decoys, which come in a variety of shapes, sizes and colors. The most popular decoys are fish shapes such as those shown here. (photo courtesy Sturgeon for Tomorrow)

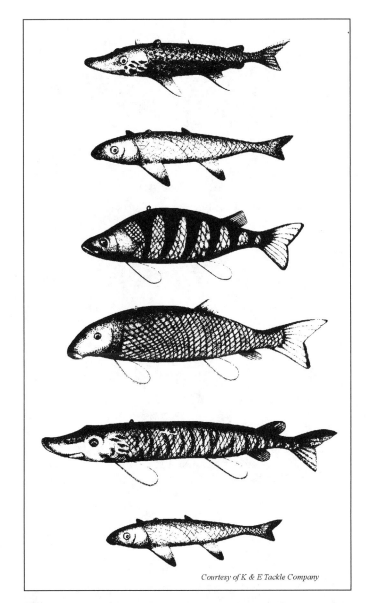

Courtesy of K & E Tackle Company

"Sturgeon decoys come in a variety of sizes, shapes and colors, but the most popular are 8- to 10-inch naturally painted models imitating perch, pike or suckers," said Jim Sprague of K&E tackle, a Michigan decoy manufacturer.

vides an excellent decoy and backdrop. Decoys also act as a reference. Since sturgeon fishing regulations require a minimum length, by making your decoy an even 1-, 2-, 5-, or 10-foot length, you have a standard to use when evaluating whether or not a fish is legal.

Regardless of what you use, your decoy must be lowered to bottom, or if the water is murky, as far down as you can see. Just remember that by law, all decoys must be removed from the lake when you're through fishing. Most spearers attach a length of monofilament or string to their decoy

for easy retrieval. However, Larry's a little more innovative.

"Remember how I explained the bolt secured with the large washer? There's a reason for that. This way when I can see bottom, I lower my decoy via a string with a large magnet attached to the washer. Once down, I pull the magnet free of the washer, leaving the decoy free of additional lines that may interfere with my spearing. At the end of the day, I use the magnet to retrieve the decoy. "Works like a charm!"

As for other accessories, a comfortable chair is a definite plus, large, sturdy gaffs are helpful when trying to lift fish from the hole, and portable heaters or wood stoves are always an asset for added comfort.

Some Additional Tips

Once you've identified your primary location and prepared your equipment, you'll need to set up. "A good spot should at least allow you to see a few sturgeon," Larry remarked, "especially if the water is clear. If you're not seeing fish, don't be afraid to move. Just be sure to mark your old hole so somebody doesn't get hurt after you leave."

For safety, spearers should mark both sides of any abandoned holes with two 4-foot lathes, preferably sprayed orange or black at the top and anchored securely within a partially drilled hole.

Spearers usually mark both sides of any abandoned holes with two 4-foot lathes, preferably sprayed blaze orange or black at the top and anchored securely within a partially drilled ice hole.

However, if you're confident of your spot, be patient. Like any trophy hunt, sturgeon spearing requires patience. You may have to wait a few seasons before you see a legal fish. But like Larry says, it's worth the wait. Just don't wait too long. "I've heard stories of people waiting 10 or 15 years to see a legal fish," Larry said. "I find that hard to believe. If people carefully search out productive areas, move periodically and are patient, most spearers should see a fish within 5 years, especially if the water clarity is cooperative."

Another tip from Larry is to fish on windy days—he feels wind may stir up currents fed by the river mouths, and this natural movement gets the food chain stirring beneath the ice. "I'm not sure why, but the windier the day, the more sturgeon seem to move," he observed. "I'd be curious to know if other spearers have noted the same phenomenon."

Spearing a Sturgeon

Now for the real action: spearing a sturgeon. First, be patient. When the target fish appears, raise your spear and throw it with a sharp, straight-on shot, then check to be sure you've got a solid hit into the fish. If you haven't obtained a solid hit, wait for the fish to come around again or apply steady pressure on the rope until it does, then throw a second spear. Either way, don't horse the fish, just apply firm, consistent pressure until it reaches the surface. At that point, open the door and force the fish out of your house quickly. Be careful about wrapping gaff or spear lines around your feet or wrists. Not only can this trip you, resulting in an ice bath with a potentially huge thrashing fish and sharp spear, but the sheer power of these fish can also break ankle and wrist bones. And amid the excitement, don't forget to mark your productive location on your GPS for future reference.

Regulations

Of course, spearing can't take place legally without a current state fishing license, spearing license and sturgeon tag. All are available from official registration stations, but get your paperwork early. In Wisconsin, no spearing licenses can be purchased after the season opens. Other-

Sturgeon tags, as shown on the tail of this fish, are used by biologists to record the fish's length, along with the date, area and time of day the fish was speared.

wise, like other game licenses, you must have your license with you at all times—and your tag, too. Never leave your tag in the spearhouse with a partner while you step out. Anyone possessing someone else's tag is in violation of the law.

While current regulations must always be checked, currently sturgeon tags require recording the overall length of your fish, along with the date, area and time of day the fish was speared. These bright orange adhesive tags must immediately be wrapped around the fish's tail after it's speared. All sturgeon must be openly displayed until the Wisconsin DNR places a carcass tag on them at an official registration station. This means unregistered fish cannot be stored in a closed trunk or even a capped truck bed with the tailgate closed. Sturgeon must also be registered by 7:00 p.m. the day of the catch. By the way, should you find a study tag on your speared fish, it pays to report it at the registration station. Not only with this assist with research, but you may also receive a nominal cash reward from Sturgeons for Tomorrow.

Cleaning the Catch

After the excitement of spearing and registering your fish, you'll want to take plenty of photos. Then you'll be ready to clean your catch. Skin the fish first. Sturgeon have no bones, but you'll want to remove the cartilage along with the brown "mudline" and fat. The meat should then be cut into steaks and boiled to remove excess fat. At this point, you can either smoke the meat, or to maintain the unique taste of sturgeon, parboil the steaks to remove any remaining fat, and freeze them in water to prevent freezer burn. The steaks can then be thawed, boiled in saltwater and served with butter, or dipped in batter and fried.

How does it taste?

"People always ask that," Larry laughed. "And I always answer the same way: Sturgeon tastes like sturgeon. If I had to compare texture, I'd say it's similar to pork chops. However, the meat tastes like sturgeon, not pork, chicken or whatever other meats sportsmen commonly compare most wild game to."

The Future of Sturgeon Spearing

All that remains to cover now is the future of sturgeon spearing. As responsible fisher-folks, we must remember sturgeon are a prehistoric, majestic, slow-growing fish. Sturgeon spearing is now unique to Lake Winnebago. We must show an interest in doing more than just spearing sturgeon. We must also have an appreciation for their uniqueness, and in their own special way, beauty. Like an avid musky fisherman, a spearer must be interested in the ecology and maintenance of their unique species.

"It takes years for sturgeon to grow to legal size," Larry pointed out. "A typical 60-pound fish will be over 40 years old. Such an amazing fish demands respect." Simple common sense factors must be practiced. Examples would include:

- Never spearing sturgeon under the minimum size. If in doubt, don't throw.
- Never spearing more fish than allowed by law.
- Whenever you don't have a good shot at a sturgeon, don't throw. Wounded fish often die later, a wasted resource.
- Promptly registering your fish.
- Becoming involved with organizations such as Sturgeon For Tomorrow, dedicated to preserving this majestic fish's future.

In short, the sturgeon's future depends on us. We must be careful. With a growing number of spearing participants, improved equipment and techniques plus water quality concerns, habitat loss and dam formation blocking spawning movements, over-harvest could burn out this precious resource quickly. This is something the Wisconsin D.N.R. is monitoring closely.

A major concern of the Wisconsin D.N.R. is the fact most people are looking for trophies. These are the same fish which maintain the best spawning stock. Consequently, numbers of the best spawners are in danger of being depleted most rapidly, and since sturgeon spawn only once every four years, the impact of this weighs heavily on the sturgeon's future. "Decisions we make over the years will surely shape decades of future sturgeon fishing," said Wisconsin fisheries biologist Ron Bruch.

Apparently other professionals agree. One study summary by Wisconsin biologists Gordy Priegel and T.L. Wirch, 1975, reads as follows:

"Once a (sturgeon) population is over-exploited, it is almost a safe assumption that the population will never recover to former abundance, as has already been shown throughout the natural geographical range of the sturgeon."

Although the Winnebago System holds the largest naturally sustaining lake sturgeon population in the world, with more people becoming interested in spearing, responsibility will be the key to maintaining the sturgeon spearing tradition and the sturgeon spearing privilege.

"It's a chance to celebrate family, and visit with no interruptions," concluded James Patt. "Just don't forget to practice for sturgeon spearing," he chided. For best results, Mr. Patt recommends "...sitting in a quiet room watching television with the thing turned off."

Chapter 13

Other Gamefish Species

Muskies resemble their cousins the northern pike, but background coloration is a greenish brown or silvery green instead of dark green, and their tails are more distinctly pointed rather than rounded.

Preceding chapters covered basic winter patterns for commonly sought winter gamefish. Yet there are some unique fish occasionally caught through the ice, usually, but not always, taken incidentally by anglers seeking other species. These include primarily muskellunge and catfish. Carp, a species rarely taken through the ice and often considered a "rough" fish is another. A pair of marine species are also taken by ice anglers. Atlantic cod and halibut are only taken in one place in the world, but they constitute "gamefish" by our definition, so we'll cover them here, too.

Muskellunge

Muskellunge are considered among the most challenging of all freshwater fishes. You've probably heard the old adage about muskies being "a fish of 10,000 casts." However, this is rarely true,

especially during winter. I can speak confidently now, because we can't cast through the ice. And even if you could, I don't think it would take that long to catch one. Yet few people concentrate their efforts fishing winter muskies.

Why? Primarily because the season often closes prior to ice formation in many areas, making pursuit opportunities limited. Secondly, with so many excellent opportunities available to catch panfish, walleyes or pike, most anglers don't think to focus on muskies. Too bad. Where the season is open, especially at first ice, muskies are probably more concentrated than any other time.

Muskellunge closely resemble their cousins the northern pike, but the muskie's background coloration is light greenish-brown or silvery-green instead of dark green, and the tips of the tail are more distinctly pointed rather than rounded. Muskies also prefer slightly warmer water, and therefore aren't as active in winter. They still feed

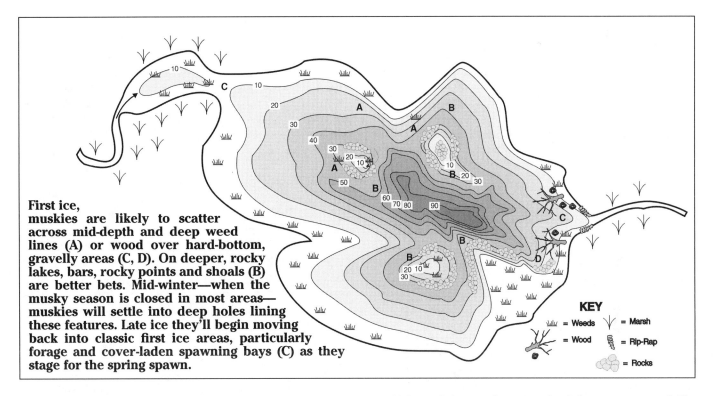

First ice, muskies are likely to scatter across mid-depth and deep weed lines (A) or wood over hard-bottom, gravelly areas (C, D). On deeper, rocky lakes, bars, rocky points and shoals (B) are better bets. Mid-winter—when the musky season is closed in most areas—muskies will settle into deep holes lining these features. Late ice they'll begin moving back into classic first ice areas, particularly forage and cover-laden spawning bays (C) as they stage for the spring spawn.

KEY

= Weeds   = Marsh

= Wood   = Rip-Rap

= Rocks

on baitfish and even larger species such as walleyes, which are often their forage of choice.

Primary Winter Musky Location Patterns

Winter muskie location varies, based primarily on how far winter has progressed, lake type and primary forage.

First ice generally offers anglers the best chance to locate active muskies, because during ice formation, most lakes are virtually inaccessible to anglers. Gaining a false sense of security, muskies tend to concentrate in easy-to-locate spots and are hungry.

One solid pattern for relatively shallow first-ice muskies is fishing lakes with a cisco forage base. Since cisco can be found relatively shallow during first ice, muskies move in. They may relate to weeds, but more commonly they are found relating to wood over hard-bottom, gravel areas. Virtually any kind of wood may produce. It could be fallen timber, brush, stumps, logs, even wooden fish cribs can be productive.

On small, weedy lakes, first-ice muskies are likely to scatter across mid-depth and deep weed lines lining deep holes or mid-lake structures where they find perch and shiners. Since these areas are often limited in size, muskies aren't usually difficult to track.

Although large, deep, rocky lakes are more difficult to fish, you can eliminate virtually all primary and secondary flats and simply target deep, mid-lake, hard-bottom, cover-laden rock bars and shoals. Focus your efforts on structures lining the deepest edge of the main-lake basin, especially where structural features such as hard-bottom, main-lake points, bars and humps supporting weeds, wood or rock meet the soft basin. Steep drops at the mouths of shallow, vegetated bays can also be good. On deep lakes, you may also notice that winter patterns closely follow those of the walleye. The main reason is muskies in these waters often are relating to their favorite forage; walleyes. Find areas where schools of these "forage" fish are roaming, and you'll also find muskies.

As the season progresses into mid-winter, muskies drop into deep holes, move very little and seldom feed. So even if the season is open, they're really not worth pursuing. But for anglers interested in trying, deep, main-lake bars or points with a variety of extensions such as deep mid-lake jogs or turns breaking quickly into deep water are most productive, simply because these areas gather baitfish.

During late-ice periods, muskies become increasingly active. In areas where the season remains open, which are few, ice anglers can do well. Start by looking near the same abrupt drop-offs along points, bars, and humps that you fished during first-ice. Gradually begin working along the edges of adjacent mid-depth flats and shelves. Muskies often utilize such locations as transition areas, as they gradually begin migrating back towards primary flats and into shallow bays and coves in search of food. You'll often find them holding there right through ice-out. Again, when the fish are using these shallow flats, look for deep-water pockets, especially those featuring weed growth, wood or rocks, to hold the most fish.

Timing

As for timing, late morning to mid-day and the hour or two just before sunset seem to provide top action, especially for the shallow wood, early-ice cisco pattern, although deep-water muskies may bite all day.

Effective Winter Fishing Strategies

Catching winter muskies is seldom easy, due to their rarity, anti-social attitude and mood-swinging activity levels. But that's the challenge. Figure out where these fish are most likely to hold and feed, and catching winter muskies can be one of the most rewarding challenges in ice fishing.

While effective presentations for icing muskies are similar to presentations commonly used for pike, muskies are a different species, and require some special variations in rigging to increase the chance of hooking legal fish. As a general rule, you'll need to use large-spooled tip-ups, heavier rods and lines, and larger, sharper hooks.

If you're following the first-ice cisco pattern, the best bet is to find a shallow to mid-depth hard-bottom, wood-strewn area adjoining deep water. Then set large-spooled PTU-5 Polar tip-ups spooled with 40- to 60-pound dacron directly over the wood. The closer the better. Get too far away, and you'll decrease your chances dramatically. Just be sure to use large-spooled tip-ups. When muskies strike and you set the hook, they'll run hard, and if you don't have adequate line backing, these fish easily straighten hooks.

As for specific rigs, make your own quick-strike rigs using 10-inch lengths of 60-pound Seven-strand wire outfitted with the highest quality, chemically sharpened #2 or #4 treble hooks you can buy. When fishing the cisco pattern, hook these into a large, dead cisco, add just enough weight to lower the bait to the bottom, and wait half an hour. If you don't get hit, lift the minnow off

the bottom and let it re-settle. You'll often get a strike. This lifting method probably works because the minnow usually falls beneath a log or piece of wood, out of the fish's sight. By repositioning the minnow, muskies are able to locate the bait. Also, if ciscos aren't available, large, 6- to 8-inch live golden shiners, featuring a shiny profile similar to the cisco, will work. While hard to come by, if you tell your local bait shop owner you're interested in these "mutants" they can usually obtain them from bait suppliers.

When fishing deeper weed or rock structures, another good method for taking consistent catches of muskies involves tip-ups. Using sonar, determine the exact tips of deep, mid-lake structures featuring suitable combinations of cover and forage. Then drill a series of holes around these deep, tapering tips, carefully covering the edges and bases of the deepest breaks featuring the best combinations of secondary cover.

To maximize efficiency and ensure water coverage, fish in small groups, and have everyone "leap-frog" their tip-ups from hole to hole, giving each hole approximately a half hour to produce before moving. Just be sure to properly set the "drag" on your unit by loosening the set screw on the cross

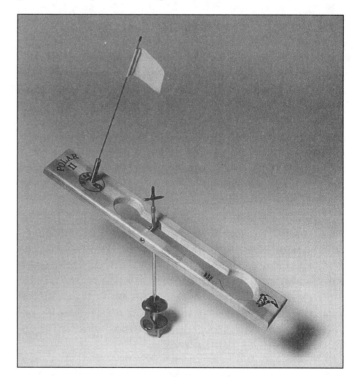

If you're following the first-ice musky-cisco pattern, your best bet is to find a shallow to mid-depth, hard-bottom, wood-strewn area adjoining deep water and set high-quality, large spooled tip-ups like this Polar II baited with a large, dead cisco. Fish near the bottom.

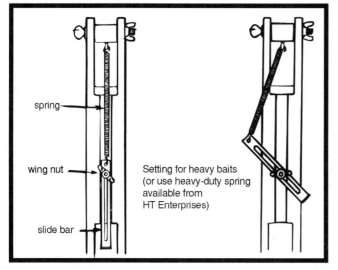

Courtesy of HT Enterprises, Inc.

spring

wing nut

Setting for heavy baits
(or use heavy-duty spring
available from
HT Enterprises)

slide bar

By using the heavy-duty spring and turning the spring tension adjustment bracket to the side, musky-sized minnows can be effectively fished on HT's Windlass tip-up—an often overlooked, highly productive winter musky catching tactic.

shaft and raising the tube slightly to increase the pressure of the flag wire against the trip shaft. This also reduces the chances of false flags.

If you're fishing really deep and need additional drag, use the PTU-10 "deep lake" Polar. Here you have the opportunity to adjust the drag adjustment feature to reduce the chance of "backlashing." With this set, large minnows won't be able to spin line from your spool without tripping the flag.

Deep-water rigs should feature a #4 or #5 ball-bearing swivel tipped with a thin, 60-pound stranded wire leader. When considering the distinct possibility of catching a hard-fighting, deep-water fish exceeding 30 pounds, stranded wire is thinner, more durable and less visible than mono of the same test. Tip your leader with an ultra-sharp hook or quick-strike style rig, using only high quality, #4 hooks like Partridge VB, Eagle Claw Lazer or Mustad Accu-Points. If you're a skilled sharpener, you may even want to touch them up a bit to ensure solid hook-ups. When fishing deep for these bony-jawed monsters, you'll be surprised by the difference quality hooks and a good sharpening job can make.

As for bait, use 8- to 12-inch golden shiners, chubs or suckers, the more aggressive the better. Don't get me wrong, deep-water muskies will pick up dead baits, too. But dead bait is a better pattern for shallow, cisco-relating muskies or scavenging pike. A large, lively chub or sucker is like a giant steak, and will appeal more to these trophy, deep-water fish.

Finally, place your hooks with the points facing the tail, in back of the dorsal with a single treble, or behind the dorsal and through the mouth with double trebles. Muskies usually eat their food head first, and this places the hooks in the highest percentage hook-setting position. For best results, send this rig down with the help of a couple large rubber-core sinkers, and fish within 5 feet of the bottom.

Wind tip-ups are a little different, and offer several presentation options that should also be looked into. Again, since you'll be fishing larger, heavier baits, set the drag tighter by adjusting the wing nut on the spool and bending the tip of the flag wire. Be sure the wind flap is properly set and jigging by turning the adjustment bracket to one side, using the extra heavy-duty spring included with each unit and experimenting with various tensions and actions until you find one that appears to work. Then secure your wind tip-up bases firmly by freezing them down with snow or slush, so if a large fish hits it won't pull these top-heavy units over.

With wind tip-ups, live bait works, but the option of using lures exists because the unit will jig your bait for you. Spoons like Bay de Noc Swedish Pimples, Vinglas or Do-Jiggers, Mepps Syclops, Bait Rig's Deep Willospoons, Reef Runner's Slender Spoons, HT's Marmooska Spoons, or Northland Fire-Eye Spoons tipped with a carefully sharpened hook and minnow are highly effective. Just remember to keep your hooks extra sharp to help maximize hooking percentages. To prevent your holes from freezing and keep snow and light from entering around your tip-ups, place a Thermal Hole Cover or Ice Guard around your unit, and use a freeze proof plastic tube around the line on your wind tip-ups to keep the bait moving freely.

Jigging muskies with the proper ice rod and equipment can also be fun, as it provides activity and helps dramatically in terms of water coverage while waiting for a flag. Use a stiff, heavy-action, heavy-power 3 or 4- foot ice rod such as HT's PL-34H Trout/Pike System. A 5- to 6-foot medium-light action summer-style fishing rod like HT's Venture, St. Croix's Premier Graphites or a similar action rod will also work.

Combine your favorite rod with a spinning or baitcasting reel spooled with 10- to 17-pound test (10- or 12-pound for spinning, 12- to 17-pound for baitcasting) tipped with a thin-strand wire leader. From here, hook a live minnow on a quick-set rig, jig and minnow or jigging lure. Set your drag tight for hook-setting purposes and switch off the anti-reverse. This way you can back-reel to better control running fish. Work your lures with delicate swimming motions and pauses interspersed with periodic, aggressive, long pulls or snaps to attract fish. Then allows the bait to fall and it should do the rest.

Finally, fish from a hole where you can conveniently watch your tip-ups, and hold on. The heart pounding excitement of jigging muskies can become addicting, and as you'll soon find, although the season may be short, it's awfully sweet.

Catfish

You may be surprised to see catfish mentioned in an ice fishing book. While catfish aren't the most active winter gamefish species, they can be caught.

Channel cats are the most common catfish species found lying on frozen surfaces across the ice fishing belt. They feature dark bluish gray to light silvery-brown sides often graced with black spots. They have two long, characteristic barbels on the upper chin and four shorter barbels emerging from the lower chin. Their tails are deeply forked. The catfish diet varies greatly, but consists mainly of fish, insect larvae and crustaceans. As scavengers, they will eat dead or rotting materials and organic debris, but are most commonly caught on live minnows or strips of fresh belly meat. Taken from winter's cold waters, you won't find many fish offering more tasty fillets.

While aggressive bottom feeders, channel catfish don't feed much in the icy waters of winter. But they do congregate in specific areas. If you can

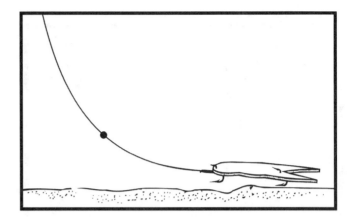

Mid-sized treble hooks baited with cut strips of oily or smelly baitfish such as smelt, cisco or bloaters make effective winter catfish tip-up rigs all winter long.

locate them and drop a bait on top of them, you'll likely catch one simply because of the sheer number of fish viewing your presentation.

At first-ice, channel catfish may be found within shallow, cover-strewn bays and coves, but are more likely to hold along the deep edges of such areas, with wood and rock seeming to be the preferred forms of cover. The steepest breaks offering bottom content changes and mixes of cover leading down to the deepest available water are often the best. By mid-winter, catfish hole up and concentrate near the base of these breaks, holding right on the bottom, usually within the deepest holes available in the main basin. In the case of rivers, deep, current-laden, frozen over river holes, eddies and pockets near the openings of deep backwater areas graced by hints of current will hold catfish.

As late ice approaches, catfish begin moving shallow again as they gather and stage in preparation for upstream spring spawning movements. They're most often found along deep primary breaks lining cover-laden flats adjoining the current of a shallow spawning inlet, outlet or river mouth. Use sonar to find where they're concentrating. Watch closely, as catfish often remain tight to the bottom in deep water and can be hard to identify. If you suspect catfish are in the area because of periodic bottom fluctuations appearing on your sonar, you might want to take advantage of an underwater camera to confirm your suspicions. If you're right, you're in business, if not, be patient, and keep moving. Since winter catfish are often so tightly concentrated, this process may take awhile, but once you're on them, the action can quickly go from nothing to good.

While catfish certainly aren't the most active of winter gamefish species, they can be caught.

As for presentation, small, lively minnows placed directly on the bottom beneath underwater or wind tip-ups work wonders. Many anglers fish with mid-sized treble hooks baited with cut strips of oily or smelly bait fish such as smelt, cisco or bloaters. Where legal, cut slices of northern pike work as well. Such baits can be successfully fished directly on the bottom with the help of lightweight split-shot placed about 18 inches up the line. Use the lightest weight you can get away with to drop the bait to bottom and hold it there. When a fish strikes, hurry to the tip-up, grab your line and set the hook with a fast, firm lift. Channel cats are often quick to drop the bait.

If you prefer to jig, a 30- to 36-inch medium-action spinning rod outfitted with 8- to 10-pound monofilament works well. Small, flashy jigging spoons tipped with cut belly meat or small minnows placed on large jig hooks and gingerly jiggled on the bottom will also produce. With any of these baits, gentle, occasional flips of your rod tip is all that's required to get their attention. Follow this by a direct drop to the bottom, jiggle the bait slightly, and keeping close contact with your lure, pause momentarily. Most strikes are just slight twitches, so watch your rod tip and line carefully. Winter catfish seldom hit hard.

Channel catfish feed best from sun-down to midnight, and again during the wee hours of the morning.

Carp

Carp have a bad reputation because of their habit of stirring up bottom sediments and ruining habitat for more desirable gamefish species. They're largely inhabitants of shallow, nutrient-rich, densely vegetated, low-oxygen, often dark or turbid environments. They're predominantly bottom feeders and scavengers, feeding on whatever is available, including insects, algae, crustaceans, silt and bottom debris. They can adapt to a wide variety of waters. They're easily identified by their large, thick, goldish-yellow-brown circular scales, down turned, fleshy mouths and two fleshy barbels on each side of the upper jaw. Their meat can be firm and well-flavored when taken through the ice and properly prepared.

While admittedly seldom caught in large numbers through the ice, some winter anglers have experienced inadvertent winter carp catches. Most often this occurs in slightly current-graced river backwaters and side channels near dams,

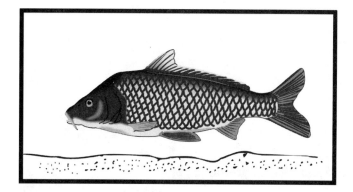

While seldom caught in number through the ice, some winter anglers have experienced inadvertent carp catches. This usually occurs in slightly current-graced river backwaters and side channels near dams, warm-water discharges, inlets and springs.

warm-water discharges, inlets and springs. Carp are most active during mid-winter "thaws" and late-ice warming trends in areas influenced by current. They feed there, but rather lethargically. Most are caught by finesse jigging small spoons, jigging minnows or live bait-tipped teardrop lures worked in a slow, jiggling motion directly on the bottom. Tip-up anglers might inadvertently hook carp by placing tip-up rigs directly on the bottom.

Atlantic Cod and Halibut

Yes, that's right. Atlantic cod and halibut.

Atlantic cod are a bottom-feeding, elongated, heavy-bodied, black-speckled tannish-brown salt-water species that feeds aggressively in cold waters. They average 3 to 5 pounds, but may grow to weights exceeding 30 pounds. Atlantic cod aren't fussy about their diet and feed on just about anything, including a variety of baitfish, mussels, worms, crabs and lobsters. It's been reported that codfish have been found with stones, glass, even oil cans in their stomachs.

Halibut are an unusual, flat-bodied, bottom-feeding saltwater species with both eyes atop their flattened bodies. Average ice fishing catches weigh between 5 and 10 pounds. Some halibut may grow to astronomical weights up to 600 pounds, but I know of none this large being taken through the ice. Table fare is excellent with both species.

Interesting. But in an ice fishing book?

Yup.

When it comes to ice fishing unique gamefish, it doesn't get much more exotic than these two

Atlantic cod are bottom-feeding, saltwater species that feed aggressively in cold water. They can be identified by their elongated, heavy bodies and black speckled tannish-brown skin.

When it comes to ice fishing gamefish, it doesn't get any more unique than the saltwater ice fishing opportunities offered in Quebec's Saguenay River.

The Atlantic cod is one of the most commonly caught gamefish on the Saguenay River.

saltwater species. They can only be caught through the ice in one location: Quebec's Saguenay River. If you read the ocean perch segment in *"Hooked On Ice Fishing II: Panfish,"* you already know the Saguenay is located just inland from the Gulf of the St. Lawrence River, where tidal action has caused this river to become a deep, brackish water, fjord-like environment. Uniquely, the Saguenay averages 300 to 800 feet deep throughout much of its length. With temperature and salinity gradients between the outflowing freshwater from Lac St. Jean and the influx of frigid saline water from St. Lawrence tidal fluctuations, a thermal layer of freshwater stratifies atop the saltwater rather than mixing. This forms a complex ecosystem.

Here, the fertile saltwater in these tremendous depths never warms beyond 2 degrees Celsius. With a continuously replenishing supply of oxygen from tidal movements, the Saguenay's depths maintain temperature, oxygen and salinity levels similar to those found in the Arctic Ocean. This enables the environment to support a viable marine fishery. Best of all, with the upper layer of freshwater allowing ice formation, anglers can enjoy ice fishing for saltwater species.

If you haven't read *"Hooked On Ice Fishing II: Panfish,"* this might throw you for a loop because ice fishing, as most people know, is limited to freshwater environments simply because saltwater has a lower freezing point than freshwater. As we all know, most marine environments tend to be large and deep, meaning the sheer volume of water impedes ice formation. In addition, most saltwater bodies are influenced by currents of some sort, perhaps even warm-water currents, which also prohibit ice formation. Thus, in most parts of the world there is no chance to go ice fishing over salt water.

But the Saguenay River is unique. Here ice anglers not only find a frozen saltwater environment, but some completely unbelievable ice fishing experiences. The miles of water feature mind-boggling depths where most cod and halibut hold along the bottom. In some of the Saguenay's most immense depths, those exceeding 500 feet, ice anglers have an incredibly serious challenge on their hands. As if these astounding depths aren't enough, the effects of currents and tidal actions influence location patterns, and water depths vary as much as 20 feet during tidal movements

Specialized rigs made from a large spool fixed on a tripod are standard for fishing cod in the immense depths of the Saguenay River. These rigs are spooled with heavy line and baited with frozen smelt.

However, once ice has formed, ice anglers can drive onto the Saguenay, and fishing from permanent shanties or portable shelters, place them strategically over points jutting out into the channel, contour turns, reefs and rock piles. To pinpoint these features, you'll need sonar. Also keep a close watch on tidal movements. When you notice the ice creaking along shore or the depth changing on your sonar, be prepared for activity. Shifting underwater tidal currents stir changes in preferred fish location, causing increased activity and improved catch rates. Depending where you're fishing and how far win-

ter has progressed, the action may improve more as the tide comes in or retreats. Learn to plan your fishing with these periods using tide-tables, and you'll soon note patterns.

In terms of presentation, the greatest challenge is finding a method allowing you to get your baits into these immense depths, while still allowing the capability to bring them back to the surface efficiently. As you might imagine, these depths have spawned numerous unique fishing methods and techniques. But most people rely on the old standby: A large-spooled tip-up. Some ice anglers use long fiberglass rods rigged with saltwater spinning

On the Saguenay River, tidal movements cause water depths to vary as much as 20 feet in just six hours. Here, the tide is moving out, exposing an icy rock ledge showing where the water level had been prior to the drop.

The Saguenay also offers some odd marine catches, such as this 500-pound, 10-foot long Greenland tall shark caught in 1995. The other fish shown is a halibut. (photo by Alain Lausie)

or baitcasting reels rigged with heavy monofilament leading to heavy, minnow-tipped jigging spoons and lures. In depths exceeding 500 feet, specialized rigs made from a large spool fixed on a tripod stand and spooled with heavy, 40- to 100-pound test monofilament tipped with, 5/0 or larger single hooks baited with frozen smelt fished on the bottom are standard fare.

In areas where tidal current is a factor, heavy weights are used to hold the bait on the bottom, and the bait is checked periodically by lifting the line. If a fish has struck, the hook is set and line is pulled in hand-over-hand. If there is no fish, the bait is lifted up and down in a jigging fashion to help attract fish, then set back on the bottom.

Other marine gamefish species are also taken on the Saguenay. Sharks exceeding 10 feet long have been caught through the ice. Other odd marine species are also occasionally caught by ice anglers, although on a less consistent basis.

Certainly no seafood lover will question the food value of baked, grilled or blackened Atlantic cod, halibut or shark steaks. Make these delicacies freshly prepared from fillets just taken from the cold, saline waters of the Saguenay, and you'll soon realize you aren't far from perfection.

Chapter 14

Putting It All Together

With the incredible changes taking place in ice fishing, our generation is discovering new winter ice fishing patterns faster than at any time in the history of our sport.

With the incredible changes taking place in ice fishing, our generation is discovering new winter patterns faster than any time in the history of our sport.

Never before has the under-ice environment been so well scrutinized by knowledgeable ice anglers. The growth and development of high-technology electronics such as hand-held GPS units are allowing us to electronically locate, save and exchange coordinates of precise, under-ice features. We can then use plotter trails to mark specific, secondary features on them. Highly specialized and increasingly sophisticated forms of sonar allow us to explore the details of these secondary features without even cutting holes. Underwater cameras allow glimpses of these magical, under-ice locations, revealing details we couldn't previously see.

Together, these developments help us better understand the constantly changing under-ice environment and how gamefish relate to it. Combine this with more knowledgeable anglers fully armed with numerous new developments in tip-ups, ice rods, lines, lures, hooks and accessories, and it's easy to understand why many undiscovered, breakthrough patterns and products are being revealed.

Whether you've never ice fished before or consider yourself a seasoned veteran, it's my hope that through reading Hooked On Ice Fishing III, you have gained an increased awareness, if not a solid understanding, of the tremendous array of variables and conditions governing winter gamefish patterns. Hopefully, you've picked up some pointers and tips for the type of winter fishing you prefer or would like to try. This awareness should make you a better ice angler. You should feel comfortable researching your waters, determining lake types and identifying specific water characteristics. I hope you also feel confident reviewing lake maps, understand how GPS, sonar and underwater cameras can enable you to quickly identify and efficiently locate "high-percentage" fishing locations and allow you to strategically establish working presentation patterns.

Yet this is just the tip of the iceberg. Unique combinations of various factors will always make ice fishing a challenge. I certainly can't cover the full gamut of winter patterns here. But whether you consider yourself a beginner, experienced veteran or advanced winter angler, the solid, skeletal winter patterns and awareness of detail we've outlined in this series should help you successfully tackle virtually any water, under a variety of conditions, anytime throughout the winter. By using and applying this foundation of elementary secrets and tricks, you should be able to confidently develop, elaborate on and fine-tune productive winter gamefish approaches, regardless of the conditions.

Along the way, the road to success can be enhanced by fishing with other good anglers, watching educational ice fishing videos, reading outdoor magazines and books and clicking through Internet pages offering helpful ice fishing tips. All of these will build on the basics and help you stay on top of the newest tactics, techniques, trends and equipment. Interacting with knowledgeable bait shop owners, guides and ice tackle manufacturers is also helpful. Like you, they're constantly experimenting, trying new twists and wrinkles in their foundations of success to stay ahead of the crowd. They realize the value and benefits of comparing notes and ideas. So should you.

Interacting with local bait shop owners to review lake maps and discuss the best approaches will always help provide a few more pieces of the puzzle when trying to assemble any winter pattern. Local anglers, guides, fishing clubs and biologists may also provide helpful information.

One of the best ways to share observations and ideas is to compare your findings at sports shows, networking with manufacturers, sales reps, resort owners, guides and fellow anglers. Ice fishing presentations and seminars by experienced ice anglers are also becoming increasingly common and can be a great way to learn.

Still, there is no better teacher than experience. To gain that experience while fishing with a seasoned veteran is beyond compare. Skilled winter guides willing to share their knowledge are worth the investment of a day's fishing. No matter who you are, a knowledgeable guide is well worth the money.

Fishing clubs are another good way to advance your knowledge. Find an active club with knowl-

Ice fishing presentations and seminars by knowledgeable ice anglers are becoming increasingly common and can be a great way to learn.

An often overlooked resource, chambers of commerce, will often be able to help lead you to excellent sources of local information regarding lodging, food, local bait shops, fishing information and guides.

edgeable members willing to share and network, and you'll make great strides learning where and how to fish a variety of waters and species in your area. Club interaction also allows the opportunity to fish with anglers of different backgrounds, expanding your wealth of knowledge. Many of these clubs also draw good speakers, allowing you to confer, perhaps even fish with, some highly skilled anglers.

Another excellent, yet often overlooked, source of information includes fisheries journals, fisheries management meetings, conferences and symposiums open to the public. Scientific studies seldom provide actual fishing information, but related technical information about various fisheries can be critically important to piecing total patterns together. At these places you'll often get information on water clarity, bottom content and cover availability. There will sometimes be information on forage species and their densities, fish movement studies, interactive competition and relationships between various fish species and their forage bases. This stuff helps.

A final means of gaining information that's becoming more and more popular is ice fishing tournaments. By organizing friendly, competitive contests between skilled anglers, numerous, knowledgeable people are facing similar condi-

tions on the same water during the same time. By comparing notes, much can be learned. Again, there is no substitute for experience. The more time you spend on the ice, the better you'll get. And as you apply and modify the basic principles presented here on various waters under a variety of conditions, the more you'll learn. You'll pick up strategic approaches often brought out only by attention to detail. It is those details that often make the difference between great catches and mediocre ones.

You've certainly experienced times when fish stubbornly refused to bite despite your best attempt to pinpoint location and presentation patterns. That's ice fishing. But as you gain experience you'll learn to deal with various situations. Using today's technology, considering options, watching and experimenting, you'll gain

There is no substitute for ice fishing experience—experience that includes mobility, versatility and an open mind—to make you a better winter angler.

It has taken awhile, but I think the pioneering theories and concepts presented in the modern "Hooked on Ice Fishing System" are finally catching on.

increased knowledge of winter's patterns—and consequently, become a better ice angler.

There is no substitute for experience that includes mobility, versatility, and an open mind. By putting the specialized, classified systems outlined in the first three volumes of *"Hooked On Ice Fishing"* together with your newfound knowledge, then putting these concepts to work on the ice, you will experience increased winter fishing success. You may even construct solid winter patterns and come to understand the building blocks for catching more and larger winter gamefish. Many of these advanced techniques which will be covered in the next *"Hooked On Ice Fishing"* book, "Advanced Ice Fishing."

Until then, I think I'm going to load some ice tackle in my truck and head for the nearest frozen lake, in the hopes of experiencing the thrill of uncovering yet another productive winter pattern. I think I'll stop to look up once or twice to watch other anglers, too. It doesn't take long to identify those familiar with the "Hooked On Ice Fishing System:" They're the ones stepping onto the ice reviewing lake maps, holding hand-held GPS units, taking sonar readings, stopping only to set up quality ice fishing gear in high-percentage locations. I smile every time I see them.

It's taken awhile, but I think the pioneering theories and concepts presented in the modern "Hooked On Ice Fishing System" are finally catching on.

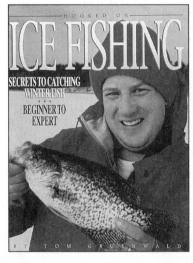
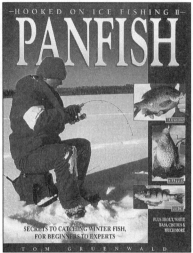
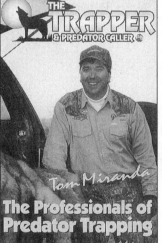

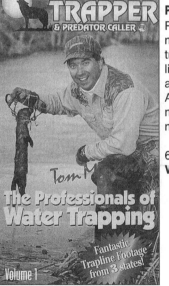